Place-Names of Northern Ireland

VOLUME FIVE

County Derry I
The Moyola Valley

LIBRARIES NI
WITHDRAWN FROM STOCK

Gregory Toner

The Northern Ireland Place-Name Project
Department of Celtic
The Queen's University of Belfast

General Editor: Gerard Stockman

D1613251

NORTH EASTERN LIBRARY SERVICE
AREA LIBRARY, DEMESNE AVENUE
BALLYMENA, Co. ANTRIM BT43 7BG

NUMBER   8877340

CLASS

RESEARCH GROUP

Professor Gerard Stockman

Fiachra Mac Gabhann MA
Dr Patrick McKay
Dr Kay Muhr
Mícheál B. Ó Mainnín MA
Dr Gregory Toner

LIST OF ILLUSTRATIONS

Cover: "The Plat of the Lands belonging to the Company of Vintners" from Sir Thomas Phillips' survey of the plantation of Co. Londonderry (1622). Reproduced with the permission of the Deputy Keeper of the Records, Public Record Office of Northern Ireland.

The cover logo is the pattern on one face of a standing stone found at Derrykeighan, Co. Antrim. The art style is a local variant of the widespread "Celtic Art" of the European Iron Age and dates to about the 1st century AD. The opposite side of the stone is similarly decorated. (Drawing by Deirdre Crone, copyright Ulster Museum).

Map of the area covered by this book (Maura Pringle, QUB)   vi

Map of the baronies of County Derry (OSI Barony map, 1938)   xviii

Townland maps:
Ballynascreen   4–5
Ballyscullion   58
Desertmartin   82
Kilcronaghan   111
Killelagh   139
Maghera   166–7
Termoneeny   212

The townland maps are based on Ordnance Survey of Northern Ireland digitized maps and reproduced with the permission of the Director of the Ordnance Survey of Northern Ireland.

ACKNOWLEDGEMENTS

In writing this book I have received assistance from many quarters, and I now express my deep gratitude to all those who helped in any way. In particular I would like to thank my fellow members in the Northern Ireland Place-Names Project for reading early drafts of the book and discussing many individual names with me. I would also like to thank the general editor of the series, Professor Gerard Stockman, for reviewing several drafts of the book, and Dr Leslie Lucas for his diligence in verifying my phonetic transcriptions and reading the proofs. Thanks are also due to the members of the Place-Names Branch of the Ordnance Survey of Ireland, Art Ó Maolfabhail, Dónall Mac Giolla Easpaig, Pádraig Ó Cearbhaill, and Pádraig Ó Dálaigh, and to Dr Nollaig Ó Muraíle of the Department of Celtic, Queen's University, Belfast, for sharing their immense knowledge of place-names with me. I would also like to express my gratitude to Mrs Maeve Walker for typing up many of the historical forms collected together in this book, and to William Johnston of the Forest Service, Department of Agriculture, Professor Pádraig Ó Riain of University College, Cork, and Anne Smyth of the Ulster Folk and Transport Museum for answering individual queries. Thanks are also due to the Place-Names Branch of the Ordnance Survey of Ireland, the Public Records Office of Northern Ireland, and the Historic Monuments and Buildings Branch of the Department of Environment for permission to consult their records and unpublished works.

The Northern Ireland Place-Names Project has received the support and assistance of many individuals too numerous to mention here, but special thanks are due to Eilís McDaniel, Dr Cathair Ó Dochartaigh, Dr Kieran Devine, and Dr Tony Sheehan for contributing towards the creation of the largest computer-based place-names project in the British Isles. We would also like to thank Mary Kelly and the staff of the Main Library at Queen's, and Angélique Day and Patrick McWilliams of the Ordnance Survey Memoir Project, Institute of Irish Studies. We are also indebted to the members of the steering committee, Michael Brand, Ronnie Buchanan, Dr Maurna Crozier, Dr Alan Gailey, Dr Ann Hamlin, Dr Maurice Hayes, Sam Corbett, and Dr Brian Walker.

Finally, I would like to express my profound thanks to all those who assisted with fieldwork in the Moyola area and who freely offered their time and energies in answering queries. In particular I would like to thank Brian and Margaret Mawhinny, Patsy Donnelly, Brian Toner, Dorothy Fleming, Eugene Keilt, Joe Doherty, and especially my mother and father, Eugene and Kathleen, whose connections with the area prompted me to undertake this study.

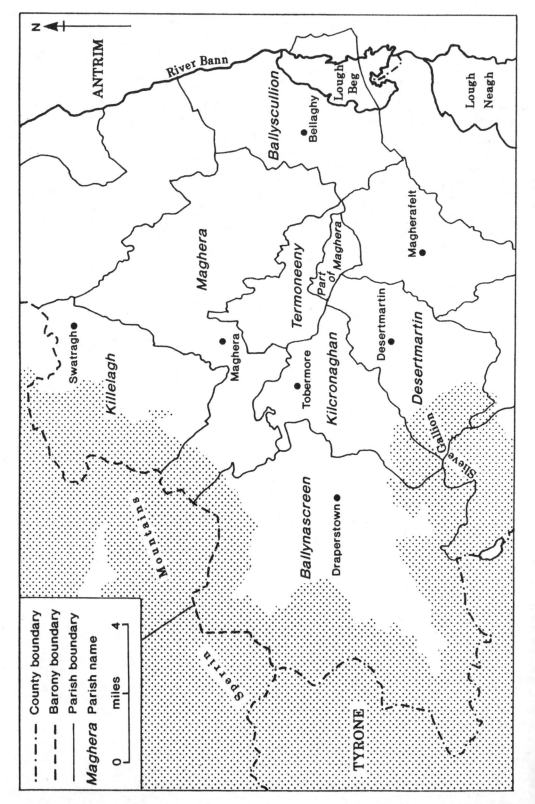

CONTENTS

	Page
General Introduction	ix
Introduction to County Derry	xix
The Barony of Loughinsholin	1
The Parish of Ballynascreen	6
The Parish of Ballyscullion	59
The Parish of Desertmartin	83
The Parish of Kilcronaghan	112
The Parish of Killelagh	140
The Parish of Maghera	168
The Parish of Termoneeny	213
Appendix A: Language	225
Appendix B: Land Units	230
Appendix C: Sources	237
Abbreviations	242
Primary Bibliography	243
Secondary Bibliography	253
Glossary of Technical Terms	260
Index to Irish forms of Place-names (with pronunciation guide)	267
Index to English forms of Place-names (with map references)	275

GENERAL INTRODUCTION

BRIEF HISTORY OF PLACE-NAME STUDY IN IRELAND

Place-name lore or *dindsenchas* was a valued type of knowledge in early Ireland, to be learnt by students of secular learning in their eighth year of study. Stories about the origin of place-names appear regularly in early Irish literature. At the end of the epic "Cattle Raid of Cooley" the triumphal charge of the Brown Bull of Cooley around Ireland is said to have given rise to names such as Athlone (Irish *Áth Luain*), so called from the loin *(luan)* of the White-horned Bull slain by the Brown Bull. In the 10th, 11th and 12th centuries legends about the naming of famous places were gathered together into a number of great collections. Frequently, different explanations of the same name are offered in these legends, usually with no preference being expressed. In an entry on the naming of *Cleitech*, the palace on the Boyne of the early king *Muirchertach mac Erca*, five separate explanations of the name are offered, none of which can be correct in modern scholarly terms. Place-name study was cultivated as a branch of literature.

Knowledge of Irish place-names was of practical importance during the English conquest and exploration of Ireland in the 16th century. Recurring elements in the place-names were noted by surveyors, and a table giving a few English equivalents appears on some maps of this period. There was concern that Irish names were "uncouth and unintelligible". William Petty, the great 17th-century surveyor and map-maker, commented that "it would not be amiss if the significant part of the Irish names were interpreted, where they are not nor cannot be abolished" (Petty 1672, 72–3). However, although the English-speaking settlers created many new names, they did not usually change the names of the lands they were granted, and the names of land units remained as they were, albeit in an anglicized form.

Interest in the meaning of Irish place-names developed further towards the end of the 18th century. The contributors to William Shaw Mason's *Parochial Survey of Ireland* often included a table explaining their local townland names, and this aspect was retained in the Statistical Reports compiled by the officers of the Royal Engineers on the parishes they surveyed for the first six-inch survey of Ireland in the late 1820s and early 1830s. Information on the spelling of place-names for the maps was collected in "name-books", and the Ordnance Survey was concerned to find that a variety of anglicized spellings was in use for many Irish place-names. The assistant director, Thomas Larcom, decided that the maps should use the anglicized spellings that most accurately represented the original Irish (Andrews 1975, 122) and he employed an Irish scholar, John O'Donovan, to comment on the name-books and recommend standard forms of names. O'Donovan was sent to the areas being surveyed to talk to local inhabitants, where possible Irish speakers, to find out the Irish forms. These were entered in the name-books, but were not intended for publication.

In 1855, a reader of *Ulster Journal of Archaeology* calling himself "De Campo" asked "that a list of all the townlands should be given in their Irish and English nomenclature, with an explanation of their Irish names" (*UJA* ser. 1, vol. iii, 25 1b). Meanwhile William Reeves, the Church of Ireland Bishop of Connor, had decided to compile a "monster Index" of all Irish townlands, which would eventually include the etymology of the names, "where attainable" (Reeves 1861, 486) . Reeves' project was cited favourably by William Donnelly, the Registrar General, in his introduction to the first Topographical Index to the Census of Ireland: "It would greatly increase the value of a publication of this nature if it were accompanied by a glossary or explanation of the names, and an account of their origin" (*Census 1851* 1, 11–12).

However, it was left to another scholar, P. W. Joyce, to publish the first major work dealing exclusively with the interpretation of Irish place-names, and in his first chapter he acknowledges his debt to both O'Donovan and Reeves *(Joyce* i 7–8, 10). At this period the progress made by Irish place-name scholarship was envied in England (Taylor 1896, 205). The high standard of Joyce's work has made him an authority to the present day, but it is regrettable that most popular books published since on Irish place-names have drawn almost entirely on the selection and arrangement of names discussed by Joyce, ignoring the advances in place-name scholarship over the last hundred years (Flanagan D. 1979(f); 1981–2(b)).

Seosamh Laoide's *Post-Sheanchas,* published in 1905, provided an Irish-language form for modern post towns, districts and counties, and research on place-names found in early Irish texts resulted in Edmund Hogan's *Onomasticon Goedelicum* (1910). Local studies have been published by Alfred Moore Munn (Co. Derry, 1925), and P. McAleer *(Townland Names of County Tyrone,* 1936). The idea of a comprehensive official survey was taken up again by Risteard Ó Foghludha in the introduction to his *Log-ainmneacha* (1935). A Place-Names Commission was founded in Dublin in 1946 to advise on the correct forms of Irish place-names for official use and this was followed by the Place-Names Branch of the Ordnance Survey. They have published the Irish names for postal towns *(AGBP* 1969), a gazetteer covering many of the more important names in Ireland *(GÉ* 1989), a townland survey for Co. Limerick (1990), and most recently bilingual lists of the place-names of a number of individual Irish counties.

John O'Donovan became the first professor of Celtic in Queen's University, Belfast, and in the 20th century members of the Celtic Department continued research on the place-names of the North of Ireland. The Ulster Place-Name Society was founded by the then head of department, Seán Mac Airt, in 1952 (Arthurs 1955–6, 80–82). Its primary aims were, (a) to undertake a survey of Ulster place-names; and (b) to issue periodically to members a bulletin devoted to aspects of place-name study, and ultimately to publish a series of volumes embodying the results of the survey. Several members undertook to do research on particular areas, much of which remains unpublished (Deirdre Flanagan on Lecale, and Dean Bernard Mooney on the names of the Diocese of Dromore).

The primary objective of the Ulster Place-Name Society was partly realized in 1987, when the Department of Celtic was commissioned by the Department of the Environment for Northern Ireland to do research into, "the origin of all names of settlements and physical features appearing on the 1:50,000 scale map; to indicate their meaning and to note any historical or other relevant information". In 1990, under the Central Community Relations Unit, the brief of the scheme was extended: to include work on all townlands in Northern Ireland, and to bring the work to publication. Although individual articles have already been published by various scholars, the *Place-Names of Northern Ireland* series is the first attempt in the North at a complete survey based on original research into the historical sources.

METHOD OF PLACE-NAME RESEARCH

The method employed by the Project has been to gather early spellings of each name from a variety of historical records written mainly in Irish, Latin and English, and arrange them in chronological order. These, then, with due weight being given to those which are demonstrably the oldest and most accurate, provide the evidence necessary for deducing the etymology. The same name may be applied to different places, sometimes only a few miles apart, and all forms are checked to ensure that they are entered under the correct modern name. For example, there are a number of references to a place called *Crosgare* in 17th-century sources, none of which refer to the well-known town of Crossgar in Co. Down, but to a townland also called Crossgar a few miles away near Dromara. Identification of forms is most readily facilitated by those sources which list adjoining lands together or give the name of the landholder. Indeed, one of the greatest difficulties in using Irish sources and some early Latin or English documents is the lack of context which would enable firm location of the place-names which occur in them.

Fieldwork is an essential complement of research on earlier written sources and maps. Sometimes unrecorded features in local topography or land use are well-known to local inhabitants. More frequently the pronunciation represented by the early written forms is obscure, and, especially in areas where there has been little movement of people, the traditional local pronunciation provides valuable evidence. The members of the research team visited their respective areas of study, to interview and tape-record informants recommended by local historical societies etc., but many others met in the course of fieldwork kindly offered their assistance and we record here our gratitude. The local pronunciations have been transcribed in phonetic script and these are given at the end of each list of historical forms. The tapes themselves will become archive material for the future. The transcription used is based on the principles of the International Phonetic Alphabet, modified in accordance with the general practice in descriptions of Irish and Scottish Gaelic dialects. The following diagram illustrates the relative position of each of the vowels used:

Front	Central	Back	
i		ʌ u	High
ï			
e		o	High-mid
	ə	ọ̈	
ɛ		ɔ	Low-mid
a		ɑ	Low

Although this research was originally based on the names appearing on the 1:50,000 scale map, it soon became clear that many townland names, important in the past and still known to people today, were not given on the published version. Townlands form the smallest unit in the historical territorial administrative system of provinces, counties, baronies, parishes, and townlands. This system, which is that followed by the first Ordnance Survey of Ireland in its name-books, has been used in the organization of the books in this series. The names of all the relevant units are explained in Appendix B. Maps of the relevant barony and parish divisions within the county are supplied for the area covered in each book, to complement the published 1:50,000 series, and to make the historical context more accessible.

In the process of collecting and interpreting early forms for the *Place-Names of Northern Ireland* each researcher normally works on a group of parishes. Some books will, therefore, have joint authorship and there may be differences of style and emphasis in the discussions within and between books. It seemed better to retain individuality rather than edit everything into committee prose. The suggested original Irish forms of the place-names were decided after group discussion with the general editor. In cases of joint authorship the members of the group responsible for the text of each book will be distinguished by name on the contents page.

All the information in this book is also preserved in a computer database in Queen's University Belfast. It is hoped that this database will eventually become a permanent resource for scholars searching for examples of a particular type of name or name element. Modern map information, lists of the townlands making up historical parishes and baronies, historical sources and modern Irish forms are all available on separate files which can be searched and interrelated. The database was designed by Eilís McDaniel, and the Project gratefully acknowledges her continuing interest.

LANGUAGE

Since Ulster was almost wholly Irish-speaking until the 17th century, most names of town-lands are of Irish-language origin. Some early names were also given Latin equivalents for use in ecclesiastical and secular documents but few probably ever gained wide currency. Norse influence on northern place-names is surprisingly slight and is largely confined to coastal features such as **Strangford Lough** and **Carlingford Lough.** The arrival of the Anglo-Normans in the 12th century brought with it a new phase of naming and its influence is particularly strong in east Ulster, most notably in the Barony of Ards. Here, the names of many of their settlements were formed from a compound of the owner's name plus the English word *tūn* "settlement" which gives us Modern English "town". Names such as **Hogstown** and **Audleystown** have retained their original form, but a considerable number, such as **Ballyphilip** and **Ballyrolly,** derive from forms that were later gaelicized.

By the time of the Plantation of Ulster in the 17th century the system of townland units and their names already existed and this was adopted more or less wholesale by the English and Scots-speaking settlers. These settlers have, nevertheless, left their mark on a sizeable body of names, particularly those of market towns, country houses, villages and farms which did not exist before the 17th century. What made the 17th-century Plantation different from the earlier ones was its extent and intensity, and it was the first time that the Irish language itself, rather than the Irish aristocracy, came under threat. The change from Irish to English speaking was a gradual one, and Irish survived into the 20th century in parts of Antrim and Tyrone. However, the language shift, assisted by an official policy that discriminated against Irish, eventually led to the anglicization of all names to the exclusion of Irish versions.

SPELLING AND PRONUNCIATION

Most of the historical sources used in this series were originally handwritten and this inevitably led to a considerable number of errors, both by contemporary copyists and by modern editors. Many of the documents, particularly grants, were copied time and again, while other sources sometimes only survive in late copies or published calendars. Mistakes could occur in any transcription but were particularly likely when the language or names being copied were unfamiliar. There is a long history of confusion in the Roman alphabet between letters of the type *i, u, n, m, w. U* and *n* are frequently confused, as are *m* and *w*. Where two or more of these letters occur together, the minims (vertical strokes) may be read in different combinations: the simple pair *ui* may be read as *iu, ni, in, m,* or *w*. Another common error is the confusion of long *s* (ʃ) and *f*. The name **Ballyhaft** (par. Newtownards, Dn) is frequently spelt in 17th-century sources with *s* instead of *f* and the modern form of the name may result from confusion of the written forms. In early sources, horizontal strokes (suspension strokes) could be written over a vowel as shorthand for a following *n* or *m*, but they were easily overlooked by scribes or editors. Spellings such as *Ballemulle* for **Ballymullan** (par. Bangor, Dn) may be explained in this way.

As well as taking account of spelling mistakes, there is sometimes difficulty in interpreting just what the spellings were intended to represent. For example, *gh*, which is usually silent in modern English dialects (e.g. night, fought) often retained its original value in the 17th century and was pronounced like the *ch* in Scots *loch* and *nicht*. Thus, *gh* was the obvious way to represent the Irish sound in words like *mullach* "summit", although both the English and Irish sounds were being weakened to [h] in certain positions at the time.

In Irish the spelling *th* was originally pronounced as in modern English *thick,* but in the 13th century it came to be pronounced [h]. The original Irish sound was anglicized as *th* or as *gh* at different periods, but where the older form of the spelling has survived the sound *th* has often been restored by English speakers. In names such as **Rathmullen** and **Rathfriland,** where the initial element represents *ráth* "a ringfort", the *th* has almost invariably been re-established.

It is clear that some spellings used in place-names no longer signify what they did when first anglicized. The *-y* in the common elements "bally-" and "derry-" was selected to represent the final vowel in the corresponding Irish words *baile* and *doire* (the same sound as the *a* in "above") but this vowel is now usually pronounced as a short *ee* as in English words such as *happy, sorry*. In modern Ulster English, the vowel in words ending in *-ane*, such as *mane, crane*, is a diphthong, but in the 17th century it was pronounced as a long *a*. Thus, Irish *bán* "white" was usually represented in anglicized forms of names as *bane* as, for example, in the names **Kinbane** (Ant.) and **Carnbane** (Arm.) and this is frequently how the names are still pronounced locally.

SOURCES

The earliest representations of Irish place-names are found in a broad range of native material, written mostly in Irish although occasionally in Latin, beginning in the 7th or 8th centuries. The Irish annals, probably begun about 550 AD (Byrne 1973, 2) but preserved in manuscripts of much later date, contain a large number of place-names, particularly those of tribes, settlements, and topographical features. Tribal names and those of the areas they inhabited frequently appear among genealogical material, a substantial proportion of which is preserved in a 12th-century manuscript, Rawlinson B 502, but is probably much older. Ecclesiastical records include martyrologies or calendars giving saints' names, often with the names and locations of their churches. The Latin and Irish accounts of the life of St Patrick, which depict him travelling around Ireland founding a series of churches, contain the first lists of place-names which refer to places owned by a particular institution. Later Irish saints' lives also may list lands dedicated to the founder of a church. Medieval Irish narrative shows a great interest in places, often giving, for example, long lists of place-names passed through on journeys. Although many of these sources may date back to the 7th or 8th centuries, the copies we have often survive only in manuscripts of the 12th century and later, in which the spelling may have been modernized or later forms of names substituted.

The administrative records of the reformed Church of the 12th century are among the first to provide detailed grants of land. There are also records from the international Church, such as the papal taxation of 1302–06 (*Eccles. Tax.*). These records are more productive for place-name study, since the names are usually of the same type (either parishes or other land units owned by the church) and are usually geographically related, making them easier to identify with their modern counterparts. However, the place-names in these documents are not usually spelled as they would be in Irish.

Paradoxically, perhaps, the 17th-century Plantation provides a massive amount of evidence for the place-names of Ulster. Grants to and holdings by individuals were written down by government officials in fiants, patents and inquisitions (in the latter case, the lands held by an individual at death). A series of detailed surveys, such as the *Escheated Counties* maps of 1609, the *Civil Survey* of 1654–6, and Sir William Petty's Down Survey (*DS (Par. Maps)*, *Hib. Del.* and *Hib. Reg.*), together with the records of the confiscation and redistribution of land found in the *Books of Survey and Distribution* (*BSD*) and the *Act of Settlement* (*ASE*), meant that, for the first time, almost all the names of smaller land units such as townlands were recorded. Unfortunately the richness of these resources has been depleted by two serious fires among the Irish public records, one in 1711 and the other in the Four Courts in Dublin in 1922. As a result, some of the original maps, and the Civil Survey covering the north-eastern counties, are lost, and the fiants, patents, inquisitions and Act of Settlement now only exist in abridged form in calendars made by the Irish Record Commission in the early 19th century. These calendars were criticized even at the time of publication for their degree of précis and for inaccurate transcription of names.

After the 17th century, little surveying of an official nature was carried out in Ireland, despite the clearance of woods and bogs and reclamation of waste land. The best sources for the 18th century, therefore, are family papers, leases, wills and sometimes estate maps, most of which remain unpublished. It became clear in the early 19th century that much of the taxation system was based on records that were out of date. The Ordnance Survey came to Ireland in 1824 and began in 1825 to do the first large-scale (six inches to the mile) survey of the country. Most of the variant spellings which they collected in their name-books were of the 18th or early 19th centuries, though in some cases local landowners or churchmen allowed access to earlier records, and these again provide a convenient and invaluable source of place-names. Minor names were also recorded in the descriptive remarks of the namebooks, in the fuller treatment of local names (water features, ancient monuments, church sites and other landmarks) in the associated Ordnance Survey Memoirs (*OSM*) and in the Ordnance Survey Revision Name-Books (OSRNB), dating from the second half of the 19th century.

Early maps are an extremely valuable source, since they show the geographical relationship between names that is often crucial for identification purposes, and in many cases they are precise enough to locate lost townlands or to identify the older name of a townland. In parts of Ulster, maps by 16th-century surveyors may antedate texts recording place-names, thus providing the earliest attestation of the names in those areas.

However, maps have their own problems. Like other written texts they often copy from each other, borrowing names or outline or both. Inaccuracies are frequent, especially in the plotting of inland water features, whether due to seasonal flooding, or the lack of a vantage point for viewing the course of a river. Frequently the surveyor of the ground was not the person who drew or published the surviving map. The great continental and English map and atlas publishers, such as Ortelius, Mercator and Speed, all drew on earlier maps, and this custom undoubtedly led to the initiation and prolongation of errors of form and orthography. Sixteenth-century maps of Lough Neagh, for example, regularly show rivers entering the lake on the south between the Blackwater and the Bann where there are known to be none (Andrews 1978, plate 22). Unsurveyed territory was not always drawn to scale. Modern Co. Donegal, for example, is usually drawn too large on 16th-century maps, while Co. Derry is frequently shown too small. The *Escheated County* maps appear to have been partly drawn from verbal information and, in the map for the barony of Armagh, the draughtsman has produced a mirror image reversing east and west (Andrews 1974, 152).

William Petty's Down Survey provided the standard map of Ireland for the 17th century. In the 18th and early 19th centuries various individuals produced local county maps: Roque (1760) Co. Armagh; Lendrick (1780) Co. Antrim; Sampson (1814) Co. Derry; Sloane, Harris, Kennedy and Williamson (1739–1810) Co. Down; Knox and McCrea (1813) Co. Tyrone. These were consulted for the place-names on their own maps by the Ordnance Survey in the 1830s. Apart from published maps, a number of manuscript maps, some anonymous, others the original work of the 16th-century surveyors Lythe and Jobson, still exist. Richard Bartlett and Thomas Raven left important manuscript maps of Ulster from the early 17th century.

HOW TO USE THIS SERIES

Throughout the series, the editors have tried to adhere to the traditional territorial and administrative divisions used in Ireland, but this has not always proved possible. The convenient unit on which to base both research and publication has been the civil parish and all townland names and minor names are discussed under the relevant parish, regardless of whether they are in the same barony or county. Each book normally deals with the parishes in one or more barony, but where the barony is too large they are split into different books, some of which may contain material from geographically adjacent baronies. Every effort has been made to accommodate the historical system in a series of volumes of regular size. Each parish, barony and county is prefaced by an introduction which sets forth its location and history, and discusses some of the sources from which the older spellings of names have been extracted.

Within each parish, townland and other names are arranged in alphabetical order in separate sections following a discussion of the parish name. The first section deals with townland names. The second section deals with names of towns, villages, hills and water features which appear on the OS 1:50,000 map, but which are not classified as townlands. This section may also include a few names of historical importance which do not appear on the map but which may be of interest to the reader. Lesser names on the 1:50,000 are only treated if relevant material has been forthcoming. An index of all the names discussed in each book is given at the back of the relevant volume.

Each name to be discussed is given in bold print on the left-hand side of the page. Bold print is also used elsewhere in the text to cross-refer the reader to another name discussed in the series. The four-figure grid-reference given under each place-name should enable it to be located on modern Ordnance Survey maps.

Beneath the map name[1] and its grid reference, all the pre-1700 spellings that have been found are listed, together with their source and date, followed by a selection of post-1700 forms. Early Irish-language forms are placed above anglicized or latinized spellings because of their importance in establishing the origin of the name. Irish forms suggested by 19th- and 20th-century scholars are listed below the historical spellings. Irish-language forms collected by O'Donovan in the last century, when Irish was still spoken in many parts of the North, require careful assessment. Some may be traditional, but there are many cases where the suggestion made by the local informant is contradicted by the earlier spellings, and it is clear that sometimes informants merely analysed the current form of the name. The current local pronunciation as collected by the editors appears below these Irish forms in phonetic script.

Spellings of names are cited exactly as they occur in the sources. Manuscript contractions have been expanded within square brackets, e.g. [ar]. Square brackets are also used to indicate other editorial readings: [...] indicates three letters in the name which could not be read, while a question mark in front of one or more letters enclosed in square brackets, e.g. [?agh], denotes obscure letters. A question mark in round brackets before a spelling indicates a form which cannot be safely identified as the name under discussion.

The dates of all historical spellings collected are given in the right-hand column, followed, where necessary, by c when the date is approximate. Here, we have departed from the normal practice, employed elsewhere in the books, because the database would otherwise have been unable to sort these dates in numeric order. In Latin and English sources a *circa* date usually indicates an uncertainty of a year or two. Irish language sources, however, rarely have exact dates and *circa* here represents a much longer time-span, perhaps of one or two centuries where the dating is based purely on the language of a text. Where no date has been established for a text, forms from that text are given the date of the earliest MS in which they appear. Following normal practice, dates in the Irish annals are given as in the source, although this may give certain spellings an appearance of antiquity which they do not deserve. The Annals of the Four Masters, for example, were compiled in the early 17th century using earlier material, and many of the names in the text were modernized by the compilers. Moreover, annals were written later for dates before the mid-6th-century, and the names, let alone the spellings, may not be that old. Another difficulty with dates concerns English administrative sources. The civil year in England and Ireland began on March 25th (Lady Day) until the year 1752, when the calendar was brought into line with changes made in the rest of Europe in 1582. Thus, the date of any document written between 1st of January and 24th of March inclusive has had to be adjusted to reconcile it with the current system by adding a year.

The original or most likely original Irish form of a name, where one is known to have existed, is given in italics on the top line to the right of the current spelling, with an English translation below. This includes Norse, Anglo-Norman and English names for which a Gaelic form once existed, as well as those of purely Irish origin. *Loch Cairlinn*, for example, was used by Irish-speakers for *Carlingford Lough* and this, rather than the original Norse, is printed on the top line. Although the name may have originally been coined at an early period of the language, standard modern Irish orthography is employed throughout, except in rare cases where this may obscure the meaning or origin of the name. The rules of modern Irish grammar are usually followed when not contradicted by the historical evidence. Where some doubt concerning the origin or form of a name may exist, or where alternatives may seem equally likely, plausible suggestions made by previous authorities, particularly the *OSNB* informants, are given preference and are printed at the top of the relevant entry. Nevertheless, where there is firm evidence of an origin other than that proposed by earlier scholars, the form suggested by our own research is given prominence.

Names for which no Irish original is proposed are described according to their appearance, that is, English, Scots etc. The form and meaning is usually obvious, and there is no evidence that they replace or translate an original Irish name. Names which are composed of two elements, one originally Irish and the other English or Scots, are described as hybrid forms. An important exception to this rule is names of townlands which are compounded from a name derived from Irish and an English word such as "upper", "east" etc. In these cases, the original Irish elements are given on the right-hand side but the later English appendage is not translated.

In the discussion of each name, difficulties have not been ignored but the basic consideration has been to give a clear and readable explanation of the probable origin of the name, and its relationship to the place. Other relevant information, on the language of the name, on other similar names, on historical events, on past owners or inhabitants, on physical changes or local place-name legends, may also be included, to set the name more fully in context.

The townland maps which appear at the beginning of each parish show the layout of all the townlands in that parish. They are based on printouts from the Ordnance Survey's digitized version of the 1:50,000 map.

The rules of Irish grammar as they relate to place-names are discussed in Appendix A, and the historical system of land divisions in Ulster is described in Appendix B. The bibliography separates primary sources and secondary works (the latter being referred to by author and date of publication). This is followed by a glossary of technical terms used in this series. The place-name index, as well as providing page references, gives the 1:50,000 sheet numbers for all names on the published map, and sheet numbers for the 1:10,000 series and the earlier 6-inch county series for townland names. The index of Irish forms gives a semi-phonetic pronunciation for all names for which an Irish form has been postulated.

SUGGESTIONS FOR FURTHER INVESTIGATION

A work like this on individual names cannot give a clear picture of any area at a particular time in the past. Any source in the bibliography could be used, in conjunction with town-land or other maps, to plot the references to a particular locality at that date, or to lands with a particular owner. Also the Public Record Office of Northern Ireland holds a considerable amount of unpublished material from the eighteenth century and later, which awaits inves-tigation for information on place-names arising at that period.

Although fieldwork forms an integral part of place-name research, it is difficult for a library researcher to acquire the familiarity with an area that the local inhabitants have. Local people can walk the bounds of their townlands, or compare boundary features with those of the early 6-inch maps. Written or tape-recorded collections of local names (especially those of smaller features such as fields, rocks, streams, houses, bridges, etc.), where exactly they are to be found, how written and pronounced, and any stories about them or the people who lived there, would be a valuable resource for the future. The Place-Name Project will be happy to talk to anyone engaged on a venture of this kind.

Footnote

(1) On the OS maps apostrophes are sometimes omitted, e.g. Mahulas Well, Deers Meadow. In this series they have been inserted when there is evidence to indicate whether the possessive is singular or plural, e.g. Mahula's Well, Deers' Meadow.

Kay Muhr
Senior Research Fellow

Map of Baronies in Co. Derry

Coleraine	Tirkeeran
Keenaght	North-East Liberties of Coleraine
Loughinsholin	North-West Liberties of Londonderry

That portion of the Barony of Loughinsholin which is discussed in this volume has been shaded to indicate its position and extent.

INTRODUCTION TO COUNTY DERRY

In January, 1610, the London Companies agreed to carry out the plantation of the old County of Coleraine, together with a portion of Donegal bordering on the city of Derry, a portion of land on the Antrim side of the Bann at Coleraine, and the barony of Loughinsholin which then lay in Co. Tyrone. When the City received a formal grant of these lands three years later they were combined to form the new county of Londonderry, thus uniting the whole of the City's property in Ulster into a single administrative unit (Camblin 1951, 22, 25; Curl 1986, 26–7; Moody 1939, 122–3).

The County of Coleraine was first marked out as a unit of English administration by Lord Deputy Perrott in 1585, but it was a county only in name and was often reckoned as part of Tyrone until the reign of James I (Moody 1939, 50). It took its name from O'Cahan's castle on the west bank of the Bann at Coleraine, near the Salmon Leap, and not from the abbey of the same name on the other side of the river. Prior to the 17th century, the territory comprising the County of Coleraine was ruled by the O'Cahans, giving rise to its alias, O'Cahan's country (Irish *Oireacht Uí Chatháin*).

Derry and Coleraine, which were separated from O'Cahan's country by the two rivers on which they stood, were essentially ecclesiastical settlements. A monastery was established at Derry by St Columcille in the 6th century (from which it was named *Doire Cholm Cille* "Columcille's oakwood"), and a monastic town grew up around it. A settlement also grew up around the 6th-century monastery at Coleraine on the eastern bank of the Bann. The inclusion of these two towns was clearly pivotal in encouraging the London Companies to take part in the plantation for in a document designed to persuade the London Companies to settle this part of Ulster, both the city of Derry, which was then in ruins, and the town of Coleraine were considered as sites which could be made "almost impregnable" by land (*ibid.* 66).

In its Charter, the city of Derry was renamed Londonderry to commemorate its association with the city of London and, according to normal practice, the name of the new county was adopted from the city which was intended to be the chief stronghold within it (*ibid.* 123). Londonderry is still the official name of both the city and county, but the form Derry has been retained by the main churches for their dioceses, and it has recently been adopted by Derry City Council in its name. It is perhaps ironic that the name London itself is of Celtic origin. It was formerly thought to derive from Celtic *Lugudunum* meaning "Lug's fort", and parallels were invoked with the Irish deity, Lugh Lámhfhada. Such an origin is clearly impossible, however, and it has more plausibly been suggested that it derives from a Celtic root *londo*-"wild, bold", possibly a personal name *Londinos* meaning "the bold one" (Ekwall 1960, 303; Gelling, Nicolaisen & Richards 1970, 128).

THE BARONY OF LOUGHINSHOLIN

Loughinsholin

Loch Inse Uí Fhloinn
"the lake of O'Flynn's island"

1. muinter Barūntacht Loch Inis Ó Luinn	Cín Lae Ó M. 11	1645c
2. go Loch Inis Í Luinn	Cín Lae Ó M. 13	1645c
3. co Loch Inis Ó Luinn	Cín Lae Ó M. 13	1645c
4. ar Inis Í Luinn	Cín Lae Ó M. 19	1645c
5. ar Loch Inis Ó Luinn	Cín Lae Ó M. 27	1645c
6. Inis Í Luinn (acc.)	Cín Lae Ó M. 28	1645c
7. Loghynisolin	Colton Vis. 125	1591
8. Loghensholin barony	CPR Jas I 376a	1609
9. Loughinsholin barony	CPR Jas I 376b	1609
10. Loughlinsholin barony (x2)	CPR Jas I 376b	1609
11. longunsholin, in baronia de	Bishop. Der. i 56	1610
12. loughunsholin	Bishop. Der. i 57	1610
13. Lougshunsholin	Bishop. Der. i 57	1610
14. Loughunsholin	Bishop. Der. i 57, 62	1610
15. Loughinsholin	Bishop. Der. i 80	1611
16. Loughinsholine	Charter of Londonderry (Reed) 81	1613
17. Loughinsholin	Charter of Londonderry (Reed) 85	1613
18. Loughinsholin Bar.	CPR Jas I 274a	1615
19. Loghinsholing Bar.	CPR Jas I 279a	1615
20. Loughinisholin	Bishop. Der. i 102	1615
21. Loughinsholin barony	CPR Jas I 314a	1616
22. Loughinisholin, in baronia de	Bishop. Der. i 121	1617
23. Lougheinsholin	Bishop. Der. i 125	1617
24. Loughensholen, barony of	CPR Jas I 479a	1620
25. Lougheinsholin	Phillips MSS (Maps) Plate 28	1622
26. Loughinisholin	Bishop. Der. i 144	1624c
27. Lowghenisholyn, the barony of	Inq. Ult. (Derry) §1 Car. I	1633
28. Lowghenisholyn, baronie of	Inq. Ult. (Derry) §1 Car. I	1633
29. Loughinsholyn, baronie of	Inq. Ult. (Derry) §1 Car. I	1633
30. Lowghenisolyn, the barony of	Inq. Ult. (Derry) §1 Car. I	1633
31. Loughnesylene	Inq. Ult. (Derry) §9 Car. I	1639c
32. Loghinsholin	Civ. Surv. iii 144, 152, 153	1654
33. Loghinsholyn	Civ. Surv. iii 167	1654
34. Loughinsholin	Civ. Surv. iii 168	1654
35. Loughinishollin	Civ. Surv. iii 175	1654
36. Loghinisholin	Civ. Surv. iii 185	1654
37. Loughinishollin	Civ. Surv. iii 189	1654
38. Loughinisholin	Civ. Surv. iii 189, 194, 196	1654
39. Loghinsholyn	Civ. Surv. iii 196	1654
40. Loghenshelleene	Civ. Surv. iii 198	1654
41. Loghinshellin	Civ. Surv. iii 215	1654
42. Loughinsholin	Bishop. Der. i 263–268	1657

43. Loghinsholin	Census 133,139,145	1659c
44. Loughinsholin	Bishop. Der. i 342	1660
45. Loughinsholin, Barony of	Bishop. Der. i 326	1661
46. Loghinsolin	Bishop. Der. i 355	1663
47. Loughinsholin	Hib. Del. Derry	1672c
48. Loughinsholin	Lamb Maps Derry	1690c
49. bar. Loghlinsholine	Forfeit. Estates 371b §11	1703
50. Lochinsholin	Sampson's Map	1813
51. Loughinshollen	OSNB No. 8	1834c
52. Lock-in-sho-'lin	OSNB Pron. No. 6	1834c
53. Loch Seal Loinn "lake on which Lyn spent a time"	OSL (Derry) 105	1834
54. Loch Sil Luinn "the lough of Lyn's seed"	OSL (Derry) 105	1834
55. Loch Annsa Linn "the lough in the bog"	OSL (Derry) 105	1834
56. Loch na Sé Linn "the lake of the six streams"	OSL (Derry) 105	1834
57. Loch Gan-Fhios Uí Loinn "hidden lough of O'Lyn"	OSL (Derry) 105	1834
58. Lough-Inch-O'Lyn "the lake of O'Lyn's island"	OSL (Derry) 107	1834
59. Loch innse Uí Loinn "lake of O'Lyn's island"	J O'D (OSNB) No. 11	1834c
60. Loch Inse Uí loinn	J O'D (OSNB) No. 8	1834c
61. Loch innse Uí Loinn "lough of O'Lynn's island"	J O'D (OSNB) No. 9	1834c
62. ˌlɔxïnʃəˈlïn	Local pronunciation	1993

Although the Barony of Loughinsholin now lies in the south-eastern portion of Co. Derry, it formed part of Co. Tyrone from its formation in 1591 until the creation of the new county of Londonderry in 1613 (Moody 1939, 51, 123). Like many other baronies, it was constructed from smaller native districts or kingdoms (*tuatha*), namely:

(1) Clandonnell in the north, extending as far south as Maghera. It was called in Irish *Clann Domhnaill* (modern *Clann Dónaill*) "Donal's offspring" after Domhnall Donn na Banna of the Clandeboy O'Neills whose father Brian mac Aodha Bhuidhe died in 1488.

(2) Glenconkeyne to the north-west, covering the present parishes of Ballynascreen, Desertmartin and Kilcronaghan. The name was explained locally in the last century as *Gleann Con Cadhain* "the valley of Cadhan's hound" and this is probably correct. Most commentators have taken the view that the valley was named after an historical person called *Cú Chadhain* or *Concadhan*, but no such name is recorded in the Irish genealogies. However, Cadhan is found as a forename in this very area, and was borne by one of the Lagans in the 19th century (see Ó Ceallaigh 1901, 200; also Ó Ceallaigh 1927, 59–60). Indeed, the *Gleann Cadhain* of some Irish romance tales can be tentatively located in this area and this may have been an early form of the name which was later augmented under the influence of the folktale to produce the current form (see *Onom. Goed.* 441).

(3) Killetra, Irish *Coill Íochtarach* "lower wood", in the south, stretching from the site of the town of Magherafelt to the Ballinderry River. Killetra and Glenconkeyne were then covered in dense forest and were considered the most inaccessible parts in the whole of Ulster.

(4) Tomlagh, a district four or five miles wide, extending from Portglenone along the Bann and Lough Beg, and bordering with Killetra on the south side of the Moyola River. The origin of the name is unclear (see *GUH* 32-37; Ó Doibhlin 1971(b) 143–4).

The name Loughinsholin was originally applied to a small lake and crannog near Desertmartin (hence *Loch Inse Uí Fhloinn* "the lake of O'Flynn's island"). The lake, and more particularly the crannog, must have been a site of some importance in the latter half of the 16th century for it to have given its name to the newly-formed barony, but there is no contemporary evidence to confirm this. The strategic importance of the site is emphasized by Chichester in a letter of 1612 concerning the building of a castle at Desertmartin to guard the road between Dungannon and Coleraine (*Anal. Hib.* viii 23):

> There is neare unto this Passage where this ffort is to be Erected a Lough which giveth Apellation unto this Barony, where was a Strong ffort and Ward of the Rebells in time of the Warr, which my self took and burned, standing in an Island as it then did. This I write, [not] only for cause of mine owne knowledge [but] also, that the place is well chosen and of great importance to be secured.

The final element in the name is the surname *Ó Floinn* (O'Flynn) which develops a byform *Ó Loinn* (O'Lynn, Lynn etc.). The O'Flynns were chiefs of Uí Thuirtre in Co. Antrim from about the middle of the 11th century until the latter part of the 14th, after which period they appear as important figures in North Down (Woulfe 1923, 587; Flanagan 1973, 65–6). According to O'Donovan, there were some O'Lynns living in Maghera in the first half of the 19th century, and Griffith records thirteen households bearing the name Lynn or Linn in this barony, but there is no trace of the name in the area among our early records (*OSL (Derry)* 105; Flanagan 1973, 67n; Byrne 1973, 125–6).

3

Parish of Ballynascreen

Townlands

Ballynure
Bancran Glebe
Brackagh
Cahore
Carnamoney
Cavanreagh
Cloane
Cloughfin
Coolnasillagh
Corick
Derrynoyd
Disert
Doon
Drumard
Drumderg
Dunlogan
Dunmurry
Duntibryan
Finglen
Glebe
Glengomna
Glenviggan
Gortnaskey
Labby
Moneyconey
Moneyguiggy
Moneyneany
Moyard
Moydamlaght
Moyheeland
Moykeeran
Mulnavoo
Owenreagh
Straw
Straw Mountain
Strawmore
Tonaght
Tullybrick

Towns

Draperstown

Based upon Ordnance Survey 1:50,000 mapping, with permission of the Director of the Ordnance Survey of Northern Ireland, Crown copyright reserved.

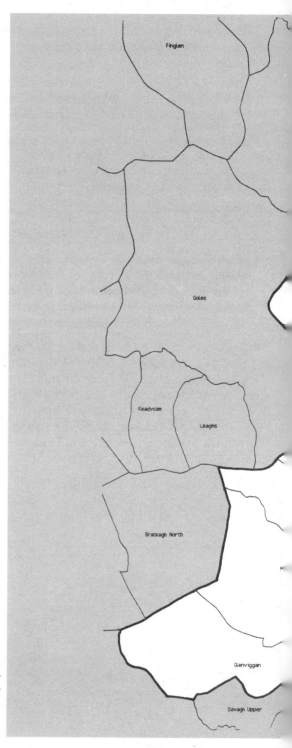

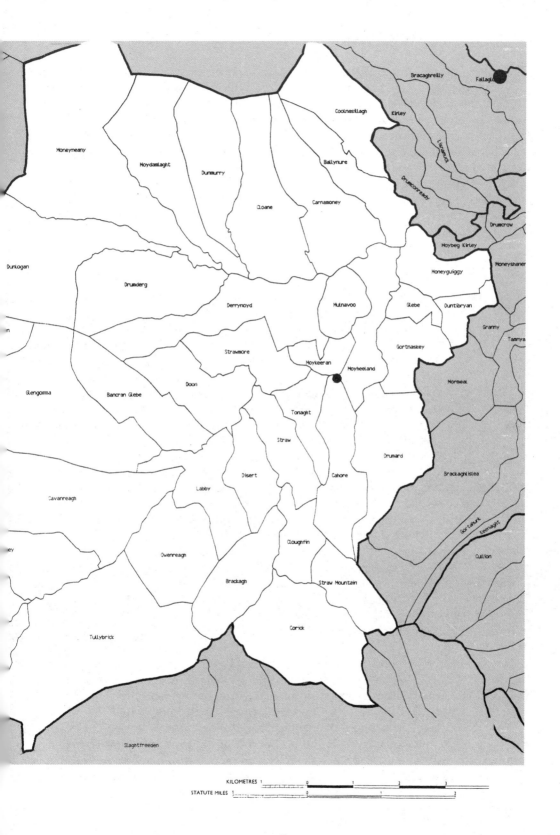

Moneyneany
Moydamlaght
Dunmurry
Coolnasillagh
Kirley
Bracaghreilly
Fallagloon
Ballynure
Carnamoney
Cloane
Lissanmuck
Drumconready
Drumcrow
Moybeg Kirley
Moneyguiggy
Moneyshaner
Dunlogan
Drumderg
Derrynoyd
Mulnavoo
Glebe
Ountibryan
Granny
Tamnya
Strawmore
Gortnaskey
Moykeeran
Moyheeland
Doon
Mormeal
Glengomna
Bancran Glebe
Tonaght
Straw
Drumard
Brackaghlislea
Disert
Cahore
Labby
Cavanreagh
Gortahurk
Keenaght
Owenreagh
Cloughfin
Cullion
Brackagh
Straw Mountain
Tullybrick
Corick
Slaghtfreeden

KILOMETRES
STATUTE MILES
0   1   2   3
0   1   2

5

THE PARISH OF BALLYNASCREEN

The ruins of the old church of Ballynascreen, the greater part of which has been dated to the 14th century, are located on the north side of the Moyola River in the townland of Moneyconey (Davies 1941(b), 60; *Colton Vis.* 82–3n). Many local traditions concerning the foundation of the church are recorded in various documents of the 19th and 20th centuries, but there is little historical evidence to substantiate any of them. Even the claim that the church was founded by St Columcille is not supported by our historical sources, and it is not even mentioned in the early 16th-century Life of St Columcille penned by Manus O'Donnell. A shrine of Columcille was kept here in the medieval period and it was from this shrine that the old name for the church, *Scrín Cholm Cille* "Columcille's shrine", is derived. The earliest reference to the church occurs in the annals under the year 1203 when Dermot, the son of Murtough O'Loughlin, plundered Ballynascreen (*AFM* iii 137).

Local tradition also associates the name of St Patrick with the church of Ballynascreen, claiming that it was first erected by the national saint as a college, and later converted into a church by St Columcille (*OSM (Loughrey)* 16). Another local legend says that Columcille tried to erect his church first in Moneyneany, then at Lough Patrick, then south of the Moyola opposite the present old ruins, but each time was prevented by a monster. Finally, in answer to a prayer, a bell fell from Heaven. Columcille ordered his assembled followers to spread out their cloaks on the ground. The bell first fell into McGillian's cloak but bounced off and gently landed on McGurk's cloak. The church was erected where the bell fell, and the McGillians and the McGurks have fought over the bell ever since (*OSL (Derry)* 82–3).

The church of Ballynascreen figures in a variety of 14th- and 15th-century ecclesiastical tracts, mostly concerning the appointment of vicars. It is valued at one mark at the beginning of the 14th century (*Eccles. Tax. (CDI)* 215), rising to three marks for its temporal lands and two marks for its episcopal lands by 1397 (*Colton Vis.* 76, 82). In 1414, Philip Ochegegan, deacon, was appointed to the vicarage of Ballynascreen following the death of Isaac Magallyn (*Cal. Papal Letters* vi 432; *Annates Ulst.* 213). Terence Oneyll was rector in 1435 if the identification of *Ballyneskyny* as Ballynascreen is correct (*Reg. Swayne* 156), and Henry Ohynnery is described as acolyte and vicar of Ballynascreen in 1445 (*ibid.* 193). The surname Hegarty becomes closely associated with the parish of Ballynascreen in the 15th century. Nicholas Ohegeartarch (Hegarty), who had previously obtained the rectory in controversial circumstances, was appointed rector by papal mandate in 1453 (*Cal. Papal Letters* x 638; cf. *Colton Vis.* 21n; *Annates Ulst.* 199). A certain Patrick Ohegerthy of Ballynascreen lost fifty cows to raiders in 1461 (*Colton Vis.* 21n), and in 1469, Eugenius Ohegrartaych (*recte* Ohegeartaych) "a native of the place" was attempting to obtain both the vicarage and the rectory of Ballynascreen (*Cal. Papal Letters* xii 336–7).

In the early 17th century, the six balliboes of Tullybrick, Moneyconey, Cavanreagh, Moyard, Dunarnon, and Owenreagh constituted the "termon or erenagh land" of Ballynascreen, and it was this territory, of course, which later became known as the Sixtowns. Five of the six balliboes can now be readily identified as modern townlands, but the sixth, Dunarnon, survives only as a minor division in Owenreagh townland (see also *Esch. Co. Map* 14; *Civ. Surv.* iii 190; *Census* 137; *HMR (Ó Doibhlin 2)* 1663, 67).

The erenagh lands passed into the hands of the Bishop of Derry during the Plantation, and most of the remaining lands in the civil parish of Ballynascreen were granted to the London companies and divided among the Skinners' and Drapers' companies (*Lond. Comp. Valuation* 309, 311). Corick was in the possession of the See of Armagh and, under the conditions of the Plantation, Bancran was allotted as glebe (*Bishop. Der.* i 145; cf. Moody 1939, 136, 292).

PARISH NAME

Ballynascreen   *Baile na Scríne*
                                                        "the land/territory of the shrine"

1. (?) na Scríne Coluim Cille (gen.)	ALC i 130	1132
2. (?) na Sgríne, airchinnech	ALC i 130	1132
3. Scrin colaim cille, ro airgset	AFM iii 136	1203
4. Scrín Coluim Cille, curro aircset	ALC i 230	1203
5. a m-Baile na Scrine	AU iii 426	1497
6. i mBoili na Sgríne	Cín Lae Ó M. 13	1645c
7. Baile na Sgrinne	Top. Frag. 82	1675c
8. Baile na Scrine	Top. Frag. 71	1680c
9. Balinmascryn, Church de	Eccles. Tax. (CDI) 215	1306c
10. Balenescrine	Colton Vis. 76	1397
11. Ballenescrine	Colton Vis. 82	1397
12. Balenascrine	Cal. Papal Letters vi 432	1414
13. Balenascrine	Annates Ulst. 213	1414
14. (?)Ballyneskyny	Reg. Swayne 156	1435
15. Balinascrine Par. Ch.	Reg. Swayne 193	1445
16. Balenagrine	Cal. Papal Letters x 283	1447
17. Balenascrine	Cal. Papal Letters x 638	1453
18. Balliscrine (Reg. Prene)	Colton Vis. 21n	1458
19. Ba[l]leiniscrine	Cal. Papal Letters xii 336	1469
20. Balleiniscrine	Cal. Papal Letters xii 337	1469
21. Balennscrine, par. ecclesie de	Annates Ulst. 199	1470
22. Ballinescrine	CPR Jas I 376b	1609
23. Ballinescrine	Bishop. Der. i 57,62	1610
24. Skrine	Speed's Ulster	1610
25. Skrine	Speed's Ireland	1610
26. Ballinescrine	Bishop. Der. i 80	1611
27. Ballinescrine	CPR Jas I 279a	1615
28. Ballinescrine	CPR Jas I 280a	1615
29. Ballinescrine parish	CPR Jas I 377a	1615
30. Ballineskrine	Bishop. Der. i 103	1615
31. Ballinescrine	Bishop. Der. i 109	1615
32. Ballynescreene, R'c'oria de	Bishop. Der. i 129	1617c
33. Skren	Phillips MSS (Maps) Plate 30	1622
34. Ballene Skren	Phillips MSS (Maps) Plate 30	1622
35. Ballineskrene	Bishop. Der. i 145	1624c
36. Ballineskreen	Civ. Surv. iii 167,177,178	1654
37. Ballina Skrine	Civ. Surv. iii 174	1654
38. Ballineskrine	Civ. Surv. iii 177	1654
39. Belleneskreen	Civ. Surv. iii 178	1654
40. Bellineskrin	Civ. Surv. iii 178,190	1654
41. Bellinskenan	Civ. Surv. iii 188	1654
42. Bellineskenny parrish	Civ. Surv. iii 372	1654
43. Ballinescrinny, the parrish of	Civ. Surv. iii 374	1654

44. The Parish of Ballenskrene	Hib. Reg. Loughinsholin	1657c
45. Ballyniskrean	Census 137	1659c
46. Bellinaskrein or Killinescreene	Bishop. Der. i 326	1661
47. Ballynesereene Parish	BSD(c) 55	1661
48. Ballineskreen Parish	HMR (Ó Doibhlin 2) 66	1663
49. Ballenescrinie	Bishop. Der. i 405	1666
50. Ballinscr'	Bishop. Der. i 415	1668
51. Balliniskreene	Bishop. Der. i 425	1669
52. Ballinascreene	Bishop. Der. ii 1	1671
53. Ballenscreen	Hib. Del. Derry	1672c
54. Ballinascreen	Bishop. Der. ii 40	1680
55. Ballinescreen	Bishop. Der. ii 43	1681
56. Ballynescreene	Bishop. Der. ii 45	1681
57. Ballyneskreen, Rec' de	Bishop. Der. ii 113	1686
58. Ballinascreen	Bishop. Der. ii 478	1688
59. Ballenscreen	Lamb Maps Derry	1690c
60. B.Screen	Lamb Maps Ulster	1690c
61. Ballinescreen, S'ti Columbe	Bishop. Der. ii 136	1692
62. Balliniskreen	Bishop. Der. ii 509	1700c
63. Baile na scríne "town of the shrine"	J O'D (OSNB) No. 16	1834c
64. Baile-na-scrin "The town of the Shrine"	Munn's Notes 43	1925
65. ˌbalnəˈskrin	Local pronunciation	1993
66. ˌbalənəˈskrin	Local pronunciation	1993

The Irish word *scrín*, a borrowing from Latin *scrinium*, denotes a shrine, usually a box or casket containing the relics of a saint (*Joyce* i 321; *DIL* sv.). The Annals of Ulster record that Columcille's shrine (*scrín*), together with his other relics, were brought to Ireland in 878 to escape the ravages of the Vikings, although the precise destination of the shrine is not revealed (*AU (Mac Airt)* 334; cf. *AFM* i 522). *Scrín* is the name of several churches containing the relics or shrine of a saint, and we may note in particular in the present context *Scrín Cholm Cille* "St Columcille's shrine" (angl. Skreen), the name given to a church in Meath where a shrine of St Columcille was also deposited, and the medieval church of *Balloneskrene de Ardo* which also held a shrine of the saint (see *Colton Vis.* 78; *BCC* §146).

The earliest reference to the shrine at Ballynascreen occurs in the annals where we are told that Dermot, the son of Murtough O'Loughlin, went on a predatory expedition and plundered the church of Ballynascreen. However, he met with fierce resistance and was eventually killed "through the miracles of the Shrine" (*AFM* iii 137). Tradition has it that the church of Ballynascreen was also called *Toigh Taisce* or "depository" because the books and treasures of the nine surrounding churches were kept there (*OSL (Derry)* 80), but this alias may, in fact, have arisen from the presence there of Columcille's shrine.

Baile is usually translated "townland" in works on Irish place-names, but the earliest sense of the word is simply "place, spot". It is first attested in place-names c.1150 in a charter relating to the lands of the monastery at Kells, Co. Meath, by which stage it seems to have developed the meaning "land, territory" (Price 1963, 119). These divisions of land later often became townlands and, where *baile* occurs in a townland name, we are quite justified in

translating it as "townland". In the case of Ballynascreen, however, there is not, and probably never was, a townland of that name, so it would be quite wrong to translate it in that way.

There is, fortunately, some indication of the area of land to which *baile* refers in this name.
A map of the lands belonging to the Company of Skinners drawn in 1622 depicts a large
tract of land called *Ballene Skren* around the church of *Skren*, and this presumably represents
the territory which is now called the Sixtowns (*Phillips MSS (Maps)* Plate 30). It appears,
therefore, that the name *Baile na Scrine* originally denoted the land held by the church of
Scrín Cholm Cille, and only later, by extension, the whole parish.

TOWNLAND NAMES

Ballynure   *Baile na nIúr*
H 7898   "townland of the yew trees"

1. B:nenoura	Esch. Co. Map 14	1609
2. Balmenoure	Charter of Londonderry 391–2	1613
3. Ba: na Nurey	Lond. Comp. Valuation 309	1613
4. Balle narre	Phillips MSS (Maps) Plate 28	1622
5. Ballinenure	Civ. Surv. iii 177	1654
6. Ballineonie, being 1½ balliboes of land	Bishop. Der. i 266	1657
7. Ballynanure	Census 137	1659c
8. Ballinenure	BSD(c) 63	1661
9. Ballmanure	HMR (Ó Doibhlin 2) 67	1663
10. Ballynun	Sampson's Map	1813
11. Ballynure	Received usage No. 16	1834c
12. Ballynure	Title Deeds (OSNB) No. 16	1834c
13. Bally'nure	OSNB Pron. No. 16	1834c
14. Baile nur "heath town or yew trees"	MacCloskey's Stat. Report 62	1821
15. Baile an iubhair "town of the yew"	J O'D (OSNB) No. 16	1834c
16. Baile-an-iubhair "The townland of the yew trees"	Munn's Notes 44	1925
17. ˌbalənˈjuːr	Local pronunciation	1993

The earliest spellings of this name indicate that the final element is plural rather than singular as previously suggested (15–16). The underlying form from the 17th-century period,
which may be taken to be something like *Ballynenure*, had given way to a shorter trisyllabic
form, *Ballynure*, by the 19th century, probably by haplology, and it was on this form that previous scholars based their interpretation (14–16).

Some of the earliest spellings seem to suggest that the name was originally pentasyllabic
(*Ballynenurey*), but these have almost certainly arisen through scribal error. The final *a* in the
form from the Escheated Counties maps (1) is probably a mistake for the *e* which appears
in the related charter of 1613 (2), and we may compare similar mistakes in **Craigmore** and
Drumlamph in Maghera. The form in the charter of 1657 (6) is probably a mistranscription of that in the earlier charter (2) and again we may compare similar errors in **Cloane** and

Killynumber below. The London Companies' valuation is not a reliable source and the spelling here (3) may be dismissed. It is fairly certain, therefore, that the underlying form from the 17th-century sources is, indeed, *Ballynenure*, and that this represents Irish *Baile na nIúr* "townland of the yew trees".

Bancran Glebe   A hybrid form
H 7394

1. banchran	Esch. Co. Map 14	1609
2. Banchran	Charter of Londonderry 391	1613
3. Banahor	Phillips MSS (Maps) Plate 30	1622
4. Banharan	Bishop. Der. i 145	1624c
5. Donaghran (x2)	Civ. Surv. iii 190	1654
6. Banchran	Bishop. Der. i 266	1657
7. Donoghan	Hib. Reg. Loughinsholin	1657c
8. Donoghan (x2)	Hib. Reg. Loughinsholin	1657c
9. Brancharan	Census 137	1659c
10. Donaghran	BSD(c) 55	1661
11. Ban Craw	HMR (Ó Doibhlin 2) 67	1663
12. Donogha	Hib. Del. Derry	1672c
13. Donoghan, Part of (x2)	Hib. Del. Derry	1672c
14. Banaghran	Sampson's Map	1813
15. Bancran	Received usage No. 16	1834c
16. Bancran	Title Deeds (OSNB) No. 16	1834c
17. 'Ban-cran	OSNB Pron. No. 16	1834c
18. Ban crann "the woody bottom"	MacCloskey's Stat. Report 62	1821
19. Bán-chrann "white tree"	J O'D (OSNB) No. 16	1834c
20. Beann-Crann "The peak, or height of the trees"	Munn's Notes 44	1925
21. 'bankran	Local pronunciation	1993
22. 'bankrən	Local pronunciation	1993

Bancran Glebe was church land from as early as c.1624. In a list of glebes allotted in the barony of Loughinsholin around that time, "1 balliboe called Banharan lying in the parish of Ballineskrene" was allotted to Gilbert Sutton, clerk (*Bishop. Der.* i 145). The editors of the text tentatively identify this as the *Donarnon* of several other early texts, but this is, in fact, one of the original six townlands of Ballynascreen and is now a subdivision of Owenreagh. Both Dunarnon, in the somewhat corrupt form *b:dounnaruarr*, and Bancran appear alongside one another on the Escheated Counties map of this part of the barony (*Esch. Co. Map* 14) and there can be little doubt that they were two distinct places.

   The origin of the name is unclear but it may be a diminutive form of *beannchar* which forms or occurs in a number of names in various parts of Ireland. Its meaning is now obscure, but perhaps the most plausible explanation to date is that it denotes some kind of palisaded enclosure (*PNI* ii 148–150).

Brackagh   *Breacach*
H 7590   "speckled place"

1. Bracka Clon Morley	Lond. Comp. Valuation 311	1613
2. Bracke Clonmorley	Phillips MSS (Maps) Plate 30	1622
3. (?)Brackagh beinge 2 sessioghes	Inq. Ult. (Derry) §1 Car. I	1633
4. Brackagh, halfe of	Civ. Surv. iii 177	1654
5. Brakagh	Civ. Surv. iii 177,178	1654
6. Brackagh, Half of	BSD(c) 63	1661
7. Brakah	HMR (Ó Doibhlin 2) 67	1663
8. Brackagh	Sampson's Map	1813
9. Brackagh	Grand Jury Pres. (OSNB) No. 16	1830c
10. Brackagh	Title Deeds (OSNB) No. 16	1830c
11. Brackagh	Received usage No. 16	1834c
12. 'Brack-agh	OSNB Pron. No. 16	1834c
13. Bracagh "spotted land"	MacCloskey's Stat. Report 62	1821
14. Brocach "a badger warren, a fox cover"	J O'D (OSNB) No. 16	1834c
15. Bracach "The speckled or broken ground"	Munn's Notes 44	1925
16. 'brakə	Local pronunciation	1993

Irish *breac* "speckled" is often employed to describe the speckled or spotted appearance of land caused by different kinds of vegetation or by the varying colours of soil or rock (*Joyce* ii 288), and is here used in conjuction with the suffix *ach* to signify "speckled land". O'Donovan's suggestion of *Brocach* "a badger warren" is not supported by the available evidence. *Brocach* does occur in names of places in various parts of the country where it is usually anglicized Brockagh etc., but although the tendency of *o* to become *a* is widespread in Ulster (O'Rahilly 1932, 192–3), this does not appear to have occurred before *c* (compare *boc, cnoc, soc*).

Cahore
H 7892

Of uncertain origin

1. Cohoire	Esch. Co. Map 14	1609
2. Cohoire	Charter of Londonderry 391	1613
3. Cohar	Lond. Comp. Valuation 311	1613
4. Cahor	Phillips MSS (Maps) Plate 30	1622
5. (?)Cahore	Civ. Surv. iii 175	1654
6. (?)Kahore	Civ. Surv. iii 176	1654
7. Cahore (x3)	Civ. Surv. iii 178	1654
8. Cohoire	Bishop. Der. i 266, 277	1657
9. Cahore	BSD(c) 64	1661
10. Cahier	HMR (Ó Doibhlin 2) 67	1663
11. Cahore	Sampson's Map	1813
12. Cahor(?)	Grand Jury Pres. (OSNB) No. 16	1830c
13. Cahore	Received usage No. 16	1834c
14. Ca-'hore	OSNB Pron. No. 16	1834c
15. Ca or "place for sheep, or for berries"	MacCloskey's Stat. Report 62	1821

16. Cath óir "golden battle"	J O'D (OSNB) No. 16	1834c
17. Cath óir (crossed out)	J O'D (OSNB) No. 16	1834c
18. Cath odhar (crossed out)	J O'D (OSNB) No. 16	1834c
19. Cathair "The townland of the circular stone fort"	Munn's Notes 45	1925
20. kʲəˈhoːr	Local pronunciation	1993

Cormac McBaron O'Neill, Hugh O'Neill's brother, wrote a letter from a place called "Cathoyr" in 1601 enquiring about his brother's progress since going to Kinsale. The editor of the letter tentatively identifies the place-name as the townland of Cattor in Co. Tyrone, but Ó Ceallaigh argues that it refers, rather, to our Cahore (*CSP Ire.* 1601–03, 463; Ó Ceallaigh 1950(a), 176). No evidence is produced by either writer, but it is perhaps noteworthy that, a short while after this, Cahore was made into a small proportion for the purposes of the Plantation (*Charter of Londonderry* 391), thereby indicating that some importance was to be attached to the place.

The origin of the name is rather obscure and none of the previous attempts to produce an etymology are very convincing. Munn's derivation from *Cathair* "a circular stone fort" is one of the more plausible suggestions but it is not supported by the evidence (19). The stress in *cathair* falls on the first syllable, but the historical spellings, which almost invariably show an *o* in the final syllable and considerable variation in the vowel of the first syllable, indicate that the name was pronounced roughly as it is still, with stress on the last syllable, as far back as the early 17th century.

Dónall Mac Giolla Easpaig, writing on the name *Leitir Catha* in Co. Donegal (1984, 53–4), suggests that the word *cath*, which appears in a number of isolated place-names, may have a meaning other than "battle" and that it may refer in these cases to a natural feature of some sort. If this is correct then this may be the initial element in this name. An origin from *Caoth* "boghole, swamp-hole" is suggested for **Caw** in Co. Derry, but the historical spellings seem to favour Mac Giolla Easpaig's *cath* (*GÉ* 201). Ó Ceallaigh (1950(a), 175–6) suggests that names such as this go back to Scottish Gaelic *cadha* "a pass" (Irish *caoi* "way, path"), but it would be strange that the element, presuming it is a borrowing from Scottish Gaelic, was so infrequent in Co. Antrim where Scottish influence was strongest. Numerous other elements are possible here, including *cabha* "hollow, cavity" (but see **Carncose** in Desertmartin), *coth* "sustenance", and *cuach* "cup" > "hollow", but there is now no way to distinguish between them with any degree of certainty. Likewise, the origin of the final element is unclear, and we might suggest *ór* "gold", *odhar* "dun, greyish brown" (but also occurring as a personal name), *fobhar* "spring, well", or possibly *fuar* "cold".

Carnamoney
H 7798

Ceathrú na Móna
"the quarterland of the bog"

1. Carramony	Esch. Co. Map 14	1609
2. Corramony	Charter of Londonderry 391	1613
3. Carn Money	Lond. Comp. Valuation 309	1613
4. Carnmane	Phillips MSS (Maps) Plate 28	1622
5. Carnemoney	Civ. Surv. iii 177	1654
6. Carramony	Bishop. Der. i 266	1657
7. Carrowmony, the small proportion of	Bishop. Der. i 277	1657

8. Carnemony	Census 137	1659c
9. Carnemoney	BSD(c) 63	1661
10. Carnomoney	HMR (Ó Doibhlin 2) 67	1663
11. Carnamoney	Sampson's Map	1813
12. Carnamoney	Grand Jury Pres. (OSNB) No. 16	1830c
13. Carnamoney	Received usage No. 16	1834c
14. Car-na-'mun-ny	OSNB Pron. No. 16	1834c
15. Carnamoney	Title Deeds (OSNB) No. 16	1834c
16. Carn a moiniadh "mound of stones in the bog"	MacCloskey's Stat. Report 62	1821
17. Cuir na moinead "the pits in the bog"	MacCloskey's Stat. Report 62	1821
18. Ceathramha na muine "quarter of the brake"	J O'D (OSNB) No. 16	1834c
19. Ceathramha na mona "bog quarter"	J O'D (OSNB) No. 16	1834c
20. "carn of the shrubbery"	Joyce iii 168	1913
21. Carn-na-muine "The cairn of the shrubbery"	Munn's Notes 45	1925
22. ˌkaːrnəˈmoːni	Local pronunciation	1993
23. ˌkɔrnəˈmoːni	Local pronunciation	1993
24. ˌkjarnəˈmo̞ni	Local pronunciation	1993

The current local pronunciation is particularly useful in determining the origin of the final element of this name. The majority of people I spoke to pronounced this part of the name with a long closed *o* (as in *bone*), indicating a derivation from *móin* "bog", rather than from *muine* "thicket" with which *móin* is often confused in place-names (see Toner 1991–3). The alternative pronunciation (with a final element sounding like *munny*) is almost certainly due to the influence of the spelling, although such confusion is at least as old as the 1830s when a local pronunciation was first collected (14). The heathy land in the north of the townland and on the slopes of Slievemoyle is probably the "bog" to which the name refers (described as "heath" in *OSNB*).

The first element is also open to a number of interpretations, many of which have been suggested by previous writers (16-21). It is perhaps not unlikely, however, that it represents Irish *ceathrú* "quarterland" (18-19). A similar shortening of *ceathrú* is witnessed in the name **Carmeen** in the parish of Clonallan, Co. Down (*PNI* i 67-8), and in the name **Carnafarn** and **Carnakilly** (Upper and Lower) in the Co. Derry parishes of Clondermot and Faughanvale respectively. Unfortunately, the frequency with which *n*, *r* and *u* are confused in early documents makes it difficult to be sure about the form of the name in the 17th century, and this makes it correspondingly harder to verify any suggested etymology. There is one spelling (7) which can only be interpreted as *ceathrú*, although little weight can be attributed to what is almost certainly a rogue spelling, as other forms in the same document and in related documents remain more ambiguous (1–2, 6).

The element *ceathrú* forms or begins the names of well over 700 townlands throughout Ireland (*Joyce* i 244). It often signifies a quarter of a ballybetagh which is here equivalent to 16 townlands, but this is hardly its sense here (see *Lond. Comp. Valuation* 309). McErlean (1983, 318) notes that in Derry, the quarter is further divided into three, or more commonly four, parts and so *ceathrú* here may be more or less equivalent to a townland or balliboe (that is, a sixteenth of a ballybetagh). A similar meaning is suggested by the name **Carrowmenagh**, Irish *Ceathrú Mheánach* "middle quarter", in the nearby parish of Killelagh.

Cavanreagh	*Cabhán Riabhach*	
H 7292	"grey hill/hollow"	
1. b:chauan	Esch. Co. Map 14	1609
2. ballychanan	Bishop. Der. i 57	1610
3. Ballychanan or Ballycanan	CPR Jas I 279a	1615
4. Ballychane	Bishop. Der. i 103	1615
5. Carnareagh	Hib. Reg. Loughinsholin	1657c
6. Cavanreagh	Census 137	1659c
7. Cannanreagh	BSD(c) 55	1661
8. Cananreagh	HMR (Ó Doibhlin 2) 67	1663
9. Carnareagh	Hib. Del. Derry	1672c
10. Cavanreagh	Sampson's Map	1813
11. Cavanreagh	Received usage No. 16	1834c
12. Cav-an-'ree-agh	OSNB Pron. No. 16	1834c
13. Cabhan reagh "the rugged plain"	MacCloskey's Stat. Report 62	1821
14. Cabhán riach "grey round dry hill"	J O'D (OSNB) No. 16	1834c
15. Cabhan-riabhach "The grey round dry hill"	Munn's Notes 45	1925
16. 'kʲavən're:jə	Local pronunciation	1993
17. 'kavən're:	Local pronunciation	1993

This name is spelt in a great variety of ways in our 17th-century sources, but most are rec-oncilable with the modern form if we correct the common error of *n* for *v*. In all probabil-ity, therefore, the origin of the modern form of this name can be identified as *Cabhán Riabhach* "grey slope/hollow". *Cabhán* originally signified a slope or hollow (O.Ir. *cobfán* < *com + fán*) but O'Donovan notes that in Down and Fermanagh it came to mean "round dry bare hill" (*O'Reilly*; cf. *Joyce* i 401), and O'Donnell translates *Cabhán an Churaigh* in north Derry as *collis cymbae* or "hill of the curragh" (*Colton Vis.* 133). However, there is no feature in the townland which might reasonably be described as a "round dry bare hill", and this meaning may be quite late. The townland is situated on the slopes of Slieveavaddy and rolls down to the Moyola River, so that *cabhán* here may mean "hollow" or more probably "slope" or "hill" (O'Donnell's *collis*). In the very earliest documents, Cavanreagh is represented by a form *Ballychauan* and the like (1–4), indicating an alternative form of the name *Baile Chabháin* "townland of the hill/hollow". The lenition of the final element here reflects the use of the name in the dative.

Cloane	*Cluain*	
H 7698	"meadow"	
1. (?)Clone, [ecclesiatical] manor of	Reg. Dowdall §60 150	1541

2. cloine	Esch. Co. Map 14	1609
3. Clony	Charter of Londonderry 391	1613
4. Agh Clon	Lond. Comp. Valuation 309	1613
5. Aghclon	Phillips MSS (Maps) Plate 28	1622
6. Cloan	Civ. Surv. iii 177	1654
7. Clony	Bishop. Der. i 266	1657
8. Cloan	BSD(c) 63	1661
9. (?)Chyen	HMR (Ó Doibhlin 2) 67	1663
10. Cloan	Sampson's Map	1813
11. Cloane	Received usage No. 16	1834c
12. Cloane	Title Deeds (OSNB) No. 16	1834c
13. 'Clone	OSNB Pron. No. 16	1834c
14. Cluain "a level recess between woods"	MacCloskey's Stat. Report 62	1821
15. Cluain "a lawn or meadow"	J O'D (OSNB) No. 16	1834c
16. Cluainte "The meadows"	Munn's Notes 45	1925
17. klo:n	Local pronunciation	1993

The derivation suggested by O'Donovan is almost certainly correct. Two of the earlier spellings (3, 7), albeit from related documents, might be taken as an indication of an old dative form of the same word, *cluanaidh* "at/by (the) meadow", but they are more likely to represent poor transcriptions from the Escheated Counties maps (see **Ballynure** above). The forms from the London Companies' Valuation and the Phillips' maps (4-5) are probably also the result of some scribal error rather than alternative forms of the name, as these two related sources are often unreliable.

Cloughfin   *Cloch Fhionn*
H 7791   "white stone"

1. Cloghlin	Sampson's Map	1813
2. Cloughfin	Grand Jury Pres. (OSNB) No. 16	1830c
3. Cloughfin	Received usage No. 16	1834c
4. Cloughfinn	Title Deeds (OSNB) No. 16	1834c
5. Clock-'fin	OSNB Pron. No. 16	1834c
6. Cloch finn "the white stone"	MacCloskey's Stat. Report 62	1821
7. Cloch fionn "white stone"	J O'D (OSNB) No. 16	1834c
8. Cloch-fionn "The white stone"	Munn's Notes 45	1925
9. klɔx'fin	Local pronunciation	1993

There are twelve townlands by the name of Cloghfin in the northern and western counties of Donegal (×4), Tyrone (×4), Antrim (×1), Armagh (×1), Monaghan (×1), and Sligo (×1), and there is another **Cloughfin** in the neighbouring parish of Kilcronaghan. In place-names *cloch* is often applied to a large and conspicuous stone, or to a stone of some historical or cultural significance, but it can also be used of a stone building, such as a castle (*Joyce* i 411; also Mac Giolla Easpaig 1984, 58; *DIL* sv. *cloch*). The final element is probably the adjective *fionn* "white", although a connection with the legendary character Finn McCool cannot be ruled out.

15

Coolnasillagh
H 7999

Cúil na Saileach
"the corner/nook of the sallow(s)"

1. Culnesellah	Esch. Co. Map 14	1609
2. Culnesellah	Charter of Londonderry 391	1613
3. (?)Clona Scilla	Lond. Comp. Valuation 309	1613
4. Coolnosilla	Phillips MSS (Maps) Plate 28	1622
5. Cullnessilagh	Civ. Surv. iii 177	1654
6. Cullnesellagh	Bishop. Der. i 266	1657
7. Cullnesillagh	Census 137	1659c
8. Cullnesillagh	BSD(c) 63	1661
9. Cullona Sealogh	HMR (Ó Doibhlin 2) 67	1663
10. Coolnasillagh	Sampson's Map	1813
11. Coolnasillagh	Grand Jury Pres. (OSNB) No. 16	1830c
12. Coolnasillagh	Received usage No. 16	1834c
13. Coolnasillagh	Title Deeds (OSNB) No. 16	1834c
14. Cool-na-'sil-agh	OSNB Pron. No. 16	1834c
15. Cuil na sailleach "the corner of willows"	MacCloskey's Stat. Report 62	1821
16. [Cuil na] sailseach "[corner of] druidical fires"	MacCloskey's Stat. Report 62	1821
17. Cuil na saileach "corner or angle of the sallows"	J O'D (OSNB) No. 16	1834c
18. Cuil-na-Saileach "The corner of the Sallows"	Munn's Notes 45	1925
19. ˌkulnəˈsïlə	Local pronunciation	1993

The two elements *cúil* "a corner, nook, or recess" and *cúl* "a back" are practically indistinguishable in their anglicized forms (*Joyce* i 530–1), but *cúil* is the more common of the two in townland names. The final element is clearly *sail*, gen. *saileach*, "sallow" which is variously anglicized as *sallagh* and *sillagh* in place-names (*Joyce* ii 357; cf. O'Rahilly 1932, 198). The latter is not usually found east of the Bann, but both forms occur side by side in Derry, Tyrone, and Fermanagh.

Corick
H 7789

Comhrac
"confluence"

1. Corock 1 sessiogh	Inq. Ult. (Derry) §1 Car. I	1633
2. Corath one Sessiogh of land	Civ. Surv. iii 188	1654
3. Gort als Corath	BSD(c) 53	1661
4. Corick	Sampson's Map	1813
5. Corick	Received usage No. 16	1834c
6. 'Co-rick	OSNB Pron. No. 16	1834c
7. Comherac "meeting of the waters"	MacCloskey's Stat. Report 62	1821
8. Comhrac "meeting of waters"	J O'D (OSNB) No. 16	1834c
9. Comhrac "The meeting of the rivers"	Munn's Notes 45	1925
10. 'korïk	Local pronunciation	1993

The rivers Black Water and White Water meet forming the north-eastern and north-western boundaries of the townland and it is almost certainly from this confluence that the townland is named. In the 17th century, it was held, along with several nearby townlands in the parish of Lissan, by the Archbishop of Armagh (*Inq. Ult* (Derry) §1 Car. I).

Derrynoyd　　　　　　　　　　　*Doire an Fhóid*
H 7696　　　　　　　　　　　　　　"oakwood of the sod"

1. derrinarde	Esch. Co. Map 14	1609
2. Derrynard	Charter of Londonderry 391	1613
3. Derrey Moy	Lond. Comp. Valuation 311	1613
4. Derenoyd	Phillips MSS (Maps) Plate 30	1622
5. Dornoyd (x2)	Civ. Surv. iii 178	1654
6. Derryward	Bishop. Der. i 266	1657
7. Dornoyd	BSD(c) 64	1661
8. Derrynoid	Sampson's Map	1813
9. Derrynoid	Grand Jury Pres. (OSNB) No. 16	1830c
10. Derrynoid	Title Deeds (OSNB) No. 16	1834c
11. Derrynoyd	Received usage No. 16	1834c
12. Derry-'noyd	OSNB Pron. No. 16	1834c
13. Doire nodh "the noble oaks"	MacCloskey's Stat. Report 62	1821
14. Doire Nuadaid "Noud's oak wood"	J O'D (OSNB) No. 16	1834c
15. Daire-Nuadht "The oakgrove of Nuat"	Munn's Notes 45	1925
16. ˌdɛriˈnɔid	Local pronunciation	1993

The first element in this name is undoubtedly *doire* "oakwood", but some doubt surrounds the final element. O'Donovan favoured an origin from the personal name *Nuadha*, which was borne by the mythical king of the Tuatha Dé Danann, as well as by other less exalted mortals (14). The name Maynooth in Co. Kildare (Irish *Maigh Nuad*) supposedly commemorates Nuadha, king of Leinster (*Joyce* i 134), and a St Nuadha has given name to the townland and parish of Estersnow (Irish *Díseart Nuadhan*) in Co. Roscommon (*ibid.* 325; *AFM* iii 546n). However, as these names demonstrate, *ua* followed by a broad consonant in Irish tends to give English [o:] or [u:], and this derivation can be dismissed. However, English *oy* may indicate an original Irish *ua* or *ó* before a palatal consonant, usually *l* or *n*. *Buaile* "summer pasturage", although usually anglicized *boley* in place-names, frequently appears in early spellings as *boyle* etc. (see **Slievenaboley** and **Ballyboley** in Co. Down; **Ballyboley** in Co. Antrim), and *ó* appears as *oy* in names such as Boyne (*An Bhóinn*), and **Lough Foyle** (*Loch Feabhail* with *abha* > *ó*).

One possible interpretation, therefore, is that the final element represents Irish *fód* "sod". It is found in a small number of place-names, including Bellanode in Co. Monaghan (Irish *Béal Átha an Fhóid*) and Castlenode (*Caiseal an Fhóid*), and is generally anglicized *-ode* (*GÉ* 189; *Onom. Goed.* 104; *Éigse* vi 204, 282; *Joyce* ii 382). Of particular interest to us is the name of the townland of **Lisoid** in Co. Down which appears to derive from *Lios Fhóid* "fort of the sod" (see *Joyce* ii 382), although this is generally spelt *Lisode* in 17th-century documents. It is perhaps difficult to account for the consistency with which the final syllable is represented as *oy* in Derrynoyd throughout the 17th century, but the exceptional spellings from the

Escheated Counties maps and related sources (1-2, 6) tend to confirm such an origin. The *r* of these forms is clearly a mistake, probably for *u*, so that we should emend these forms to *Derrinaude* or the like. English *au* in words like *cause* is very close in sound to the long-*o* in Irish *fód*, and it is not unlikely that this is the sound intended here (see Barber 1976, 300–1).

I have also considered a possible connection with the rare and obscure element which we find in the name *Sliabh Fuaid*, a mountain between Armagh and Dundalk which is usually identified with Deadman's Hill near Newtownhamilton (Arthurs 1954(b), 33). This name has not survived into modern times but early 17th-century spellings such as *Slewfoed* and *Slewboed*, if not mistranscriptions of a form *Slewfood*, make a striking parallel to the anglicized form of Derrynoyd. However, it is no more likely to produce the range of spellings which we see here than *fód* and perhaps less likely to give forms such as our reconstructed *Derrinaude*. Furthermore, we would not normally expect to find the article accompanying what is clearly an obsolete element.

Disert
H 7692

Díseart
"hermitage"

1. b:desart	Esch. Co. Map 14	1609
2. Desart	Lond. Comp. Valuation 311	1613
3. Desart	Phillips MSS (Maps) Plate 30	1622
4. (?)Deisary	Civ. Surv. iii 177	1654
5. Dissert	Census 137	1659c
6. Diesary	BSD(c) 63	1661
7. Desert	Sampson's Map	1813
8. Dysert	Grand Jury Pres. (OSNB) No. 16	1830c
9. Dyzert	Received usage No. 16	1834c
10. Dysert	Title Deeds (OSNB) No. 16	1834c
11. 'Dy-zert	OSNB Pron. No. 16	1834c
12. Des art "stony land"	MacCloskey's Stat. Report 62	1821
13. Dís Chert "two just church wardens"	OSL (Derry) 86	1834
14. Dísert "a desert or wilderness"	J O'D (OSNB) No. 16	1834c
15. Disert "a wilderness, a hermitage"	OSM (Loughrey) 60	1837c
16. Disert "The Hermitage"	Munn's Notes 46	1925
17. 'di:zərt	Local pronunciation	1993
18. 'daizərt	Local pronunciation	1993

O'Donovan cites a fanciful tradition which was then current in the county that places called Desert (or Disert) were named from two just church wardens (*Dís Chert*) who were appointed by the clergy to distribute alms to the poor (*OSL (Derry)* 56, 86), and he quite rightly dismisses this notion. In fact, it derives from Irish *díseart*, a borrowing from Latin *desertum*.

Deirdre Flanagan has suggested that the use of *díseart* in place-names may have begun as early as the 6th century with the meaning "hermitage" and that by the 8th and 9th centuries it had developed a more specialized meaning "a place apart: a monastic house observing a stricter rule" which may be related to the spread of the Culdee movement (1981–2(c), 72).

18

The place-name remains as the only evidence of an early ecclesiastical presence on this site, and tradition mentions only a mass rock at "Lub-na-hAltora" where the White Water flows into the Moyola (*Coulter's Ballinascreen* 45).

Doon   *Dún*
H 7594   "fort"

1. dounagilliduf	Esch. Co. Map 14	1609
2. Donagilleduff	Charter of Londonderry 391	1613
3. Dodd Gilduff	Lond. Comp. Valuation 311	1613
4. Donkilduff	Phillips MSS (Maps) Plate 30	1622
5. Dungillduffe	Civ. Surv. iii 177	1654
6. Honnagillyduffe	Bishop. Der. i 266	1657
7. DunoGilduffe	Census 137	1659c
8. Dungillduffe	BSD(c) 63	1661
9. Dunnigilladuff	HMR (Ó Doibhlin 2) 67	1663
10. Doon	Sampson's Map	1813
11. Doon	Grand Jury Pres. (OSNB) No. 16	1830c
12. Doon	Title Deeds (OSNB) No. 16	1834c
13. 'Doon	OSNB Pron. No. 16	1834c
14. Dun "the hill"	MacCloskey's Stat. Report 62	1821
15. Dún "an earthern fort"	J O'D (OSNB) No. 16	1834c
16. Dun "The fortress"	Munn's Notes 46	1925
17. du:n	Local pronunciation	1993

The remains of a fort were excavated here by Desmond McCourt in c.1955 and the site was found to contain a substantial farmhouse of the early Christian period (G. Mawhinney, pers. comm.; see also Speer 1990, 10). Ó Ceallaigh's assertion that it was once called *Dún an Ghiolla Dhuibh* (1927, 60) is supported by the historical spellings assembled here, but his identification of the eponymous owner of the fort as one Giolla Dubh Ó Ceallaigh (Kelly), whose family still then exclusively occupied the half townland of Doon called Crieve, is open to doubt (*ibid.*). The family appears to have had a long association with the area for a Thirlo O'Kelly of Doon appears in the Hearth Money Rolls of 1663 (*HMR (Ó Doibhlin 2)* 67). However, Giolla Dubh Ó Ceallaigh lived only some 200 years ago and assured the preservation of his name in local tradition by marrying the daughter of a Protestant minister (Ó Ceallaigh 1901, 201) so he cannot possibly be the person who gave name to the fort.

Drumard   *Droim Ard*
H 7993   "high ridge"

1. ⅓ dromard	Esch. Co. Map 14	1609
2. Dromard, ⅓ part of a balliboe	Charter of Londonderry 392	1613
3. Dromard & Money grogon	Lond. Comp. Valuation 311	1613
4. Dromard	Phillips MSS (Maps) Plate 30	1622
5. Drumard Munyqugan	Civ. Surv. iii 177	1654
6. Drumard	Civ. Surv. iii 177,188	1654
7. Dromard	Bishop. Der. i 266	1657

8. Drumard	BSD(c) 63	1661
9. Drummard	HMR (Ó Doibhlin 2) 67	1663
10. Drimard	Sampson's Map	1813
11. Drumard	Grand Jury Pres. (OSNB) No. 16	1830c
12. Drimard	Received usage No. 16	1834c
13. Drimard	Title Deeds (OSNB) No. 16	1834c
14. Drim'ard	OSNB Pron. No. 16	1834c
15. Druim ard "the lofty back"	MacCloskey's Stat. Report 62	1821
16. Druim ard "high ridge"	J O'D (OSNB) No. 16	1834c
17. Driuim ard "high ridge"	OSM (Loughrey) 60	1837c
18. Druim-Ard "The high ridge"	Munn's Notes 46	1925
19. drọm'ɑːrd	Local pronunciation	1993

There can be little doubt about the derivation of this name. The high ridge along the southern boundary of the townland is very probably the feature referred to in the name.

Drumderg   *Droim Dearg*
H 7396   "red ridge"

1. dromvlderige (?)	Esch. Co. Map 14	1609
2. Dromohderigg	Charter of Londonderry 391	1613
3. (?)Drom Lirge	Lond. Comp. Valuation 311	1613
4. (?)Dromlyrg	Phillips MSS (Maps) Plate 30	1622
5. Dromlerick	Civ. Surv. iii 177	1654
6. Dromderrick	Civ. Surv. iii 215	1654
7. Drinuliderrigg	Bishop. Der. i 266	1657
8. Drumlierge	Census 137	1659c
9. Dromlerrick	BSD(c) 63	1661
10. Drimderg	Sampson's Map	1813
11. Drumderig	Received usage No. 16	1834c
12. Drumderig	Title Deeds (OSNB) No. 16	1834c
13. Drum-'dearg	OSNB Pron. No. 16	1834c
14. Druim dearg "the red back"	MacCloskey's Stat. Report 62	1821
15. Druim a' Deirg "the ridge of Dergo"	OSL (Derry) 85	1834
16. Druim dearg "red ridge"	J O'D (OSNB) No. 16	1834c
17. Druim-a-Deirg "The ridge of Deirg"	Munn's Notes 46	1925
18. drọm'dɛːrg	Local pronunciation	1993

Munn recounts a tale of a certain giant whom he calls *Deirg-much-a Draoigneain*, one of the sons of Finn McCool who fought in Scotland against the Romans about 300–400 AD, and was buried here in the south-east corner of the townland (*Munn's Notes* 46). MacCloskey states that the grave of a giant was located on the hill known as *Kill na hough* which he interprets as "the cemetery among the caves" (*MacCloskey's Stat. Report* 14), and Munn cites this tradition in support of his interpretation of the townland name. Deirg was killed by Goll mac Morna after they fought for eight days and nights without resting. This story supports Munn's suggestion that the name derives from an Irish form meaning "the ridge of Deirg", but the account smacks of folk etymology and should probably be dismissed. O'Donovan recounts a slightly different version of this tale but notes that it was only very faintly remembered in his day (*OSL (Derry)* 85–6). According to this version, Dergo (as he calls him) was a mighty warrior who came over from Scandinavia to conquer all of Finn McCool's men single-handedly. The tale is also recounted in the Ordnance Survey Memoirs where it is stated that the giant was killed by Cú Chulainn, and that the place where he was buried is called Killé Aheuma "the tomb burial ground" (*OSM (Loughrey)* 18-19, 37).

Given this tradition of a giant's grave apparently called *Cill na hUamha* "graveyard of the cave/grave", it is tempting to accept the earliest spellings as representative of a form *Droim Uamha Deirg* "ridge of Derg's grave" (1–2, 7). However, all these spellings occur in closely related sources and do not offer independent evidence of the pronunciation of the name. Furthermore, although these sources generally supply us with interesting and illuminating forms, they frequently contain significant scribal errors, and in the absence of any corroborating evidence we must discount such an origin.

A much more likely interpretation is offered by O'Donovan, namely, that the name simply means "red ridge" (Irish *Droim Dearg*). The 17th-century spellings generally vary between *-der(r)igg* and *-der(r)ick*, showing the pronunciation of the *ea* in the original Irish *dearg* as [ɛ] (O.Ir. *derg*), and the presence of an epenthetic vowel between the *r* and *g* of *dearg*. The latter group of spellings seems to show devoicing of original [g] to [k], but this has probably occurred in English rather than Irish (see O'Rahilly 1932, 147n; cf. **Aghaderg** in Co. Down). Although final, unstressed *g* is normally devoiced in a small number of words in Ulster Irish, the phenomenon is generally restricted to parts of north-west Donegal and is not consistently attested in East Ulster (Ó Dochartaigh 1987, 161–4, 305–7).

Dunlogan   Of uncertain origin
H 7097

1. Don Lewan	Lond. Comp. Valuation 309	1613
2. Donlewan	Phillips MSS (Maps) Plate 30	1622
3. Dunlogan, half town	HMR (Ó Doibhlin 2) 66	1663
4. Dunlogan	Sampson's Map	1813
5. Dunlogan	Received usage No. 16	1834c
6. Dunlogan	Title Deeds (OSNB) No. 16	1834c
7. Dun-'lo-gan	OSNB Pron. No. 16	1834c
8. Doonlogan "the brown district"	MacCloskey's Stat. Report 62	1821
9. Dún-logáin "Logan's fort"	J O'D (OSNB) No. 16	1834c
10. Dun-Ghluagain "The fort of the Monster Toad"	Munn's Notes 46	1925
11. ˌdɔnˈloːgən	Local pronunciation	1993

The *dún* "fort" which forms the first element in this name may be the enclosure which stands on a local eminence between two streams in this townland (Speer 1990, 1; *NISMR (Derry)* sh.35 §8). Unfortunately, the name is absent from many of our 17th-century sources and the form of the second element is not easily ascertained. The early spellings we have fall into two groups, one of which agrees with the modern form (3). The earlier group, which is contained in two closely-related sources, yields a form *Donlewan* (1–2). This should perhaps be emended to *Donlowgan* or the like, but the lack of any early authority for this change must cast serious doubt over any subsequent interpretation. It is important, however, in that it indicates that the name has always been pronounced much as it is, with a long-*o* in the second syllable. Thus, we can reject an origin from *logán* "little hollow" which has a short-*o*.

There seems to be no word or personal name in the Irish language which suitably explains this element and we can only conclude that it has suffered some degree of corruption, probably before it was even anglicized. The surname Logan is common in Ulster, and where it is of Irish origin it represents the name *Ó Leocháin* (MacLysaght 1982, 147), so we might propose an origin here from the personal name *Leochán*. The anglicization of Ó Leocháin as Logan goes back a long way in Ulster for both Logan and O'Louchan were used by members of the clergy of Armagh and Down in the first half of the 15th century (*ibid.*). However, the normal anglicization of the surname would be O'Loughan or O'Loghan and it clearly only became Logan by confusion with the Anglo-Norman name, de Logan, which appears in medieval documents relating to the Carrickfergus area as early as 1190 (*ibid.*). Logan in Ulster can also have come from Scotland where it is probably derived from the place-name Logan in Ayrshire (*ibid.*; Black 1946, 436), and this doubtless further strengthened the tendency in later times to anglicize the Irish surname as Logan.

Dunmurry　　　　　　　　　　　*Dún Muirígh*
H 7599　　　　　　　　　　　　　"Murray's fort"

1. (?)b:dounnaruarr	Esch. Co. Map 14	1609
2. Don Mura whey	Lond. Comp. Valuation 309	1613
3. Donmurahy	Phillips MSS (Maps) Plate 28	1622
4. Dunnemury	Civ. Surv. iii 177	1654
5. Donmurry	Census 137	1659c
6. Dunnemurry	BSD(c) 63	1661
7. Drimberry	HMR (Ó Doibhlin 2) 66	1663
8. Dunmurry	Sampson's Map	1813
9. Dunmurry	Received usage No. 16	1834c
10. Dunmurry	Title Deeds (OSNB) No. 16	1834c
11. Dun-'mur-ry	OSNB Pron. No. 16	1834c
12. Dun muraim (marus) "the fenced hill"	MacCloskey's Stat. Report 62	1821
13. Dún Muireadaigh "Murray's fort"	J O'D (OSNB) No. 16	1834c
14. Dun-Mhuireadhaigh "The fort of Murray"	Munn's Notes 46	1925
15. ˌdɒnˈmɔri	Local pronunciation	1993

This name appears to derive from *Dún Muirígh* "Murray's fort", although one group of early spellings (2-3) is perhaps suggestive of the personal name *Murchadh*. However, it is unlikely that the *ch* of *Murchadh* would have been lost in the anglicization process, and these spellings are probably corruptions. It is possible, however, that the *w*(*h*) in these rogue spellings represents the *dh* of *Muireadhach* (modern *Muiríoch*) which was still faintly pronounced in some words into the 20th century and occasionally appears in other place-names (cf. **Fallagloon**

22

in Maghera parish, and the pronunciation of the surname as Murrihy in Woulfe 1923, 621). There is now no trace of a fort in the townland, nor is there any indication of the identity of the eponymous owner of the fort.

Duntibryan	*Dún Tí Bhriain*	
H 8096	"fort of Brian's house"	
1. Dountibrian	Esch. Co. Map 14	1609
2. Domituibrian	Charter of Londonderry 391	1613
3. Donte Brean	Lond. Comp. Valuation 309	1613
4. Dontebrean	Phillips MSS (Maps) Plate 28	1622
5. Duntibrean	Civ. Surv. iii 177	1654
6. halfe Duntibrean	Civ. Surv. iii 177	1654
7. Duntibrien	Civ. Surv. iii 177	1654
8. Duntibrian	Civ. Surv. iii 190	1654
9. Dromtibrion	Bishop. Der. i 266	1657
10. Half Duntibreane	BSD(c) 63	1661
11. Duntiburne half town	HMR (Ó Doibhlin 2) 67	1663
12. Duntybryan	Sampson's Map	1813
13. Duntybrian	Received usage No. 16	1834c
14. Duntybrian	Title Deeds (OSNB) No. 16	1834c
15. Dunty'bri-an	OSNB Pron. No. 16	1834c
16. Dunlig breon "the spotted hill"	MacCloskey's Stat. Report 62	1821
17. Dún Tíghe Bhriain	OSL (Derry) 85	1834
18. Dún tíghe Bhriain "fort of Brian's house"	J O'D (OSNB) No. 16	1834c
19. Dun-tighe-Bhriain "fort of Brian's house"	Joyce iii 343	1913
20. Dun-tighe-Bhriain "The fort of ... house of Brian"	Munn's Notes 47	1925
21. ˌdͻnti'braiən	Local pronunciation	1993

The rath at the western end of the townland (H 8095), described in the Ordnance Survey Name Book for this parish as "Duntybrian Fort", is probably the structure referred to in this name as a *dún* "fort" (cf. Speer 1990, 41). In the last century, it was believed locally that the owner of the house was Brian Carrach O'Neill, and some old men remembered its ruins, although these had disappeared by the time O'Donovan visited Ballynascreen in 1834 (*OSL (Derry)* 85).

Finglen	*Fionnghleann*	
H 7095	"white/fair valley"	
1. ffinglen-o Mullegan	Civ. Surv. iii 168	1654
2. Finniglen Omulligan	Civ. Surv. iii 372	1654
3. Finnyglenn Omullan	Civ. Surv. iii 374	1654
4. Finglen	Received usage No. 16	1834c
5. 'Fin-glen	OSNB Pron. No. 16	1834c

6. Fionn-ghleann "fair or white glen"	J O'D (OSNB) No. 16	1834c
7. Fionn-gleann "The white glen, or the narrow, or straight glen"	Munn's Notes 47	1925
8. 'fīni̩glɛn	Local pronunciation	1993
9. 'fīnglɛn	Local pronunciation	1993

The townland obviously takes its name from the valley (Irish *gleann*) which runs through it. The pronunciation obtained from some local people shows an epenthetic vowel between the two elements which was not recorded by the Ordnance Survey in the 1830s but which is found in some of our earliest sources (2–3).

The early references to the name also show that it was known as *Fionnghleann Ó Maolagáin* "white/fair valley of the O'Mulligans" in the latter half of the 17th century. O'Mulligan was the name of an important sept in Co. Donegal who lost their lands during the Plantation of Ulster in the early 17th century (MacLysaght 1957, 233–4). The surname was common in Monaghan and Fermanagh in the mid-17th century, and one Art O'Mulligan was found resident in the townland of Brackagh in Ballynascreen in 1663 (*ibid.* 234; *HMR (Ó Doibhlin 2)* 67).

Glebe
H 7995
An English form

1. Glebe	Received usage No. 16	1834c
2. gli:b	Local pronunciation	1993

Part of the glebe of Ballynascreen was formerly situtated in the parish of Lissan, but this was exchanged in 1793 for parts of the townlands of Moyheeland and Gortnaskey out of which was formed the townland of Glebe (*Der. Clergy* 111; see also Curl 1986, 187).

Glengomna
H 7194
Gleann Gamhna
"valley of the calf"

1. Glanganny	Hib. Reg. Loughinsholin	1657c
2. Glangawny	Hib. Del. Derry	1672c
3. Glengawna	Sampson's Map	1813
4. Glengomna	Grand Jury Pres. (OSNB) No. 16	1830c
5. Glengomna	Received usage No. 16	1834c
6. Glengomna	Title Deeds (OSNB) No. 16	1834c
7. Glen-'gom-na	OSNB Pron. No.16	1834c
8. Glengavney (x2)	OSM (Loughrey) 32	1836
9. Glean gabhanagh "the close glen"	MacCloskey's Stat. Report 62	1821
10. Gleann Gamhna "the glen of the calf"	OSL (Derry) 86	1834
11. Gleann gamhnach "Glen of the strippers or milch cows"	J O'D (OSNB) No. 16	1834c
12. Gleann-gamhnach "glen of milch cows"	Joyce iii 367	1913

13. Gleann-gamhnach "The glen of the calf"	Munn's Notes 47	1925
14. ˌglɛnˈgamnə	Local pronunciation	1993
15. ˌglɛnˈgɔmnə	Local pronunciation	1993

The *gleann* here is clearly the valley through which the Glengomna Water now runs. The identity of the second element is slightly more problematic. O'Donovan (followed by Joyce) opts for *gamhnach* "a stripper or milch cow" but none of the anglicized forms show any sign of a final spirant (Irish *ch*). While the *ch* in unstressed *-ach* tends to disappear in Ulster, it is generally well-preserved in spellings of the 17th century (see O'Rahilly 1932, 210, and compare **Brackagh** and **Tonaght** in this parish). Munn seems to have *gamhain* in mind when he translates the Irish as "calf", although historically this word was never declined in the manner that he indicates (13).

One of the many stories collected by O'Donovan during his visit to Ballynascreen accounts for the name in the following way. The famous cow called Glasgavlin had a calf in the valley of Glengomna and, having calved, her milk poured forth from her udder in such torrents that the whole valley was flooded by it. It was in commemoration of this that the local inhabitants called the valley *Gleann Gamhna* "the glen of the calf" (*OSL (Derry)* 86).

Glenviggan	*Gleann Bhigín*	
H 6988	"Bigín's glen"	
1. Glenviggan	Sampson's Map	1813
2. Glenviggan	Received usage No. 16	1834c
3. Glen-ˈvig-gan	OSNB Pron. No. 16	1834c
4. Glean beagan "the little glen"	MacCloskey's Stat. Report 62	1821
5. Gleann bhigin "Biggin's glen or valley"	J O'D (OSNB) No. 16	1834c
6. Gleann-Bheichcean "The glen of St. Beccan"	Munn's Notes 47	1925
7. ˌglɛnˈvĭgən	Local pronunciation	1993

Both O'Donovan and Munn take the second element in this name to be a personal name, and Munn goes so far as to identify the bearer of the name as St Beccán, a descendant of Colla Uais and companion of Columcille (5–6). However, Irish *ea* would not be expected to give [ĭ] here and this possibility can be dismissed (Ó Dochartaigh 1987, 75–8). The most likely origin seems to be from the personal name *Bigín*. Although it is not common it appears in the genealogy of the *Uí Dhúdhíorma* of Inishowen in Co. Donegal (*CGH* 146b47; Woulfe 1923, 514). It is attested in the place-name *Cluain Bhigín* in Uí Maine (see *Onom. Goed.* sv.), and may be the second element in the townland name **Dunbiggan** in Co. Tyrone.

Gortnaskey	*Gort na Sceach*	
H 7995	"the field of the hawthorns"	
1. Gort Skeagh	Lond. Comp. Valuation 309	1613
2. Gortskeah	Phillips MSS (Maps) Plate 28	1622

3. Gortneskey	Civ. Surv. iii 177	1654
4. Gortaskey	Census 137	1659c
5. Gortnaskey	BSD(c) 63	1661
6. Gortnarkie	HMR (Ó Doibhlin 2) 67	1663
7. Gortnaskey	Sampson's Map	1813
8. Gortnaskea	Received usage No. 16	1834c
9. Gortnaskea	Title Deeds (OSNB) No. 16	1834c
10. Gort-na-'skee	OSNB Pron. No. 16	1834c
11. Gort na sciog "field of thorns"	MacCloskey's Stat. Report 62	1821
12. Gort na sgeach "field of the briers"	J O'D (OSNB) No. 16	1834c
13. Gort na Sgeach "field of the briars"	OSM (Loughrey) 60	1837c
14. Gort-na-sceach "The field of the white thorns"	Munn's Notes 47	1925
15. ˌgɔrtnəˈskiː	Local pronunciation	1993
16. ˌgɔrtnəˈskeː	Local pronunciation	1993

The elements which go to make up this name are fairly transparent, and the historical spellings support the form suggested by previous authorities. Traces of the final *ch* are still visible in some early spellings (1–2), but the weakening of non-palatal *ch*, which is characteristic of Ulster Irish (O'Rahilly 1932, 210), soon becomes apparent (3 *et seq.*).

Labby　　　　　　　　　　　　　　*An Leaba*
H 7592　　　　　　　　　　　　　　"the bed"

1. b:nellapah	Esch. Co. Map 14	1609
2. Ballmelappagh	Charter of Londonderry 391	1613
3. Ba: lappie	Lond. Comp. Valuation 311	1613
4. (?)Ba: Lagye	Phillips MSS (Maps) Plate 30	1622
5. Laby	Civ. Surv. iii 177	1654
6. Ballinelappagh	Bishop. Der. i 266	1657
7. Lebby	Census 137	1659c
8. Labban	BSD(c) 63	1661
9. Labby	Sampson's Map	1813
10. Labby	Grand Jury Pres. (OSNB) No. 16	1830c
11. Labby	Received usage No. 16	1834c
12. Labby	Title Deeds (OSNB) No. 16	1834c
13. 'Lab-by	OSNB Pron. No. 16	1834c
14. Leaba "a bed, a druidical altar"	MacCloskey's Stat. Report 62	1821
15. leabaidh "a bed; a grave"	J O'D (OSNB) No. 16	1834c
16. Leaba	Joyce i 341	1869
17. Leaba "The bed"	Munn's Notes 48	1925
18. 'labi	Local pronunciation	1993

A few early sources record a form from *Baile na Leapa* "townland of the bed" but this has given way to *Leaba* (or dative *Leabaidh*) meaning simply "a bed". The term *leaba Dhiarmada agus Ghráinne* "the bed of Diarmaid and Gráinne" is frequently applied in folk tradition to passage-graves which were imagined to be places where the young couple slept during their flight from the jealous Finn McCool. However, a separate tradition recorded locally by Munn claims that Labby was the location of *Leabaidh na Glaise* "bed of the grey cow" which was named after the fabulous cow, Glasgavlin, which belonged to the smith of the mythical Tuatha Dé Danann, Goibhniu (*Munn's Notes* 48). In either case, the name probably originally referred to a passage-grave which has since disappeared (cf. *Joyce* i 340-2).

Moneyconey		*Móin an Chongna*	
H 7191		"bog of the antler"	
1.	b:vanachonie	Esch. Co. Map 14	1609
2.	ballidonachony	Bishop. Der. i 57	1610
3.	Ballyvonachony	CPR Jas I 279a	1615
4.	Ballyvounachony	Bishop. Der. i 103	1615
5.	Monnecheny	Hib. Reg. Loughinsholin	1657c
6.	Moyneconif	Census 137	1659c
7.	Manecheny	BSD(c) 55	1661
8.	Moynaconey	HMR (Ó Doibhlin 2) 67	1663
9.	Moneycheny	Hib. Del. Derry	1672c
10.	Meenacony	Sampson's Map	1813
11.	Moneyconey	Received usage No. 16	1834c
12.	Mun-ny-'coe-ny	OSNB Pron. No. 16	1834c
13.	Muine Comhnuidhe "hill of rest"	OSL (Derry) 85	1834
14.	Muine connaidh "brake of the fire-wood"	J O'D (OSNB) No. 16	1834c
15.	Muine-comhnuidhe "The hill of rest, ... graveyard"	Munn's Notes 48	1925
16.	ˌmǫniˈkoːni	Local pronunciation	1993

Moneyconey was one of the six church townlands in Ballynascreen and the ruins of the medieval parish church dedicated to St Columcille still stand here. O'Donovan and Munn have both given the first element of this name as *muine* "shrubbery", but there is considerable evidence among the historical spellings to show that we are, in fact, dealing with the word *móin* "bogland, moor" (see Toner 1991–3, 53-4). This seems particularly apt here as Moneyconey is dominated by the heathy mountain which rises to the west of the old church.

O'Donovan was told that the Irish form of the name was *Muine Comhnuidhe* (modern *Muine Cónaí*) "hill of rest" because it was here that the bodies of the dead were laid to rest (*OSL (Derry)* 85). The modern pronunciation, which is apparently echoed by the pronunciation recorded by the Ordnance Survey in the last century, shows a long closed-o, and this might be cited in support of this interpretation. O'Donovan favoured an origin from the better attested *connadh* "firewood" (14), but we would not expect it to be anglicized *-coney* (*Joyce* ii 351–2) and it is perhaps significant that we do not find something like *cunny* among the early spellings. However, *cónaí* is rarely used of habitation features and only two place-names containing this element have so far been located in early Irish documentation (*Onom. Goed.* 634 sv. *tilach na comhnaigi*; *Cranoc na Comhnaigh* in *Top. Frag.* 71). In this context it might be said to express the peculiarity of what might have normally been considered uninhabitable bog.

Some of the early spellings show signs of lenition of this element (1–5, 7), and as a number of these appear to contain an inflected form of *móin* we can infer the presence here of the gen. sing. masc. of the definite article. This would rule out the possibility of a final element *cónaí* as this is feminine, but we might suggest *codhnach* (masc.) "lord, master", although its earlier meaning "(sensible) adult" is perhaps inappropriate. However, the most plausible origin is from the word *congna* (masc.) "horn, antler". The *ng* in the consonant group *ngn* has disappeared with lengthening of the preceding vowel in every dialect of Irish, and the loss appears in MSS as early as the 16th century (O'Rahilly 1932, 183). We may imagine, therefore, that the antlers of some giant deer (*Megaloceros giganteus*) were dug up in the bog here at some time in the medieval period, thousands of years after the animal had perished.

Moneyguiggy
H 8096

Maigh na gCúigeadh
"the plain of the fifths"

1. moynagogie ⅓	Esch. Co. Map 14	1609
2. Monegog	Lond. Comp. Valuation 309	1613
3. Monegoge	Phillips MSS (Maps) Plate 28	1622
4. Munegiugie	Civ. Surv. iii 177	1654
5. Muniguigie	Civ. Surv. iii 177	1654
6. Muneguigie	Civ. Surv. iii 177	1654
7. Moneguigie	Civ. Surv. iii 190	1654
8. Moynagogy, being ⅓ balliboe in 3 parts divided	Bishop. Der. i 266	1657
9. ½ Moyneguigye	Census 137	1659c
10. Moyneguigye, ye other ½ of	Census 137	1659c
11. Monegingee	BSD(c) 63	1661
12. Moynaquigge	HMR (Ó Doibhlin 2) 67	1663
13. Moneyguigy	Sampson's Map	1813
14. Moneyguigy	Grand Jury Pres. (OSNB) No. 16	1830c
15. Moneyguiggy(?)	Received usage No. 16	1834c
16. Munny-'guig-gy	OSNB Pron. No. 16	1834c
17. Moneyguiggy	Title Deeds (OSNB) No. 16	1834c
18. Moin a quagiu "the shaking bog"	MacCloskey's Stat. Report 62	1821
19. Móin na g-cuigeadh "Bog of the Quiggs or Fivers"	J O'D (OSNB) No. 16	1834c
20. Muine-gcuigeadh "brake of the fives"	Joyce iii 511	1913
21. Muine-g'cuigeadh "The Shrubbery of the fives"	Munn's Notes 48	1925
22. ˌmọniˈgwïgi	Local pronunciation	1993

The representation of this name in some of our early sources suggests an initial element *maigh* "plain" (1, 8–10, 12), although *móin* "bog" is occasionally anglicized *moyn(e)* (see **Moneyconey** and **Moneyneany** in this parish). However, the relatively level nature of this tract of land, which was described in the last century as "nearly all arable", favours an origin from *maigh* "a plain" (*OSNB* No. 16).

The final element appears to be *cúigeadh* "a fifth (part)" which also appears in the Co.

Donegal name Cronaguiggy (*Cró na gCúigeadh*). Mac Giolla Easpaig compares the use of *cúigeadh* in the Donegal name to the use of terms such as *leath* "half", *trian* "third", *ceathrú* "quarter", etc., and suggests that it was a unit of land (1986, 77-8). In the 17th century, Moneyguiggy was described as "being ⅓ balliboe of land" (8, cf. 1), and elsewhere it was said to have been further divided into two halves (9–10).

Moneyneany

H 7497

Móin na nIonadh
"bog of the wonders"

1.	Monaneney	Phillips MSS (Maps) Plate 30	1622
2.	Moynin	Civ. Surv. iii 177	1654
3.	Moyneniny (x3)	Civ. Surv. iii 178	1654
4.	Mononiny	Civ. Surv. iii 190	1654
5.	Moyneegne	Census 137	1659c
6.	Moyneniny	BSD(c) 64	1661
7.	Munaneny	HMR (Ó Doibhlin 2) 66	1663
8.	Moninientagh	Sampson's Map	1813
9.	Moneyneany	Received usage No. 16	1834c
10.	Munny-'nean-y	OSNB Pron. No. 16	1834c
11.	Moin a monach "the spotted mountain"	MacCloskey's Stat. Report 62	1821
12.	Móin na n-Iongantas "the bog of wonders"	OSL (Derry) 84	1834
13.	Magh na n-iongnadh "plain of the wonders"	J O'D (OSNB) No. 16	1834c
14.	Meen na neenthus "the plains of wonders"	OSM (Loughrey) 21	1836
15.	Muine-na-n-iongantas "The hill of the wonders"	Munn's Notes 48	1925
16.	Móin na nIonadh	GÉ 254	1989
17.	ˌmọniˈnʲini	Local pronunciation	1993
18.	ˌmọniˈnʲiːnə	Local pronunciation	1993
19.	ˌmọniˈiːnə	Local pronunciation	1993

O'Donovan, probably following local advice, derived this name from an Irish original, modern *Maigh na nIonadh*, meaning "the plain of the wonders" (*OSNB*, cf. *OSL (Derry)* 84) and he relates many wonders and miracles associated with the townland. Denis O'Hagan of White Water told him that the fairies existed here in the time of his mother. One evening, she came on horseback to a certain stream in the townland where the horse stopped to drink. It was drinking for some time, so the woman struck it with a switch to get it to move on. Immediately, the switch caught fire and the horse's mane appeared to burn. The teller of this tale attributed this wonder to the fairy folk who "used to amuse themselves by many little pranks of this nature" (*OSL (Derry)* 84). There was also a well in Moneyneany, called *Tobar an Mhadaidh Léith* or *Tobar an Mhadaidh Mhaoil* ("the grey or cropped dog's well") the water of which would curdle new milk, and if all the mad dogs of the country were pursued, they would make their way to this well (*ibid.* 84–5, 91, 97; *OSM (Loughrey)* 21).

Munn cites a tradition that, at some remote period, King Arthur and Merlin were here and that headless monsters, pigs, etc. were seen wandering about (*Munn's Notes* 48). A separate tradition is recorded in the Ordnance Survey Memoirs, according to which the valleys of Moneyneany were a favourite place with old Irish warriors in which to perform great exploits and tricks by magic, and so it was called *Meen na neenthus* (properly *Mín na nIontas*) "the plains [sic] of wonders" (*OSM (Loughrey)* 21).

Unfortunately, this name is not well documented among our 17th-century sources so that an authoritative derivation cannot be offered. The first element may be either *maigh* "plain" as suggested by O'Donovan, or *móin* "moor, bog" as has been more recently proposed (16). The townland is largely mountainous, but there is an area of flat land in the south-eastern corner around Moneyneany village (cf. **Moydamlaght** below; also **Moyard**).

An explanation of the final element produces problems in equal proportions. According to the Ordnance Survey Memoirs, a cattle-fair had been held in Moneyneany prior to the founding of Draperstown (*OSM (Loughrey)* 5), and this may suggest the element *aonach* "fair", although there is no indication that the fair was of any great antiquity. However, an origin from *ionadh* "wonder" is not as peculiar as it may first appear and there is evidence of another identically named place in the parish of Aghaderg (see *PNI* vi forthcoming). It is spelt *Moenynnie* etc. in 16th- and 17th-century sources and on one early map it is translated "the strange marish" (*ibid.*). Harris translates the name as "the wonderful bog" and explains this as referring to a stream in the bog which divides and then runs in opposite directions (*Harris Hist.* 115; *OSM* xii 3–4).

Moyard	*Maigh Ard*	
H 6990	"high plain/field"	
1. b:wey	Esch. Co. Map 14	1609
2. Ballinwey	Bishop. Der. i 57	1610
3. Ballniwey or Ballinwey	CPR Jas I 279a	1615
4. Ballinvey	Bishop. Der. i 103	1615
5. Bellnevay	Civ. Surv. iii 190	1654
6. Moyoieragh, Pt of	Hib. Reg. Loughinsholin	1657c
7. Moyoghtearagh, Part of	Hib. Reg. Loughinsholin	1657c
8. Moghertragh	Census 137	1659c
9. Moyoghterragh	BSD(c) 55	1661
10. Moyard & Dunaron	HMR (Ó Doibhlin 2) 67	1663
11. Moyoghtragh	Hib. Del. Derry	1672c
12. Moyotragh	Hib. Del. Derry	1672c
13. Moyard	Sampson's Map	1813
14. Moyard	Grand Jury Pres. (OSNB) No. 16	1830c
15. Moyard	Received usage No. 16	1834c
16. Moy'ard	OSNB Pron. No. 16	1834c
17. Mágh Aird	OSL (Derry) 90	1834
18. Magh ard "high plain or table land"	J O'D (OSNB) No. 16	1834c
19. Magh-ard "The high plain"	Munn's Notes 49	1925
20. mɔi'a:rd	Local pronunciation	1993
21. mɛ'ja:rd	Local pronunciation	1993

This relatively straightforward name has a very varied and interesting history. If the spellings collected here are correctly assigned to this name then it was called *Baile an Mhaí* "townland of the plain" (1–5) and *Maigh Uachtarach* "upper plain" (6–9, 11–12) in the 17th century. The modern form of the name is, of course, more or less synonymous with this latter form. In his letters, although not in the Name Books, O'Donovan takes the second element to be *ard* meaning "a height, hill" and claims that the townland took its name from the hill called *Ard a' Ghuail* "the hill or height of the coal" (*OSL (Derry)* 90). The hill apparently was so called because charcoal for the smelting of iron was made there (*ibid.*). In O'Donovan's time, many old men still remembered the sites of several iron mills and recalled a number of people who were engaged in the charcoal trade (*ibid.*).

No extensive area of flat or level land is to be found within the current bounds of the townland, and we might better translate *maigh* here as "field" (see *DIL* sv. *magh*). However, the absence of references in our 17th-century sources to the adjoining townland of **Glenviggan**, which does contain a large plain, may indicate that Moyard once included that area.

Moydamlaght	*Maigh dTamhlachta*	
H 7597	"plain of the plague-cemetery"	
1. b:madaullaght	Esch. Co. Map 14	1609
2. Ballymadaulaght	Charter of Londonderry 391	1613
3. Madonka	Lond. Comp. Valuation 309	1613
4. Madawlat	Phillips MSS (Maps) Plate 28	1622
5. Moydaumphle	Civ. Surv. iii 177	1654
6. Moydaumphlagh	Civ. Surv. iii 177	1654
7. Maytallatt	Civ. Surv. iii 198	1654
8. Ballimadaughlaght	Bishop. Der. i 266	1657
9. Moydoucaght	Census 137	1659c
10. Moydamplett	BSD(c) 63	1661
11. Moytamlatt	HMR (Ó Doibhlin 2) 66	1663
12. Moydowmalaght	Sampson's Map	1813
13. Moydamlaght	Received usage No. 16	1834c
14. Moydamlaght	Title Deeds (OSNB) No. 16	1834c
15. Moy-'dam-laght	OSNB Pron. No. 16	1834c
16. Magh dam lachd "the milk house on the plain"	MacCloskey's Stat. Report 62	1821
17. Magh tamhlachta "plain of the burial place"	J O'D (OSNB) No. 16	1834c
18. Magh-dtaimhleachta "plain of the plague-cemetery"	Joyce iii 514	1913
19. Magh-d-taimhleachta "The plain of the plague-monuments, or cemetery"	Munn's Notes 49	1925
20. ˌmɔiˈdamlət	Local pronunciation	1993

There is little doubt that the second element in this name is the word *tamhlacht* which Dinneen translates "a plague burial-ground" (*Dinneen* sv.). Joyce reports that this element is fairly common throughout Ireland where it is variously anglicized as Tamlaght, Tamlat,

Tawlaght, Towlaght and Toulett (*Joyce* i 162), and Tallaght in Co. Dublin represents a further manifestation. Joyce also suggests that it is of pagan origin and is only applied to Christian burial sites by adoption (*ibid.*). In the early part of the last century a large number of skulls and bones were unearthed in a fort in this townland marked by two ancient thorns (*OSM (Loughrey)* 17). Without citing his source, Munn claims that there was a great plague in this area during the time of St Patrick (*Munn's Notes* 49) although, even if the tradition can be substantiated, there is no necessary connection with the name.

The form of the name in the various historical sources cited above is of some interest. The predominant form shows the prefix of an initial *d* to this element, a process known in Irish grammar as eclipsis or nasalization. In Old Irish, neuter nouns such as *magh* nasalized the following word, a phenomenon which became largely obsolete after c.1000 AD. However, traces of the old neuter in the form of nasalization were retained in certain fixed phrases and particularly in place-names well after this date and this name probably represents a further example of this phenomenon. The existence of two spellings with *t* for *d* might suggest that the nasalization is the result of repeated use of the name in the accusative (a further and more prolonged cause of nasalization), but this is unlikely and these isolated occurrences probably represent mere scribal errors. Moydamlaght is mostly mountain and the *maigh* or "plain" may refer to a flat piece of ground at the lower end of the townland near the river, or we should perhaps translate "field" (see **Moyard** above).

Moyheeland	*Maigh Chaoláin*	
H 7995	"plain of the marshy stream"	
1. moychellan	Esch. Co. Map 14	1609
2. Moychellan	Charter of Londonderry 391	1613
3. Moykelan	Lond. Comp. Valuation 309	1613
4. Moykillare	Civ. Surv. iii 177	1654
5. Moychellan	Bishop. Der. i 266	1657
6. ½ Moycelan	Census 137	1659c
7. (?)Makillan	Census 137	1659c
8. Moyekillare	BSD(c) 63	1661
9. Moykillan	HMR (Ó Doibhlin 2) 67	1663
10. Moyheelan	Sampson's Map	1813
11. Moyheeland	Grand Jury Pres. (OSNB) No. 16	1830c
12. Moyheeland	Received usage No. 16	1834c
13. Moyheeland	Title Deeds (OSNB) No. 16	1834c
14. Moy'heeland	OSNB Pron. No. 16	1834c
15. Magh callean "the beautiful plain"	MacCloskey's Stat. Report 62	1821
16. Magh Chaolain "the plain of the small guts"	OSL (Derry) 78	1834
17. Magh Chaoilain "Caylan's plain"	OSL (Derry) 79	1834
18. Magh Shioláin "Sillan's plain or Heeland's plain"	J O'D (OSNB) No. 16	1834c
19. Magh-Chaolain "The plain of the Intestines"	Munn's Notes 49	1925
20. ˌmɔiˈhiːlən(d)	Local pronunciation	1993
21. ˌmɔiˈhiːln	Local pronunciation	1993

O'Donovan cites a tradition that a monster hound was slain in Glenconkeyne, and that Moyheeland was named *Magh Chaolain*, which he translates "the plain of the small guts", because the hound's intestines fell out here (*OSL (Derry)* 78). However, he rejects this fanciful interpretation and proposes instead that the second element is a man's name *Caolán* (*ibid.* 79). *Caolán*, which means "slender lad", is borne by a number of historical personages, including St Caolán of Lough Derg, and while no one of that name can be linked with Moyheeland or the surrounding district, *maigh* "plain" is frequently qualified by a personal name (Ó Corráin & Maguire 1981, 40, *Onom. Goed.* 511 ff.).

It is perhaps more likely, however, that the second element here is a diminutive form of the common noun *caol. Caol*, and the diminutive form *caolán*, have a wide range of meanings, but in general they can denote anything narrow or slender. Meanings such as *caolán* "creek" can be immediately dismissed as unsuitable, but we are still left with a considerable number of possible interpretations. The townland becomes quite narrow in the middle, and we might consider *caolán* in the sense of "a narrow piece of land", although this meaning is not recorded in the dictionaries and there seems to be little evidence of its use in placenames (but see *PNI* iii 16). Dinneen records the meaning "a small rod or wattle", and it is possible that the name refers to some form of wattle structure on this low-lying plain (*Dinneen* sv.; cf. *caol* "osier, twig" and *caolach* "osiers, twigs, wattle"). *Caol* can also mean "a marshy stream, a marsh" and is used as such in some place-names, so a diminutive form of this, *caolán*, is perhaps the most likely of all the possibilities (*Dinneen* sv.; *Joyce* ii 418–9). The Drumard Water flows along the eastern boundary of the townland and it is quite likely that the land on either side of it was formerly liable to flooding.

Moykeeran
H 7795

Maigh Chaorthainn
"plain of the rowan"

1. moycherin ⅓	Esch. Co. Map 14	1609
2. Moycherrin ⅓ part of a balliboe	Charter of Londonderry 391	1613
3. Moy Kerran	Lond. Comp. Valuation 309	1613
4. Moyker	Phillips MSS (Maps) Plate 28	1622
5. Moykarne	Civ. Surv. iii 177	1654
6. Moychirhin	Bishop. Der. i 266	1657
7. MoyKiran	Census 137	1659c
8. Moykarne	BSD(c) 63	1661
9. Moykeerin	Sampson's Map	1813
10. Moykeeran	Grand Jury Pres. (OSNB) No. 16	1830c
11. Moykeeran	Received usage No. 16	1834c
12. Moykeeran	Title Deeds (OSNB) No. 16	1834c
13. Moy-'kee-ran	OSNB Pron. No. 16	1834c
14. Magh caeran "the marshy plain"	MacCloskey's Stat. Report 62	1821
15. Magh Chaorthainn	OSL (Derry) 77-8	1834
16. Mágh caorthainn "plain of the rowan trees"	J O'D (OSNB) No. 16	1834c
17. Magh-mic-Chaerthainn "plain of the son of Kieran"	Munn's Notes 49	1925
18. ˌmɔiˈkiːrən	Local pronunciation	1993
19. ˌmɔiˈkiːrn	Local pronunciation	1993

33

The first element here is clearly *maigh* "plain", and undoubtedly denotes the area of flat land in which the townland stands. There can be little doubt, either, that O'Donovan was correct in taking the final element to be *caorthann* "mountain ash, rowan", although various different interpretations have been put forward in the past (14, 17).

The suggestion by Munn that the final element derives from the name of the great-grandson of Colla Uais, who allegedly gave his name to the barony of Tirkeeran, is highly unlikely and must be dismissed (*Munn's Notes* 49). Ó Ceallaigh claims to have also heard *Ciarán* (1927, 60), but there is no evidence of an *á* in the final syllable among the historical forms (see **Curran** in the parish of Maghera). *Caorán* "moor", which is now confined to parts of Donegal, does not appear to have been widely used in place-names, and it is not cited by either Joyce in his *Irish Names of Places* or Hogan in his *Onomasticon Goedelicum*. There may be some examples in East Ulster (see *An Caorán* for Keerhan in Co. Louth, *L. Log. Lú* 10), and it was known to Tadhg Ó Brolcháin of Maghera c.1700 (*DCCU* 426; cf. O'Rahilly 1932, 185). However, it is unlikely to lie behind this name as there is no indication among the historical spellings of a long-*a* in the last syllable.

Mulnavoo   Of uncertain origin
H 7896

1. Mulla an Voto	Lond. Comp. Valuation 311	1613
2. Mullanahoy	Phillips MSS (Maps) Plate 30	1622
3. Mullanvoy	Civ. Surv. iii 177	1654
4. Mullinevo	Civ. Surv. iii 190	1654
5. Mollanvoy	BSD(c) 63	1661
6. (?)Mullanamore (ed. Mullaghmore)	HMR (Ó Doibhlin 2) 66	1663
7. Mulnavoo	Sampson's Map	1813
8. Mulnavoo	Received usage No. 16	1834c
9. Mulnawoo	Title Deeds (OSNB) No. 16	1834c
10. Mull-na-'voo	OSNB Pron. No. 16	1834c
11. Mual na bea "hill of cattle"	MacCloskey's Stat. Report 62	1821
12. Mullan a' bhuaidh "hill of the victory"	J O'D (OSNB) No. 16	1834c
13. Mullach-an-bhuat "The summit of the plateau"	Munn's Notes 50	1925
14. ˌmolnəˈvuː	Local pronunciation	1993

The first element in this name is by no means certain, but it is probably one of the several words meaning "hill" (cf. *maoil* "rounded summit; hillock, knoll"; *maoileann* (similar in meaning); *maolán* (similar again); *mol* "crown"; *mullán* "elevated ground, hillock"; *mullach* "summit"), or possibly *muileann* "mill". Mulnavoo consists largely of a low ridge of land overlooking the Moyola River so that of the hill-words listed here, *mullán* is probably the most suitable (see further *Joyce* i 393).

The origin of the final element is not altogether clear either. References to the name are unfortunately absent from a number of important 17th-century sources, and the remaining spellings are inconsistent. The Hearth Money Rolls are generally unreliable and the peculiar form cited here may be ignored (6). The form from Phillips' maps (2) may be reconciled with the majority of early spellings if we read *v* for *h* (remembering that *v* is generally written much like *b* in documents of this period), and our earliest form (1) should probably be emended to give a similar reading. In short, therefore, the 17th-century spellings seem to be mere variants of a form *Mullanavoy*.

The development of *-voy* to modern *-voo* suggests a final element ending in *ua* or *ú* + a palatal consonant. O'Donovan suggests the word *bua* "victory, triumph" which has an early variant gen. sing. *buaidhe* (*DIL* sv. 1 *búaid*), and this does indeed correspond quite neatly to what we know of the pronunciation of the name (cf. Carnew in Co. Wicklow from *Carn an Bhuadha*, Price 1945–67, vi 342–3). However, there are several other possible interpretations, such as *bú* "hyacinth" and *bóitheach*, gen. sing. *bóithigh* "cowhouse, byre", and a definitive derivation cannot be proposed.

| **Owenreagh** | *An Abhainn Riabhach* | |
| H 7491 | "the grey river" | |

1. b:nehounreogh	Esch. Co. Map 14	1609
2. Ballinehounreagh	Bishop. Der. i 57	1610
3. Ballinehoureagh; except 3a...		
glebe	CPR Jas I 279a	1615
4. Ballinehon'reagh	Bishop. Der. i 103	1615
5. (?)Bellinecoragh	Civ. Surv. iii 190	1654
6. Pt of Balliowenreagh	Hib. Reg. Loughinsholin	1657c
7. (?)Balliweneagh	Hib. Reg. Loughinsholin	1657c
8. Onereagh	Census 137	1659c
9. Ballyowenreagh, pt: of	BSD(c) 55	1661
10. Ballyowenreagh	BSD(c) 55	1661
11. Owenreigh	HMR (Ó Doibhlin 2) 67	1663
12. Balliowenreagh	Hib. Del. Derry	1672c
13. BalliOwenreagh	Hib. Del. Derry	1672c
14. Oanreagh	Sampson's Map	1813
15. Owenreagh	Received usage No. 16	1834c
16. O-en-'ree-agh	OSNB Pron. No. 16	1834c
17. Abhuin reagh "the rugged plain"	MacCloskey's Stat. Report 62	1821
18. Abhainn riach "greyish river"	J O'D (OSNB) No. 16	1834c
19. Abhainn-riabhach "The grey river"	Munn's Notes 50	1925
20. ˌoːnˈreːʲa	Local pronunciation	1993
21. ˌoːnˈreː	Local pronunciation	1993

The 17th-century references to Owenreagh largely reflect a form *Baile na hAbhann Riabhaí* or the like, "the townland of the grey river", but the modern name comes from a form *An Abhainn Riabhach* "the grey river". It is not clear which river gave rise to the name but it was possibly the Moyola which forms the northern boundary of the townland.

| **Straw** | *Srath* | |
| H 7693 | "river-meadow" | |

1. dromdallagan	Esch. Co. Map 14	1609
2. Dromealegan, ⅓ part of a		
balliboe	Charter of Londonderry 391	1613

3. Shrahdum Dolgan	Lond. Comp. Valuation 311	1613
4. shredromdalye	Phillips MSS (Maps) Plate 30	1622
5. Strathdrum:Dellian	Civ. Surv. iii 177	1654
6. Dromealegan, being ⅓ balliboe ...in 3 parts	Bishop. Der. i 266	1657
7. Straghdrund & Algone	Census 137	1659c
8. Shrathdrum Dellian	BSD(c) 63	1661
9. Stragh	HMR (Ó Doibhlin 2) 67	1663
10. Strath	Sampson's Map	1813
11. Straw	Grand Jury Pres. (OSNB) No. 16	1830c
12. Straw	Title Deeds (OSNB) No. 16	1834c
13. 'Straw	OSNB Pron. No. 16	1834c
14. Straith "the marsh"	MacCloskey's Stat. Report 62	1821
15. Srath "a holm or strath"	J O'D (OSNB) No. 16	1834c
16. Srath "The swampy meadow...along the river bed"	Munn's Notes 50	1925
17. strɔ:	Local pronunciation	1993

Irish *srath* often denotes a stretch of low-lying, usually marshy, land beside a river and here it clearly refers to the land lying on either side of the White Water. The development of Irish *sr* into English *str* is widely attested in Ulster place-names, most notably in the name **Strabane** from Irish *An Srath Bán* "the white river-meadow" (*Joyce* i 60–2).

The earliest references to the townland show that the modern name was formerly compounded with another, now obsolete, name. The inconsistency in the spelling makes it impossible to ascertain its meaning with any certainty. One element, *droim* "ridge" is, however, clearly visible, and it undoubtedly refers to the ridge in the southern end of the townland. See also **Strawmore** and **Straw Mountain**.

Straw Mountain	*Áit Tí Néill*	
H 7890	"place of Niall's house"	
1. Aughtyneal	OSRNB 20 sh. 40	1850c
2. "Neal's place"	OSRNB 20 sh. 40	1850c
3. Ait tighe Néill "place of Niall's house"	OSRNB 20 sh. 40	1850c
4. strɔ 'məuntn	Local pronunciation	1993
5. atʃə'nel	Local pronunciation	1995

The name Straw Mountain does not occur in any of our early sources and was undoubtedly named from the townland of **Straw**. This is the form of the name used in official documents etc., but locally it was, and indeed still is, known as Attyneill, from Irish *Áit Tí Néill* "place of Niall's house".

Strawmore	*Srath Mór*
H 7695	"large river-meadow"

1. laghtmeskie	Esch. Co. Map 14	1609
2. Laghtmesky	Charter of Londonderry 391	1613
3. Shragh Moore latiniskey	Lond. Comp. Valuation 311	1613
4. Slatmone Latmiske	Phillips MSS (Maps) Plate 30	1622
5. Strathmore	Civ. Surv. iii 177,178	1654
6 Laghtmesky	Bishop. Der. i 266	1657
7. Shrathmore	BSD(c) 63	1661
8. Strainmore	HMR (Ó Doibhlin 2) 67	1663
9. Strath more	Sampson's Map	1813
10. Strawmore	Grand Jury Pres. (OSNB) No. 16	1830c
11. Strawmore	Received usage No. 16	1834c
12. Straw'more	OSNB Pron. No. 16	1834c
13. Stramore	Title Deeds (OSNB) No. 16	1834c
14. Striath mor "the great marsh"	MacCloskey's Stat. Report 62	1821
15. Srath mór "great strath or holm"	J O'D (OSNB) No. 16	1834c
16. Srath-mor "The great swampy meadow land along the river bed"	Munn's Notes 50	1925
17. strə'mo:r	Local pronunciation	1993
18. strɔ'mo:r	Local pronunciation	1993

The name Strawmore is obviously of similar origin to those of the nearby townlands of **Straw** and **Straw Mountain**. It is occasionally compounded, perhaps accidentally, with the name of another land unit in some 17th-century documents. The first element in the affix is *leacht* or *sleacht* "gravemound", and this may be the megalithic tomb now known as Slaght Illeran (*NISMR* sh.40 §8; cf. Slaughte in *OSM (Loughrey)* 19, 33). The remainder of the name is more difficult to interpret, but it may represent *an uisce* "of the water", *na sceiche* "of the thornbush" or, possibly, a personal name.

Tonaght   *Tonnach*
H 7793   "enclosure/mound" (?)

1. tonnagh	Esch. Co. Map 14	1609
2. Tonnagh	Charter of Londonderry 391	1613
3. Tulla Tuna	Lond. Comp. Valuation 311	1613
4. Tulla Tuna	Phillips MSS (Maps) Plate 30	1622
5. Tamnaghtullagh	Civ. Surv. iii 177	1654
6. Taumnagh &c.	Civ. Surv. iii 177	1654
7. Tennagh	Bishop. Der. i 266	1657
8. Tonnagh	Census 137	1659c
9. Tumnaghtullagh	BSD(c) 63	1661
10. Tonnogh	HMR (Ó Doibhlin 2) 67	1663
11. Tonagh	Sampson's Map	1813
12. Tonaght	Grand Jury Pres. (OSNB) No. 16	1830c
13. Tonaught	Received usage No. 16	1834c
14. 'Ton-aught	OSNB Pron. No. 16	1834c
15. Tonnach "wavy ground"	MacCloskey's Stat. Report 62	1821

16. Tonnach "a mound"	J O'D (OSNB) No. 16	1834c
17. Tamnach "The green field producing fresh sweet grass"	Munn's Notes 51	1925
18. ˈtɒnə	Local pronunciation	1993
19. ˈtɒnəx	Local pronunciation	1993

According to a late version of the story of Cadhan Ó hInneirghe and the terrible hound which terrorized the valley of Glenconkeyne, the injured beast made three great leaps. The first was to Tonnagh Hill where it cast up blood and, so the story goes, it was from this that the hill was called *Cnoc an Tonnaigh* "the hill of the Vomiting" (Ó Ceallaigh 1927, 59).

The name Tonaght has a particularly unusual and interesting history. The final -*t* does not appear in the 17th-century spellings, nor is it reflected in the current local pronunciation, and it clearly has no bearing on the origin of the name. The 17th-century forms fall into three distinct categories. The largest body of these, which includes a number of independent sources, represents the name fairly much as it is today but without the final *t*. The Valuation of 1613 and the closely related Phillips' maps have a distinctive spelling *Tulla Tuna*, while the Civil Survey and Book of Survey and Distribution yield forms such as *Tamnaghtullagh* and *Taumnagh* (5–6, 9). Both these forms appear to contain the element *tulach* "mound", but the difference in order of the elements suggests that Tonnagh has been accidentally compounded with another name in these sources.

Forms such as *Taumnagh* might suggest an origin in *tamhnach* "field", but these spellings are exceptional and are confined to a single group of sources (5–6, 9). Although *tamhnach* is sometimes anglicized *Tonnagh* in modern place-names, examination of 17th-century spellings quite often reveals this to be a late development (e.g. **Tonaghmore** in par. Magherally and **Tonaghmore** in par. Saintfield, Co. Down). In such cases, the shortening of the original diphthong is almost certainly due to the fact that this syllable is unstressed, but in this instance, there is no qualifying adjective to take the stress and it remains on the first syllable. I would suggest, therefore, that these spellings represent corruptions of an original *Tunnagh* or the like, perhaps by conscious analogy with names containing *tamhnach*.

O'Donovan clearly did not hear anything like *tamhnach* when he was there, and he unquestioningly writes *Tonnach* which he translates "a mound". Joyce conjectures, probably correctly, that this *tonnach* is a by-form of *sonnach* (*Joyce* ii 220), the original meaning of which was "an enclosure, palisade" (*DIL* sv.), although there is another word *tonnach* (apparently from *tonn* "wave") meaning "quaking bog, quagmire" (*Ó Dónaill*; *Dinneen* sv.). In this particular case, unfortunately, there is no trace of either a fort or a bog within the bounds of the modern townland, and it is impossible to ascertain to which type of feature the townland owes its name.

A parasitic final *t* appears in a small number of names elsewhere in Ulster. **Desertcreat** in Co. Tyrone comes from Irish *Díseart Dá Chríoch* "hermitage of the two boundaries/territories" and the final *t* there does not appear until the 18th century (McCann 1981–82). A parasitic *t* appears in several names after *r*, notably **Ballywhollart** and **Ballystockart** in Co. Down (*PNI* ii 129–30).

Tullybrick
H 7289

An Tulaigh Bhric
"the speckled hill"

1. b:netallabrick	Esch. Co. Map 14	1609
2. Ballinetollabrick	Bishop. Der. i 57	1610

3. Ballynetollabrick	CPR Jas I 279a	1615
4. Ballinetullabrick	Bishop. Der. i 103	1615
5. Bellitullibricke	Civ. Surv. iii 190	1654
6. Ballitullibrick (x2)	Hib. Reg. Loughinsholin	1657c
7. Ballytullybrick	BSD(c) 55	1661
8. Cullyboke	HMR (Ó Doibhlin 2) 67	1663
9. Ballitullibrick (x2)	Hib. Del. Derry	1672c
10. Tullybrick	Sampson's Map	1813
11. Tullybrick	Received usage No. 16	1834c
12. Tully-'brick	OSNB Pron. No. 16	1834c
13. Tulla breac "the speckled field"	MacCloskey's Stat. Report 62	1821
14. Tulaig bruic "badger hill"	J O'D (OSNB) No. 16	1834c
15. Tulaigh-breac "The speckled hill"	Munn's Notes 51	1925
16. ˌtoˌli'brïk	Local pronunciation	1993
17. ˌtoˌlə'brïk	Local pronunciation	1993

This name, in all likelihood, goes back to an old dative form *An Tulaigh Bhric* (nom. *An Tulach Bhreac*). O'Donovan's suggestion of a final element based on the word *broc* "a badger" (14) may have been an attempt to explain the quality of the vowel in the final syllable, but a dative form of the adjective *breac*, such as suggested here, would equally well explain this feature. That the final element is an adjective is confirmed by the earliest sources which represent something like *Baile na Tulaí Brice* "townland of the speckled hill". The position of the article *na* "the" here clearly shows that the final element is an adjective.

The Ordnance Survey Memoirs relate that a stone column called Brackan Naglisha (*Breacán na Glaise*) or Brackanglashgevlin (*Breacán Ghlas Gaibhleann*) then stood in Tullybrick. It was said locally that Columcille's cow, the Glasgevlin, was kept tethered to that stone and that it was on account of this that it got its name "the grey cow's tedder [tether] stake" (*OSM (Loughrey)* 42).

OTHER NAMES

Altalacky River   A hybrid form
H 7597

1. (?)the River of Oweneny	Civ. Surv. iii 178	1654
2. Altayiacky Water	OSM (Loughrey) 11	1836
3. ˌɑltə'laki	Local pronunciation	1993

Altalacky River takes its name from a precipitous glen on the western edge of Moydamlaght Forest which was known in Irish as *Allt an Leacaigh* "glen of the rocky place/river". The word *allt* originally denoted a height or cliff, but O'Donovan recorded the meaning "a glen, a woody glen" in Co. Derry in 1834 (*DIL* sv. *2 alt; OSL (Derry)* 21). This latter is the sense in which it is to be understood in this and several other similar names in this area, and we note in particular the bilingual name **Altdoo** or **Black Glen**. The final element is *leacach* which frequently denotes "a place of flat rocks" in place-names, but it is probably in the sense of a "rocky river" that it is to be understood here for the upper reaches of Altalacky River are strewn with large flat rocks (*Joyce* i 417–8; *leacach* appears to be masc. as a river name in *AFM* iv 919n).

A much earlier name for the river is recorded in the Civil Survey of 1654. Two rivers are mentioned in the description of the bounds of the townland of Moneyneany, namely, *Owin beg* and *the River of Oweneny* which formed respectively the northern and eastern boundaries of the townland (*Civ. Surv.* iii 178). The former is now Owenbeg Burn (*Abhainn Bheag* "small river"), a tributary of the Dunlogan River which forms the southern boundary of Moneyneany. Therefore, although the boundary descriptions in the Civil Survey are often wildly inaccurate, *the River of Oweneny* can almost certainly be identified with Altalacky River. The first element in this name is clearly *abhainn* "river", and it is tempting to relate the final element to the name of the townland through which it passes (see **Moneyneany** above).

Sampson calls the glen through which the Altalacky River runs by the name Evishgore Glen on his map of 1813, but this seems to be a corruption of the name Innisgore recorded by the Ordnance Survey in the 19th century and which was understood then as *Inis Gabhar* "island of the goats" (*OSRNB* 61 sh. 35). Clearly, the glen was known in Irish as *Allt an Leacaigh* "glen of the rocky river", and it is possible that part or all of the same glen was called Innisgore Glen in English.

Altaturk Glen	*Allt an Toirc*	
H 6989	"glen of the boar"	
1. ˌaltəˈhərk glɛn	Local pronunciation	1993
2. ˌaxəˈtərk glɛn	Local pronunciation	1993

Altaturk Glen would have been known in Irish as *Allt an Toirc* "glen of the boar". Wild boars were once common in Ireland and the element *torc* is found in a great number of names throughout the country (*Joyce* i 479). A wild boar is also remembered in the name of the nearby summit of Mullaghturk (Irish *Mullach Tuirc* "hilltop of the boar") on the border between Cos Derry and Tyrone (OS H 6789), but the two names may not be related.

The two local pronunciations recorded here were heard from the same speaker, a native of the Six Towns, on two different occasions, and appear to show a degree of corruption.

Altbane Burn	A hybrid form	
H 6788		
1. altˈbɑːn	Local pronunciation	1993

Altbane Burn rises on the slopes of Mullaghturk and flows southwards into Broughderg Burn in Co. Tyrone through a small southerly-facing gully. The gully or glen from which the burn takes its name was known in Irish as *Allt Bán* "white glen".

Altdoo or **Black Glen**	*Allt Dubh*	
C 7201	"black glen"	
1. Alt Dubh "Black glen"	OSRNB 61 sh.35	1850c

Altdoo or Black Glen is formed by low ground between the two peaks of Crockalougha and Mullaghmore. The two names, one Irish and one English, are wholly synonymous.

| **Altihaskey** | *Allt Átha Easca* | |
| H 7289 | "glen of the ford of the sedgy bog" | |

1. Alta-easga	Sampson's Map	1813
2. Altayeskey, the 'Eshka' in...	OSM (Loughrey) 22	1836
3. Alt (Altus) easge "the narrow glen with waters"	MacCloskey's Stat. Report 62	1821
4. Allta Easgaidh	JRSAI lxxx 178	1950
5. ˌaltəˈɛski	Local pronunciation	1993
6. ˌaltiˈɛski	Local pronunciation	1993

A clue to the origin of this name lies in the Ordnance Survey Memoirs for the parish of Ballynascreen. There, the writer remarks on certain parts of the parish which then possessed a character of great wildness, including the "approach to the 'Eshka' in the townland of Altayeskey" (*OSM (Loughrey)* 22). He unfortunately does not point to the exact location of the "Eshka" (Irish *easca* "wet sedgy bog"), but it would appear to have lain east of the small wooded glen (*allt*) on the hillslope which faces Altayeskey Primary School.

The Ordnance Survey has adopted the spelling Altihaskey, apparently following several local authorities, but it is locally pronounced and spelt Altayeskey (*Coulter's Ballinascreen* 34, *OSL (Derry)* 88). The reason for this difference is unclear, but the two forms can largely be reconciled if we assume an original form *Allt Átha Easca* "glen of the ford of the sedgy bog". The popular form represents a natural development from the Irish with intervocalic *th* giving [j] (see Stockman & Wagner 1965, 198) and the pronunciation of *ea* as [ɛ] before *s*. We might argue that the official form represents a slight variation on this whereby the *th* (=[h]) has become attached to the final element where it would have been protected from loss (*ibid.*). However, the *a* of the final element in this form is rather more difficult to explain, and it possibly represents a mistranscription of original *e*.

A number of previous writers have pointed to a place called *(E)askylaw O Laraghan* in the Civil Survey of 1654-6 as an earlier form of this name but the identification is problematic (*Coulter's Ballinascreen* 34; Ó Ceallaigh 1950(a), 178; Ó Cíobháin 1978, 66). In the description of the bounds of the barony of Loughinsholin, this place is located in the most westerly part of the parish of Ballynascreen, dividing the baronies of Loughinsholin and Strabane, and a similar location is suggested by the description of the bounds of the parish of Ballynascreen (*Civ. Surv.* iii 168, 177). A description of the bounds of the parish of Lissan includes a reference to the same name (*ibid.* 173), and while the geographical context is less clear here, it is not irreconcilable with a location on or near the boundary between Glenviggan in the parish of Ballynascreen and Broughderg in the parish of Lissan, Co. Tyrone. Thus, there seems to be no demonstrable link between these two names.

| **Altmore Burn** | A hybrid form | |
| H 7698 | | |

1. Alt Mór "great glen"	OSRNB 61 sh.35	1850c

There can be little doubt that this name originates from Irish *Allt Mór* which here probably signifies "great glen" (1). The glen through which Altmore Burn runs is not particularly large but it is long and steep, and so it is in the sense of "great" rather than "big" that we must understand *mór* here.

Ballynacross Bridge H 7597	A hybrid form	
1. Baile na Croise "town of the cross"	OSRNB 61 sh.35	1850c
2. ˌbalnəˈkrɔs	Local pronunciation	1993

The feature originally denoted by the name Ballynacross is not clear. The final element is undoubtedly *crois* "cross", but it is unclear whether it signifies a crossroads or an ecclesiastical cross. The first element may well be *baile* as previously suggested (1), with which we may compare *Baile na Croise* "town of the cross", a name used among Irish speakers until the present century for **Draperstown**, but its meaning here cannot be ascertained with any great certainty. *Baile* is often found in names of subdivisions of townlands, and many people still consider some subdivisions to be townlands even though they are not officially designated as such. Many divisions, such as Dunarnon in the townland of **Owenreagh**, which were deemed townlands in the 17th century, are not now recognized as such by officialdom, and the translation "townland" may be most appropriate here.

However, I would tentatively suggest that the name Ballynacross was originally applied to the small village of Moneyneany, less than a mile south-west of Ballynacross Bridge. This was the site of the local cattle fair until 1798 when it was transferred to Draperstown, and it is perhaps not unlikely that the name accompanied the fair to its new location (*OSM (Loughrey)* 5). A similar transfer is seen in the name of the village of Dungloe, Co. Donegal, which was originally known as *An Clochán Liath* and, indeed, still is among the Irish-speaking population. The name Dungloe was originally applied to a fort near the village where a fair was customarily held, but it was transferred to its current location when the fair was moved there in the late 18th century (Mac Giolla Easpaig 1984, 57–8). Such transfers can be easily understood as the name would have been as much associated with the fair as with the place.

Banty Bridge H 7996	An English form	
1. ˈbanti ˈbrïdʒ	Local pronunciation	1993

Banty Bridge was probably named from people by the name of McKenna who are locally given the nickname Banty, apparently on account of their small stature.

Bealnamala Bridge H 6989	A hybrid form	
1. "The ford [mouth -O'D] of the sack"	OSRNB 22 sh.45	1850c
2. ˌbɛlnəˈmalə ˈbrïdʒ	Local pronunciation	1993

The initial element in the Irish part of this name seems to be *béal* which primarily means a "mouth" but is used in a secondary sense to denote an entrance, approach, or face (*Joyce* i 357; *Ó Dónaill* sv.). It is found alongside *áth* "a ford" in numerous place-names, such as

Ballinamallard in Co. Fermanagh (from *Béal Átha na Mallacht*) and Ballyshannon, Co. Donegal (from *Béal Átha Seanaidh*), and it is quite possible that a similar construction lies behind this name. Joyce notes that constructions of this sort are so common that *béal* often has the same meaning when used on its own (*Joyce* i 357) and, indeed, this seems to have been how the name was locally understood in the last century (1). The final element is clearly *mala* "slope" rather than *mála* (masc.) "sack" as has previously been implied (1), so we may suggest an original Irish form *Béal na Mala* "(ford)mouth of the slope".

Bealnaslaght Bridge H 7189	A hybrid form	
1. Béal na Sleacht	OSRNB 20 sh.40	1850c
2. ˌbalïnəˈslat	Local pronunciation	1993

Eugene Bradley of Moyard informs me that there was a ford at Bealnaslaght Bridge in his time, and there remain some large flat stones a few yards downstream from the bridge at a place evidently still used as a crossing for cattle. Although the current local pronunciation may be suggestive of *béal átha* "fordmouth", there is no indication of this extra syllable in the 19th-century form and it may be dismissed as a corruption by analogy with *baile*-names such as Ballynascreen. The final element appears to be *sleacht* which is a northern variant of *leacht* "gravemound, monument" (*Joyce* i 66), although there is now no evidence of any such monuments here. Bealnaslaght, therefore, probably derives from Irish *Béal na Sleacht* "(ford)mouth of the gravemounds".

Black Fort H 7497	An English form	
1. blak ˈfort	Local pronunciation	1993

Black Fort derives its name from an old ring-fort of that name. The ring-fort appears on sheet 35 of the 1926 revision of the Ordnance Survey 6-inch series, but it has since been built over. The derelict house which stands opposite Black Fort was formerly owned by a man named Cassidy whose son now occupies the bungalow at Black Fort (Mary Cassidy, pers. comm.). It was known as Lisdoo Cottage, from Irish *Lios Dubh* "black fort", and although it does not occur anywhere in our sources before Black Fort makes its appearance, it almost certainly represents the old Irish name for the fort (*OS 1:10,000* sh. 76).

Black Glen C 7201	See **Altdoo**	

Black Hill, The H 8096	*Cnoc na Daróige Duibhe* "hill of the black oak"	
1. Cnoc na Daróige Duibhe "hill of the black oak"	OSL (Derry) 130	1834
2. (ðə) ˈblak ˈhïl	Local pronunciation	1993

43

It was said that The Black Hill was formerly covered with heath which, being of a dark colour, gave name to the hill (*OSRNB* 39 sh. 36). In Irish it was known as *Cnoc na Daróige Duibhe* "hill of the black oak", after an ancient oak tree which once stood there called *Daróg an Oireachtais* "the oak of the assembly" (*OSL (Derry)* 130–1).

Black Water	*Dúghlas*	
H 7589	"black stream"	
1. Blackwater River	Sampson's Map	1813
2. Dhu Glass or Blackwater	MacCloskey's Stat. Report 2	1821
3. 'blak,watər'brïdʒ	Local pronunciation	1993
4. ðə ,blak 'watər	Local pronunciation	1993
5. ,blak 'wɔtər	Local pronunciation	1993

Blackwater or Black Water is a common name for rivers in Britain and Ireland, and it usually denotes a stream with dark, muddy water or of a general dark appearance (Ekwall 1928, 35-6). MacCloskey's variant indicates that there was a synonymous Irish form of the name, *Dúghlas* (from *dubh* "black" and *glas* "a stream"), which is found in various guises throughout Ireland and Scotland (*Joyce* i 456).

Boheradaile Bridge	A hybrid form	
H 7796		
1. Bothar a Doill "Blind man's road"	OSRNB 61 sh.35	1850c

This peculiar name is explained by the Ordnance Survey as *Bóthar an Daill* "the blind man's road" (1) but no tradition about the name is recorded and its origin is not known. *Srath Daill* in Glenlark, Co. Tyrone, which was the location of a penal mass site, was explained locally as "the blind or hidden holm", and clearly was of importance in the selection of the site (Morton 1959, 56).

Boley	*Buaile Cholm Cille*	
H 7489	"Columcille's pasturage"	
1. Bolea	Sampson's Map	1813
2. Bolie Columbkille	OSM (Loughrey) 17	1836
3. Bolie Columkill	OSM (Loughrey) 19	1836
4. Bolie Colum Kille	OSM (Loughrey) 36	1836
5. Boulie[Collumkille – scored out]	OSCNB 20 sh.40	1850c
6. Boley only [in pencil]	OSCNB 20 sh.40	1850c
7. Boleycolumbkille JOD	OSCNB 20 sh.40	1850c
8. Buaile Choluim Chille		
"Columbkille's bolie"	OSL (Derry) 119	1834
9. "St Columbkille dairy place"	OSCNB 20 sh.40	1850c
10. "Herds Place"	OSRNB 20 sh.40	1850c
11. Buaile "a Dairy place"	OSRNB 20 sh.40	1850c
12. 'boːlji	Local pronunciation	1993

The original Irish form of this name was recorded by John O'Donovan in 1834 (*OSL (Derry)* 119). He describes it as "a green spot in the mountain" immediately above Lough Patrick, and the Ordnance Survey Memoirs record a tradition that it was chosen by Columcille "as a place of meditation and prayer" (*OSM (Loughrey)* 17, 36). *Buaile*, which refers to summer pasturage often high in the mountains, is rarely qualified by a saint's name, but Joyce cites the example of Boultypatrick in Co. Donegal which he takes to mean "Patrick's booleys" (*Buailte Phádraig*) (*Joyce* i 240). MacCloskey states that booleying was the common practice in this area up until 60 years before the date of his survey (1821), and that every May, all the families in the district removed with their flocks and herds to "the woody glens and upland heights then rich with the most luxuriant herbiage" (*MacCloskey's Stat. Report* 16). The Memoirs state that there was a standing stone here, called in Irish the "grey cow's tether-stake", which was believed to be the stake to which Columcille's cow was tethered when she was out grazing (*OSM (Loughrey)* 19).

Bonnety Bush   An English form
H 7288

  1. 'bɔnəˌti 'bʊʃ   Local pronunciation   1993

Bonnety Bush is described c. 1850 as a white thorn growing on a rocky spot on the south-east side of Altihaskey Hill: the top was quite flat and broad on account of the westerly winds "which cut it as evenly as a knife could do" and its resulting resemblance to a Scottish bonnet thus gave rise to the name (*OSRNB* 22 sh. 45). There is another Bonnety Bush in the townland of Cloghogue, Co. Antrim (*OS 6-inch* sh. 37).

Carricknashinnagh   *Carraig na Sionnach*
H 7193   "the rock of the foxes"

  1. "Foxes Rock"   OSCNB 20 sh.40   1850c
  2. Carraic na Sionnach "rock of the
     foxes"   OSCNB 20 sh.40   1850c

Sionnach, meaning "fox", is found in a number of Irish place-names where it is frequently anglicized *shinnagh* (*Joyce* i 483).

Cockhill   An English form
H 7392

  1. kɔk'hïl   Local pronunciation   1993
  2. kɔk'hïl 'məuntn   Local pronunciation   1993

Cockhill is the name of a number of places in Ireland and Britain. In England it probably refers to the haunts of the woodcock, the habits of which have been closely studied by country people for centuries (Field 1972, 49). In Ireland, it may be a translation of a native name. **Cock Mountain** in the Mournes, for example, is a translation of the original Irish *Sliabh an Choiligh* "mountain of the cock" (*PNI* iii 131).

Cornafarna   *Corr na Fearna*
H 7495   "round hill of the alder-tree"

1. ˌkɔrnə'fɛːrn(ə)	Local pronunciation	1993

The final element in this name, *fearn* "alder(-tree)", is masculine in Modern Irish (*Ó Dónaill*, *Dinneen* sv.), but it was originally feminine (*DIL* sv.), and is clearly feminine here. The first element, *corr*, has a wide variety of meanings, but it most frequently signifies "a round hill" in place-names (see, for example, *Dinneen* 249-50 sv.; *Joyce* i 397). Here, it denotes a small, round outcrop of Crockmore rather than an isolated round hill.

Cow Lough	An English form	
H 7488		

1. ðə 'kəu ˌlɔx	Local pronunciation	1993

This small lake was named from the practice of watering cattle here (*OSRNB* 22 sh. 45). The hill on which it lies was formerly known in Irish as *Buaile Cholm Cille* (see **Boley** above), a name which relates to the custom of pasturing cattle on hills during the summer.

Craigagh Hill	A hybrid form	
H 7198		

1. "Rocky Hill"	OSRNB 60 sh.35	1850c
2. 'krɛgə 'hil	Local pronunciation	1993
3. 'kreːgə	Local pronunciation	1993

Many of the hill-names in this locality, such as **Craigbane**, **Rock Hill**, **Carrick-nashinnagh**, and **Stone Hill**, are derived from words relating to "rock". The eastern slope of Craigagh Hill is quite rocky and it is clearly from this feature that the element *Creagach* "rocky place" derives. The English word "hill" is certainly a late addition, and there is no indication whether the name *Creagach* was ever applied to the hill as a whole, or if the hill was ever known by a different name in Irish.

Craigbane	*Creag Bhán*	
H 7196	"white rock"	

1. "White Rock"	OSRNB 60 sh.35	1850c
2. Creag Bhán "white rock"	OSRNB 60 sh.35	1850c

Crockacahir	*Cnoc na Cathaoireach*	
H 7689	"hill of the chair"	

1. "The Chair Hill"	OSRNB 20 sh.40	1850c
2. Cnoc a Chathaoir	OSRNB 20 sh.40	1850c

In the middle of the 19th century, it was believed that this hill was named from a stone which resembled a chair (*OSRNB* 20 sh. 40) and, indeed, there is still a stone chair there (Sean Brolly, pers. comm.). It is not unusual for resemblances to people or things to give rise to names for rocks, and there are several other examples of rocks being likened to chairs. Munn refers to a large rock in Glengomna called *Cathaoir Ruairí* "Rory's chair" where Rory

O'Donnell used to sit when watching his sheep (*Munn's Notes* 47). A natural rock formation in the townland of Carrowmenagh in the parish of Killelagh resembling a large chair was known as a giant's chair, as was a similar stone in the townland of Iniscarn in Desertmartin, and a large stone in the parish of Ballintoy, Co. Antrim, resembling an armchair was known locally as the Giant's Chair (*OSM* xxvii 98, xxxi 57; xxiv 23).

The anglicized form of the name shows nothing of the Irish inflection, but this is probably purely the result of the anglicization process, and the underlying form is almost certainly *Cnoc na Cathaoireach* "hill of the chair". We see the *n* of the article *na* "(of) the" being lost after *c* or *t* in the names Crockalyre in the Glenelly district, Co. Tyrone, from Irish *Cnoc na Laidhre* "the hill of the fork" (Mac Aodha 1986(b) 90), and Altacree Burn which comes from *Allt na Críche* "glen of the boundary" (*OSRNB* 54 sh. 31), and an almost exact parallel may be provided by the name Laghtacahir in the townland of Legatonegan and parish of Termonamongan, Co. Tyrone (Irish *Leacht na Cathaoireach* "gravemound of the chair"). In this last example, we also see the shortening of the last element from three to two syllables.

Crockaghole
H 7090

Cnoc an Ghuail
"hill of the charcoal"

1. "Coal Hill"	OSCNB 20 sh.40	1850c
2. Cnoc a Chuaille "hill of the pole"	OSCNB 20 sh.40	1850c

Gual can mean either "coal" or "charcoal" but in place-names it always seems to denote the latter as the introduction of coal as a fuel is comparatively recent (*Joyce* ii 205). About half a mile to the west of Crockaghole lies the similarly named Ardnagoole which comes from Irish *Ard an Ghuail* "height of the charcoal". O'Donovan was told that this place was named from the fact that charcoal was manufactured here, and many old men remembered the production of charcoal in the area before the importation of coal began (*OSL (Derry)* 90). We might consider an alternative explanation from *gabhal* "fork" which appears in numerous place-names, but this does not have the support of local authority (1).

Crockataggart
H 7397

Cnoc an tSagairt
"the priest's hill"

1. "The Priests Hill"	OSRNB 60 sh.35	1850c
2. Cnoc a tSagairt "hill of the priest"	OSRNB 60 sh.35	1850c
3. ˌkrɔxəˈtɛgərt	Local pronunciation	1993

It was said that the village of Crockataggart derived its named from a priest who once lived there, and it was also claimed as the birth place of a clergyman called Rodgers who distinguished himself at the Siege of Clonmel (*OSRNB* 60 sh. 35). The modern pronunciation may suggest an initial element *cruach* "stack" or possibly *croch* "gallows", but it seems quite likely that this is merely a corruption of earlier *cnoc* "hill".

Crockawilla
H 7498

Cnoc an Bhaile
"hill of the town"

1. "Hill Town"	OSRNB 60 sh.35	1850c
2. Cnoc a bhaile "hill of the town"	OSRNB 60 sh.35	1850c
3. ˌkrɔkə'wïljə	Local pronunciation	1993
4. ˌkrɔknə'wïlə (?)	Local pronunciation	1993

One local informant suggested to me that this name derives from the Irish word for a cattle-pen (*buaile*), but this does not accord particularly well with the anglicized form (cf. **Boley** above). It seems to have been understood locally as "hill town" in the last century (1) and this line of argument is certainly defensible. In the Irish of Tyrone, the internal vowel in *baile* was usually pronounced [ɔ] and sometimes [ï] (Stockman & Wagner 1965, 52), and even in the 17th century it was, in certain sources, frequently anglicized *Belly*. *Baile* here probably signifies some form of settlement, probably a clachan, rather than "townland".

Crockbrack   *Cnoc Breac*
H 7195   "speckled hill"

1. Cnoc Breac "speckled hill"	OSCNB 59 sh.35	1850c
2. krɔk'brak	Local pronunciation	1993

The adjective *breac* normally means "speckled" or "dappled", and in place-names it generally refers to the speckled or spotted appearance of land caused by different kinds of vegetation (*Joyce* ii 288).

Crockmoran   *Cnoc Uí Mhuireáin*
H 7088   "Moran's hill"

1. "Moran's Hill"	OSRNB 22 sh.45	1850c
2. Cnoc Moráin	OSRNB 22 sh.45	1850c
3. krɔk'mɔrn (bre:)	Local pronunciation	1993

The final element in this place-name is clearly the surname Moran which is still common in the area to this day. A certain Murtagh O Murren was living in the townland of Owenreagh in 1663, and the surname was numerous here in the last century (*Griffith's Val.* 277 where is is spelt Morrin). It also appears in another place-name, that of Moranstown, which was located in the Six Towns (*Sampson's Map*). The anglicized form Moran is used for several distinct Irish surnames, but the 17th-century reference to Murtagh O Murren of Owenreagh cited above, together with forms of the name found in the 17th century in Co. Antrim, may indicate that in this area it derives from Irish *Ó Muireáin* (cf. MacLysaght 1985, 221, 230; Woulfe 1923, 621; *PNI* iv 99).

Crockmore   *Cnoc Mór*
H 7295   "big hill"

1. krо̨k'mo:r	Local pronunciation	1993
2. krɔk'mo:r	Local pronunciation	1993

Despite its name, Crockmore is smaller than the neighbouring hills of Crockbrack and Spelhoagh. Nevertheless, its prominent position and its sheer bulk give it an impression of size which the other hills lack.

Crocknacreeha *Cnoc na Críche*
H 7287 "hill of the boundary"

Crocknacreeha sits on the boundary between the parishes of Ballynascreen and Lissan, as well as on the county boundary, and it is clearly from this fact that the hill has been named.

Douglas Bridge An English form
Douglas River
H 7596, H 7696

1. Douglas Bridge	Sampson's Map	1813
2. ðə 'duɡləs 'rïvər	Local pronunciation	1993
3. (ðə) 'duɡləs 'brïdʒ	Local pronunciation	1993

The surname Douglas has a long association with this area, dating back at least to Robert Douglasse of Moydamlaght who is mentioned in the Hearth Money Rolls of 1663 (*HMR (Ó Doibhlin 2)* 66). It is probably from the surname rather than an Irish form *Dúghlas* "black stream" that the river and bridge are named (cf. **Black Water** above). The surname is of Scottish origin and, in Ulster, is most common in counties Antrim and Derry (Bell 1988, 57).

Doyles Bridge An English form
H 7596

1. 'dɔilz 'brïdʒ	Local pronunciation	1993

This bridge was named from a person called Doyle who lived here in the mid-19th century (*OSRNB* 61 sh. 35).

Draperstown An English form
H 7894

1. i mBaile na Croise	Sgéalta Mh. L 122	1930c
2. Cross	Sampson's Map	1813
3. The village of Moyheelan more usually called the Cross	MacCloskey's Stat. Report 9	1821
4. Moyheelan	MacCloskey's Stat. Report 9	1821
5. The Cross of Ballynascreen, locally called	Munn's Notes 43	1925
6. Borbury or the "yellow road"	OSM (Loughrey) 5	1836
7. Baile na Croise	GÉ 215	1989
8. 'drɛpərz'təun	Local pronunciation	1993
9. 'drïpərz'təun	Local pronunciation	1993

The name Draperstown was first given to the town of **Moneymore** which was founded by the Drapers' Company early in the 17th century. The modern Draperstown was not founded until 1798 (*OSM (Loughrey)* 5), and did not take its current name until 1818 (*Munn's Notes* 43; Curl 1986, 189–91, 203). Despite the adoption of the name Draperstown, the village was more usually called "the Cross" (signifying the crossroads where the market was held), as well as "the Cross of Ballynascreen" and "Moyheelan" (**Moyheeland** being a townland in which the town now partially stands). The Ordnance Survey Memoirs also state that the village was first called Borbury (Irish *Bóthar Buí*) meaning "yellow road" (*OSM (Loughrey)* 5). In Irish it was known as *Baile na Croise* "town of the crossroads" (1).

Glashagh Burn	*Glaise*	
H 7292	"stream"	
1. Glaise "a brook or streamlet"	OSRNB 20 sh.40	1850c
2. 'glaʃə 'börn	Local pronunciation	1993

The local pronunciation, with no trace of a final *gh*, supports O'Donovan's suggestion of *Glaise* signifying a rivulet or stream (1), and this was probably the original Irish name for the burn. *Glaiseach* normally denotes a place of streams or watery bogland (*Ó Dónaill* sv.) and may appear in this sense in place-names (see, for example, Mac Giolla Easpaig 1986, 79).

| **Kilcraigagh** | *Coill Chreagach* |
| H 7299 | "rocky wood" |

Even with the best documentation, it is usually impossible to distinguish between *coill* "a wood" and *cill* "a church" if no authentic Irish form is forthcoming. However, the absence of any evidence of a church or graveyard in this area, coupled with its location on the hill, renders the former interpretation more likely. The rocky nature of the area gives the name its second element, *creagach* "rocky".

Legmore	*Log Mór*	
H 7599	"big hollow"	
1. "Big Hollow"	OSRNB 60 sh.35	1850c
2. Lag Mór "great hollow"	OSRNB 60 sh.35	1850c

According to Joyce, *Leg* begins the names of about 100 townlands, mostly in the northern half of Ireland, and he generally interprets this as meaning a hollow (from Irish *log*) (*Joyce* i 431). Legmore is formed by a conspicuous cliff and indentation in the face of a hill (*OSRNB* 60 sh. 35).

Lough Ouske	*Loch Uaisce*	
H 7093	"lake of the yearling ewe(s)"	
1. Loghharsh	Civ. Surv. iii 374	1654
2. Loch-uisce "The lake of the water"	Munn's Notes 47	1925
3. lɔx 'uːsk	Local pronunciation	1993

The bog surrounding Lough Ouske is still traversed by sheep and a derivation from *Loch Uaisce* "lake of the yearling ewe(s)" must be considered the most likely origin of the name (see Hamilton 1974, 336; Wagner 1959, 76; and cf. *uascán* "a hogget", Stockman & Wagner 1965, 109; see also *DIL* sv. *óisc*). However, many lakes in Ireland are named from the blackness of their water, and Lough Ouske possibly derives from Irish *Loch Dhubhuisce* "lake of the black water". This mountain-top lake is surrounded on all sides by bog, and its boggy water is made to appear all the darker by the presence of black algae over large parts of its surface.

Lough Patrick	*Loch Phádraig*	
H 7490	"St Patrick's lake"	
1. lɔx ˈpatrïk	Local pronunciation	1993

MacCloskey describes an "assemblage" on the banks of Lough Patrick which was held each year on St John's Eve:

> Numerous crowds of both sexes assemble, and while the neighbouring hills and the plain below are blazing with the midsummer bonfires, indulge themselves in rustic amusements, dances, and thus pass the evening in harmless pleasures. But the priests seem to think it has ceased to be harmless: they now exert themselves to prohibit such meetings. (*MacCloskey's Stat. Report* 24–5).

He also records that its water was believed to have been blessed by St Columcille (*ibid.* 24).

The association with St Patrick is made clear only in the Ordnance Survey Memoirs. It was said that when St Patrick was journeying through this district, he and several others began a station on the site of the lough. Some of his followers became thirsty and demanded a drink from him, so the saint performed a miracle. He thereby caused a spring to burst forth and the lough was formed, and a station was subsequently held annually at it for penances and cures (*OSM (Loughrey)* 27).

McConnamys Bridge	An English form	
H 6888		
1. ˌməˈkɔnəˌmiz ˈbrïdʒ	Local pronunciation	1993

The bridge was named after a man called McConnamy who formerly resided in a house east of it (*OSRNB* 21 sh. 44). The surname is still common in the area.

McNally's Bridge	An English form	
H 6787		
1. ˌməkənˈaːliz ˈbrïdʒ	Local pronunciation	1993
2. ˌmakˈnɑliz ˈbrïdʒ	Local pronunciation	1993

This bridge was named after Hugh McNally who formerly resided in a house south of it (*OSRNB* 21 sh. 44). The surname McNally, which here probably derives from Irish *Mac Con Allaidh* (see *GUH* 115n), is frequently pronounced locally as McAnally.

Mile Mountain H 7091	An English form	
1. ðə 'mail ˌməuntn	Local pronunciation	1993

A number of hills and mountains throughout the country, such as **Five Mile Hill** in Co. Down, have received their names from their distance from some important centre (*PNI* i 111). Mile Mountain may have been named from the fact that it is approximately one mile from the old church of Ballynascreen at Sixtowns.

Mill Lough H 7488	An English form	
1. ðə 'mïl ˌlɔx	Local pronunciation	1993

This small isolated lake was once used as a mill pond (*OSRNB* 22 sh. 45).

Milltown H 7996	An English form	
1. (ðə) 'mïltəun	Local pronunciation	1993

Cf. **Milltown** in the parish of Maghera. The element "town" in such names does not always denote a large urban centre, but frequently signifies a small settlement or a cluster of houses. In Scots, town can still mean "farmstead and its buildings" (*EPNS* i pt 2, 61).

Mountain View H 7493	An English form	
1. 'məunʔn 'vju:	Local pronunciation	1993

This place clearly derives its name from its location in the shadow of the surrounding hills.

Moyola River H 7491	*Abhainn na Scríne* "Ballinascreen river"	
1. ō Bir co Camus	CGH LL 333c35	1125c
2. ó Bhior go hAbhainn Mhóir	Céitinn iii 302	1633c
3. Skrine flu:	Bartlett Maps (Esch. Co. Maps)	1603
4. (?)Skinne flu	Speed's Ulster	1610
5. Miola, rivelet...called	Boate's Hist. 103	1652
6. Moyolla River	Civ. Surv. iii 168	1654
7. Moyola River	Civ. Surv. iii 170	1654
8. the River of Moyola	Civ. Surv. iii 170,177,178	1654
9. Monola River	Civ. Surv. iii 187	1654
10. the River of Monola	Civ. Surv. iii 187,191	1654
11. Moyola River	Civ. Surv. iii 174,176,180	1654
12. Minola River	Sampson's Map	1813

13. Minola or Mayola (original obliterated)	Received usage No. 16	1834c
14. 'Moy-o-la	OSNB Pron. No. 11	1834c
15. My-'o-la	OSNB Pron. No. 16	1834c
16. Abhainn na Scríne	GUH 25	1951
17. Abhainn na Scríne	GÉ 256	1989
18. ðə mɔi'oːla (rïvər)	Local pronunciation	1993
19. ðə mɔi'oːlə	Local pronunciation	1993

The Moyola River rises in Moyard in the parish of Ballynascreen and, after passing by Tobermore and Castledawson, falls into Lough Neagh. The name is comparatively late in its application to the river and is derived from the Moyola estate, originally granted to Sir Thomas Phillips, at the north-west corner of Lough Neagh where the river flows into the lake (see **Moyola Park** in the parish of Ballyscullion).

It is generally accepted that the river was known in the medieval period as *Bior*. This means simply "water" and is a common appellation for streams and rivers. The Synod of Rath Breasail, which was held in 1111, fixed the boundary of the diocese of Armagh at the *Bior* (*Céitinn* iii 302), and although the boundary of the modern diocese follows the Moyola for a distance of only one mile near Castledawson, Ó Cíobháin (1978, 63–4) plausibly argues that the original boundary followed the Moyola as far as the Sperrins.

Ó Ceallaigh recalls that the Moyola was called *Abhainn na Scríne* "the river of Ballynascreen" by some old people in his time (*GUH* 25). On Bartlett's map of Ulster, which dates from 1603, a river called "Skrine flu:" is depicted flowing into the Bann at Lough Beg (3), and this is undoubtedly the Moyola, although the Moyola actually enters Lough Neagh to the south of Lough Beg. Speed, in his Map of Ulster (4), draws another river further north flowing into the Bann at Kilrea and calls this "Skinne Flumen" (a river is also depicted by Speed running from "Skrine" past "Maharry" (Maghera) into Lough Beg, and this is clearly the Moyola).

Mullaghlahan
H 7795

Mullach Leathan
"broad hilltop"

1. Mullach Leathan "broad summit"	OSRNB 60 sh.35	1850c

This settlement was named from its position on top of a small, flat-topped hill.

Mullaghmore
C 7300

Mullach Mór
"big hilltop"

Mullaghmore is the highest peak in the northern end of the parish, rising to a height of 555.9 metres.

Mullaghshuraren
H 7089

Of uncertain origin

1. Mullach Siúradhráin in the western extremity of Glenconkeine	OSL (Derry) 85	1834

2. Mullach Siudharáin...a mountain
in the south of the Sixtowns of
Ballinascreen called Mullagh
Shoorin   Ó Ceallaigh 1901, 201   1901

3. 'mǫlə   Local pronunciation   1993

This name is known locally only by its shorter version (Irish *Mullach* "hilltop").The second
element in the official form of the name has never been satisfactorily explained, but Ó
Ceallaigh (1901, 201), citing a note by O'Donovan on the extent of Brian Carragh's lands
as his source, gives an Irish form which may be rendered into standard Irish as *Mullach
Siúráin* which he identifies with "a mountain in the south of the Sixtowns of Ballinascreen
called Mullagh Shoorin".

Old Church Bridge, The   An English form
H 7390

1. ðə ˌold 'tʃərtʃ ˌbrïdʒ   Local pronunciation   1993

Named after the old parish church of Ballynascreen.

Parkaveadan Burn   A hybrid form
C 7200

1. ˌparkə'vi.dʒən   Local pronunciation   1995

Parkaveadan Burn is clearly named after a nearby field known in Irish as *Páirc an Mhíodúin*
"field of the meadow". We may compare here Altaveedan Burn in the nearby district of
Glenelly, Co. Tyrone, from Irish *Alt an Mhíodúin* "the ravine of the meadow" (Mac Aodha
1986(b), 89).

Ranaghan   *Raithneachán*
H 7398   "ferny place"

1. 'ranəˌhən   Local pronunciation   1993

Ranaghan occurs as a place-name throughout Ireland and usually derives from Irish
Raithneachán "ferny place, place of ferns" (*Joyce* ii 331). Even to this day there is an abun-
dance of ferns in this area. Coulter identifies the *Coulraine* of the Civil Survey as Ranaghan,
but the context makes it quite clear that it lies on the north-eastern boundary between
Ballynascreen and Maghera (*Coulter's Ballinascreen* 34; *Civ. Surv.* iii 177). *Coulraine* is probably the same place as the *Cúl Rathain* in the parish of Kilcronaghan mentioned in *Cín Lae
Ó Mealláin* and previously identified as the town of Coleraine (*Cín Lae Ó M.* lch 5).The text
here is defective and I would suggest the following reading: ...*agus fuair ceathramha maith.
[Do cuiredh techta] ón Ghen. go Cúl Rathain i bporraist[e] Cill Cruinechan.*, "...and he got good
quarter. Messengers were sent by the General to Coulraine in the parish of Kilcronaghan..."
There is some slight discrepancy between the two locations suggested by these two texts, but
the distance involved is negligible and we must allow for some degree of error.

Rock Hill H 7195	An English form	
1. ˌrɔk'hïl	Local pronunciation	1993
2. ðə 'rɔksəz məun?n	Local pronunciation	1993

A rocky mountain. See **Crockbrack**.

Six Towns, The H 7290	An English form	
1. Na Sé Bhaile	GÉ 271	1989
2. ðə sïks 'təunz	Local pronunciation	1993

The Six Towns derives its name from the fact that it comprises the six townlands of Cavanreagh, Glenviggan, Moneyconey, Moyard, Owenreagh and Tullybrick. This plot of land, called "termon or erenagh land", formerly belonged to the church of Ballynascreen, and it was this factor which gave them their distinct identity. The name Glenviggan does not appear in our 17th-century sources but instead we find reference to a place called Dunarnon which survives now only as a minor division of Owenreagh townland.

Sixtowns Lodge
H 7391

An English form

See **Six Towns, The**.

Slievemoyle
H 7799

Sliabh Maol
"bare mountain"

This may have been an older name for what is now Coolnasillagh Mountain, but on modern maps it is applied only to the southern spur of the mountain. *Sliabh* can mean "a mountain or mountain-range" or "a moor" in early Irish (*DIL* sv. *sliab*) and, in topographical usage, is applied to a wide variety of physical features from isolated hills and mountains to extensive plateaus and raised bogs (de hÓir 1970(a), 2). In place-names, it is frequently of great antiquity, as, for example, in the name **Slieve Gallion**, but in many cases it may well be of much more recent date (*ibid.* 4).

According to the legend of the hound which terrorized the valley of Glenconkeyne, when Cadhan O'Henery undertook to kill the monster he was to signal his success to the people who had fled east of the Bann by lighting two fires, one on Slievemoyle on the northern side of the glen and one on Slieve Gallion (*OSL (Derry)* 136). As a result, so the tradition goes, both places were named *Teinnteacha* meaning "fires". *Teinnteach* (properly *Tinteach*) is, in fact, a derivative of *tine* "fire" and the adjectival suffix *(e)ach*, and may be translated "a place of fire; a place where a fire is lit". There is a townland and mountain called **Tintagh**, which derives from *tinteach* "fire", in the parish of Lissan, and this is probably the origin of the legend. O'Donovan, perhaps correctly, argues that the *Tinteacha* were more probably named after fires lit at Bealtaine (May 1st) (*ibid.*).

Spelhoagh
H 7097

Speal Chuach
"scythe of the *Cuach* (bowl/hollow)"

1. Spellhoagh	MacCloskey's Stat. Report 8	1821
2. Spell-'hoagh	OSNB Pron. No. 16	1834c
3. Spell Hoagh Gap	OSM (Loughrey) 29	1836
4. Speal cuach "Scythe or crooked mountain of cuckoos"	J O'D (OSNB) No. 16	1834c
5. Spallnachoigha or Cucoo Sythe	OSCNB 59 sh.35	1850c
6. Speal Chuach "scythe of the cuckoos"	OSRNB 61 sh.35	1850c
7. Speal Chuach	Ó Ceallaigh 1927, 59	1927
8. 'spalθ	Local pronunciation	1993

The hill denoted by this name curves gently northwards in the shape of a scythe, and an origin from Irish *speal*, or some form of it, seems quite plausible. The final element in the written form of the name, which goes back to the early part of the last century, has been widely interpreted as the word *cuach* "cuckoo", but it is highly unlikely that cuckoos would be found in such a high and exposed location (568 metres above sea level). Furthermore, if the composition of the name is as recent as we might reasonably suppose, we would probably expect to find evidence of the article *na* "the" before the final element, and this only appears in one highly stylized form in which there appears to have been a deliberate attempt to show the origin of the name (5).

It might be suggested, therefore, that we have here an instance of the word *cuach* "bowl; goblet, drinking cup" being used to describe a hollow, and such a feature is indeed to be found between Spelhoagh and Craigbane to the south. Linguistically, a much stronger case can be made for a connection with this word, as *Speal Chuach* is likely to be a shortened version of a once longer name so that we would not necessarily expect to find the article. *Cuach* "bowl" is not widely used in place-names and it is hardly surprising that a more obvious interpretation should have been sought.

We should also consider the possibility that we have here a hybrid of Irish *Speal* "scythe" and English dialect *hough* or *how* "hill". However, Irish was spoken in this district possibly into this century (Ó Ceallaigh 1927, 59n), and it is unlikely that such a name would not be wholly Gaelic in origin, particularly as it was widely understood to be Irish by local people in the last century.

While the written forms of the name are compatible with the suggested Irish form, the modern pronunciation is wholly at odds with both, although it is clearly somehow related to the earlier forms.

Sruhanleanantawey *Sruthán Léana an tSamhaidh*
H 7888 "the stream of the sorrel meadow"

1. "The sorrel meadow Burn"	OSRNB 22 sh.45	1850c
2. Sruthan Leana an tSamhaigh	OSRNB 22 sh.45	1850c

Léana generally means a "low-lying grassy place, water-meadow" (*Ó Dónaill* sv.) but in Derry it is used of any green field, meadow or pasture-land (*OSL (Derry)* 21), and this is probably the sense in which it is used here. Sorrel, Irish *samhadh*, is plentiful in Ireland and has given name to a great number of places (*Joyce* ii 341–2).

Sruhannaclogh
H 7789

Sruthán na gCloch
"the stream of the stones"

1. Srothán na g-cloch "streamlet of
the stones"

OSRNB 20 sh.40

1850c

There are several megaliths in the vicinity of Sruhannaclogh but the name is more probably derived from the fact that the stream is full of stones.

Stone Hill
H 7489

An English form

1. ston 'hïl
2. 'sto:n hïl

Local pronunciation
Local pronunciation

1993
1993

This hill appears to have been named from naturally occurring rock in the area (*OSRNB* 20 sh. 40), although we should note the presence of several stone monuments nearby.

Teal Lough
H 7388

An English form

1. ðə 'ti:l ˌlɔx

Local pronunciation

1993

This small lake derives its name from the fact that it was much frequented by a type of duck known as teal (*OSRNB* 22 sh. 45).

Weddell Bridge
H 7897

An English form

1. 'wadəl ˌbrïdʒ
2. 'wɛdəl ˌbrïdʒ

Local pronunciation
Local pronunciation

1993
1993

The surname Weddell, which is of Scottish origin, is a variant of the name Waddel (Black 1946, 796-7). Although written Weddell, the earlier pronunciation is used locally in connection with the bridge.

White Fort
H 8196

An English form

1. 'wait 'fort

Local pronunciation

1993

So called from the nearby rath of that name.

White Water
H 7790

An Abhainn Bhán
"the white river"

1. Whitewater River
2. Awain Ban or White Water
(Whitewater)

Sampson's Map

MacCloskey's Stat. Report 2, 5

1813

1821

3. ðə 'wait 'watər

Local pronunciation

1993

The more or less synonymous Irish name of the river is suggested by a form used by MacCloskey (2) but, unlike the **Black Water,** there is no certainty that the English name is a translation from the Irish.

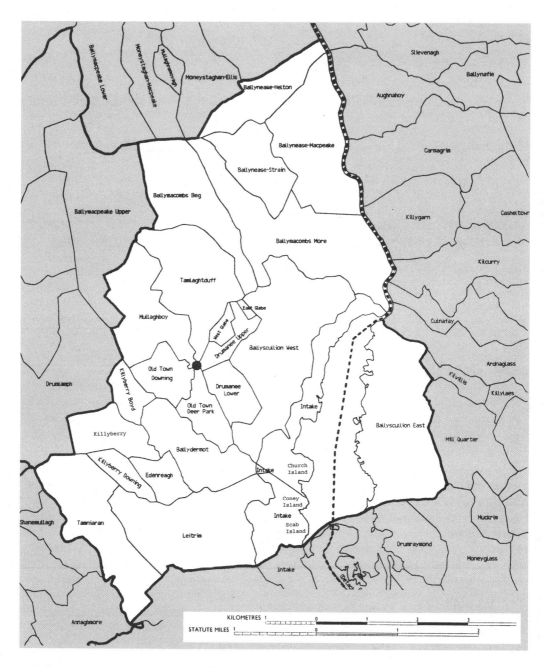

Parish of Ballyscullion

Townlands

Ballydermot	Ballyscullion East	Glebe West	Old Town Deer Park	Church Island
Ballymacombs Beg	Ballyscullion West	Killyberry	Old Town Downing	Coney Island
Ballymacombs More	Drumanee Lower	Killyberry Boyd	Tamlaghtduff	Scab Island
Ballynease-Helton	Drumanee Upper	Killyberry Downing	Tamniaran	
Ballynease-Macpeake	Edenreagh	Leitrim		*Towns*
Ballynease-Strain	Glebe East	Mullaghboy	*Islands* (intaken)	Bellaghy

Based upon Ordnance Survey 1:50,000 mapping, with permission of the Director of the Ordnance Survey of Northern Ireland, Crown copyright reserved.

THE PARISH OF BALLYSCULLION

The ruins of the medieval parish church of Ballyscullion lie in an overgrown graveyard on Church Island in Lough Beg. Both the island and the church were formerly called *Inis Taoide* "St Taoide's island" after the church's patron, and the name persists in our records well into the 17th century. Little is known of the patron saint, save that his feast day was celebrated on September 7 (*Colton Vis.* 83n). Reeves, following the Martyrology of Donegal, spells the name without the final *e* (modern Irish *Taoid*), but the earlier Martyrology of Gormán supports the spelling *Taoide* (*Mart. Gorm.* 172).

References to the church are few and far between in the medieval period. It was plundered by the Ulaid with the loss of many lives in 1129 (*AIF* 292, *AU (Mac Airt)* 576), and in 1458 the Primate of Armagh forbade various members of the clergy from disturbing Patrick O'Kegan, the rector, in his duties (*EA* 374). After the Plantation, the majority of the lands in the civil parish were held by the Vintners' Guild, while the Salters were possessed of the townland of Ballydermot and the half townland of Edenreagh (*Lond. Comp. Valuation* 308). By way of compensation for the surrender of his interests in and about Coleraine Sir Thomas Phillips argued for and obtained a grant of 500 acres around the river Moyola opposite his castle at Toome, including the townlands of Leitrim and Tamniaran in Ballyscullion (Moody 1939, 108, 115; *CPR Jas I* 286b).

PARISH NAME

Ballyscullion   *Baile Uí Scoillín*
                                     "Scullion's townland"

1. Innis Taoyde sive Baile Sguilin	Top. Frag. 83	1675c
2. Balle Oskullyn	Colton Vis. 76	1397
3. Balleoskullyn	Colton Vis. 83	1397
4. de Ynistayde	Annates Ulst. 113	1500
5. Ballynescallen otherwise Inistide	CPR Jas I 376b	1609
6. Ballynescullen otherwise Inistide	CPR Jas I 377a	1609
7. Ballinscollin alias Inishtide	Bishop. Der. i 57,62	1610
8. Ballinescullin al's Inishtide	Bishop. Der. i 80	1611
9. Ballinscollin otherwise Inistide, the termon ...	CPR Jas I 279a	1615
10. Ballinescollin	CPR Jas I 280a	1615
11. Ballinscollin al's Inishtide	Bishop. Der. i 103	1615
12. Ballynesculline, R'c'oria de	Bishop. Der. i 129	1617c
13. Ballinescullen	CPR Jas I 567b	1623
14. Ballineskullin	Bishop. Der. i 145	1624c
15. Ballineskullen	Bishop. Der. i 146	1624c
16. Balluskullan Parish	Civ. Surv. iii 167	1654
17. Balluskallen, Parish of	Civ. Surv. iii 168	1654
18. Belliostullen, the pish of	Civ. Surv. iii 180	1654
19. Balliskullan, Parish of	Civ. Surv. iii 192	1654
20. Balliscullen Parish	Hib. Reg. Loughinsholin	1657c
21. Ballyscullen	Bishop. Der. i 326	1661
22. Ballyscullen Parish	BSD(c) 50	1661

23. Ballewskallan Parish	BSD(c) 58	1661
24. Balliskullion, The Parish of	HMR (Ó Doibhlin 2) 66	1663
25. Ballyscillin, parish of	Bishop. Der. i 376	1664
26. Ballyscullin, parish of	Bishop. Der. i 377	1664
27. Balliscullin	Bishop. Der. i 398	1665c
28. Ballinescallin	Bishop. Der. i 405	1666
29. Inistida	Bishop. Der. i 405	1666
30. Balliscullin	Bishop. Der. i 415	1668
31. Ballineskullin	Bishop. Der. i 425	1669
32. Balliniscullen	Bishop. Der. i 425	1669
33. Ballinascullin	Bishop. Der. ii 1	1671
34. Balliscullin	Hib. Del. Derry	1672c
35. Ballyneskullen, Rec' de	Bishop. Der. ii 113	1686
36. Balliscullin	Lamb Maps Derry	1690c
37. Ballinescullin, S'te Tide	Bishop. Der. ii 136	1692
38. Ballinescullen	Bishop. Der. ii 136	1692
39. Inistedah	Bishop. Der. ii 509	1700c
40. Ballyscuglin R.	Sampson's Map	1813
41. Baile-Scoilain "Townland of the O'Scollans"	Munn's Notes 56	1925
42. Baile-Ui-Scoláin "O'Scollan's town"	Joyce iii 118	1925
43. ˌbaləˈskǫljən	Local pronunciation	1993
44. ˌbalənəˈskǫljən	Local pronunciation	1993

The name Ballyscullion is clearly derived from the Scullions who are believed to have been the medieval erenaghs of the parish's church lands (*Colton Vis.* 83n). They were among the principal Irish families in Loughinsholin in the early second half of the 17th century, and the name is still common in the parish to this day (*Census* 139; cf. *HMR (Ó Doibhlin 2)* 66). MacLysaght (1985, 266) takes this surname to represent Irish *Ó Scolláin*, but both the early spellings of the surname and the modern pronunciation favour something like an otherwise unattested *Ó Scoillín*. The wide range of early references to the place-name adds support to this interpretation, and it is surely significant that there is virtually no indication of a long-*a* in the final syllable (cf. **Curran** in Maghera).

It is often difficult to distinguish between singular and plural forms of Ó-surnames in place-names for the principal distinguishing feature, the form of the surname marker, becomes indistinct before the main stress. Indeed, the difference would be obscured even in Irish and the distinction could only be maintained by the effect of the surname marker on the following consonant. In the case of Ballyscullion, the following *sc* would have remained unaffected by either a gen. sing. or gen. pl. form, so no convincing case can be argued in favour of either possibility on these grounds. The *O* which appears in the very earliest references to the name seems merely intended to indicate that the final element is a surname. There is evidence that the parish name **Desertoghill**, which is frequently spelt with an *O* in early sources, derives from Irish *Díseart Uí Thuathail*, and there is good reason to believe that **Tamlaght O'Crilly**, despite its modern form, also contains a gen. sing. form of a surname.

As should be clear from the early references to the parish assembled above, Ballyscullion Parish was formerly known as *Inis Taoide* "Taoide's island" from the church and island of that name on Lough Beg (see above). However, it seems to have adopted the name Ballyscullion, which originally probably denoted just the erenagh lands, at an early date, although both names continued to be used alongside one another for some time. A similar development is witnessed in several other parishes such as **Ballynascreen**, and seems in general to be due to the close connection which clearly existed between the church and its lands.

TOWNLAND NAMES

Ballydermot
H 9494

Baile Uí Dhiarmada
"O'Dermody's townland"

1. b. dermody	Esch. Co. Map 13	1609
2. Ballydermody	Charter of Londonderry 392	1613
3. Ballidermond	Civ. Surv. iii 168	1654
4. Bellidermond	Civ. Surv. iii 168	1654
5. Bellidermond (x2)	Civ. Surv. iii 170	1654
6. Ballydermody	Bishop. Der. i 267	1657
7. Ballydermott	Census 135	1659c
8. Ballidermond one Town	BSD(c) 58	1661
9. Ballydermot	Duff's Lough Neagh	1785
10. Ballydermot	Sampson's Map	1813
11. Bally-'der mot	OSNB Pron. No. 5	1834c
12. Baile Diarmada "Dermot's town"	J O'D (OSNB) No. 5	1834c
13. Baile-Diarmada "The townland of the Clann Diarmada, or Diarmaids, or Dermots"	Munn's Notes 57	1925
14. ˌbaliˈdɛrmət	Local pronunciation	1993

In general, the forms listed above support an origin from Irish *Baile Uí Dhiarmada* "O'Dermody's townland" (note particularly 1–2, 6). The surname O'Dermody is scattered throughout Ireland but is most numerous in Cos Cavan, Westmeath, Kilkenny and Galway (MacLysaght 1985, 80). It had probably become obsolete in Derry by the 17th century for it is not mentioned in the Hearth Money Rolls, and it is hardly surprising that it is supplanted by a better known name in some of our 17th-century sources (3-5, 8). These related documents appear to reflect the Donegal and Derry surname *Ó Dúdhíorma* (earlier *Ó Duibhdhíorma*), which was borne by the ancient lords of Brédach in Inishowen, Co. Donegal (Woulfe 1923, 514; MacLysaght 1982, 75). Its association with Ballyscullion is also very early, for an Ó Duibhdhíorma was among the people slain on Church Island by the Ulaid in 1129 (*AU (Mac Airt)* 576). The descendants of the lords of Brédach anglicized their name as O'Dermond in the 17th century, and this form of the name was recorded among the principal Irish names in the barony of Inishowen in the Census of c.1659 (*Census* 64), and is recorded in south Derry in the parish of Killelagh in 1663 (*HMR (Ó Doibhlin 2)* 66).

Ballymacombs Beg
H 9599

Baile Mhic Giolla Chóimdhe Beag
"MacIlcomey's townland, little"

1. (?)b:g	Esch. Co. Map 13	1609

2. Ballgillthony	Charter of Londonderry 392	1613
3. 2 BalleMc:qilcomes	Lond. Comp. Valuation 308	1613
4. 2 Balle McKillconeys	Phillips MSS (Maps) Plate 24	1622
5. Bellimcillcomees two townes	Civ. Surv. iii 168	1654
6. Ballygilchony	Bishop. Der. i 267	1657
7. Bally McLecombmoore	Census 135	1659c
8. Bally McLecombebeg	Census 135	1659c
9. Ballimckillkonis	BSD(c) 58	1661
10. Ballimacome	Duff's Lough Neagh	1785
11. Ballymacombs	Sampson's Map	1813
12. Bal-ly-ma-'combs	OSNB Pron. No. 5	1834c
13. Baile mic Coma "Mac Combs town"	J O'D (OSNB) No. 5	1834c
14. Baile-mac-Combil "The townland of the McCombees"	Munn's Notes 57	1925
15. ˌbaliməˈkoːmz ˈbɛːg	Local pronunciation	1993

The earliest spellings clearly show that the final element in this name is a surname of the form *mac* + *giolla* + a third element which, unfortunately, is not altogether clear. The forms assembled here show a great deal of confusion, but it is apparent that the final element was disyllabic. It is not clear, however, if this element contained an *m* as in the modern name or an *n*, as even those sources which are related to one another vary between the two.

If we accept that the name was pronounced with an *n*, then we are faced with the difficulty of identifying the surname. A similar name, McGilleconnye, was borne by a gallowglass family, two members of which, Shane and Owen McHenry McGilleconnye, were pardoned by Queen Elizabeth in 1585 (*Fiants Eliz.* §4747), but there is no firm evidence linking the two forms. The name *Mac Giolla Chainnigh*, which is thought to have originated in West Ulster, is usually anglicized McElhenny and McIlhinny in Donegal and Derry, and it is hardly the surname in question (MacLysaght 1982, 137–8). However, if we assume that, apart from the loss of a final syllable, the pronunciation of the name has not substantially changed, then we can point to the old Cavan surname Comey, Irish *Mac Giolla Chóimdhe* (see Woulfe 1923, 370).

The surname MacComb is most common in Cos Derry, Antrim and Down (Bell 1988, 98), and it was almost certainly under its influence that Ballymacombs took on its present form. The English plural *-s* is apparent in some of our earliest spellings where it indicates the division of the townland into two parts, one large (*mór*) and the other small (*beag*) (see forms 7–8 above). It is interesting that the modern form of the name has ungrammatically interposed the English plural ending between the root Irish name and its qualifier, and this is doubtless due to the use of a simple plural form Ballymacombs beside forms like Ballymacomb Beg and Ballymacomb More.

Ballymacombs More
H 9699

Baile Mhic Giolla Chóimdhe Mór
"MacIlcomey's townland, big"

1. ˌbaliməˈkoːmz ˈmoːr	Local pronunciation	1993

See **Ballymacombs Beg**.

Ballynease-Helton   *Baile Naosa*
Ballynease-Macpeake   "Neice's townland"
Ballynease-Strain
C 9601, C 9700, C 9600

1. b:nener	Esch. Co. Map 13	1609
2. Ballemenoew, two balliboes	Charter of Londonderry 392	1613
3. 2 Balle Neav	Lond. Comp. Valuation 308	1613
4. Balleneas	Phillips MSS (Maps) Plate 24	1622
5. Bellinees, two townes	Civ. Surv. iii 168	1654
6. Ballinees	Civ. Surv. iii 182	1654
7. Ballinenoen, being 2 balliboes	Bishop. Der. i 267	1657
8. Upper Ballyneas	Census 135	1659c
9. Lower Ballyneas	Census 135	1659c
10. Ballines	BSD(c) 58	1661
11. Ballyneese	Sampson's Map	1813
12. Bally-'neese	OSNB Pron. No. 5	1834c
13. Baile Aonghusa "Aeneas's town"	J O'D (OSNB) No. 5	1834c
14. Baile-Aenghuis "The townland of		
the Aengus"	Munn's Notes 57	1925
15. Baile Naos	JRSAI lxxx 176	1950
16. Baile Naosa	GÉ 186	1989
17. ˌbaliˈniːs	Local pronunciation	1993

The 17th-century references to this name tend to confuse rather than clarify its origin. The final *s* is largely absent from the very earliest spellings, and one might suppose that, where it does occur, it represents the English plural ending found in many other Irish place-names, as the townland was at that stage divided into two parts. However, one form without the *s* (3) is clearly a mistranscription, for the name appears in a closely related source with the final *s* (4). Moreover, there is great potential for confusion between *s*, *r*, *n*, etc., in the script of this period, and we are probably justified in rereading the group of anomalous forms as *Ballynanees* or the like (1-2, 7; the latter two forms also show confusion of *o* and *e*).

The earliest group of spellings (1-2, 7) shows traces of what looks like a form of the article meaning "the" which would suggest a formation *baile* "townland" + article + noun. Such a combination could have been reduced to the modern form by haplology, but it would be wrong to place so much weight on a group of forms which we have already seen is corrupt in other regards.

All previous interpretations of the name have centred on the personal name *Naos*, a contracted form of *Aonghas* (Stand. Ir. *Aonas*), and the general body of forms collected above, with the exception of the anomalous group discussed previously, tends to support such an origin. *Baile* "townland" is more commonly found with a surname in Co. Derry, but numerous examples of personal names occurring in this position appear elsewhere in the country (see Price 1963, 121-2). In any case, no known surname matches the pronunciation suggested by the historical spellings, and although the surname McNeice may be considered, we would really expect to find some trace of the *mac* in the modern form.

Ballynease is now divided into three parts, each of which is distinguished by a surname. McPeake is indigenous to the area and is still common in the parish (see **Ballymacpeake**

Upper in the parish of Maghera). The remaining two surnames have no known connection with the parish but Hilton, here corrupted to Helton, is found in the parish of Tamlaght O'Crilly in the 19th century (*OSM* xviii 137).

Ballyscullion East	*Baile Uí Scoillín Beag*	
H 9995	"Scullion's townland, little"	

1. Ballyscullinbeg	Bishop. Der. ii 479	1688
2. Ballyscullenbeg	Bishop. Der. ii 482	1703
3. Ballyscullenbegg	Reg. Deeds 27-154-16203	1714
4. Ballyscullens. Ballyscullen begg	Duty Bk Grange	1733
5. Ballyscullen Beg, Termon or Erenagh land of	Reg. Deeds 94-186-65851	1738
6. Ballyscullan	Duff's Lough Neagh	1785

The townland of Ballyscullion East in the Barony of Toome and County of Antrim faces Ballyscullion West across Lough Beg. Together, the two townlands formerly comprised the church lands of Ballyscullion Parish (McKay 1990, 283). For a fuller discussion of the name see **Ballyscullion West** below.

Ballyscullion West	*Baile Uí Scoillín Mór*	
H 9697	"Scullion's townland, big"	

1. (?)b:kolly	Esch. Co. Map 13	1609
2. O Skullannestown	Bishop. Der. i 33	1610
3. Ba: Skullin	Phillips MSS (Maps) Plate 24	1622
4. Belliskallan Church land (x2)	Civ. Surv. iii 168,170	1654
5. Belliskullan one bellibo or towne land	Civ. Surv. iii 192	1654
6. Balliscullen	Hib. Reg. Loughinsholin	1657c
7. Ballyscullin	Census 135	1659c
8. Ballyscullen	BSD(c) 50	1661
9. Ballyscullinmore	Bishop. Der. ii 479	1688
10. Ballyscullen	Duff's Lough Neagh	1785
11. Ballyscullin	Sampson's Map	1813
12. Bally-'scul-i-on	OSNB Pron. No. 5	1834c
13. Baile Ui Scuillín "O'Scullion's town"	J O'D (OSNB) No. 5	1834c
14. Baile-ui-Scoilain "townland of the O'Scullions"	Munn's Notes 57	1925

For greater clarity, references to the two townlands of Ballyscullion East and West have been separated from those concerning the church and parish of Ballyscullion where possible. The two townlands are occasionally distinguished from each other in the 17th and 18th centuries, but not according to the modern divisions of East and West. Rather, the adjective *mór* "big" is used to identify Ballyscullion West, and Ballyscullion East is qualified by the adjective *beag* "small".

Church Island	*Inis Taoide*	
H 9794	"St Taoide's island"	
1. [Inse] Toitae for Loch Echach	Mart. Tal. Sep 7 69	830c
2. Arcun Insi Taite	AIF 292	1129
3. i nInis Taiti	AU (Mac Airt) 576	1129
4. Insi Toite (gen.) for Loch Bec	Mart. Gorm. Sep 7 172n	1630c
5. Iniscidy	Eccles. Tax. (CDI) 215	1306c
6. Einsh Tyd	Phillips MSS (Maps) Plate 24	1622
7. Inish Tid	Hib. Reg. Loughinsholin	1657c
8. Inishtid	Hib. Del. Derry	1672c
9. Church Island	Duff's Lough Neagh	1785
10. Church Island	OSM vi 42	1836
11. Inis-Toide	Munn's Notes 59	1925
12. Inis-Tatti	Munn's Notes 59	1925
13. Inis-Tede	Munn's Notes 59	1925

Church Island is the original location of the church of Taoide. Taoide was the parish's patron saint, and it was from him that the island took the name *Inis Taoide* "St Taoide's Island". In 1788, the Earl of Bristol, then Bishop of Derry, erected a steeple and spire close to the ruins of the old church in order to improve the view from his mansion at Ballyscullion, and the name of the island was then changed to the present one (*Colton Vis.* 83n, *Munn's Notes* 59; *OSM* vi 65). In the early part of the 19th century, the island shed its religious past and became a haunt for smugglers and illegal distillers (*OSM* vi 56). Since the lowering of the level of Lough Beg, Church Island has ceased to be an island proper and has become attached to the mainland.

Church Island Intake	An English form
H 9796	

See **Church Island** above and **Intake** below.

Coney Island	An English form	
H 9793		
1. Cuney Island	Phillips MSS (Maps) Plate 24	1622
2. Cunny Id.	Duff's Lough Neagh	1785
3. Coney Island or Small Island	OSRNB 42 sh.42	1850c
4. "Rabbit Island"	OSRNB 42 sh.42	1850c
5. Comhnaidhe "Residence Island"	Munn's Notes 59	1925
6. ðə 'koni ˌailən	Local pronunciation	1993

It has been suggested that the initial element in this name is of Irish origin (5) but there seems to be little doubt that it is simply the English word "coney" meaning "rabbit". The same word occurs in a number of island names, as well as in transparent names such as

Coneyburrow (in Tyrone and Derry) and Coneywarren (Tyrone and Fermanagh). Rabbits were numerous here in the last century (*OSRNB* 42 sh. 42).

It appears from a footnote in the Ordnance Survey Memoirs that the island was called "Deenish or Coney Island" in a document of 1633 concerning the sale of Dudley and George Phillips' lands to Thomas Dawson (*OSM* vi 50-1). The second element is almost certainly *inis* "island", but the first element is uncertain. Joyce cites examples of Irish *Dubhinis* "black island" giving Dinish and Deenish, but such a development is unlikely in Ulster Irish (*Joyce* ii 269; *CMR* 131n; cf. O'Rahilly 1932, 24). Ó Máille dismisses such an interpretation for Dynish in Co. Galway and proposes instead an origin from *daingean* "fortified, secure" + *inis* "island" (1962(b), 56-7; cf. 1989–90, 126, 131), but this is again unlikely here as *daingean*, as in the Galway name, tends to give [dain] rather than [di:n].

Drumanee Lower   *Droim an Fhia* (?)
Drumanee Upper   "ridge of the deer"
H 9696, H 9596

1. (?)b: dromen	Esch. Co. Map 13	1609
2. Ballydromenew	Charter of Londonderry 392	1613
3. Drumney	Civ. Surv. iii 168	1654
4. Ballydromenen	Bishop. Der. i 267	1657
5. Drumany	Census 135	1659c
6. Drumney	BSD(c) 58	1661
7. Drumanee	Duff's Lough Neagh	1785
8. Drum-a-'nee	OSNB Pron. No. 5	1834c
9. Druim an Fhiaidh "Ridge of the deer"	J O'D (OSNB) No. 5	1834c
10. "the deer's hill"	Joyce i 476	1869
11. Druim-an-fiadh "The hill-ridge of the deer"	Munn's Notes 59	1925
12. ˌdrɒmə'ni:	Local pronunciation	1993

The first element in this name is almost certainly a form of *droim* "ridge" and may have originally denoted the long low ridge of land which dominates Drumanee Lower. Unfortunately, we have a rather poor range of early spellings of the name, some of which are clearly corrupt, and the final element defies a definitive interpretation. Several suitable words may be suggested, but the most likely is probably *fia* "deer" which is similarly anglicized in a number of other place-names in various parts of the country (*Joyce* i 476-7).

Edenreagh   *An tÉadan Riabhach*
H 9494   "the grey hillface"

1. neadenreogh	Esch. Co. Map 13	1609
2. Nedanreagh	Charter of Londonderry 392	1613
3. Teden Reah, Dromar &	Lond. Comp. Valuation 308	1613
4. Edinreagh, halfe of the towne called	Civ. Surv. iii 168	1654
5. Nedanaeogh	Bishop. Der. i 267	1657

6. Edenreagh	Census 135	1659c
7. Edenreagh, half of ye Town called	BSD(c) 58	1661
8. Edenreagh	Sampson's Map	1813
9. Eden-'ree-agh	OSNB Pron. No. 5	1834c
10. Eadan Riach "Grey brow or brae"	J O'D (OSNB) No. 5	1834c
11. Eudan-riabhach "The grey hill brow or face"	Munn's Notes 59	1925

The ridge which forms the western boundary of this townland slopes gently to the south-east, and it is almost certainly this slope which has given rise to the name of the townland. The earliest spellings of this name are particularly interesting in that they clearly reflect two different forms of the name, one nominative *An tÉadan Riabhach* (3) and the other proba-bly dative *(ar) An Éadan Riabhach* (1-2, 5).

Glebe East An English form
Glebe West
H 9697, H 9597

1. glib	Local pronunciation	1993

The Downing family purchased the Glebe lands for the parish, as well as providing an annu-ity for the support of the parish, a Communion service and a fine church bell (*Munn's Notes* 59; *Der. Clergy* 114).

Intake An English form
H 9793

Following the lowering of Lough Beg, several large portions of land, amounting to several hundred acres, were reclaimed. The new portions, of which there are three in the parish of Ballyscullion, are each known as Intake. See also **Church Island Intake** above.

Killyberry *Coillidh Bhearaigh* (?)
Killyberry Boyd "wood of the place of stakes/spits"
Killyberry Downing
H 9395, H 9496, H 9394

1. keillbarry	Esch. Co. Map 13	1609
2. Keil-Ibary	Charter of Londonderry 392	1613
3. Colberey	Lond. Comp. Valuation 308	1613
4. Coolberrey	Phillips MSS (Maps) Plate 24	1622
5. Killbarry	Civ. Surv. iii 168	1654
6. Keil Ibary	Bishop. Der. i 267	1657
7. Killaberry	Census 135	1659c
8. Killbarry	BSD(c) 58	1661
9. Kiltyberry	Duff's Lough Neagh	1785
10. Killyberry	Sampson's Map	1813
11. Kil-ly-'ber-ry	OSNB Pron. No. 5	1834c
12. Coill Uí Bhearaigh "O'Berry's woods"	J O'D (OSNB) No. 5	1834c

13. Coille-ui-Bhearaigh "The Woods of the Berry's or Barry's"	Munn's Notes 60	1925
14. Coill-Ui-Bhearaigh "O'Berry's wood"	Joyce iii 417	1925
15. ˌkïliˈberi	Local pronunciation	1993

The first element in this name is almost certainly a form of *coill* "wood", probably the dative *coillidh*. *Cill* "church" may also be considered, but there is no evidence of a religious foundation here, and some variant spellings may suggest the broad initial of *coill* "wood" (3–4), although these possibly originate from the common error of *o* for *e*. Possible further alternatives based on these two spellings, such as *cúil* "corner, recess", may be rejected. We have seen elsewhere that there is a tendancy for the scribe of the Phillips maps to write *Cool-* where it is not warranted (see **Calmore** in the parish of Kilcronaghan), and this has doubtless occurred here as well. The townland was still covered with native oak wood at the end of the 18th century, and it was said that a man might almost have walked on the trees from Killyberry to Bellaghy (*OSM* vi 44).

While the form of the final element can be readily established, its exact meaning is unclear. O'Donovan understood it to be a surname and this is apparently supported by some of the early forms, but there are no suitable surnames in the North. The name suggested by O'Donovan is not otherwise recorded, while the surname *Ó Beargha* seems to have been confined to Cos Limerick and Mayo (Woulfe 1923, 435). Indeed, northern instances of Berry in our 17th-century documents seem always to be of English origin. The personal name *Bearach* was a relatively common name in early Ireland and was borne by a number of saints, including one who gave name to Kilbarry in Co. Roscommon (Ó Corráin & Maguire 1981, 31), but although *coill* is frequently compounded with personal names in place-names, an origin from a common noun is perhaps more likely.

There is another **Killyberry** in Co. Tyrone, and both names have a similar appearance in the 17th century, and the two names may have identical origins. The word *bearach* signifying "heifer" seems to lie behind the name **Dromara** in Co. Down (Irish *Droim mBearach* "ridge of the heifers"). However, a gen. sing. form would be required here and this is perhaps unlikely in the circumstances. For that reason we must consider the rare element *bearach* which occurs most notably in the name of the village of **Beragh** in Co. Tyrone. The meaning of this word is unfortunately not altogether clear, however, but it probably relates to *bior* "point, spike, spit", so that *bearach* may denote a place where stakes or spits could have been cut.

Leitrim
H 9593

Liatroim
"grey ridge"

1. b: letrim	Esch. Co. Map 13	1609
2. Lyetrum	CPR Jas I 286b	1612
3. Leitrim	Charter of Londonderry (Reed) 66	1613
4. Lyetrum	Charter of Londonderry (Reed) 74	1613
5. Balleletrim	Charter of Londonderry 392	1613
6. Ballyletrim	Bishop. Der. i 267	1657
7. Litram	Bishop. Der. i 269	1657
8. Lyetrum	Bishop. Der. i 274	1657
9. Leitrim	Duff's Lough Neagh	1785

10. Leitrim	Sampson's Map	1813
11. 'Let-rim	OSNB Pron. No. 5	1834c
12. Liathdhruim "Grey ridge"	J O'D (OSNB) No. 5	1834c
13. Liath-druim "The grey hill-ridge"	Munn's Notes 60	1925
14. 'litrïm	Local pronunciation	1993

This is a compound of *liath* "grey" and *droim* "ridge" which is frequently found throughout Ireland, most notably in the name of the county of Leitrim. It almost certainly denotes the prominent ridge of land which traverses the townland from north-west to south-east. On the highest part of the hill stands the site of a ring-fort (Speer 1990, 16).

Mullaghboy　　　　　　　　　　*Mullach Buí*
H 9497　　　　　　　　　　　　　"yellow hilltop"

1. b:fualliweg	Esch. Co. Map 13	1609
2. Bally-Inallewey	Charter of Londonderry 392	1613
3. Mulla Boy	Lond. Comp. Valuation 308	1613
4. Mullaboy	Phillips MSS (Maps) Plate 24	1622
5. Mullimoy	Civ. Surv. iii 168	1654
6. Bally Inallewey	Bishop. Der. i 267	1657
7. Cullanavea	Census 135	1659c
8. Mullimoy	BSD(c) 58	1661
9. Mullaghbuy	Sampson's Map	1813
10. Mul-lagh-'buoy	OSNB Pron. No. 5	1834c
11. Mullach buidhe "yellow summit or hill-top"	J O'D (OSNB) No. 5	1834c
12. Mullach-buidhe "The yellow hill, or summit"	Munn's Notes 60	1925
13. ˌmọləˈbɔi	Local pronunciation	1993

The origin of this name is clearly from Irish *Mullach Buí* "yellow hilltop". A number of peaks in the townland rise to over 50 metres, but the feature to which the name originally referred is probably the large unnamed hill which lies in the northern part of the townland (H 9498). An early variant form, *Baile (an) Mhullaigh Bhuí* "townland of the yellow hilltop", is witnessed by some of our earliest sources (1–2, 6).

Oldtown Deerpark　　　　　　An English form
Oldtown Downing
H 9595, H 9496

1. Oldtown	Duff's Lough	1785
2. Deerpark	Sampson's Map	1813
3. 'Old-town	OSNB Pron. No. 5	1834c
4. 'oltəun 'dirpark	Local pronunciation	1993
5. 'oltəun 'dəunïŋ	Local pronunciation	1993

Oldtown, formerly Bellaghy, is of English origin. The suffix "Downing" is derived from the family of that name who settled here. Captain Adam Downing of Bellaghy was included in the Act of Attainder passed by the Parliament called in Dublin by King James II on 7th May, 1689 (*Munn's Notes* 60). One of the Downing family resided in Oldtown Downing in a house the site of which was later occupied by the residence of John Leonard (*ibid.*).

Scab Island	An English form	
H 9794		
1. Scabby Id.	Duff's Lough Neagh	1785
2. Oilean-na-scuab "The island of the besom"	Munn's Notes 60	1925
3. ðə 'skʲab	Local pronunciation	1993

Earlier called "Scabby Island", the name seems to refer to the condition of the land. Scabbed is used in some English dialects to refer to land which has thin, bare, gravelly soil interspersed with rocks etc. (*Eng. Dial. Dict.* v 230). It was believed in the 19th century that the island took its name from the fact that there are some loose stones on it (*OSRNB* 42 sh. 42).

Tamlaghtduff	*Tamhlacht Dubh*	
H 9598	"black burial ground"	
1. b:haulagh Iga	Esch. Co. Map 13	1609
2. Ballyhowlaght-Igane	Charter of Londonderry 392	1613
3. Tawlat	Phillips MSS (Maps) Plate 24	1622
4. Tawlaught Duff	Bishop. Der. i 146	1624c
5. Taumphcagh duffe	Civ. Surv. iii 168	1654
6. Tawlagh-due	Civ. Surv. iii 192	1654
7. (?)Ballyhawlaght Ioane	Bishop. Der. i 267	1657
8. Tamboughdood	Census 135	1659c
9. Taunophcaghduffe	BSD(c) 58	1661
10. Tamnaduff	Duff's Lough Neagh	1785
11. Tamlaghduff	Sampson's Map	1813
12. Tam-laght-'duff	OSNB Pron. No. 5	1834c
13. Tamhlacht Dubh "Black burial place"	J O'D (OSNB) No. 5	1834c
14. Taimhleacht-dubh "The black plague monument"	Munn's Notes 60	1925
15. ˌtamlə'dǫf	Local pronunciation	1993

The element *tamhlacht* is thought usually to denote a pagan burial ground, but it occurs surprisingly often in names of early Christian sites (*IPN* 145). It is largely confined to the North of Ireland and is most common in Co. Derry where it occurs in the names of four early churches (*ibid.*). *Tamhlacht* varies in both inflection and gender, but the forms from the Escheated Counties maps and related sources (1–2, 7) appear to show a longer form of the name *Baile Thamhlachta Dhuibh* indicating that it was masc. here (we should probably emend these forms to *Ballyhawlaghtiguv* or the like).

| **Tamniaran** | *Tamhnaigh Uí Eararáin* | |
| H 9393 | "O'Herreran's field" | |

1.	tanniarhuran	Esch. Co. Map 13	1609
2.	Taunarran	CPR Jas I 286b	1612
3.	Tannarran	Charter of Londonderry (Reed) 66	1613
4.	Tannarran	Charter of Londonderry (Reed) 74	1613
5.	Tanngarharan	Charter of Londonderry 392	1613
6.	Taumphiararan	Civ. Surv. iii 168	1654
7.	Taumniharawan	Civ. Surv. iii 170	1654
8.	Towne Arran	Civ. Surv. iii 170	1654
9.	Tannyarharran	Bishop. Der. i 267	1657
10.	Tannaran	Bishop. Der. i 269	1657
11.	(Mayela)tannaran	Bishop. Der. i 274	1657
12.	Tamimaran	Census 135	1659c
13.	Tamnayaran	Duff's Lough Neagh	1785
14.	Tam-ni-'ar-an	OSNB Pron. No. 5	1834c
15.	Tamhnach Ui Eaghráin "O'Haran's field"	J O'D (OSNB) No. 5	1834c
16.	Tamnach-ui-h-Eaghrain "The field, or residence of the O'Haran's"	Munn's Notes 60	1925
17.	Tamhnach Uí Fhuradhráin	GUH 27n	1951
18.	ˌtamniˈarən	Local pronunciation	1993
19.	ˌtamniˈarn	Local pronunciation	1993

On the meaning and significance of the first element, see **Tamnymartin** in the parish of Maghera below. Two independent groups of 17th-century sources show the presence of an extra syllable in the final element in this name (1, 5, 9; 6-7) which has since been lost by haplology, so we can safely discount the possiblity of surnames such as *Ó Feáráin* and *Ó hEáráin*, the names of two Oriel septs (MacLysaght 1985, 105, 155). Ó Ceallaigh suggests the obsolete surname *Ó Furadhráin* which occurs in two medieval genealogical compilations (*GUH* 27n, 57), and Ó Doibhlin posits a link between this surname and a progenitor of the Uí Thuirtre who inhabited this area in the early Christian period (1971, 143). However, there is a problem with this suggestion in that the *u* in the patronymic is unlikely to give *a*, and we need to look elsewhere for a solution. The rare surname O'Herreran, Irish *Ó hEararáin*, is associated with Derry and Donegal, and this is very probably the final element in this name (MacLysaght 1985, 155). Its association with Derry is very old for it was borne by one Mael Brighte Ua hEaráin, a monk at Derry, who was made bishop of Clonfert in 1205 (Woulfe 1923, 563).

OTHER NAMES

Annagh	*Eanach*
H 9694	"marsh island"

1. Anagh	Duff's Lough Neagh	1785
2. "Island"	OSRNB 42 sh.42	1850c
3. Eanach "a marsh"	OSRNB 42 sh.42	1850c
4. 'anə	Local pronunciation	1993

Irish *eanach* normally signifies a marsh, but successive English writers have equated it in place-name usage with English "island", and it frequently appears in names of bog-bound hills (Ó Mainnín 1989–90, 204–5). Our Annagh is a small hill almost entirely surrounded by bog, and it is probably from this circumstance that it derives its name.

The transference of *eanach* from the surrounding marsh to the cultivated land which it encloses is hardly surprising, but what is in dispute is whether or not this happened in Irish (*ibid.*). There is some strong circumstantial evidence, however, to suggest that it occurred in Irish, although the sense "island" is not attested in the Irish lexicon.

There is a dense cluster of Annagh-names in the eastern portion of the Barony of Loughinsholin, the majority of which are described as "islands" or hills almost wholly surrounded by bog (*OSRNB* 63 sh.37 (×4), 42 sh.42 (×2), 43 sh.46). More importantly, none is described as a bog or marsh. There are a number of names in Ulster which derive from Irish *Eanach an Bhogaigh*, namely, **Annaghavogey** in the parish of Longfield West and **Annaghavoggy** in the parish of Dromore, both in Co. Tyrone, and **Annaghavoggy** in the parish of Tamlaght O'Crilly, Co. Derry, and **Annaghaboggy** which borders the parishes of Ballyscullion and Maghera, also in Co. Derry. The final element in all these names is *bogach* "soft, boggy ground", and this suggests that the first element cannot mean "marsh". More compelling evidence is found in the name of another marsh island in the parish of Maghera, namely, **Annaghfad**. This long narrow piece of cultivated land is almost entirely surrounded by bog and its name in Irish was *Eanach Fada* which can only mean in these circumstances "long marsh island".

It seems, therefore, that *eanach* did come to mean "marsh island" in Irish. It should be noted that all the places cited by name above in support of this conclusion are minor names, and this would seem to allow us to postulate a relatively late date for the transition. It is true that not all minor names are of recent origin, and some hill and river names are extremely archaic, but on the whole many are indeed late and this is probably the case here.

Bellaghy
H 9596

Baile Eachaidh (?)
"Eochy's townland"

1. go Boile Achadh	Cín Lae Ó M. 2	1645c
2. cūirt B[oile] Eachaidh	Cín Lae Ó M. 2	1645c
3. b: aghy	Esch. Co. Map 13	1609
4. Ballyaghy	Charter of Londonderry 392	1613
5. Ba: Aghey	Lond. Comp. Valuation 308	1613
6. Ba: Aghee	Phillips MSS (Maps) Plate 24	1622
7. Vintners Town	Phillips MSS (Maps) Plate 24	1622
8. Ballaghy	Civ. Surv. iii 168	1654
9. Bellaghy	Civ. Surv. iii 168	1654
10. Ballyaghey	Bishop. Der. i 267	1657
11. Balliachy house (added above line) and Church	Hib. Reg. Loughinsholin	1657c

12. Ballyagheg	Census 135	1659c
13. Ballaghy	BSD(c) 58	1661
14. Ballyaghy	Bishop. Der. i 362	1663
15. Ballyaghy	Bishop. Der. i 371,374	1664
16. Vintners Towne alias Ballyaghy	Bishop. Der. i 377	1664
17. Balliaghy	Bishop. Der. i 398	1665c
18. Balliaghy	Bishop. Der. i 415	1668
19. Balliachy	Hib. Del. Derry	1672c
20. Balliaghy	Bishop. Der. ii 34	1677
21. Balliaghy, church of	Bishop. Der. ii 35	1677
22. Balliaghy	Bishop. Der. ii 40	1680
23. Ballyhagie	Bishop. Der. ii 113	1686
24. Ballyaghie	Bishop. Der. ii 113	1686
25. Ballachy	Lamb Maps Derry	1690c
26. Ballachy	Lamb Maps Ulster	1690c
27. Balliaghy	Bishop. Der. ii 136	1692
28. Belliaghy	Bishop. Der. ii 136	1692
29. Bellaghy	Duff's Lough Neagh	1785
30. Bellaghy	Sampson's Map	1813
31. Bel-'lagh-e	OSNB Pron. No. 5	1834c
32. Baile Eachadha "Eochy's town"	J O'D (OSNB) No. 5	1834c
33. Béal Lathaigh "mouth or entrance of the mire"	Joyce i 357	1869
34. Baile-lathaighe "The mouth...of the miry place"	Munn's Notes 57	1925
35. Baile Eachaidh	GÉ 189	1989
36. ˌbəˈlahi	Local pronunciation	1993

Bellaghy was founded by the Guild of Vintners and the building of the new settlement with its castle, church, mill and main street was largely complete by 1622 as is clear from the plan of the town in the Phillips' manuscripts (*Phillips MSS (Maps)* Plate 25). The name Bellaghy was originally applied only to the townland while the town was called Vintners Town, but it soon extended to cover the settlement as well.

Joyce derives its name from Irish *Béal Lathaigh* "mouth or entrance of the mire" and was followed in this interpretation by Munn (33-4). The earliest spellings, and particularly the available Irish forms, clearly show that this cannot be correct. Unfortunately, these Irish forms, both of which are from the same 17th-century source, are ambiguous, but in all probability they represent an underlying form *Baile Eachaidh* "Eochy's townland", for the scribe writes *Achaidh* for *Eachaidh* in other parts of the text (thus, *Tuath hAchaidh* for *Tuath Eachaidh*), and does not always attempt to distinguish between broad and slender final consonants.

However, Ó Mealláin would hardly have been able to distinguish between *Baile Achaidh* "townland of the field" and *Baile Eachaidh* "Eochy's townland", as both are pronounced exactly the same. Indeed, given the prevalence of the formation *baile* + Gaelic surname, we must also consider an origin from *Baile Uí Eachaidh* "O'Haghey's townland" as this, again, would be indistinguishable from the previous two possibilities in pronunciation. An inquisition of 1609 found that a family of this name were in possession of the townland of

Cavanballaghy in Co. Armagh (*Church Lands Arm.* 86), and the townland name there still preserves the memory of their association with it (*Cabhán Bhaile Uí Eachaidh* "the hollow of O'Haghey's townland"). The name is recorded in the form *O'Heaghy* in the extreme south of Co. Derry in the latter half of the 17th century (*HMR (Ó Doibhlin 2)* 71), although there is no evidence of any connection with this immediate area.

Names of the type *Baile Eachaidh* "Eochy's townland" are well attested, and this form has much to recommend it. However, an origin from *Baile Achaidh* cannot be ruled out even though there is no trace of the article in the name. Although we normally expect to see evidence of the article in names of the type *baile* + qualifying noun in the genitive, we do occasionally find examples where it is omitted and, indeed, Hogan lists three other places with precisely this name (*Onom. Goed.* 73).

Bishops Canal H 9797	An English form	
1. ðə 'bɪʃəps kə'nal	Local pronunciation	1993

Bishops Canal was cut at the expense of the Earl of Bristol, Bishop of Derry, from which circumstance it gets its name (*OSRNB* 62 sh. 37).

Brough H 9392	*Bruach* "bank"	
1. Broagh	Sampson's Map	1813
2. "Broken bank"	OSRNB 42 sh.42	1850c
3. Bruach "a brink or margin"	OSRNB 42 sh.42	1850c
4. brox	Local pronunciation	1993

Brough takes its name from its location on the bank of the Moyola River (*OSRNB* 42 sh. 42).

Crillys Town C 9600	An English form	
1. 'krɪliz ˌtəun	Local pronunciation	1993

This was named after tenants called Crilly who formerly occupied the whole of the subdivision (*OSRNB* 63 sh. 37). The family is long established in the barony of Loughinsholin, most notably as erenaghs of the parish of **Tamlaght O'Crilly**, and the name is still prominent in the area.

Culbane C 9700	*Cúil Bhán* "white recess"	
1. Culbane, Ballyneasemacpeake or	OSCNB 62 sh.37	1850c
2. kol'ba:n	Local pronunciation	1993

In the Ordnance Survey Memoirs, Culbane is described as a large bog, said to be 14 feet deep in parts (*OSM* vi 43–4). The name apparently derives from the fact that turf-cutting exposed a whitish clay beneath the bog (*ibid.*). The alias cited above is simply the name of the townland in which Culbane lies.

Curly Hill	Of uncertain origin	
H 9497		

In the Revision Name Books, Curly Hill is said to take its name from the place being covered by brushwood of a curly or dwarfish nature until it was cleared about the year 1778 or 1792 (*OSRNB* 62 sh. 37), but we must consider several possible alternatives. It may relate to the surname Curley (Irish *Mac Thoirealaigh*) which, as a variant of the Ulster name Turley, is found mainly in Cos Galway and Roscommon, but also in Co. Derry (MacLysaght 1985, 70; Mitchell 1992, 30). It may otherwise be an Irish name, in which case it might derive from the Irish *Corrbhaile* "prominent townland". **Curley** in the parish of Newry, Co. Down, can be shown through documentary evidence to have evolved from such a name and it is possible that a similar development occurred here (*PNI* i 18–9).

Cut of the Hill	An English form	
H 9798		

1. ˌkɒt ə ðə ˈhïl	Local pronunciation	1993
2. ðə ˈkɒt	Local pronunciation	1993

So called from the road leading to Newferry which was cut through the hill here (see *OSM* vi 67; *OSRNB* 62 sh. 37).

Downings Borough	An English form	
H 9494		

1. ˈdəunïŋz ˈbə:r	Local pronunciation	1993

On the Downings see **Oldtown Downing** above.

Folly Hill	An English form	
H 9497		

1. ˈfɔli ˈbre:	Local pronunciation	1993

Folly Hill, or Folly Brae as it is better known locally, takes its name from a large house built on this hill by two men called Rankin about the year 1750, the ruins of which were removed about 1820 (*OSRNB* 62 sh. 37). More recent tradition relates the name to the building of Frederick Hervey's fabulous palace on the shores of Lough Beg. Sitting on his horse on Folly Brae, Bishop Hervey, Earl of Bristol, picked the site for his palace beside Lough Beg. In the castle he made 365 windows, one for every day of the year. The introduction of the "window tax" soon afterwards made the castle impractical to live in and he never did (Toner 1990, 2). It is reputed to have cost £100,000, and was pulled down in 1813 after having been only 8 years standing (it was begun in 1787 and finished in 1805) (*OSM* vi 48).

Grove Hill H 9492	An English form	
1. 'grov hïl	Local pronunciation	1993

Named from a circular plantation on top of the hill (*OSRNB* 42 sh. 42).

Half Quarter C 9600	An English form	
1. 'hɛf ˌkwartər	Local pronunciation	1993

A quarter is usually the quarter part of a ballybetagh, but in this instance it may represent a townland (see **Carrowmenagh** in Killelagh). Half Quarter then is the half part of that quarter.

Hill Head H 9597	An English form	

Hill Head is the name of a great number of place-names in Ireland and usually denotes a settlement on top of a hill. Our Hill Head is partly situated on the summit of a hill.

Hill Head H 9393	An English form	
1. ðə 'hïl 'hɛd	Local pronunciation	1993

See **Hill Head** above, but this village is at the foot of Warren Hill.

Iniscarn Forest	See **Moyola Wood**	
Lake View H 9594	An English form	
1. 'le:k vju	Local pronunciation	1993

So called because of its view of Lough Beg.

Long Point H 9795	An English form	
1. 'lɔŋ pɔənt	Local pronunciation	1993

Long Point stretches out into the wet land which borders on Lough Beg. Before the lowering of the level of Lough Beg, it would have projected into the lake.

Lough Beg H 9894	*Loch Beag* "little lake"	
1. for Loch Bec i Úibh Tuirte	Mart. Gorm. Sep 7 172n	1630c

2. Lo Beg	Bartlett Maps (Esch. Co. Maps)	1603
3. Logh beg	Esch. Co. Map 13	1609
4. Loghbegg	Bishop. Der. i 33	1610
5. Lo Beg	Speed's Ulster	1610
6. Lo. Beg	Speed's Antrim & Down	1610
7. Loughbegge	Bishop. Der. i 138	1621
8. Lough Begge	Phillips MSS (Maps) 148	1622
9. Lough Begg	Phillips MSS (Maps) Plate 24	1622
10. Lough Begg	Phillips MSS (Maps) Plate 26	1622
11. Loughbegg	Civ. Surv. iii 168	1654
12. Lough-begg	Civ. Surv. iii 168	1654
13. Lough Begg	Hib. Reg. Loughinsholin	1657c
14. Lough Beg	Hib. Del. Derry	1672c
15. Lough Beg	Duff's Lough Neagh	1785
16. Lough Beg	Sampson's Map	1813
17. An Loch Beag	GÉ 126	1989

Ó Doibhlin incorrectly posits a relationship between this name and the name of one of the ancestors of the Uí Thuirtre (1971(b), 143), but there can be little doubt that the name derives from *Loch Beag* "little lake". Ó Doibhlin asserts that it is called *Loch Beic* in Irish sources, but he gives no references and I have found no such form. Neither is it recorded by Hogan in his *Onomasticon Goedelicum*. He may simply have followed Ó Ceallaigh who uses the forms *Loch Beic* and *Loch Beice* which, apparently, are his own constructions (*GUH* 35, 41, 91).

Moyola Park	A hybrid form	
H 9293		
1. Moyallagh 2.bb.	Esch. Co. Map 13	1609
2. Mayola	CPR Jas I 286b	1612
3. Moyelogh, two balliboes	Charter of Londonderry 392	1613
4. Moyola	Charter of Londonderry (Reed) 66	1613
5. Mayola	Charter of Londonderry (Reed) 74	1613
6. Moiolah	Lond. Comp. Valuation 308	1613
7. Moyolak, Sir Thomas Phillips' Lands of	Phillips MSS (Maps) Plate 24	1622
8. Moyola, Sir Thomas Phillips' Lands of	Phillips MSS (Maps) Plate 26	1622
9. Two Moylaghes	Civ. Surv. iii 170	1654
10. Moyollagh, being 2 balliboes of land	Bishop. Der. i 268	1657
11. Moyola, 2 townes of	Census 138	1659c
12. Moylaghes, Two	BSD(c) 59	1661
13. Moyollys, [the two]	HMR (Ó Doibhlin 2) 72	1663
14. 'Moy-o-la	OSNB Pron. No. 11	1834c
15. My-'o-la	OSNB Pron. No. 16	1834c
16. Magh Dola "Dola's plain"	J O'D (OSNB) No. 9, 16	1834c

17. Mugh dala "plain of Dola"   J O'D (OSNB) No. 11   1834c

18. ðə mɔiˈoːlə   Local pronunciation   1993

Moyola Park is not named from its position overlooking the Moyola River as is sometimes thought. Originally, the name Moyola was applied to two balliboes at the southern end of Lough Beg now called The Creagh (Etre and Otre). Sir Thomas Phillips subsequently borrowed the name for his estate here, and it was retained by the Dawsons after Phillips sold the estate to Thomas Dawson in 1622 (Curl 1986, 432).

The name Moyola has frequently been identified with the *Magh Dula* which occurs in the Life of St Patrick, an assertion which is still repeated despite Séamus Ó Ceallaigh's convincing refutation of the notion (*GUH* 21–25). Ó Ceallaigh points to some 17th-century spellings of the name which show a final *h* or *gh*, and suggests that the name was corrupted from an early date by English speakers (*ibid.* 26–29). He then ventures the suggestion that it represents an original *Magh Locha* "plain of the lake" and that it was here that the tribe of *Fir Mhuighe Locha* ("the men of Magh Locha") once dwelt (*ibid.* 29).

However, the earliest forms show there to have been another syllable in the middle of the name and, while Ó Ceallaigh's thesis is attractive, we need to look further for a satisfactory explanation of the name. Ó Doibhlin (1971(b), 144) circumvents this problem to a certain degree by supposing that the original form of the name was actually *Magh-dhá-loch* "plain of the two lakes", that is, the plain between Lough Neagh and Lough Beg, but like Ó Ceallaigh before him, he fails to satisfactorily explain all the evidence.

For the most part, the 17th-century spellings collected here show little variation in the representation of the vowel in the second syllable, a feature which we would expect only if the stress fell on this syllable. We should also note that although there are some indications of a final guttural (Irish *ch*), it is totally absent from a great many forms. Again, this is not consistent with a pronunciation with stress on the last syllable. Thus, there can be little doubt that the stress pattern has remained unchanged. Furthermore, it is quite clear that the pronunciation has not substantially changed since the 17th century, save perhaps that we have lost a final guttural (Irish *ch*).

It is clear that the first element here is *maigh* "plain", but the final element still poses some problems of interpretation. I have considered a form of *abhaill* "apple-tree", perhaps an adjectival form *abhlach* "of (many) apple trees", but we might expect to see forms like *Moyowla* in the 17th century (cf. **Magherally**, Co. Down; *Joyce* i 516). We might also consider an origin from the personal name *Foghlaidh* (gen. *Foghlú*) which was borne by one of the chiefs of the Uí Thuirtre who formerly inhabited this district (*CGH* LL 338d45), but then again we might expect a slightly different anglicization (*Moyoley* or the like). Perhaps the most likely explanation, therefore, is from *foghail*, gen. sing. *foghla* and *foghlach*, "plundering, pillaging", so that we might posit an original Irish *Maigh Fhoghlach* "plain of the plundering". The old balliboes of Moyola must have been very vulnerable to raids in the past located as they are on the banks of both Lough Beg and Lough Neagh and just across the Bann from Toome.

In the late version of the Glenconkeyne story, an avowedly fanciful interpretation of the name Moyola is presented (Ó Ceallaigh 1927, 59). The hound, having been fatally injured, made three leaps, the last of which brought it to the River Moyola where it died, and as it passed away it cried *Mo fhola* "my blood" which, as the storyteller admits, "was very poor grammar".

Moyola Wood   A hybrid form
H 9394

This Forest Service plantation takes its name from **Moyola Park** in which it is located. A rather curious situation has arisen here where the wood known locally as Moyola Wood is marked on the Ordnance Survey's 1:50,000 series map as Iniscarn Forest. There is another Iniscarn Forest on the slopes of Slieve Gallion from where Moyola Wood was formerly managed, and it seems that the name of that forest has been mistakenly transferred to Moyola Wood (William Johnston pers. comm.).

Mulhollands Town	An English form	
H 9499		

Mulhollands Town gets it name from its former inhabitants (*OSRNB* 63 sh. 37; cf. *Griffith's Val.* 147–8).

Newferry	An English form	
H 9897		
1. New Ferry	Duff's Lough Neagh	1785
2. New ferry	Sampson's Map	1813
3. (ðə) ˌnjuˈferi	Local pronunciation	1993

Named from a ferry which was established here by the Earl of Massereene about 1756, replacing an older one about 220 yards further south (*OSM* vi 66). It saved three miles on a journey between Bellaghy and Ballymena, and a similar distance between Bellaghy and Randalstown, affording great advantage to inhabitants of both sides of the Bann (*ibid.*).

Roe's Gift	An English form	
H 9495		
1. Rosegift	Duff's Lough Neagh	1785
2. Rosegift	Sampson's Map	1813
3. ˈroz ˈgïft	Local pronunciation	1993

The Rev. Simon Rowe was rector of this parish in the early part of the 18th century and left behind several monuments bearing his name (*OSM* vi 45–6). When his daughter Anne married John Downing, a son of Adam Downing, the Rev. Rowe presented the residence, which he had acquired from the Skeffington family, to the couple who thereupon named it Rowe's Gift (*Munn's Notes* 57).

Rose Hill	An English form	
H 9495		
1. ˈroz ˈhïl	Local pronunciation	1993

Rose Hill was said to take its name from the fact that the place was well planted with many shrubs and flowers (*OSRNB* 42 sh. 42), but it seems more likely that, like **Roe's Gift** here, it was named from the Rev. Simon Rowe.

Sandy Mount	An English form	
H 9798		

1. 'sandi ˌmaunt ·	Local pronunciation	1993

Takes it name from its location on a sandy hill (*OSRNB* 62 sh. 37).

Seawright's Hill   An English form
H 9799

The inhabitants of this village were principally of the name Seawright, for which reason it was called Seawright's Hill (*OSRNB* 62 sh. 37; cf. *OSM* vi 71).

Sheep Hills   An English form
C 9400

1. Sheep hill	OSM vi 42	1836
2. Sheep hills	OSM vi 70	1836

A number of small undulating hills surround a larger one here, and they are collectively called Sheep Hills (*OSCNB* 62 sh. 37). The largest of these was itself known as Sheep Hill on account of the large quantities of sheep which were always kept on it (*OSCNB* 62 sh. 37).

Slugawn Bridge   A hybrid form
H 9692

1. Slugán "a gulley or swallow hole"	OSRNB 41 sh.42	1850c
2. (ðə) 'slǫgən (dre:n)	Local pronunciation	1993

The Slugawn Drain is a narrow, man-made channel passing through rough pasture towards Lough Beg. The Irish *Slogán* is translated by Dinneen as "a vortex or quagmire", and possibly refers to the land on either side of the channel which, before the lowering of the Bann, was probably marsh land. An attractive alternative meaning "a gully or swallow hole" is given by O'Donovan, but the meaning "gully" is not attested in the dictionaries (*OSRNB* 41 sh. 42). See further **Sluggan Moss** in Co. Antrim (*PNI* iv 75–6).

Spring Well Bridge   An English form
H 9797

The bridge is named from a nearby well (*OSRNB* 62 sh. 37).

Thornstown   An English form
C 9701

1. 'θɔrnztəun	Local pronunciation	1993

It has been suggested that Thornstown gets its name from being formerly fenced round with hawthorn trees (*OSRNB* 63 sh. 37; cf. Field 1972, 229). However, if this were the case we might expect a form Thorntown (cf. English Thornton) and it seems not unlikely that we have here an instance of the surname Torrens (Irish *Ó Toráin*) which is a common name in Co. Derry (Woulfe 1923, 653; MacLysaght 1982, 203).

Tory Island   An English form
H 9799

1. ˌtori ˈailən   Local pronunciation   1993

Tradition has it that this island was at one time the haunt of a gang of robbers or "tories" (*OSM* vi 71; *OSRNB* 62 sh. 37), and it would seem that the island subsequently took its name from these occupants.

Warren Hill   An English form
H 9493

1. ˈwarn ˈhïl   Local pronunciation   1993

Gets its name from being at one time a rabbit warren (*OSRNB* 42 sh. 42).

Wood, The   An English form
H 9598

Gets its name from being formerly wooded (*OSRNB* 62 sh. 37).

Woodhill   An English form
C 9501

The place was once wooded and it is from this fact that it takes its name (*OSRNB* 63 sh. 37).

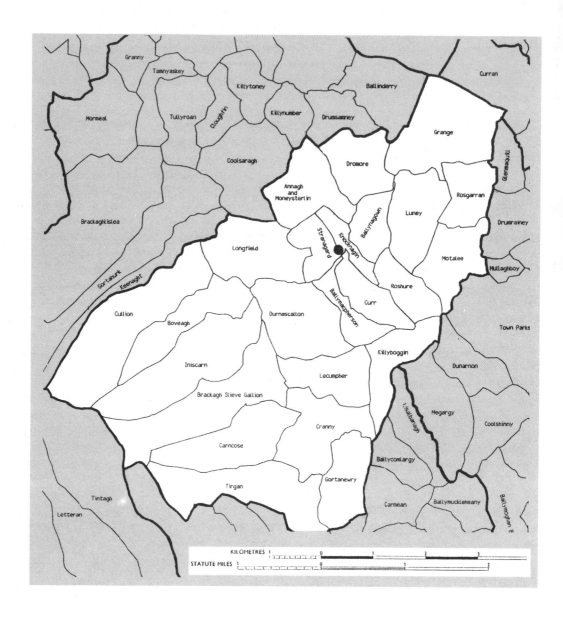

Parish of Desertmartin

Townlands
Annagh and Moneysterlin
Ballymacpherson
Ballynagown
Boveagh
Brackagh Slieve Gallion
Carncose
Cranny
Cullion
Curr
Dromore
Durnascallon
Gortanewry '
Grange
Iniscarn
Killyboggin
Knocknagin
Lecumpher
Longfield
Luney
Motalee
Rosgarran
Roshure
Stranagard
Tirgan

Towns
Desertmartin

Based upon Ordnance Survey 1:50,000 mapping, with permission of the Director of the Ordnance Survey of Northern Ireland, Crown copyright reserved.

THE PARISH OF DESERTMARTIN

A few remains of the ancient parish church of Desertmartin lie on damp ground in the bend of the Grange Water near the village of Desertmartin in the townland of Knocknagin (Hamlin 1976, ii 566). Many large dressed polygonal blocks of red sandstone, presumably from the church, were reused in the northern part of the west wall of the graveyard, and a portion of the church was taken down in 1820 to provide materials for building the parochial schoolhouse (*ibid.*; *Munn's Notes* 128). Although the name of the church is probably early Christian, no reference is made to it before the Papal Taxation of 1302–6.

The four townlands of Ballymacpherson, Curr, Knocknagin, and Stranagard (then called Moydrowne) were church lands (*Bishop. Der.* i 57, 103, 172; *CPR Jas I* 279a). The O'Doells (Irish *Ó Dúghaill*) were erenaghs of the parish, and had a long association with the parish. In a letter addressed to the Bishop of Derry, the Rev. Oliver Mather identifies the last erenagh of Desertmartin as one "Patrick O Doell" (*Bishop. Der.* i 182), and various members of the family held ecclesiastical office at least as early as 1454 when Roger O'Dubayll was rector (*Cal. Papal Letters* x 706). The name of the townland of **Ballymacpherson** appears to be connected with this family, and perhaps directly to Owen O'Doell who was parson there.

A number of place-names appear in a list of the rents of the Deanery of Tullaghoge in the Register of Archbishop Swayne (c.1500) which the editor, D.A. Chart, cautiously identifies as townlands in the parish of Desertmartin (*Reg. Swayne* 103). *Ballymagumfrech* is identified as Ballymacpherson, *Kyllbeggan* as Killyboggin, and *Drummagyn* with Knocknagin. However, the similarity that the early names bear to the modern townland names is misleading, for 17th-century spellings of the townland names bear little resemblance to the former, and in any case Desertmartin lay outside the Deanery of Tullaghoge. In a fascinating analysis of the territories and history of the Deanery of Tullaghoge, Éamon Ó Doibhlin identifies *Ballymagumfreck* (Chart's *Ballymagumfrech*) as Ballymurphy and *Drummagyn* as Drumenny, both of which were erenagh lands in the parish of Ardboe and Deanery of Tullaghoge (Ó Doibhlin 1971(b) 161). *Kyllbeggan* is less confidently identified with Killoon, the name of a parish which was situated near Coagh and which appears in some medieval documents (*ibid.*).

PARISH NAME

Desertmartin	*Díseart Mhártain* "St Martin's hermitage"	
1. Dīsiort Mhārtain	Cín Lae Ó M. 2	1645c
2. Disert Martuin	Top. Frag. 83	1675c
3. Cill Mhartan	Top. Frag. 72	1680c
4. Disarthmartan	Eccles. Tax. (CDI) 215	1306c
5. Disertmartyn	Colton Vis. 76	1397
6. Dysertmartyn	Colton Vis. 83	1397
7. Discertmarcham	Cal. Papal Letters x 706	1454
8. Disertmartin	CPR Jas I 376b	1609
9. Diesertmarten	Bishop. Der. i 57	1610
10. Disertmarten	Bishop. Der. i 62	1610
11. Disertmartyn	Bishop. Der. i 80	1611

12. Disertmartin, the termon or erenagh land of	CPR Jas I 279a	1615
13. Disertmartine	CPR Jas I 280a	1615
14. Disertmartin parish	CPR Jas I 377a	1615
15. Disantmarten	Bishop. Der. i 103	1615
16. Disertmartin	Bishop. Der. i 109	1615
17. Disertm'tin, R'c'oria de	Bishop. Der. i 129	1617c
18. Desert Martin	Phillips MSS (Maps) 162	1622
19. Disert Martin (x2)	Bishop. Der. i 144	1624c
20. Disert-Martin	Bishop. Der. i 171,172	1633
21. Disert Martin	Bishop. Der. i 172	1633
22. Disert Martin	Bishop. Der. i 182	1634?
23. Dissertmartin	Civ. Surv. iii 167,189	1654
24. Disertmartin	Civ. Surv. iii 174	1654
25. Dissert-Martin	Civ. Surv. iii 187	1654
26. Dissertmartine	Civ. Surv. iii 189	1654
27. T: of Desert martin	Hib. Reg. Loughinsholin	1657c
28. Desert martin, The Parish of	Hib. Reg. Loughinsholin	1657c
29. Dissert Marten, 4 townes of	Census 136	1659c
30. Desert Martin	Bishop. Der. i 326	1661
31. Desertmartin	Bishop. Der. i 331,332	1661
32. Desert Martin Parish	BSD(c) 54	1661
33. Desertmartine	Bishop. Der. i 354,355	1663
34. Desertmartin	Bishop. Der. i 354,357	1663
35. Desert Martine	Bishop. Der. i 355	1663
36. Desertmartin Parish	HMR (Ó Doibhlin 2) 68	1663
37. The four towns of Desertmartin	HMR (Ó Doibhlin 2) 68	1663
38. Dizirtmartin	Bishop. Der. i 405	1666
39. Desertm'	Bishop. Der. i 415	1668
40. Desertmartin	Bishop. Der. i 425	1669
41. Desertmartyn	Bishop. Der. i 425	1669
42. Desertmartyn	Bishop. Der. ii 1	1671
43. Desertmartin	Hib. Del. Derry	1672c
44. Desertmartyn	Bishop. Der. ii 34	1677
45. Desertmartyn, church of	Bishop. Der. ii 35	1677
46. Desertmartin	Bishop. Der. ii 40	1680
47. Dessertmartin, Rec' de	Bishop. Der. ii 114	1686
48. Desartmartin	Bishop. Der. ii 479	1688
49. Desermartin	Lamb Maps Derry	1690c
50. Dissermatrin, S'ti Covelli	Bishop. Der. ii 136	1692
51. Dissertmartine	Bishop. Der. ii 136	1692
52. Disertmartin	Bishop. Der. ii 509	1700c
53. Desertmartin R.	Sampson's Map	1813
54. Desertmartin	Sampson's Map	1813
55. Desertmartin	Custom of County (OSNB) No. 8	1834c
56. Desartmartin	Sampson's Stat. Sur. (OSNB) No. 8	1834c
57. Dísert Martain "Martin's desert or wilderness"	J O'D (OSNB) No. 8	1834c

58. Dishert-Martin "St. Martin's Hermitage"	Munn's Notes 128	1925
59. Díseart Mhártain	GÉ 213	1989
60. ˌdɛzərt'martn	Local pronunciation	1993

The name of the parish is clearly derived from the Irish *Díseart Mhártain* "St Martin's hermitage", after St Martin of Tours whose name is linked with the church here by early 19th-century tradition (*MacCloskey's Stat. Report* 13; *OSL (Derry)* 108; *AFM* i 139n). The cult of St Martin was widespread in the early Irish church and he is closely associated with St Patrick and St Columcille. It was believed that St Patrick was Martin's maternal uncle, and that his grave was discovered by Columcille (Ó hÓgáin 1990, 293). William Reeves adverts to a cemetery and holy well at Derry dedicated to St Martin, and to a copy of the Gospels called the Gospel of St Martin, traditionally believed to have been brought to Ireland by St Patrick, which was preserved for some time at Derry (*Colton Vis.* 83; cf. *AFM* iii 60n; also Ó hÓgáin *loc. cit.*).

A *díseart* or "hermitage" was normally attached to, or lay in close proximity to, a monastic church, and it was a place where the more devout monks and the pilgrims from other establishments might lead the life of recluses and at the same time share in the religious work of the church (Kenney 1929, 469). As a place-name element *díseart* is most common in Leinster and Munster, and Flanagan suggests that the distribution of the element may point to a connection with the ascetic Culdee movement of the 8th and 9th centuries (Flanagan 1981–2(c) 72). Several *díseart*-sites, such as Desertoghill in Co. Derry, are alleged to have earlier associations, and we may reasonably suppose that a number of *díseart*-names have superseded earlier church names. Although the name Desertmartin suggests associations with Martin of Tours, the parish church has been dedicated to St Comgall from at least the 17th century and the present Church of Ireland church still bears his name (*Bishop. Der.* ii 136; i 405; cf. *Colton Vis.* 83n; *Adomnán* 319). It seems quite likely, therefore, that the name Desertmartin was transferred to the parish church from the nearby hermitage dedicated to St Martin.

Todd identifies *uaim Martain* in the Irish Nennius as Desertmartin, but this seems unlikely (Todd 1848, 212n). The story goes that an Irish pilgrim arrived at Tours on his way to Rome. There he saw his mother distributing food to the poor, although in actual fact she was at home at *Ros Ailithir* (Roscarbery). He took the lid from the vessel she held and, a year later when he arrived home, showed it to her. She recognized the lid and it fitted her vessel "So that it is manifest from this that every distribution of alms that is made in Martin's Cave (*a n-uaim Martain*) is as effectual as if distributed at Tours" (*ibid.* 213). It appears from this that *uaim Martain* was probably near Roscarbery, Co. Cork.

TOWNLAND NAMES

Annagh and Moneysterlin   *Eanach* "marsh"
H 8493

1. lissanny	Esch. Co. Map 14	1609
2. Lysanny	Charter of Londonderry 391	1613
3. Annah	Lond. Comp. Valuation 309	1613
4. Anna	Phillips MSS (Maps) Plate 28	1622
5. Cullkanna Arrnagh being two towne lands	Civ. Surv. iii 176	1654

6. Lysarny	Bishop. Der. i 265	1657
7. Annagh and Culcam	Census 136	1659c
8. Arrnagh	BSD(c) 62	1661
9. Annagh	Bishop. Der. i 355	1663
10. Annagh, Calcam and	HMR (Ó Doibhlin 2) 69	1663
11. Annagh	Sampson's Map	1813
12. Annagh & Moneysterlin	OSNB No. 8	1834c
13. Annagh & Moneysterling	Bar. Coll. (OSNB) No. 8	1834c
14. 'An-nagh, Munny-'ster-lin	OSNB Pron. No. 8	1834c
15. Aonach "the public meeting"	MacCloskey's Stat. Report 60	1821
16. Eanach "a marsh or cut out bog"	J O'D (OSNB) No. 8	1834c
17. Eanach "The Marsh"	Munn's Notes 128	1925
18. 'anəx	Local pronunciation	1993

As the name implies, the modern townland of Annagh and Moneysterlin originally comprised two separate townlands, Annagh to the north-east and Moneysterlin to the south-west (*Esch. Co. Map* 14; *Phillips' MSS (Maps)* Plate 28). Both townlands are named separately in documents of the first half of the 17th century when they were in the possession of the Drapers' Company. In the second half of the century, however, the name Moneysterlin largely disappears from the records. Contemporary with this development, forms of the name **Coolcalm** begin to appear in our documents, and it is probable that this was considered as an alias for Moneysterlin. Even on Sampson's map of 1813, Coolcalm and Annagh are marked side by side with no mention of Moneysterlin. See **Moneysterlin** below.

The name Annagh is derived from Irish *Eanach* "marsh", but our earliest documented forms suggest that this portion of the townland was also called *Lios Eanaigh* "fort of the marsh" (1–2, 6). There is a fort situated on a long hill in the east of the townland (Speer 1990, 11), although it is not certain that this is the structure denoted by the name. The land in the immediate vicinity of the fort is described as "rough pasture" (*ibid.*) but there is a large area of bog to the north east (*Munn's Notes* 129).

Ballymacpherson
H 8590

Machaire Bhaile Phearsúin
"plain of the parson's townland"

1. magheryvallaforsan	Esch. Co. Map 14	1609
2. Magheryvally Farsan	Bishop. Der. i 57	1610
3. Magheryvallyfarson	CPR Jas I 279a	1615
4. Magherivallifarson	Bishop. Der. i 103	1615
5. Magheriballifarson	Bishop. Der. i 172	1633
6. Magheribelliperson	Civ. Surv. iii 189	1654
7. Magheryballypson	BSD(c) 54	1661
8. Ballymacaferson	Sampson's Map	1813
9. Ballymacpherson	Custom of County (OSNB) No. 8	1834c
10. Ballymacpherson	Bar. Coll. (OSNB) No. 8	1834c
11. Bally-mac-'ferson	OSNB Pron. No. 8	1834c
12. Baile magh fearshion "the plain for meadows"	MacCloskey's Stat. Report 60	1821

13. Baile mic a' Phearsuin "town of Macpherson"	J O'D (OSNB) No. 8	1834c
14. Baile-mac-Fheargusa "townland of the Fergusons"	Munn's Notes 129	1925
15. ˌbaliməkˈfɛrsᵻn	Local pronunciation	1993

The original form of this name is quite clearly shown by our earliest spellings to have been *Machaire Bhaile Phearsúin* "plain of the parson's townland" (on the possible connotations of *machaire* see **Maghera** below). Ballymacpherson is described as "termon or erenagh land" in various documents of the early 17th century (*Bishop. Der.* i 57, 103, 172; *CPR Jas I* 279a), and a letter addressed to the Bishop of Derry by the Rev. Oliver Mather regarding the townland of Ballynagown identifies the last parson of the parish as "Owen O Doell, alias Parson Odoell" (*Bishop. Der.* i 182). The O'Dowells (Irish *Ó Dúghaill*) were erenaghs of the parish, and had a long association with it. The Rev. Mather, in the same letter referred to here, further identifies the last erenagh of Desertmartin as one Patrick O Doell, and Roger O'Dubayll was rector of the parish in 1454 (*Cal. Papal Letters* x 706). It seems certain, therefore, that the townland took its name from Owen O Doell or one of his predecessors. The modern form of the name has undoubtedly been adopted by analogy with the surname MacPherson, which in Ulster is usually of Scottish origin (cf. Woulfe 1923, 316).

The absence of the article *an* "the" from this name requires some explanation as we would normally expect it to qualify a late borrowing such as *pearsún* (from Mid. Eng. *persoun*). Although the *n* of the article is normally retained after a vowel (as in *baile*) in place-names, there is no evidence for it among the historical spellings collected here. It is perhaps not unlikely, therefore, that the name is a shortened version of something like *Machaire Bhaile Phearsúin Dhíseart Mhártain* "the plain of the townland of Desertmartin's parson" (cf. examples cited in *DIL* sv. *persún*).

Ballynagown
H 8592

Baile na nGamhna (?)
"townland of the calves"

1. ballingowne	Esch. Co. Map 14	1609
2. Ballyngam	Charter of Londonderry 391	1613
3. Ballynegawnagh	Bishop. Der. i 182	1634
4. Ballinagow	Civ. Surv. iii 176	1654
5. Bellinagow	Civ. Surv. iii 176	1654
6. Ballinegow	Civ. Surv. iii 176	1654
7. Bellimcgowne	Civ. Surv. iii 177	1654
8. Ballingona	Bishop. Der. i 265	1657
9. Ballynegowne	Census 136	1659c
10. Ballinegow	BSD(c) 62	1661
11. Cullingowne	HMR (Ó Doibhlin 2) 69	1663
12. Ballinagown	OSNB No. 8	1834c
13. Ballynagown	Bar. Coll. (OSNB) No. 8	1834c
14. Bally-na-'gown	OSNB Pron. No. 8	1834c
15. Baile na gobhan "town of the pointed stone"	MacCloskey's Stat. Report 60	1821
16. Baile na ngabhan "town of the smiths"	J O'D (OSNB) No. 8	1834c

17. Baile-na-g-cananach "The townland of the canons"	Munn's Notes 129	1925
18. Baile-na-ngabhan "the town of the smiths"	Joyce iii 111	1925
19. ˌbalənəˈgəun	Local pronunciation	1993

There are numerous places called Ballygowan or Ballygown in various parts of the country, and it is interesting that approximately half of these lie in Ulster, mostly in Co. Down. The majority are probably related to the word *gabha* (gen. sing. *gabhann*) "smith", either directly or indirectly through surnames such as *Ó Gabhann* and *Mac Gabhann* (see *PNI* iii 23; *L. Log. Lú* 28; *L. Log. C. Chainnigh* 56; *Joyce* i 222–3).

However, a chance reference in a letter written by a local clergyman (3) indicates that this name has a quite different origin. In his letter to the bishop of Derry, dated 22 September, 1634, the Rev. Oliver Mather displays a profound knowledge of local parish affairs and in particular of the ownership and history of the townland of Ballynagown which was then the subject of some dispute, and so his spelling of the name must be considered authoritative. It might be argued that Mather's spelling shows evidence of a final *ch*, thereby indicating *gamhnach* "stripper (cow)", but *gh* is sometimes intended to be silent in place-names, and the remaining 17th-century forms can be much more easily explained if we accept that this is the case here. We would almost certainly expect Irish *-ach* to appear more or less consistently in anglicized forms as *-agh*, whereas final unstressed *a* is nearly always lost. Thus, *gamhna* from *gamhain* "calf" can account for the form in the Rev. Mather's letter as well as the general spread of 17th-century forms.

It might be objected that the remainder of the 17th-century spellings show no sign of the features normally associated with the sound *amh* such as the frequent emergence of the nasal (cf. **Drumsamney**, **Gortamney** in Kilcronaghan; **Longfield** below; **Cloghanramer** *PNI* i 14), and particular parallels could be drawn with the name **Glengomna**, Irish *Gleann Gamhna*, in the parish of Ballynascreen. However, there is irrefutable evidence from elsewhere that *gamhain* can give *gowan* etc. in anglicized place-names, for it is clear from the Irish annals that Ballynagowan in Co. Limerick derives from *Bealach an Ghamhna* "the way of the calf", and that Clonygowan in Co. Laois comes from *Cluain na nGamhain* "the meadow of the calves" (Ó Maolfabhail 1990(a), 68; *Joyce* i 471; see also **Luney** below).

The first element is, in many ways, as problematic as the last, and a definitive derivation can hardly be offered. The parallel example from Co. Limerick cited above might suggest *bealach* "pass, path", and there is perhaps a suitable site for this on the minor road which runs between the two peaks of Ballynagown Hill, but there is no evidence among the historical forms of the final *ch* of this word.

Baile "townland" must be considered as the most probable origin, but we can hardly reject possibilities such as *béal átha* "mouth of the ford" which is anglicized in numerous other place-names as *Bally*. Ballynagown is bounded on the north and west by the Grange Water, and it is distinctly possible that the name has something to do with a ford (*áth*). *Áth* is often found in conjunction with names of animals in place-names, probably because they would frequently have been brought across fords and watered there. Annamoe in Co. Wicklow, for example, comes from *Áth na mBó* "ford of the cows", and Annamult in Co. Kilkenny from *Áth na Molt* "ford of the wethers" (see also *Onom. Goed.* 67). It is possible, therefore, that a ford over the Grange Water may once have borne the name *Áth na nGamhna* "ford of the calves", and that the element *baile* "townland" was subsequently tacked on at some later date, a process of accretion which is seen in many other names such as *Baile Átha Cliath* (now Dublin), earlier *Áth Cliath* "ford of the hurdles", and *Baile Átha Troim* (now Trim), earlier *Áth Troim* "ford of the elder tree".

Boveagh	*Both Bheitheach*	
H 8291	"birch hut"	

1. Boveah	Lond. Comp. Valuation 309	1613
2. Boveah	Phillips MSS (Maps) Plate 28	1622
3. Bovevagh	Civ. Surv. iii 176	1654
4. Boveagh	Civ. Surv. iii 177	1654
5. Boveagh, 1/2 towne of	Census 136	1659c
6. Half Bouea	BSD(c) 62	1661
7. Bobagh	HMR (Ó Doibhlin 2) 68	1663
8. Boveagh	Sampson's Map	1813
9. Boveagh	Custom of County (OSNB) No. 8	1834c
10. Boveagh	Bar. Coll. (OSNB) No. 8	1834c
11. Boveagh	Rent Roll Drapers (OSNB) No. 8	1834c
12. Bo-'vieagh	OSNB Pron. No. 8	1834c
13. Bev beog "the young cattle"	MacCloskey's Stat. Report 60	1821
14. Both beithe "booth or hut of the birch"	J O'D (OSNB) No. 8	1834c
15. Both-bheithigh "booth of birches"	Joyce iii 147	1913
16. Both-bheithigh "The hut of the Birches"	Munn's Notes 129	1925
17. ˌboˈveːjə	Local pronunciation	1993

Both "hut" is relatively common in Irish place-names and, not surprisingly, it frequently occurs with a personal name. Here, however, it appears to be qualified by a form of the word *beith* "birch tree". The final *gh* in the early spellings could be silent, but the pronunciation recorded locally in the last century appears to suggest that it was still heard then (12) and this suggests that the final element is the adjective *beitheach* which here probably denotes "(made of) birch". The final *gh* has probably been accidentally omitted from form 6 as it is found in related sources (3-4).

Brackagh Slieve Gallion	*Breacach* "speckled place"	
H 8288	+ *Sliabh gCallann*	

1. brackagh	Esch. Co. Map 14	1609
2. Vrackah	Charter of Londonderry 391	1613
3. Brackhah	Lond. Comp. Valuation 309	1613
4. Brackah	Phillips MSS (Maps) Plate 28	1622
5. Beakagh	Civ. Surv. iii 176	1654
6. Brackagh	Civ. Surv. iii 177	1654
7. Wrackeigh	Bishop. Der. i 266	1657
8. Brackagh	Census 136	1659c
9. Brackagh	BSD(c) 62	1661
10. Bokach	HMR (Ó Doibhlin 2) 69	1663

11. Brackaghsliavgallon	Sampson's Map	1813
12. Brackaghsliebhgallion	Custom of County (OSNB) No. 8	1834c
13. Brackaghslievegallon	Bar. Coll. (OSNB) No. 8	1834c
14. Brackagh-Sliebh-'Gal-lion	OSNB Pron. No. 8	1834c
15. Bracagh "spotted land"	MacCloskey's Stat. Report 60	1821
16. Bracach Sléibhe Challainn "Badger warren or fox cover of Slieve Gallion"	J O'D (OSNB) No. 8	1834c
17. Breacach-sliabh-G-Callainn "The greyish, or speckled mountain of Callan or Colla"	Munn's Notes 129	1925
18. 'brakə sliv 'galjin	Local pronunciation	1993

On the identity and meaning of the element *breacach* "speckled place" see **Brackagh** in the parish of Ballynascreen. There were a number of townlands in the Barony of Loughinsholin called Brackagh and suffixes were sometimes added in order to help to distinguish between them (see **Brackaghlislea** in Kilcronaghan parish, **Bracaghreilly** in Maghera parish, and see also **Brackagh** in Lissan parish). See also **Slieve Gallion**.

Carncose	*Carn Chua* (?)	
H 8388	"Cua's cairn"	
1. Carn Coo	Lond. Comp. Valuation 309	1613
2. Carne	Phillips MSS (Maps) Plate 28	1622
3. Cornekoe	Civ. Surv. iii 176	1654
4. Carnto	Census 137	1659c
5. Cornekoe	BSD(c) 62	1661
6. Carnecrosse	HMR (Ó Doibhlin 2) 69	1663
7. Carncoes	Sampson's Map	1813
8. Carncose	Bar. Coll. (OSNB) No. 8	1834c
9. Carncose	Rent Roll Drapers (OSNB) No. 8	1834c
10. Carn-'coes	OSNB Pron. No. 8	1834c
11. Carn cois "the mound at the foot of the hill"	MacCloskey's Stat. Report 60	1821
12. Carn cuas "the carn of the caves"	J O'D (OSNB) No. 8	1834c
13. Carn-ic-Uais "The cairn of the son of Uais"	Munn's Notes 130	1925
14. karn'ko:s	Local pronunciation	1993

Some of our earliest writings make reference to the custom of raising a heap of stones (Irish *carn*) over the graves of the dead (*Joyce* i 332). Many were built on mountains in various parts of the country and, as a result, many mountains have taken their names from them (*Joyce* i 332–3). The absence of a cairn from the townland of Carncose is hardly of any significance as such structures were often destroyed in the past in order to provide building material.

Only one early spelling, and that from a very unreliable source (6), shows any trace of the *s* which we find in the modern form of the name, and we may safely conclude that it is not original. It is not uncommon for the English plural ending *-s* to be added to Gaelic names, frequently as the result of the division of the unit into two or more parts, but also sometimes as a reflex of an original plural in the Irish (*Joyce* i 32; *PNI* ii 232).

Nevertheless, the final element is difficult to determine with certainty, although it may well be the same as the final element in the now obsolete name *Legekoe* which seems to have marked the south-western boundary of the parish (*Civ. Surv.* iii 173, 174). *Cabha* "hollow" may be dismissed out of hand as it appears to be a late borrowing (it is absent from *DIL*, *Onom. Goed*, and *Joyce*; cf. Ó Murchadha 1964). It appears from certain 19th-century references that Slieve Gallion was also known by the name *Cnoc an Cheo* "the hill of the mist", but again this is unlikely to be the origin of the element under consideration here as this variant has very much the appearance of a late composition, and the article *an* "the" is noticeably absent from the townland name (*OSCNB* 43 sh. 46).

A more plausible derivation is from the now obsolete word *cua* which can mean "hollow, cavity" (*DIL* sv. *cúa* and cf. *cúad*), which might aptly describe the hollow interior of a cairn. However, the element *carn* "cairn" is frequently qualified by the name of the person who is believed to be entombed there, and it is perhaps here that we should look for the most likely origin of the name. The personal name *Mo Chua*, a pet-form of *Crónán*, is occasionally shortened to *Cua* in place-names (*PNI* iii 103), but it is almost exclusively borne by saints whereas cairns are generally associated with warriors and warlords (see Ó Corráin & Maguire 1981, 62–3, 137, *Onom. Goed.* 159ff.). However, the legendary warrior of Ulster, Cú Chulainn, is occasionally given the name *Cua* in some early Irish texts (*DIL* sv. *Cúa*), and it is distinctly possible that the cairn became associated with him. Indeed, the association may have been prompted by the potential pun on the name, Cú Chulainn, and the name of the mountain on which the townland is situated, Slieve Gallion. The absence of any traditions concerning the occupant of the cairn, even in the 19th century, is hardly surprising given the fact that it had evidently been destroyed by that stage.

Cranny
H 8588

Crannaigh
"wooded place"

1. Crannagh	Esch. Co. Map 14	1609
2. Crannagh	Charter of Londonderry 391	1613
3. Greena	Lond. Comp. Valuation 309	1613
4. Grenagh	Phillips MSS (Maps) Plate 28	1622
5. Cranny	Civ. Surv. iii 176	1654
6. Crannagh	Bishop. Der. i 266	1657
7. Crainy	Census 136	1659c
8. Cranney	BSD(c) 62	1661
9. Crannie	HMR (Ó Doibhlin 2) 68	1663
10. Cranny	Sampson's Map	1813
11. Cranny	Bar. Coll. (OSNB) No. 8	1834c
12. 'Cran-ny	OSNB Pron. No. 8	1834c
13. Crannidh "the trees"	MacCloskey's Stat. Report 60	1821
14. Crannach "arborous"	J O'D (OSNB) No. 8	1834c
15. Crannagh "The townland full of trees"	Munn's Notes 130	1925

16. 'krani	Local pronunciation	1993

This name derives from *Crannaigh*, a dative or accusative form of *Crannach* which primarily denotes "a wooded place" but, by extension, various wooden objects and structures (*DIL* and *Ó Dónaill* sv. *crannach*). Woods are depicted in this very townland on the Escheated Counties map of this part of the barony of Loughinsholin (*Esch. Co. Map* 14). However, the woods that are now present in the townland are probably no older than the extensive plantation made by the Drapers' Company in the early 19th century (on which see *MacCloskey's Stat. Report* 3).

Cullion *An Chuilleann*
H 8191 Meaning uncertain

1. b:negullan	Esch. Co. Map 14	1609
2. Ballmegallan	Charter of Londonderry 391	1613
3. Guillen	Lond. Comp. Valuation 309	1613
4. Quillin	Phillips MSS (Maps) Plate 28	1622
5. Collunn	Civ. Surv. iii 176	1654
6. Cullan	Civ. Surv. iii 176	1654
7. Ballingallan	Bishop. Der. i 265	1657
8. Cullan	Census 136	1659c
9. Cullane	BSD(c) 62	1661
10. Callan	HMR (Ó Doibhlin 2) 68	1663
11. Cullien	Sampson's Map	1813
12. Cullion	Custom of County (OSNB) No. 8	1834c
13. Cullion	Bar. Coll. (OSNB) No. 8	1834c
14. Cullion	Rent Roll Drapers (OSNB) No. 8	1834c
15. 'Cull-e-on	OSNB Pron. No. 8	1834c
16. Cuilean "the holly trees"	MacCloskey's Stat. Report 60	1821
17. Cuillean "holly, land of holly"	J O'D (OSNB) No. 8	1834c
18. Cuillion "The townland of the holly"	Munn's Notes 130	1925
19. 'kọljïn	Local pronunciation	1993

Cuileann "holly" is often confused in place-names with the now obsolete word *cuilleann* which Ó Máille takes to signify "a steep (unbroken) slope" (1960, 61), but Cullion's location on the northern slope of Slieve Gallion is clearly suggestive of the latter. Moreover, *cuileann* "holly" rarely stands on its own in place-names (*PNI* i 75), whereas *cuilleann* frequently does so.

The earliest available spellings (1–2, 7), all of which occur in related sources, seem to suggest a form of the name which includes *baile* "townland" and a form of the article meaning "(of) the". This might be thought to be an important diagnostic for although *cuileann* "holly" is frequently found with the article (note in particular *Baile an Chuilinn* "townland of the holly", *Onom. Goed.* 81), *cuilleann* "steep slope" is generally accepted as an element of some antiquity and of all the instances cited in Hogan's *Onomasticon Goedelicum* none contain the article. Nevertheless, it is possible that *cuilleann* continued to be productive into the Middle Ages when the article was becoming increasingly common in place-name formations. We might also consider the use of the article with ancient names such as **Navan** in Co. Armagh which appears first without the article as *Eamhain* or *Eamhain Mhacha*, traditionally explained as "the twins of Macha". In the 17th century, however, we find a mixture of forms in both Irish and English, many of which include the article, and a number of English forms suggest a close parallel to the name under discussion here, namely, *Baile na hEamhna* "townland of *An Eamhain*".

This group of spellings approximates most closely to an underlying Irish form *Baile na gCuileann* "townland of the hollies", but elsewhere *cuileann* is invariably employed in the singular (see *Onom. Goed.* passim). Thus, whatever the underlying form actually is, we must assume that the *g* of these spellings is an error for *q*. We could argue, therefore, that they represent a form *Baile an Chuilinn* "townland of the holly", but it is perhaps unlikely that the *ne* of forms 1–2 represents anything other than *na* (fem.) "(of) the". *Cuilleann* is usually fem., so that the form of the article does not present any problems in this case (I hope to discuss this element in greater detail in a forthcoming article in *Ainm*).

Curr	*An Chora*	
H 8691	"the weir"	
1. b:necorrew	Esch. Co. Map 14	1609
2. Ballinecorrew	Bishop. Der. i 57	1610
3. Ballinecorrewe	CPR Jas I 279a	1615
4. Ballinecorrewe	Bishop. Der. i 103	1615
5. Ballinecorren	Bishop. Der. i 172	1633
6. Bellinecurr	Civ. Surv. iii 189	1654
7. Ballynecur	BSD(c) 54	1661
8. Curr	Sampson's Map	1813
9. Curr	Custom of County (OSNB) No. 8	1834c
10. Curr	Bar. Coll. (OSNB) No. 8	1834c
11. Curr	OSNB Pron. No. 8	1834c
12. Curr "the corner, or, the pool"	MacCloskey's Stat. Report 60	1821
13. Corr "a pit"	J O'D (OSNB) No. 8	1834c
14. Corr "The round hill"	Munn's Notes 130	1925
15. kǫr	Local pronunciation	1993

The 17th-century forms for Curr show that the name originates from *Baile na Coradh* "townland of the weir". There is no trace of the weir, which was probably of wooden construction, but the likely location for it would have been on the Grange Water which runs close to the northern boundary of the townland. The subsequent development is difficult to ascertain given the paucity of available forms from the late 17th and 18th centuries, but the indications are that it was shortened to *Ballynacurr* or the like in the latter half of the 17th century, and that this was further truncated at a later date to give something resembling the modern form. These changes have considerably obscured the origin of the name and this doubtless led O'Donovan to postulate an Irish form *Corr* which he translates "pit" (it can, however, often mean "a round hill": Munn notes that there are no apparent pits or hollows in the townland, *Munn's Notes* 130).

A number of similar names occur elsewhere in Ireland, most notably Ballinacor in Glenmalure, Co. Wicklow, and **Ballynacor** in the parish of Seagoe, Co. Armagh, both of which derive from *Baile na Cora* "townland of the weir" (*Joyce* i 367; *GÉ* 186; Price 1945–67, 56–7). There is a Ballinacurra (divided into three parts) in Co. Limerick, but its origin appears to be from *Béal Átha na Cora* "the fordmouth of the weir" (Ó Maolfabhail 1990(a), 70).

Dromore	*Droim Mór*	
H 8593	"big ridge"	
1. drommore	Esch. Co. Map 14	1609
2. Dromore	Charter of Londonderry 391	1613
3. Drommor	Phillips MSS (Maps) Plate 28	1622
4. Drom'ore	Bishop. Der. i 144	1624c
5. Dromore	Civ. Surv. iii 174,189	1654
6. Dromore	Bishop. Der. i 265	1657
7. Dromore	Hib. Reg. Loughinsholin	1657c
8. Drumore	Census 136	1659c
9. Dromore	BSD(c) 54	1661
10. Dromore	Hib. Del. Derry	1672c
11. Dromore(?)	Sampson's Map	1813
12. Dromore	Custom of County (OSNB) No. 8	1834c
13. Dromore	OSNB No. 8	1834c
14. Dromore	Bar. Coll. (OSNB) No. 8	1834c
15. Dro'more	OSNB Pron. No. 8	1834c
16. Drom mor "the great back"	MacCloskey's Stat. Report 60	1821
17. Druim mór "great ridge"	J O'D (OSNB) No. 8	1834c
18. Druim-mor "The great ridge"	Munn's Notes 130	1925
19. ˌdrọˈmoːr	Local pronunciation	1993

The townland of Dromore is dominated by a large ridge overlooking lower ground to the east, and it is doubtless from this feature that the townland has been named.

Durnascallon	*Doire na Sceallán*	
H 8490	"oakwood of the seeds"	
1. derryneskellan	Esch. Co. Map 14	1609
2. Derryneskellan	Charter of Londonderry 391	1613
3. Derr ne Skellan	Lond. Comp. Valuation 309	1613
4. Dirreneskallam	Phillips MSS (Maps) Plate 28	1622
5. Durneskillean	Civ. Surv. iii 176	1654
6. Derrineskellan	Bishop. Der. i 266	1657
7. Derrynoscallan	Census 136	1659c
8. Durneskilleane	BSD(c) 62	1661
9. Derieneskalla	HMR (Ó Doibhlin 2) 68	1663
10. Derrynaskelan	Sampson's Map	1813
11. Durnascallon	Custom of County (OSNB) No. 8	1834c

12. Durnascallion	Bar. Coll. (OSNB) No. 8	1834c
13. Durnascallon	Rent Roll Drapers (OSNB) No. 8	1834c
14. Dur-na-'scal-lon	OSNB Pron. No. 8	1834c
15. Doir na sgalain "the huts in the waters"	MacCloskey's Stat. Report 60	1821
16. Doire na sgeallán "oakwood of the small acorns"	J O'D (OSNB) No. 8	1834c
17. Doire-na-sceallan "oakwood of the kernels/acorns"	Munn's Notes 130	1925
18. ˌdərnəˈskaljïn	Local pronunciation	1993

The array of early spellings supports the origin suggested by O'Donovan and Munn. Both translate *sceallán* as "acorn", although this normally has the more general connotation of a seed or pip (*Ó Dónaill* sv.). The normal word for acorn is *dearcán*, and mast was indicated by the word *meas*. *Sceallán* can also mean "small potato", but as the potato was not commonly grown in Ireland until perhaps the 1670s (Mitchell 1990, 188), this is hardly the sense here. Acorns and other nuts were, of course, of great importance to the economy of medieval Ireland, primarily as food for pigs, and the annals are replete with references to the size of the mast crop (Ó Corráin 1972, 56–7).

Gortanewry
H 8587

Gort an Aoire
"the shepherd's field"

1. gortIncrew	Esch. Co. Map 14	1609
2. Gortmeren	Charter of Londonderry 391	1613
3. Gortenare	Lond. Comp. Valuation 309	1613
4. Gortenare	Phillips MSS (Maps) Plate 28	1622
5. Gorterny	Civ. Surv. iii 176	1654
6. Gortnerenny	Civ. Surv. iii 189	1654
7. Gortnerei	Bishop. Der. i 265	1657
8. Gortneery	Census 136	1659c
9. Gorterney	BSD(c) 62	1661
10. Gortenowry	HMR (Ó Doibhlin 2) 69	1663
11. Gortinure	Sampson's Map	1813
12. Gortanewry	Custom of County (OSNB) No. 8	1834c
13. Gortanewry	Bar. Coll. (OSNB) No. 8	1834c
14. Gortanewry	Rent Roll Drapers (OSNB) No. 8	1834c
15. Gort-a-'newry	OSNB Pron. No. 8	1834c
16. Gort an ur "field of heath, or yews"	MacCloskey's Stat. Report 60	1821
17. Gort an iubhraighe "field of the yew"	J O'D (OSNB) No. 8	1834c
18. Gort-an-iubhraigh "The tilled field of the yew grove"	Munn's Notes 131	1925
19. Gort-an-iubhraigh "field of the yew"	Joyce iii 373	1925
20. ˌgɔrtïˈnjuri	Local pronunciation	1993

The first element in this name, *gort*, denotes a field of arable or pasture land, and is very common in Irish place-names (*DIL* sv. 1 *gort*; *Joyce* i 230). Previous commentators have taken the final element to relate to the word *iúr* "yew", but the 17th-century forms offer little or no support for this interpretation. Although there are substantial differences between the early spellings, even within groups of related sources, an underlying form something like *Gortenery* can be discerned, and this may reflect an Irish element *aoire* "shepherd" which is similarly anglicized at this period in the name **Ballaghanery** in Co. Down, from Irish *Bealach an Aoire* "pass of the shepherd" (*PNI* iii 20–1). The vowel *ao(i)* is frequently anglicized *e*, and later *ee*, in place-names, but developed into an unrounded [u:] in Ulster Irish and is occasionally anglicized *oo* (see **Balloo**, *PNI* ii 150–1). Thus, we can establish a clear line of development from the 17th-century forms recorded here down to the modern form.

The word *aoire* can be used in the extended sense of "pastor", and it is possible that this is the intended meaning here, for a *gort* or "garden" was often attached to the parish church for the benefit of the local vicar (*Colton Vis.* 118). However, there is no evidence that Gortanewry was ever held by the Church, and it fell into the hands of the Drapers' Company at the Plantation.

Grange

H 8794

An Ghráinseach

"the grange/granary"

1.	Aighiter two towns	CPR Jas I 377a	1609
2.	aghieghter	Esch. Co. Map 14	1609
3.	Agh Eter	Lond. Comp. Valuation 307	1613
4.	Agheter	Phillips MSS (Maps) Plate 24	1622
5.	Gravany	Civ. Surv. iii 176	1654
6.	Grange	Census 136	1659c
7.	Granoney	BSD(c) 63	1661
8.	Grainge	HMR (Ó Doibhlin 2) 69	1663
9.	Grange	Sampson's Map	1813
10.	Grange	Custom of County (OSNB) No. 8	1834c
11.	Grange	Bar. Coll. (OSNB) No. 8	1834c
12.	Grainge "cornland, from grainseach a barn"	MacCloskey's Stat. Report 60	1821
13.	Grainseach "The Grange"	Munn's Notes 131	1925
14.	(ðə) greːnʒ	Local pronunciation	1993

Both Grange and the neighbouring townland of Ballinderry were held by the Abbey of St Peter and St Paul at Armagh, and this is doubtless the origin of the name of this townland for the word *grange* usually denotes a unit of land held as farm-land by a monastery of the 12th- or post-12th-century period (*CPR Jas I* 376b-377a; Flanagan 1981-2(c), 75). English/French *grange* was borrowed into Irish as *gráinseach*, but in anglicized forms of place-names the English form is frequently substituted for the Irish form, and it is often difficult to tell whether or not the name is of Irish origin. **Gransha** in the parish of Newry, Co. Down, is written *Grange* in the 16th and 17th centuries, but the 19th-century forms indicate an underlying form *An Ghráinseach* (*PNI* i 27–8). A more telling example, also from Co. Down, is that of **Grangee** in Donaghadee parish (*PNI* ii 191). This is variously written in the 17th century as *Ballinegrangee* etc. which clearly indicates an Irish form *Baile na Gráinsi* "townland of the grange" and is once written *Granshagh* (Irish *Gráinseach*). In this particular instance, it would be remarkable if the name had not been gaelicized in the locality, although we cannot be certain that it was not originally coined by English speakers at Armagh.

It seems that Grange was originally a parcel of land of which *Agheter* was the only subdivision (*Lond. Comp. Valuation* 307; cf. *Phillips MSS (Maps)* Plate 24; *Esch. Co. Map* 14). The land here is low and flat, being bounded on the south by the Grange Water, and we might reasonably suggest that this form comes from Irish *Achadh Íochtair* "lower field".

Iniscarn
H 8290

Inis Cairn
"high meadow of the cairn"

1.	Inishgarna	Esch. Co. Map 14	1609
2.	Enish Crann	Lond. Comp. Valuation 309	1613
3.	Eniskarm	Phillips MSS (Maps) Plate 28	1622
4.	Enishcarne	Census 136	1659c
5.	Inneskerne	HMR (Ó Doibhlin 2) 68	1663
6.	Inishcairn	Sampson's Map	1813
7.	Inniscarn	Custom of County (OSNB) No. 8	1834c
8.	Inniscarran	Bar. Coll. (OSNB) No. 8	1834c
9.	Inniscarn	Rent Roll Drapers (OSNB) No. 8	1834c
10.	Innis-'carn	OSNB Pron. No. 8	1834c
11.	Inniscarn "the insulated mound"	MacCloskey's Stat. Report 60	1821
12.	Inis cairn "island or holm of the carn"	J O'D (OSNB) No. 8	1834c
13.	Inis-carn "The island of the cairn"	Munn's Notes 131	1925
14.	ˌinïs'kaːrn	Local pronunciation	1993

The cairn referred to in this name is located on the northern peak of Slieve Gallion (OS H 8189), and is probably the cairn called the Giant's Grave in the Ordnance Survey Memoirs (*OSM* xxxi 57). It was four feet high and 14 yards in diameter at the base, and when it was excavated by Francis Quinn, parish priest of Omagh, in 1825, a grave 8½ feet long was found inside (*ibid.*). Tradition relates that the giant, Tadhg Mór, whose powers were given to him by St Patrick, slew a great black bull in a bog hole on top of Slieve Gallion. The local people, fearing his strength, prayed to the saint to reduce him to his former powers whereupon he died and was buried in the Giant's Grave. The saint had apparently not known that Tadhg had previously dined on the remains of the black bull and when Tadhg's stature was reduced his stomach could not cope with the meal and he died of indigestion (*ibid.* 57–8).

The first element may be any of a number of similar words. The most obvious is *inis* which is normally applied to islands, but by extension it can also denote "a water-meadow" (also *inse* from the old dative form). The meaning "island" is usual in the large number of names containing that element in Upper and Lower Lough Erne in Co. Fermanagh, although it appears to denote a peninsula on two occasions (Inish Dacharne and Inishkeen). Where *inis* is used outside Fermanagh, it is more often of a place, usually low-lying, near or partially surrounded by a river (e.g. **Inish Pool** on the River Roe, **Inshaleen** beside the Agivey River, and **Inishrush** on the Clady River, Co. Derry), implying the sense of "water-meadow".

However, the word is not wholly restricted to low-lying places, and we may note *insí cnoc* "grassy places (along streams, etc.) in hills" and *inseachas* "low-lying mountain pasturage; a sheltered place in the mountains for cattle" (*Ó Dónaill, Dinneen* svv.; also *PNI* ii 85). Munn notes that the northern part of the townland "is practically, by the rivers rising in it, separated into 3 Islands", but these so-called islands are not at all clear, and *inis* here probably denotes a grassy place on Slieve Gallion near the cairn (*Munn's Notes* 131).

Inis from O.Ir. *indes* "byre, milking place" must also be considered (*DIL* sv.). The slopes of Slieve Gallion were noted for the height at which traces of ancient culture have been found (*MacCloskey's Stat. Report* 2), but the top of a mountain is an unlikely location for a milking place. Nevertheless, it might be plausibly argued that *inis* is here used fancifully or metaphorically of the milking place of some mythical cow (cf. **Boley** in Ballynascreen). Yet another possibility is the element *ionnas* which Ó Máille takes to be a compound of O.Ir. *ind, inn* "top, high part" + the suffix *as* (1989–90, 133–4), but although the meaning is clearly suitable in the present context, there is very little firm evidence for its existence.

Killyboggin	*Cúil an Bhogáin*	
H 8690	"recess of the quagmire"	
1. (?)B: tauniloure	Esch. Co. Map 14	1609
2. (?)Ballytannylour	Charter of Londonderry 391	1613
3. Calabogan	Lond. Comp. Valuation 308	1613
4. Coolabogan	Phillips MSS (Maps) Plate 28	1622
5. Callovogan	Civ. Surv. iii 176	1654
6. Collovogan	Civ. Surv. iii 177	1654
7. (?)Ballytametoure	Bishop. Der. i 265	1657
8. Cullabogan	Census 136	1659c
9. Callovogan	BSD(c) 63	1661
10. Culleboghan	HMR (Ó Doibhlin 2) 68	1663
11. Kilbogan	Sampson's Map	1813
12. Killyboggin	Custom of County (OSNB) No. 8	1834c
13. Killybogin	OSNB No. 8	1834c
14. Killyboggan	Bar. Coll. (OSNB) No. 8	1834c
15. Killy-'bog-in	OSNB Pron. No. 8	1834c
16. Coill bog "the wet wood"	MacCloskey's Stat. Report 60	1821
17. Coill a'bhogain "wood of the bog"	J O'D (OSNB) No. 8	1834c
18. Coill-a-bhogain "The woods of the little bog"	Munn's Notes 131	1925
19. Coill-a'-bhogáin "wood of the bog or quagmire"	Joyce iii 417	1925
20. ˌkʲiliˈbɔgïn	Local pronunciation	1993

Dinneen records *bogán* in the sense of "quagmire" in Co. Derry, and this is probably the sense of the final element here (*Dinneen* sv. *bogán*). Munn points out that the eastern part of the townland is boggy (*Munn's Notes* 131). A number of 17th-century forms indicate that the initial element should probably be taken to be *cúil* "corner, nook, recess", rather than *coill* "wood" or *cill* "church". A similar development of *cúil* occurs in the name **Killynumber** in the parish of Kilcronaghan.

It appears from the Escheated Counties Maps that Killyboggin was formerly known by the name *Ballytauniloure* or the like (1). No authoritative derivation can be offered for this name as all the attestations are found in related sources (1–2, 7).

Knocknagin
H 8592

Cnoc na gCeann
"hill of the heads"

1. moydroune	Esch. Co. Map 14	1609
2. Moydrowne	Bishop. Der. i 57	1610
3. Moydrowne	CPR Jas I 279a	1615
4. Moydrowne	Bishop. Der. i 103	1615
5. Moyedron	Civ. Surv. iii 189	1654
6. Moydron	BSD(c) 54	1661
7. Knocnagin	Sampson's Map	1813
8. Knocknaghin	Custom of County (OSNB) No. 8	1834c
9. Knocknagin	OSNB No. 8	1834c
10. Knocnegin	Bar. Coll. (OSNB) No. 8	1834c
11. Knock-na-'ghin	OSNB Pron. No. 8	1834c
12. Cnoc na gin "wedge shaped hill"	MacCloskey's Stat. Report 60	1821
13. [Cnoc na gCeann] "place of execution"	OSL (Derry) 107	1834
14. Cnoc na gceann "hill of the heads"	J O'D (OSNB) No. 8	1834c
15. Cnoc-na-gceann "the hill of the heads"	Joyce i 221	1869
16. Cnoc-na-g-ceann "The hill of the heads"	Munn's Notes 131	1925
17. ˌnɔknəˈgjïn	Local pronunciation	1993

In the early 19th century, the inhabitants of Desertmartin pointed out the site and remains of a gaol to John MacCloskey and noted the adjacent height of Knocknagin as the place of execution (*MacCloskey's Stat. Report* 9; cf. *OSL (Derry)* 107). Parallel traditions and beliefs may have been connected to other similarly named sites such as **Tullynagin** in the parish of Lisnadill, Co. Armagh, which appears to derive from *Tulaigh na gCeann* "hillock of the heads". Human remains were found in the last century at Knocknagin near Balrothery, Co. Dublin, also from *Cnoc na gCeann* (*Joyce* i 221–2).

Throughout the 17th century, the townland now called Knocknagin was known as *Moydrowne*, as can be seen from the Escheated Counties Maps where it is pictured beside Stranagard, Ballymacpherson, Curr, Rosgarran, Ballynagown, and Moneysterlin.

Lecumpher
H 8589

Leac Iomchair (?)
Meaning uncertain

1. licke Imaghare	Esch. Co. Map 14	1609
2. Lickmahary	Charter of Londonderry 391	1613
3. Lacklumhore	Lond. Comp. Valuation 309	1613
4. Leckvmhor	Phillips MSS (Maps) Plate 28	1622

5. Lockumcher	Civ. Surv. iii 176	1654
6. Leckumcher	Civ. Surv. iii 176	1654
7. Lickemagherie	Bishop. Der. i 266	1657
8. Leckonicher	Census 136	1659c
9. Leeckvmcher	BSD(c) 62	1661
10. Leakm'cur	HMR (Ó Doibhlin 2) 69	1663
11. Lekumpher	Sampson's Map	1813
12. Lecumpher	Custom of County (OSNB) No. 8	1834c
13. Lecumpher	Bar. Coll. (OSNB) No. 8	1834c
14. Lecumpher	Rent Roll Drapers (OSNB) No. 8	1834c
15. Leck-'hum-fer	OSNB Pron. No. 8	1834c
16. Leac omur "the stone"	MacCloskey's Stat. Report 60	1821
17. Lag umair "hollow of the trough"	J O'D (OSNB) No. 8	1834c
18. Lag-umhair "The hollow of the cup"	Munn's Notes 131	1925
19. ˌləˈkọmfər	Local pronunciation	1993

The first element in this rather unusual name is almost certainly the word *leac* which primarily denotes "a flat stone or rock", but the sense "gravestone" is probably also common in place-names. The variation in the representation of the vowel in the historical spellings seems to suggest a dative form *lic* (1–2, 7) and renders an origin from *leaca* "hillside" unlikely. There is no record of a rock of any special significance in the townland but this is hardly surprising.

The origin of the second element is not altogether clear. The pronunciation suggested by the historical forms may indicate an origin from *iomchar* which has a variety of meanings, the most likely of which in this case is "support", and it might be imagined that a stone (*leac*) was used as a support in some structure such as a passage grave, although this does seem improbable. There were several words in O.Ir. which are similar in form and meaning to *iomchar*, and one of these, *immarchor*, appears in the obsolete name *Cluain Immorchair* where it may mean "practising, playing" or "ferry, passage" (*DIL* sv.; *Onom. Goed.* 265). Another meaning of *immarchor* is "casting, throwing" (possibly related to *airchor*, Mod. Ir. *urchar*, "cast, shot"), and it is conceivable that the *leac* was used in games as a test of strength or, more probably, that it was associated with some great giant in local tradition. Joyce remarks that there are several places in Ireland containing the word *urchar* "cast, shot", and that in "every such place there is a legend of some remarkable cast of a weapon, memorable for its prodigious length, for killing of some great hero, a wild animal, or infernal serpent" (*Joyce* i 168). There is a tradition of a giant's grave and chair in the townland of **Iniscarn**, and a story was recalled locally in the last century about the occupant of the grave, although there is no mention of the stone (*OSM* xxxi 57). Another 19th-century tradition relates that Finn McCool cast an enormous stone from Slieve Gallion to Seefin in the parish of Maghera (*OSL (Derry)* 87). A striking parallel is found in *Leac an Urchair* "the rock of the cast" on Tory Island, Co. Donegal, which clearly preserves a memory of some fabulous throw (Ó hUrmoltaigh 1967, 103). Unfortunately, we can no longer establish the exact significance of the name Lecumpher, nor any possible associated traditions.

Longfield *Leamhchoill*
H 8392 "elm wood"

1.	laaghell	Esch. Co. Map 14	1609
2.	Langhell	Charter of Londonderry 391	1613
3.	Lamwhill	Lond. Comp. Valuation 309	1613
4.	Lamwhill	Phillips MSS (Maps) Plate 28	1622
5.	Loghfield	Civ. Surv. iii 176	1654
6.	Longfield	Civ. Surv. iii 177	1654
7.	Laughell	Bishop. Der. i 265	1657
8.	Longfield	Census 136	1659c
9.	Longfeelde	BSD(c) 62	1661
10.	Longfield	HMR (Ó Doibhlin 2) 68	1663
11.	Longfield	Sampson's Map	1813
12.	Longfield	Custom of County (OSNB) No. 8	1834c
13.	Longfield	Bar. Coll. (OSNB) No. 8	1834c
14.	'Longfield	OSNB Pron. No. 8	1834c
15.	Leamhchoill "Elmwood"	J O'D (OSNB) No. 8	1834c
16.	Leamh-choill "The elm woods"	Munn's Notes 132	1925
17.	'lɔŋfil	Local pronunciation	1993

Despite the English appearance of this name, it is Irish in origin, and its form (a noun + noun compound) suggests that it may be at least as old as the 6th century (Mac Giolla Easpaig 1981, 151–2). *Leamhchoill* is anglicized in various ways throughout Ireland (*Joyce* i 509), and we may compare in particular Longfields in Antrim, Armagh, and Fermanagh, as well as **Longfield Beg** and **Longfield More** in the parish of Faughanvale, Co. Derry.

The *mh* had already been vocalized by the time our earliest form was recorded (1, 7), but it undoubtedly left a strong nasal trace on the preceding vowel which later re-emerged as *m* or *ng*. Some time before the second half of the 17th century, the *ch* (a guttural sound as in *lough*) became *f* under the influence of the preceding *m* (cf. **Lecumpher** above). The final transformation, by false etymology, to its modern form had already taken place by the middle of the 17th century, at which time we begin to see the unhistorical final *d* appearing.

Luney
H 8792

Leamhnaigh
"place of elms"

1.	Sauony	Esch. Co. Map 14	1609
2.	Lawny	Charter of Londonderry 391	1613
3.	Lemaney	Lond. Comp. Valuation 307	1613
4.	Lemaney	Phillips MSS (Maps) Plate 24	1622
5.	Leavany	Civ. Surv. iii 176	1654
6.	Leavanny	Civ. Surv. iii 177	1654
7.	Leovoyne	Civ. Surv. iii 177	1654
8.	Lawney	Bishop. Der. i 265	1657
9.	(?)Senany	Census 136	1659c
10.	Leavanny	BSD(c) 63	1661
11.	(?)Bremie	HMR (Ó Doibhlin 2) 68	1663
12.	Lewny	Sampson's Map	1813
13.	Luney	Custom of County (OSNB) No. 8	1834c
14.	Luney	Bar. Coll. (OSNB) No. 8	1834c

15. 'Loo-ne	OSNB Pron. No. 8	1834c
16. Luaneach "marshy, from lua water"	MacCloskey's Stat. Report 60	1821
17. Leamhnaigh "elm plain"	J O'D (OSNB) No. 8	1834c
18. Leamhnach "The elm land or plain"	Munn's Notes 132	1925
19. 'luni	Local pronunciation	1993

O'Donovan's Irish form, *Leamhnaigh*, which is an oblique form of *Leamhnach* "place of elms", is fully supported by the historical forms. The 17th-century spellings show a large degree of variation, quite apart from some obvious corruptions. Nevertheless, we can distinguish three major types: *Lawney*, *Leavany*, and *Lemaney*, although this range of spellings may simply reflect orthographic variations of an underlying form *L(e)awaney*. The modern form of the name is somewhat irregular, and we might properly expect to find something like Lawney or Lowney (see Quiggin 1906, 57). It is possible that the pronunciation has been corrupted by English speakers, probably on the basis of the written form, but it is worth noting that *leamhan* is pronounced "loon" in Achill, Co. Mayo (G. Stockman, pers. comm.).

Moneysterlin, Annagh and
H 8493

Maigh Inse Uí Fhloinn
"plain of O'Flynn's island"

1. moyinisholin	Esch. Co. Map 14	1609
2. Momisholm	Charter of Londonderry 391	1613
3. Monisholin	Lond. Comp. Valuation 309	1613
4. Moinsholin	Phillips MSS (Maps) Plate 28	1622
5. Monysholin	Bishop. Der. i 265	1657
6. Monashallin	Bishop. Der. i 355	1663
7. Moneysterlin, Annagh &	OSNB No. 8	1834c
8. Moneysterling, Annagh &	Bar. Coll. (OSNB) No. 8	1834c
9. Munny-'ster-lin	OSNB Pron. No. 8	1834c
10. Monaster-O'Lyn [O'Lyn's monastery]	OSL (Derry) 100	1834
11. Mainistir Fhloinn "Lyn's monastery"	J O'D (OSNB) No. 8	1834c
12. Mainistir OFhloinn	Colton Vis. 77n	1850
13. Muinister-ui-Fhlainn "Monastery of the O'Lynns"	Munn's Notes 128	1925
14. Magh Innse Uí Fhloinn	GUH 27n	1951
15. ˌmoni'stɛrlɪŋ	Local pronunciation	1993

O'Donovan derives Moneysterlin from Irish *Mainistir Fhloinn* which he translates "Lyn's monastery" (10-11) and he is followed in this by Reeves (12). However, this interpretation is not supported by any of our 17th-century spellings, which appear to indicate an original *Maigh Inse Uí Fhloinn* "plain of O'Flynn's island". This townland is, of course, the location of *Inis Uí Fhloinn* "O'Flynn's island", the crannog which gave name to both the lake and subsequently the barony of Loughinsholin (*Loch Inse Uí Fhloinn*).

The development of the name into its current form is worthy of comment but in the absence of any references which would link the 17th-century spellings to the 19th-century forms we cannot make any definitive statements in this matter. Any theory of the development must take into account the shift in stress from the last syllable to the penultimate, as well as the intrusion of the *t* and *r* which we see in the modern form. The shift in stress may well have been facilitated by the same obvious analogy with English "money" and "sterling" (or perhaps the Scottish place-name Stirling) which has also led to the pronunciation of the final consonant as *ng*. Perhaps the simplest explanation is that the name was reanalysed, presumably in the 18th century, but what form this may have taken is uncertain.

Motalee　　　　　　　　　　　　Of uncertain origin
H 8792

1. monnaghtallen	Esch. Co. Map 14	1609
2. Monaghtolea	Charter of Londonderry 391	1613
3. Me Va Tulley	Lond. Comp. Valuation 307	1613
4. Mavatully	Phillips MSS (Maps) Plate 24	1622
5. Moyachultie	Civ. Surv. iii 176	1654
6. Moyochilty	Civ. Surv. iii 177	1654
7. Monatoola	Bishop. Der. i 265	1657
8. Moyatelly	Census 136	1659c
9. Moyachulty	BSD(c) 63	1661
10. Moytally	HMR (Ó Doibhlin 2) 69	1663
11. Motalee	Sampson's Map	1813
12. Mottalee	Custom of County (OSNB) No. 8	1834c
13. Mottalee	Bar. Coll. (OSNB) No. 8	1834c
14. Mot-ta-'lee	OSNB Pron. No. 8	1834c
15. Mota lia "the stone mount, or grey mount"	MacCloskey's Stat. Report 60	1821
16. Móta laoich "the hero's moat"	J O'D (OSNB) No. 8	1834c
17. Mota-laoic "The moat of the hero"	Munn's Notes 132	1925
18. Mota-laogh "moat of calves"	Joyce iii 513	1925
19. ˌmɔtəˈliː	Local pronunciation	1993

The early spellings show quite clearly that this name cannot have originated from *Móta Laoich* or the like, but unfortunately, they do not give us a clear enough picture of the 17th-century pronunciation to offer a more authoritative derivation. They do, however, show that the *t* of the modern form is a reduced form of *cht*, a characteristic feature of East Ulster Irish.

Rosgarran　　　　　　　　　　*Ros Gearrán*
H 8893　　　　　　　　　　　　　"wooded height of the horses"

1. Rosgaveon	Lond. Comp. Valuation 307	1613
2. Rosgaron	Phillips MSS (Maps) Plate 24	1622
3. Rosskarran	Civ. Surv. iii 176	1654
4. Rossgarron	Civ. Surv. iii 189	1654
5. Rossegarran	Census 136	1659c

6. Rosskarran	BSD(c) 63	1661
7. Ragharron	HMR (Ó Doibhlin 2) 68	1663
8. Rosgarren	Sampson's Map	1813
9. Rosgarron	Custom of County (OSNB) No. 8	1834c
10. Rosgarran	OSNB No. 8	1834c
11. Rosgarron	Bar. Coll. (OSNB) No. 8	1834c
12. Ross-'gar-ron	OSNB Pron. No. 8	1834c
13. Rosgaran "beautiful underwood"	MacCloskey's Stat. Report 60	1821
14. Ros Garráin "point of the copse or shrubbery"	J O'D (OSNB) No. 8	1834c
15. Ros-garran "The point, or wood of the shrubbery"	Munn's Notes 132	1925
16. ˌrozˈgjarlən	Local pronunciation	1993
17. ˌrosˈgarən	Local pronunciation	1993

The word *ros*, which is cognate with Welsh *rhos* "moor" and Middle Breton *ros* "hill", usually denotes a wooded height or a promontory, and is commonly used in place-names (Lewis & Pedersen 1937, 21; *DIL* sv. 1 *ros*). Joyce notes that in the southern half of Ireland, *ros* is generally understood only in the sense wood, while in the north, this application is lost, and it means only a peninsula (*Joyce* i 443). It is indeed true that the sense peninsula is dominant in the North. A glance at the townland index reveals that the vast majority (approximately 70%) of names beginning with or comprising *Ros(s)* are found in the two counties of Fermanagh and Donegal. In Fermanagh, the high proportion of *Ros(s)*-names appears to be related to the large stretches of inland water that are to be found there, while in Donegal, the rugged coastline accounts for many such names. There is only a handful of *Ros(s)*-names in Cos Derry, Antrim, Down and Tyrone, and there are none at all in Armagh. Despite long stretches of coastline around Derry, Antrim and Down, few of these names appear to be associated with promontories, and *ros* must have been used in the sense "wooded height". The first element in the name Rosgarran is certainly used in this sense, for the townland stands at the western edge of high ground overlooking lower, flat land to the west and north.

The analysis of the second element presents more serious problems. Two 17th-century forms, albeit from related sources, seem to indicate that this element may have begun with a *c* rather than a *g*, and a further independent form could be amended to give *Raskarron* (3, 6–7). In Irish, *sc* and *sg* are interchangeable, but this does not apply across word boundaries where *c* and *g* normally remain distinct. Nevertheless, there is probably some room for confusion, particularly in the anglicization process, and it is not unlikely that a few incorrect spellings should arise.

Two possibilities therefore present themselves, *garrán* "grove" and *gearrán* which is the normal word for horse in East Ulster Irish (cf. **Lisgarron Point** *PNI* iii 61). O'Donovan's suggestion of *garrán* "grove" would have been treated sceptically by Joyce who notes that he could not find the word *garrán* "grove" in Ulster outside Monaghan (*Joyce* i 498). It does, indeed, appear to be absent from the recorded dialects of Ulster, but it does not follow that it was never used in the North. The existence of minor names such as **Garranbane** and **Garrane** in Co. Fermanagh, may indicate that the element did have some currency in the North at some stage, but it is worth noting that a mountain near Limerick was called *Gearrán Bán* (*O'Reilly* 701), and in the name **Garron Tower** in Co. Antrim we appear to be dealing with a metaphorical use of the word *gearrán* "gelding, horse". *Ros* is frequently qualified by names of animals in place-names, and where this is the case, the animal name frequently, although not exclusively, appears in the plural (see *Onom. Goed.* 584ff.), and so a form *Ros Gearrán* "wooded height of the horses" seems most probable here.

Irish *ros* is not uncommonly corrupted to "rose" in place-names (*PNI* i 154), and the name under discussion is now spectacularly corrupted to "Rosegarland", although the older pronunciation prevails in normal speech.

Roshure	*Ros Iúir*	
H 8691	"wooded height of the yew tree"	
1. rosuire	Esch. Co. Map 14	1609
2. Rosiare	Charter of Londonderry 391	1613
3. Rossara	Civ. Surv. iii 176	1654
4. Rosseacre	Bishop. Der. i 265	1657
5. Roshure	Census 136	1659c
6. Rossarra	BSD(c) 63	1661
7. Rosuer	HMR (Ó Doibhlin 2) 68	1663
8. Rossure	Sampson's Map	1813
9. Roshure	Custom of County (OSNB) No. 8	1834c
10. Roshure	Bar. Coll. (OSNB) No. 8	1834c
11. Rosure	OSNB No. 8	1834c
12. Rosh-'shure	OSNB Pron. No. 8	1834c
13. Ruis ur "beautiful valley (Cur vallis Hebraire, or wood of yew)"	MacCloskey's Stat. Report 60	1821
14. Ros iubhar "point of the yew"	J O'D (OSNB) No. 8	1834c
15. Ros-iubhair "The point/wood of the yew trees"	Munn's Notes 133	1925
16. rọˈʃuːr	Local pronunciation	1993

The first element *ros* here undoubtedly has the same meaning as in **Rosgarran**, namely, "wooded height", and again Roshure is situated on high ground overlooking low-lying land to the north and east. The final element is almost certainly *iúr* "yew tree". There are numerous occurrences of this word in place-names, and it is almost always used in the singular rather than the plural. Of almost 30 names containing the element listed in Hogan's *Onomasticon Goedelicum*, only one, *Achad na n-Iubhar*, contains a plural form (*Onom. Goed.* passim). Yew trees are, of course, thinly spread in Ireland, and this may partially account for the predominant use of the singular, but it is surely the great age which these trees can attain that marks them out as special. The 12th-century Book of Leinster makes reference to a place called *Senibar* "old yew tree" (*LL* iv 1.29162), and the Annals of the Four Masters describe the burning in 1146 of the yew tree "which Patrick himself had planted" at Newry (Irish *an tIúr* "the yew tree") (*PNI* i 1).

Stranagard	*Srath na gCeardaithe*	
H 8592	"river-meadow of the craftsmen"	
1. shruinishnagrrdie	Esch. Co. Map 14	1609
2. Sha Inishnagardy	Bishop. Der. i 57	1610

3.	Shra-Inishnagardy	CPR Jas I 279a	1615
4.	Shra-Inishuagardy	Bishop. Der. i 103	1615
5.	Strafinshnagardy	Bishop. Der. i 172	1633
6.	Strathnecarrie	Civ. Surv. iii 189	1654
7.	Stratnecarny & Moydron	BSD(c) 54	1661
8.	Stranagard	Sampson's Map	1813
9.	Stranagard	Custom of County (OSNB) No. 8	1834c
10.	Stranagard	OSNB No. 8	1834c
11.	Stranagard	Bar. Coll. (OSNB) No. 8	1834c
12.	Stran-a-'gard	OSNB Pron. No. 8	1834c

13.	Sraith na gairbhe "the rough marsh"	MacCloskey's Stat. Report 60	1821
14.	"the holme of the guard"	OSL (Derry) 107	1834
15.	Sráth na garda "holm of the guard"	J O'D (OSNB) No. 8	1834c
16.	Sraith-na-garda "The meadow of the guard houses"	Munn's Notes 133	1925

17.	ˌstranə'ga:rd	Local pronunciation	1993

O'Donovan notes that the ruins of a guard house of assizes stood in that part of the village of Desertmartin which was in the townland of Stranagard and translates the name "the holme of the guard" (OSL (Derry) 107). However, the name clearly predates the building of the guard house and, more importantly, garda "guard" is a late loan-word in Irish, borrowed from English or French (DIL sv. gárda). Hogan cites only a single example of this word in his corpus of Irish place-names, for **Ballynagard** in the parish of Templemore, Co. Derry, but unfortunately the reference he supplies is incorrect and the form cannot be verified (Onom. Goed. 86).

A more likely origin is from Srath na gCeardaithe "river-meadow of the craftsmen" which derives some support from two 17th-century sources which show -c- for -g- (6–7). Joyce cites several names which apparently contain references to the presence of craftsmen at various sites, most notably **Tullynagardy** in the parish of Newtownards, Co. Down, Irish Tulaigh na gCeardaithe "hillock of the artisans/artificers" (Joyce i 223-4; PNI ii 236).

Our 17th-century documentation points to an earlier form of the name, Srath Inis na gCeardaithe. As we have seen (**Iniscarn** above), inis is often used of a low-lying place near or partially surrounded by a river, and is thus frequently synonymous with srath "river-meadow". The land described here is undoubtedly the area of low-lying land to the south-west of Desertmartin between Keenaght Water and Grange Water.

Tirgan
H 8387

Torgán
"little tower"

1.	Torngan	Esch. Co. Map 14	1609
2.	Torrigan	Charter of Londonderry 391	1613
3.	Turgan	Lond. Comp. Valuation 309	1613
4.	Turgan	Phillips MSS (Maps) Plate 28	1622
5.	Turegan	Civ. Surv. iii 173	1654
6.	Tiretian	Civ. Surv. iii 176	1654

7. Tornagan	Bishop. Der. i 265	1657
8. Tirregan	Census 137	1659c
9. Tirretian	BSD(c) 62	1661
10. Tirrigan	HMR (Ó Doibhlin 2) 69	1663
11. Tirgan	Sampson's Map	1813
12. Tyrgan	Bar. Coll. (OSNB) No. 8	1834c
13. 'Tyr-gan	OSNB Pron. No. 8	1834c
14. Tir gain "the sandy land"	MacCloskey's Stat. Report 60	1821
15. Tír gann "scarce country, hungry country"	J O'D (OSNB) No. 8	1834c
16. Tuirgean or Turraichin or Torraigan	Munn's Notes 133	1925
17. "The land of the little peaks or round hills"	Munn's Notes 133	1925
18. 'tərgən	Local pronunciation	1993

The 17th-century spellings present a reasonably consistent picture of the pronunciation of this name throughout that period, with only a small number of obvious corruptions. There is a certain amount of fluctuation between a disyllabic and a trisyllabic form, and this suggests that there was an epenthetic vowel between the *r* and the *g* (O'Rahilly 1932, 190ff.). The vowel in the first syllable is written *o* and *u* in the earliest forms, but this soon gives way to the modern *i*. English *i* and *u* were originally distinct before *r*, but in the course of the 17th century the two sounds fell together under the influence of the *r* to give a centralized vowel [ə] (Barber 1976, 305–6), and this is doubtless the reason why *i* begins to appear in our forms at this stage.

All this points to an original Irish form *Torgán*, probably meaning "little tower", from *tor* "tower". *Tor*, from Latin *turris*, originally signified a "tower" or "fortified building", but in many parts of Ireland, most notably in Co. Donegal, it is applied to a tall rock resembling a tower (*DIL* sv. 2 *tor*; *Joyce* i 399). The ground at Tirgan rises to a high rocky point which is now called **Windy Castle**, and this might be taken as an indication that *tor* here denotes a "steep rocky height". The diminutive suffix does not always have a strictly diminutive meaning and is commonly used in place-names in the sense of "place" (e.g. *creagán* "rocky place").

Tor "bush" might also be considered a possible root of the name, although it does seem less likely (compare, however, the use of *muine* "thicket" and *craobh* "tree" in townland names). Nevertheless, the presence here of a feature such as Windy Castle invites the translation offered above, although there is not necessarily any continuity between the two names.

OTHER NAMES

Coolcalm House   A hybrid form
H 8592

1. Cullkanna Arrnagh being two towne lands	Civ. Surv. iii 176	1654
2. Cullkanna	Civ. Surv. iii 177	1654
3. Cullkanny	Civ. Surv. iii 177	1654

4. Culcam, Annagh and	Census 136	1659c
5. Cullkanna	BSD(c) 62	1661
6. Calcam and Annagh	HMR (Ó Doibhlin 2) 69	1663
7. Coolcam	Sampson's Map	1813
8. kul'ka:m	Local pronunciation	1993

Coolcalm House was formerly the residence of Mr Henry Kelly who built and named it (*OSRNB* 40 sh. 41). O'Donovan took it to be a fancy name, a compound of the English words "cool" and "calm" (*ibid.*), but there is ample evidence to show that the name is derived from that of a subdivision of the townland of Annagh and Moneysterlin which is documented as early as the 17th century. There are other townlands called Coolcam in Roscommon and Wexford, and three townlands called Coolcaum in Cork.

Unfortunately, the Irish form of the name is unclear. The second element is variously represented in the 17th-century sources, but as all the forms with *nn* occur in related documents (1-3, 5) we may safely conclude that the pronunciation of this element has not substantially changed (reading *nna* as *mm*). Joyce interprets the Coolcams in Roscommon and Wexford as *Cúl an Chaim* "back of the curve" (*Joyce* iii 242), but Price, probably correctly, takes the second element to be the adjective *cam* "bent" in a number of similar names in Wicklow (Price 1945-67, 168, 214, 224). The form of the Cork names and of some of the variants of the Wicklow names suggests the diphthongization of *a* before *m* that we find in southern dialects of Irish, so that only the adjective may be considered likely in those cases (O'Rahilly 1932, 49–50).

Dan's Brae
H 8191

A Scots form

1. dɛnz 'bre:	Local pronunciation	1993

Desertmartin
H 8592

See PARISH NAME

The origins of the village of Desertmartin lie in the early 17th century. As early as 1611, plans were being discussed for the erection of a fort here "fit for the King's service and the serving of travellers between Colraine and all parts of Tyrone and Armagh" (*Cal. Carew MSS* 1603–23 224–5). The fort was erected soon after 1613, and is depicted alongside the church and two houses on a map of the lands belonging to the Drapers' Company drawn up in 1622 (Moody 1939, 151; *Phillips' MSS (Maps)* Plate 28). Phillips encouraged the expansion of Desertmartin in order to counter the political and economic instability of the region at this time (Curl 1986, 186). For further discussion of the later history of the village see Fleming 1991; *Lewis' Top. Dict.* i 456–7.

Drummuck
H 8288

Droim Muice
"pig's back"

1. "Pig's Back"	OSRNB 43 sh.46	1850c
2. Druim Muice "pig's back"	OSRNB 43 sh.46	1850c

Drummuck was called *Droim Muice* "pig's back" on account of the hill's fancied resemblance to a pig's back (*OSRNB* 43, sh. 46).

Glenview	An English form
H 8588	

This name was given to the house by the man who built it, the Rev. James Wilson, a Presbyterian minister of Lecumpher meeting house, on account of the view of Reubens Glen (*OSRNB* 43 sh. 46).

Holly Mount	An English form
H 8591	

Undoubtedly named from the presence of holly trees on one of the flanking hills. The name was coined by a Mr Leper who came to live here about 1841 (*OSRNB* 40 sh. 41).

Iona House	An English form
H 8691	

Iona House was built about 1920 by Michael Hegarty who chose to name it after the island of Iona where St Columcille founded a monastery in 563 (D. Fleming, pers. comm.).

Lough Aber	*Loch Abair*
H 8794	"lake of the boggy ground"

All that is left of the lake which gave name to Lough Aber, Irish *Loch Abair* "lake of the boggy ground", is a marsh surrounded on all sides by bog.

Loughinsholin	See BARONY NAME
H 8492	

This small lake near the village of Desertmartin has given name to the Barony of Loughinsholin.

Reubens Glen Bridge	An English form
H 8588	

1. 'rubïnz ˌglɛn	Local pronunciation	1993

It is believed locally that Reubens Glen is named from a farmer called Reuben Archer who used to keep watch over the plantation in the glen. Nothing further is known about Mr Archer, but the ruins of his house are still pointed out on the Iniscarn Road (D. Fleming, pers. comm.). The 19th-century Revision Name Books claim, however, that the glen is named from a Reuben Thom (the surname is unclear) who formerly owned the land about it (*OSRNB* 43 sh. 46). This is surely more likely to be correct, and it seems that local tradition about the name has been revised to include reference to a better known character (cf. **Folly Hill** in the parish of Ballyscullion above).

Windy Castle	An English form
H 8287	

The Windy Castle is the name given to a portion of Slieve Gallion on account of its imagined resemblance to a castle. **Pierce's Castle** in the Mournes in Co. Down is also said to take its name from its similarity to a castle, and the element appears in a number of names of natural rocks in that same area (*PNI* iii 125, 129, 141, 147). Windy Castle may be a partial translation of *Torgán* "little tower" which is the Irish name for the townland of **Tirgan**, although it is possible that both names were applied independently to the same feature.

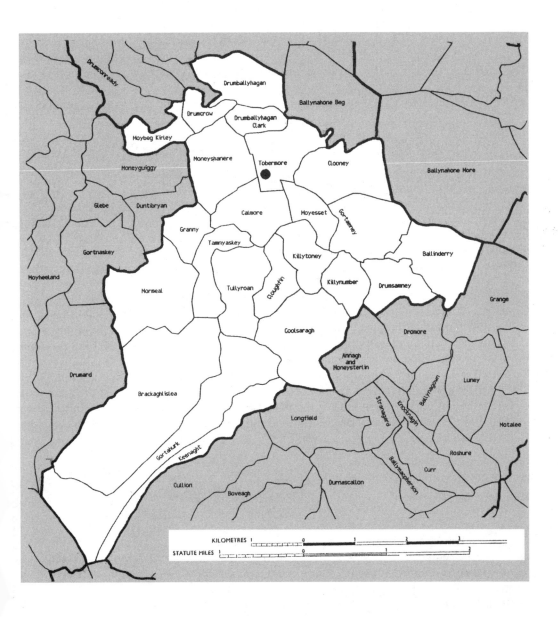

Parish of Kilcronaghan

Townlands	Drumcrow	Mormeal
Ballinderry	Drumsamney	Moybeg Kirley
Brackaghlislea	Gortahurk	Moyesset
Calmore	Gortamney	Tamnyaskey
Clooney	Granny	Tobermore
Cloughfin	Keenaght	Tullyroan
Coolsaragh	Killynumber	
Drumballyhagan	Killytoney	*Towns*
Drumballyhagan Clark	Moneyshanere	Tobermore

Based upon Ordnance Survey 1:50,000 mapping, with permission of the Director of the Ordnance Survey of Northern Ireland, Crown copyright reserved.

THE PARISH OF KILCRONAGHAN

The earliest references to the church of Kilcronaghan occur in various ecclesiastical documents stretching back as far as the beginning of the 14th century. It was a minor benefice, valued at only 6s. 8d. in the papal taxation of 1302-6 (*Eccles. Tax. (CDI)* 215), although it includes some of the richest portions of the valley of the River Moyola. Fragments of the medieval church seem to have been incorporated into an early 19th-century church, the ruins of which now stand in a neglected graveyard in the townland of Mormeal (Hamlin 1976, ii 577–8).

Under the conditions of the plantation, termon or erenagh land was retained by the bishops to whom rent was payable (Moody 1939, 88). In Kilcronaghan, the bishop's land comprised the four townlands of Granny, Tamnyaskey, Tullyroan, and Mormeal, and are so named as early as the middle of the 17th century (*Civ. Surv.* iii 187). Prior to this, the four townlands which constituted the termon or erenagh land are called "ballintrolla, Derreskerdan, Dirrygrinagh et Kellynahawla" (*Bishop. Der.* i 57) with some variation in spelling. There can be no doubt that these townlands are the same as the later church townlands, as they appear in precisely the right position on the Escheated Counties map (*Esch. Co. Map* 14) and are consistently identified as lands of the Bishop of Derry, but it is now impossible to match them to any of the modern townlands with any degree of certainty.

Following the plantation by the London Companies, the lands of the parish, excluding those held by the Church, were divided mainly between the Vintners and the Drapers, with a freehold at Tobermore and Grenan (obsolete) going to William Rowley (Curl 1986, 368). The Vintners were granted lands in the north and east of the parish, but the Drapers received by far the largest portion, constituting the remainder of the secular lands in the parish. The townland of Drumsamney was, under the conditions of the plantation, given as glebe by the Company of Drapers (*Bishop. Der.* i 145).

PARISH NAME

Kilcronaghan   *Cill Chruithneacháin*
                                 "St Cronaghan's church"

1. go Cill Cruineachāin	Cín Lae Ó M. 10	1645c
2. go Cill Cruinechan	Cín Lae Ó M. 5	1645c
3. I bporraist[e] Cill Cruinechan	Cín Lae Ó M. 5	1645c
4. Cill Cruinnechan	Top. Frag. 83	1675c
5. Cill Chroilichain	Top. Frag. 71	1680c
6. Kellcruchnathan	Eccles. Tax. (CDI) 215	1306c
7. Kylcronechan	Colton Vis. 76	1397
8. Kyllecronechan	Colton Vis. 82	1397
9. Killermiechan	Cal. Papal Letters x 283	1447
10. Kyllecimechan	Cal. Papal Letters x 375	1453
11. Killerunechan	Cal. Papal Letters x 706	1454
12. Kyllerunechan	Cal. Papal Letters x 726	1454
13. Kylcrunechayn, the rectory of	Annates Ulst. 225	1511
14. Killcronighan	CPR Jas I 376b	1609
15. Kilcronighan	CPR Jas I 376b	1609
16. Killcrunighan	Bishop. Der. i 57	1610
17. Kilcrinaghen	Bishop. Der. i 80	1611

18. Kilcrunighan, the termon or erenagh land of	CPR Jas I 279a	1615
19. Kilcrunighan	CPR Jas I 280a	1615
20. Kilcrunighan	Bishop. Der. i 102	1615
21. Kilcrinaghan	Bishop. Der. i 109	1615
22. Killcrenaghan, R'c'oria de	Bishop. Der. i 129	1617c
23. Killcronohan	Bishop. Der. i 145	1624c
24. Killcronahan	Bishop. Der. i 145	1624c
25. Killcrenehan	Bishop. Der. i 180	1634?
26. Kilkrenaghan	Civ. Surv. iii 167	1654
27. Killkrenaghan	Civ. Surv. iii 174	1654
28. Killcranughan	Civ. Surv. iii 175	1654
29. Killcrenaghan	Civ. Surv. iii 175,176	1654
30. Killrenaghan	Civ. Surv. iii 175,176	1654
31. Killkrenaghan	Civ. Surv. iii 175,177,178	1654
32. Killkranaghan	Civ. Surv. iii 187	1654
33. Killnarahan, Part of the Parish of	Hib. Reg. Loughinsholin	1657c
34. Kilcranaghan	Census 135	1659c
35. Killcronaghan	Bishop. Der. i 342	1660
36. Kilcronaghan	Bishop. Der. i 326	1661
37. Kilcrennaghan	Bishop. Der. i 331	1661
38. Kilcrennan	Bishop. Der. i 331,332	1661
39. Kilcrenaghan	Bishop. Der. i 333	1661
40. Killcronaghan	Bishop. Der. i 343	1661
41. Killranaghan Parish	BSD(c) 52	1661
42. Killkrenaghan Parish	BSD(c) 61	1661
43. Killecronaghan	Bishop. Der. i 345	1661c
44. Kilcrenehan	Bishop. Der. i 359	1663
45. Kilcronaghan, The Parish of	HMR (Ó Doibhlin 2) 74	1663
46. Kilcrenanghan	Bishop. Der. i 398	1665c
47. Killighrumachan	Bishop. Der. i 405	1666
48. Kilcronaghan	Bishop. Der. i 415	1668
49. Killcronaghan	Bishop. Der. i 425	1669
50. Killcrenaghan	Bishop. Der. i 425	1669
51. Killecronaghan	Bishop. Der. ii 1	1671
52. Killcranaghan, Rec' de	Bishop. Der. ii 114	1686
53. Kilcranaghan	Bishop. Der. ii 479	1688
54. Killcrenaghan, S'ti Chirmachani	Bishop. Der. ii 136	1692
55. Killecrananagha'	Bishop. Der. ii 137	1692
56. Kilcrenaghan	Bishop. Der. ii 509	1700c
57. Killcronaghan	Par. Tithe Bk (OSNB) No. 9	1767
58. Killcronaghan R.	Sampson's Map	1813
59. Cill Cruithneacháin "St Cronachan's Church"	J O'D (OSNB) No. 9	1834c
60. Cill Cruithneachain	Colton Vis. 82n	1850
61. Cill-Cruithnechain "The church of St. Cronaghan"	Munn's Notes 183	1925

113

62. Cill Chruithneacháin	GÉ 235	1989
63. ˌkʲilˈkrɔnəxən	Local pronunciation	1993

The eponymous patron of the church of Kilcronaghan is assumed to have been the priest, called Cruithneachán in Irish, who fostered St Columcille as a child (*Adomnán* 466; *Colton Vis.* 82n). The name does not appear in any of the calendars of Irish saints and, in order to make a place for him in the calendar, Colgan has identified him with Cairiotan of Druim Lara, whose feast was celebrated on March 7 (*Acta SS Colgan* 600–1 [recte 510–11]), although there is no demonstrable connection between the two characters (*Reeves' Ad.* 191n).

TOWNLAND NAMES

Ballinderry
H 8695

Baile an Doire
"townland of the oakwood"

1. B:Derry	Esch. Co. Map 14	1609
2. Derrey	Lond. Comp. Valuation 307	1613
3. Derrey	Phillips MSS (Maps) Plate 24	1622
4. Ballinderry	Civ. Surv. iii 174	1654
5. Ballinderry, ye ½ towne of	Census 135	1659c
6. Ballinderry	BSD(c) 62	1661
7. Ballydery, half	HMR (Ó Doibhlin 2) 74	1663
8. Balenderry	Par. Tithe Bk (OSNB) No. 9	1767
9. Ballinderry	Sampson's Map	1813
10. Bal-lin-ˈder-ry	OSNB Pron. No. 9	1834c
11. Bal an doire "place of oaks"	MacCloskey's Stat. Report 61	1821
12. Baile an doire "town of the oak wood"	J O'D (OSNB) No. 9	1834c
13. Baile-an-daire "The townland of the oakgroves"	Munn's Notes 183	1925
14. Droichead Bhaile an Doire	GÉ 180	1989
15. Abhainn Bhaile an Doire	GÉ 180	1989
16. ˌbalənˈdɛri	Local pronunciation	1993

MacCloskey reports that wood, mostly fir but including some oak, had been found in the bog at Ballinderry (*MacCloskey's Stat. Report* 2). Although the name clearly derives from Irish *Baile an Doire* "townland of the oakwood", two of our earliest sources refer to it simply as *Derrey* (2-3), but as these documents are related there can be no doubt that this form represents a corruption of the original whereby an initial *B:* standing for *Bally* or *Ballin* has been omitted.

Brackaghlislea
H 8092

An Bhreacach "the speckled place"
+ *Lios Liath* "grey enclosure"

1. b:nebracky	Esch. Co. Map 14	1609

114

2. lislea	Esch. Co. Map 14	1609
3. Lislea, ⅔ parts of the ballibo of	Charter of Londonderry 391	1613
4. Ballymebracky	Charter of Londonderry 391	1613
5. Lislea, 1/3 part of the ballibo of	Charter of Londonderry 391	1613
6. Lisleah	Lond. Comp. Valuation 309	1613
7. Lisleah	Phillips MSS (Maps) Plate 28	1622
8. Breakagh-Lisslea	Civ. Surv. iii 175	1654
9. Ballynebracky	Bishop. Der. i 266	1657
10. Lislea	Bishop. Der. i 266	1657
11. Brackagh Listea	Census 135	1659c
12. Breakaghlissa	BSD(c) 62	1661
13. Brucklagh	HMR (Ó Doibhlin 2) 74	1663
14. Brackaghlislea	Sampson's Map	1813
15. 'Brack-agh-'lis-le	OSNB Pron. No. 9	1834c
16. (?)Brauagh "a spotted land"	MacCloskey's Stat. Report 61	1821
17. Breacach lis léith "speckled land of...grey fort"	J O'D (OSNB) No. 9	1834c
18. Breacach-lis-leith "The speckled grey fort"	Munn's Notes 183	1925
19. ˌbraklïs'le:	Local pronunciation	1993
20. ˌbrakrïs'le:	Local pronunciation	1993
21. ˌbrakïs'le:	Local pronunciation	1993

The townland of Brackaghlislea appears to be an amalgamation of two 17th-century town-lands called *Baile na Breacaí* "townland of the speckled place" and *Lios Liath* "grey fort", the latter being a very common townland name, particularly in the North. They appear side by side on the Escheated Counties map (1–2), and are separately listed in a number of other early sources. In the Charter of 1613, *Ballymebracky*, being one balliboe, and ⅓ part of the balliboe of *Lislea* are considered part of the proportion called *Cohoire*, while the remaining ⅔ of *Lislea* are reckoned as part of the proportion of *Cynah* (3–5). *Lisleah* alone appears in the Valuation of the lands of the London Companies and the 1622 map of the lands belong-ing to the Drapers' company (6–7). There is no sign in either of these sources of Ballynebracky and it is unclear whether this has been accidently omitted or whether Lisleah is meant to include both areas. The townland next crops up in the Civil Survey in 1654 where we find, for the first time, something similar to the modern form of the name (8).

The modern name has resulted from the compounding of the names of the two earlier townlands, although the first element clearly reflects an underlying shortened form *An Bhreacach* "the speckled place", which is possibly represented in the Hearth Money Rolls (13), rather than the better attested *Baile na Breacaí* "townland of the speckled place". This type of variation between forms with and without the element *baile* "townland" is not uncommon in the place-names of this area (see **Cavanreagh, Labby, Owenreagh, Moyard** and **Tullybrick** in the parish of Ballynascreen).

Calmore   *An Coll Mór*
H 8295   "the great/large hazel"

1. san Chall Mōr	Cín Lae Ó M. 5	1645c
2. Calemore	Esch. Co. Map 14	1609
3. Culemoire	Charter of Londonderry 391	1613
4. Call Moore	Lond. Comp. Valuation 309	1613
5. Coolmor	Phillips MSS (Maps) Plate 28	1622
6. Kallmore	Civ. Surv. iii 174	1654
7. Callmore	Civ. Surv. iii 175,176	1654
8. Calemore	Bishop. Der. i 265	1657
9. Calmoore & Cloghfin	Census 136	1659c
10. Kallmore	BSD(c) 62	1661
11. Culmore	HMR (Ó Doibhlin 2) 74	1663
12. Calmore	Par. Tithe Bk (OSNB) No. 9	1767
13. Calmore	Sampson's Map	1813
14. Caul-'more	OSNB Pron. No. 9	1834c
15. Coll mer "the great head"	MacCloskey's Stat. Report 61	1821
16. Coll mór "great hazel"	J O'D (OSNB) No. 9	1834c
17. Coll-mor "The townland of the great hazel tree"	Munn's Notes 183	1925
18. "great hazel"	Joyce iii 160	1925
19. kal'mo:r	Local pronunciation	1993
20. kɔl'mo:r	Local pronunciation	1993

Calmore appears to have formerly been a place of some importance, although little is known of its early history. There was a crannog here until the beginning of the 19th century when it was dismantled (Speer 1990, 43). Crannogs were defensive structures built on artificial islands, and seem to have been inhabited by the more powerful members of society (Mallory & McNeill 1991, 124–5). There was also once a castle here west of Tobermore, although nothing now remains of it as the rubble was carried off by the tenant, John McKee, for building work (*NISMR* sh. 36 §17; *Munn's Notes* 183). According to local tradition, the castle was built by Shane More O'Hagan, who was succeeded in it by his son William O'Hagan and later by Owen Roe O'Hagan (*OSM* xxxi 69). It was inhabited by the Rowleys at the outbreak of the rebellion of 1641, but seems then shortly afterwards to have fallen back into Irish hands. It was finally burnt by the Irish in 1689 or 1690 (*ibid.* 87; *MacCloskey's Stat. Report* 13; *Munn's Notes* 183). It was known by several names: O'Hagan's Castle after its first occupants, but later Rowley's Castle and Calmore Castle.

Despite a few anomalous 17th-century spellings (on which see below), there can be little doubt that the name Calmore derives from Irish *Coll Mór* "great or large hazel", as suggested in the last century by John O'Donovan. Ó Ceallaigh (1950(a), 177), a native of Ballynascreen, claims that the spelling found in Ó Mealláin's Journal (1) "does not conform to the local pronunciation of *coll*, "a hazel tree", but the change of *o* to *a* is a well-attested phenomenon in certain words in Northern Irish. *Coll* was frequently spelt *call* in medieval Irish (*DIL* sv. 1 *coll*), and is still pronounced *call* in Donegal (O'Rahilly 1932, 192–3). The pronunciation with *a* is also apparent in some place-names. **Shankill** in the parish of Aghaderg in Co. Down, for example, was always spelt with an *a* in the second syllable until more recent times, and is probably derived from *Seancholl* meaning "old hazel" (see also *Joyce* iii 160). J.B. Arthurs (1956(b), 31) appears to reject the possibility of *coll* "a hazel" in this and other names in the North and proposes a variety of unattested elements meaning something like either "marsh" or "high ground", but his evidence is scant and inconclusive.

O'Donovan records a tradition that a very extensive wood once stood in Calmore and cites the testimony of Maelseaghlin McNamee who claimed that a large oak tree was felled by a storm in this townland in his father's time. It was called the Royal Oak from its majestic appearance and was so large that two men on horse-back, on both sides of it, could not see each other's heads over its trunk as it lay stretched along the ground (*OSL (Derry)* 111). However, it is unlikely that this oak is in any way related to the name of the townland.

The majority of the 17th-century spellings are spelt with *a* in the first syllable, indicating the sort of origin suggested here. There are a small number of anomalous spellings which apparently would indicate an original first element *cúil* "corner, nook", but all the variations can easily be accounted for. The most remarkable form is that from the Phillips' map of the Drapers' lands (5), but the place-names on this map are copied from the Valuation of 1613 or a closely related source so that this spelling must be a mistake. There are only two other anomalous forms, in both of which *u* is written for *a* in this element. This variation is open to a number of interpretations but the most probable cause is that *a* has been misread as *u*, either by the modern editors of the texts concerned, or by the early scribes who made the copies on which we depend. This is almost certainly the case in the Hearth Money Rolls (11) where *u* is elsewhere written for *a* (see **Brackaghlislea** above). The Charter of 1613 (3), in which the other misspelling occurs, is closely related to both the Escheated Counties Maps and the Charter of 1657 and, as both these documents contain an *a* in this element, we may safely conclude that the *u* in the earlier charter is a mistake.

Clooney
H 8496

An Chluanaidh
"the meadow"

1. B:neclouy	Esch. Co. Map 14	1609
2. Ballmeclom	Charter of Londonderry 391	1613
3. Ba: ne Clon	Lond. Comp. Valuation 307	1613
4. Belliclan	Civ. Surv. iii 174	1654
5. BelliClan	Civ. Surv. iii 174	1654
6. Ballinacleny	Bishop. Der. i 265	1657
7. Clone, Ye ½ towne of	Census 135	1659c
8. (?)Cloane	HMR (Ó Doibhlin 2) 76	1663
9. (?)Clone	HMR (Ó Doibhlin 2) 77	1663
10. Clooney	Par. Tithe Bk (OSNB) No. 9	1767
11. Cloan	Sampson's Map	1813
12. 'Clo-ne	OSNB Pron. No. 9	1834c
13. Cluain "a level recess between woods"	MacCloskey's Stat. Report 61	1821
14. Cluain "a lawn, meadow or bog island"	J O'D (OSNB) No. 9	1834c
15. Cluainidhe "The Meadows"	Munn's Notes 184	1925
16. 'klo:ni	Local pronunciation	1993
17. 'kloni	Local pronunciation	1993

While working on this parish for the Ordnance Survey, John O'Donovan recommended that the modern form of the name should be spelt "Cloan", but in the Ordnance Survey Name

Books this has been scored out and replaced by a form "Cloney" based on the "received usage" of the time. The spelling was again reviewed at some later stage and emended further to produce the modern form Clooney. Clearly, the two variants were in use at this time, and both are based on different forms of the word *cluain* "meadow".

The 17th-century spellings reveal yet another form of the name. The Escheated Counties map of Loughinsholin and the charters of 1613 and 1657 are all related, and the spellings contained therein are doubtless corruptions of an original *Ballyneclony* or the like, representing Irish *Baile na Cluana* "townland of the meadow". The form in the 1613 Valuation (3) provides independent evidence in support of this etymology.

Cloughfin
H 8394

Cloch Fhionn
"white stone"

1. cloghom	Esch. Co. Map 14	1609
2. Cloghom	Charter of Londonderry 391	1613
3. Cloghfine	Lond. Comp. Valuation 309	1613
4. Cloughtym	Phillips MSS (Maps) Plate 28	1622
5. Clowghfin	Civ. Surv. iii 176	1654
6. Cloughfin	Civ. Surv. iii 176	1654
7. Cloghony	Bishop. Der. i 265	1657
8. Cloghfin	Census 136	1659c
9. Clohtine	HMR (Ó Doibhlin 2) 74	1663
10. Cloughfin	Par. Tithe Bk (OSNB) No. 9	1767
11. Cloghfin	Sampson's Map	1813
12. Clock-'fin	OSNB Pron. No. 9	1834c
13. Clochfinn "the white stone"	MacCloskey's Stat. Report 61	1821
14. Cloch fionn "white stone"	J O'D (OSNB) No. 9	1834c
15. Cloch-fionn "The White Stone"	Munn's Notes 184	1925
16. klɔx'fïn	Local pronunciation	1993

There seems no reason to doubt the suggested origin of this name despite the presence of some irreconcilable forms in a group of related sources (1–2, 7: the absence of *f* reflects lenition of this consonant, and the *m* may be read as *in* but the *o* is peculiar). The second element is almost certainly *fionn* "white", although some connection with the legendary character Finn McCool cannot be ruled out (cf. **Cloughfin**, parish of Ballynascreen). There appears to be no trace now of the rock to which the name originally referred.

Coolsaragh
H 8393

Cúil Sáráin (?)
"Sárán's recess"

1. Cowsaran	Esch. Co. Map 14	1609
2. Consaran	Charter of Londonderry 391	1613
3. Colsanan	Lond. Comp. Valuation 309	1613
4. Coolsaram	Phillips MSS (Maps) Plate 28	1622
5. Cullsarran	Civ. Surv. iii 174	1654
6. Consaren	Bishop. Der. i 265	1657
7. Coolesahan	Census 135	1659c

8. Cullsaran	BSD(c) 61	1661
9. Culfanum	HMR (Ó Doibhlin 2) 74	1663
10. Culsaragh	Par. Tithe Bk (OSNB) No. 9	1767
11. Coolsarah	Sampson's Map	1813
12. Cool-'sarragh	OSNB Pron. No. 9	1834c
13. Coile scarra "corna for mowing scarra, scythe"	MacCloskey's Stat. Report 61	1821
14. Cul Sharuighthe "the back place of violence"	OSL (Derry) 131	1834
15. Cul saraide "Sara's back hill"	J O'D (OSNB) No. 9	1834c
16. Cul-saruighthe "The hill back of the slaughter"	Munn's Notes 184	1925
17. ˌkulˈsɑrə	Local pronunciation	1993

In a letter from Moneymore dated September 29th, 1834, John O'Donovan recounts a tradition that the name Coolsaragh derives from a massacre that took place there shortly after that at Island Magee (*OSL (Derry)* 131). Eighteen Scottish families, the story goes, settled in the neighbourhood, slaughtering the Irish occupants of the land, whence the name *Cul Sharuighthe* "the back place of violence, slaughter or massacre" (see also *Munn's Notes* 184).

However, the earliest available evidence clearly shows that this cannot be the origin of the name. The 17th-century documents contain several obvious spelling errors, notably *n* for *r* in the Valuation of 1613 (3), *h* for *r* in the Census of c.1659 (7), and *f* for *s* in the Hearth Money Rolls (9), but a form something like *Culsaran* or *Coolsaran* can easily be discerned. Loss of final *n* is not a regular development but it is attested in other Irish place-names. Islandeady in Co. Mayo has lost its final *n*, a development which is even reflected in the form used among Irish speakers of the last century, *Oileán Éadaí* (Ó Muraíle 1985, 50), and the townland of **Ednego** in Co. Down has lost its final *n*. It is perhaps best explained in the present context as the result of an omission in writing of the contraction frequently used to represent *n* in early documents.

It is quite possible that the final word here is *során* "wireworm", with the common development in this dialect of *o* to *a* (cf. *sor* "louse, tick" which has early variant forms *sor* and *sar*, *DIL* sv. 2 *sor*), suggesting an original Irish form *Cúil Során* "recess of the wireworms". Wireworms attack the roots of tuberous plants and are a formidable pest to farmers, so that it is not unlikely that they would have been deemed worthy of notice in place-names. Indeed, various other insects have left their mark on Irish place-names (see *Joyce* ii 291ff.), but perhaps of greatest note in this regard is the name of the townland of **Culnagrew** in the parish of Killelagh which appears to derive from *Cúil na gCnumh* "recess of the maggots". See also **Killysorrell** in Co. Down.

However, the absence of the article meaning "the" from this place-name may suggest that the final element is either an obsolete noun or a personal name. The personal name *Sárán* was borne by, among others, several saints and an early king of Ulster (Ó Corráin & Maguire 1981, 161). The parish of Kilsaran (*Cill Sáráin* "Sárán's church") in Co. Louth is named after one saint of the name, as is Tisaran (*Teach Sáráin* "Sárán's house") in Co. Offaly (*L. Log. Lú* 2; *L. Log. Uíbh Fhailí* 3; *Onom. Goed.* 211, 626). Thus, while we cannot be certain about the origin of this name, we might reasonably propose an original *Cúil Sáráin* "Sárán's recess".

Drumballyhagan
H 8298

Droim Bhaile Uí Ágáin
"ridge of O'Hagan's townland"

1. dromballiagan	Esch. Co. Map 14	1609
2. Dromballyagan	Charter of Londonderry 391	1613
3. Balle Hagan	Lond. Comp. Valuation 307	1613
4. Balle Hagan	Phillips MSS (Maps) Plate 24	1622
5. Drombellihaggon	Civ. Surv. iii 174,175	1654
6. Drumbellihaggan	Civ. Surv. iii 175	1654
7. Dromballiagan	Bishop. Der. i 266	1657
8. Drumballyhagan	Census 136	1659c
9. Drombellihaggan	BSD(c) 62	1661
10. Drumbolehagan	HMR (Ó Doibhlin 2) 74	1663
11. Drumballyhagan	Par. Tithe Bk (OSNB) No. 9	1767
12. Drumballyhagan	Sampson's Map	1813
13. Drum-bally-'haygan	OSNB Pron. No. 9	1834c
14. Druim baile "place on the back"	MacCloskey's Stat. Report 61	1821
15. Druim bhaile Uí Agáin "Ridge of O'Hagan's town"	J O'D (OSNB) No. 9	1834c
16. Druim-baile-ui-Again "The hill-ridge of the O'Hagans"	Munn's Notes 184	1925
17. ˌdrǫmˌbaliˈhagən	Local pronunciation	1993

The proposed origin of this name is reasonably certain. O'Hagan is recorded as one of the principal Irish names in the barony of Loughinsholin in the so-called Census of c.1659 (*Census* 139), and the castle at **Calmore** was occupied by O'Hagans (see above). A report on the tenantry of the Drapers' proportion, drawn up by John Rowley in 1614, shows that many balliboes were then let to Irish, including the O'Hagans (Moody 1939, 332), and the name seems to have been particularly common in the neighbouring parishes of Ballynascreen and Desertmartin (*HMR (Ó Doibhlin 2)* 82).

The inflection of the surname is of some interest. In the nominative form of Ó-names, the Ó causes *h* to be prefixed to a following vowel (Hagan < *Ó hÁgáin*, Henry < *Ó hInnéirghe*, O'Higgin < *Ó hUiginn*), but this is dropped in the genitive singular (*Uí Ágáin, Uí Innéirghe, Uí Uiginn* in the above examples). This dropping of the *h* is reflected in some of our early forms (1–2, 7), but has been restored in the later forms by analogy with the nominative form of the surname (O'Hagan).

The first element, which is clearly *droim* "a ridge", has been omitted in two early sources (3–4). However, these two documents are closely related and it is virtually certain that this shortened form of the name is the result of an accidental omission in a single exemplar.

More serious reservations must be expressed in relation to the *bally* part of the name. It is often difficult to distinguish between *baile* "a townland" and *béal átha* "approach to a ford" in place-names as both are frequently anglicized *bally* (Ballyshannon in Co. Donegal, for example, comes from Irish *Béal Átha Seanaidh*). Indeed, Drumballyhagan is bordered on the south by the Moyola River, although there is no evidence of a ford here. An *e*, perhaps suggesting *béal átha*, occurs in several related sources (5–6, 9) but this frequently represents *baile* in these sources. However, *béal átha* is rarely qualified by personal or surnames in place-names (see *GÉ* 31–34), whereas *baile* is frequently found in such combinations, and we can reasonably propose an original *Droim Bhaile Uí Ágáin* "ridge of O'Hagan's townland".

Drumballyhagan Clark   A hybrid form
H 8297

See **Drumballyhagan**. Drumballyhagan Clark is not documented in the 17th century and it is clearly a later formation. The affixing of native and planter surnames to pre-existent place-names in order to create new divisions is not uncommon (see **Moneystaghan-Ellis** and **Moneystaghan-Macpeake** in the parish of Tamlaght O'Crilly, and **Ballynease-Helton**, **Ballynease-Macpeake** and **Ballynease-Strain** in the parish of Ballyscullion).

Drumcrow   *Droim Cró*
H 8197   "bloody ridge"

1.	Drum Crowor	Lond. Comp. Valuation 307	1613
2.	Drom Crow	Phillips MSS (Maps) Plate 24	1622
3.	Drumcrow	Civ. Surv. iii 174	1654
4.	Drumcroe	Census 136	1659c
5.	Half Dromcrow	BSD(c) 62	1661
6.	Drumero	HMR (Ó Doibhlin 2) 74	1663
7.	Drumcrow	Par. Tithe Bk (OSNB) No. 9	1767
8.	half Drumcro	Sampson's Map	1813
9.	Drum-'crow	OSNB Pron. No. 9	1834c
10.	Druim cro "back of the hill with nuts"	MacCloskey's Stat. Report 61	1821
11.	Druim cró "ridge of the hovel or fold for cattle"	J O'D (OSNB) No. 9	1834c
12.	Druim-cruadh "The hard ridge"	Munn's Notes 184	1925
13.	drọm'kro:	Local pronunciation	1993

There are numerous places called Drumcrow in the northern half of Ireland, mostly in Ulster. There are Drumcrows in Antrim, Armagh, Donegal, Fermanagh, Monaghan, and Tyrone, with the highest incidence being in Cavan where there are six distinct occurrences. In addition, we may also consider in this category **Drumcro** and **Drumcro and Drumo** in Co. Down. While not all these names are necessarily of the same origin, the frequency with which the name type occurs suggests that there may be some obvious connection between the two elements.

The suggestion that the second element in this name represents Irish *cnó* "nut" (10) is not supported by the earliest forms. *Cnó* is, indeed, pronounced *cró* in modern Northern Irish, but the change is comparatively late and there is little trace of it in anglicized names of the late 16th and early 17th centuries (O'Rahilly 1932, 22–3). The majority of our townland names containing the element *cnoc* "a hill" are anglicized as *Knock* (the *k* in English *kn* was pronounced until well into the 17th century), while in more recently anglicized names of hills it is frequently represented as *Crock* (*ibid.* 23).

Irish *ua* is frequently anglicized [o:] in townland names and so Munn postulates an origin from *crua* "hard" (12). However, *crua*, historically *cruaidh*, is pronounced [kru:i] in Ulster, and in the few names where it occurs it is anglicized *croy* (*Joyce* ii 477; *PNI* iii 35; see also **Carrowcroey**, Ballintoy, Co. Antrim).

Mac Giolla Easpaig (1986, 78) notes that *cró* is a common element in west Donegal where it signifies "a glen enclosed on three sides", but O'Donovan records the more usual mean-

121

ing of "a small hovel; a fold for sheep" in Derry (*OSL (Derry)* 22; cf. *Ó Dónaill* sv. *cró* 1 "hollow, hole"). Joyce cites a number of names containing the element which he thinks normally denotes "hut, fold, pen for cattle" in place-names (*Joyce* ii 225).

However, there are serious problems with this interpretation. *Cró* "hut, fold, enclosure" gives gen. sing. *craoi* up until the end of the Early Modern Irish period (Greene 1983, 4), and we might expect this inflection to appear in the earliest forms (note in particular the 16th-century forms for **Drumcro** in the parish of Kilkeel, cited *PNI* iii 35). Moreover, although the article does not appear in the earliest Irish place-names, it was widely adopted in names of this type after the 11th century (Flanagan 1980, 41). If Drumcrow belongs to the earlier phase with no article, then we should almost certainly expect it to have shown signs of the earlier inflection, yet it cannot belong to the later phase with the article for there is no indication of it in any of the historical forms. These difficulties might be avoided by taking *cró* in these names as a plural rather than singular, and supposing that they all belong to the earlier phase.

Hogan cites a number of names containing a gen. form *cró* and the early dates of his sources indicate that it cannot be singular, although a plural form may be acceptable in a number of cases (as in *Achad na Cró*, cited *Onom. Goed.* 10). However, the context of several of these names clearly suggests that we have here the noun *cró* "blood, gore" (earlier *crú*, gen. sing. *cró*). Early Irish *crú* was frequently used in the gen. with the effect of an adjective and the article would not be expected in such a construction (cf., for example, *Cnoc Fola* for Bloody Foreland in Donegal). Of particular interest here is the name *Druim Cró* which is given in an early Irish poem as an older name for Drumcree in Co. Westmeath. It was the site of a battle and the editor of the text concludes, probably quite rightly, that the intended meaning of the final element was "blood, gore" (*Met. Dinds.* iv 386).

Another *Droim Cró* is mentioned in a poem on Domhnall Óg Ua Domhnaill, king of Tír Chonaill, by Giolla Brighde Mac Con Midhe, but there is no clear evidence of a battle having being fought here (*Poems Giolla Brighde* 78). The editor of the poem takes it to be the same name as that cited by Hogan (*ibid.* 287) but the subject matter makes it quite clear that it was located in Donegal and it is almost certainly the townland of Drumcrow in the barony of Raphoe.

Clearly, further research into other similar place-names might help to shed some light on the name currently under discussion, but from the available evidence an origin from *Droim Cró* "bloody ridge" seems most likely. It would be particularly interesting to know if battles can be associated with any of the sites. A ridge is, in many ways, an ideal defence-attack position in a medieval battle. The area to be defended on top of the hill is small, and any aggressor must first face an uphill struggle against a barrage of missiles thrown from above. Moreover, the defending army can easily and swiftly switch to an attacking force and launch an attack with all the additional momentum and advantage of a downhill charge. Of course, it could be objected that it would be curious if some memory of an ancient battle were not preserved in a place which takes its name from it, and we should not lose sight of the possibility that *cró* may be used in a metaphorical sense. It is perhaps significant in this regard that there are 12 townlands, exclusively in the North, called Drumderg, most of which probably come from *Droim Dearg* "red ridge" (see **Drumderg** in Ballinascreen parish).

Drumsamney	*Droim Samhna*	
H 8594	"ridge of *Samhain*"	
1. dromsauna	Esch. Co. Map 14	1609
2. Dromsanna	Charter of Londonderry 391	1613

3. Drumsawne	Phillips MSS (Maps) Plate 28	1622
4. Dromsany	Civ. Surv. iii 174,189	1654
5. Drumsany	Civ. Surv. iii 189	1654
6. Dromsaima	Bishop. Der. i 265	1657
7. Drumsanny	Hib. Reg. Loughinsholin	1657c
8. Dromsany	BSD(c) 54	1661
9. Drumsavunia	HMR (Ó Doibhlin 2) 74	1663
10. Dromsana	Hib. Del. Derry	1672c
11. Drumsamney	Sampson's Map	1813
12. Drum-'sam-ne	OSNB Pron. No. 9	1834c
13. Druim samhna "the pleasant back of the hill"	MacCloskey's Stat. Report 61	1821
14. Druim Samhna "ridge of Allhallowtide sports	J O'D (OSNB) No. 9	1834c
15. Druim-samhna "The ridge of Samhain"	Munn's Notes 184	1925
16. ˌdrọm'samni	Local pronunciation	1993

The initial element in this name is undoubtedly *droim* "a ridge" and probably refers to the hill now known as Drumsamney Hill. The second and final element is not as immediately obvious but there seems to be no good reason for departing from the form suggested by previous authorities. *Samhain*, which fell on the 1st of November, was a pagan festival and it appears to have left its mark on a number of place-names throughout the country (*Joyce* i 202-4). We may compare in particular **Drumsawna Beg** and **Drumsawna More** in Co. Fermanagh (*ibid.* 203–4).

The range of historical spellings collected here clearly requires some explanation. One of the best forms is that found on the Escheated Counties map of 1609 (1), but this has been corrupted in the related charters of 1613 and 1657 (2, 6). Similar errors occur in the documents relating to the Civil Survey (4-5) and the Down Survey (7, 10) with *nn* giving *n* in some cases. The degree to which modern editors are responsible for this confusion is uncertain, but there seems to be little doubt that all these variations represent an original form, *Dromsauna*. The remaining forms tend to confirm our idea of the pronunciation of this name in the 17th century (3, 9). The latter appears still to be somewhat corrupt, again due to confusion of minims in letters such as *u* and *n*, but it is probably intended to represent something like *Drumsawna*.

Gortahurk
H 8191

Gort an Choirce
"field of the oats"

1. gortIchorchy	Esch. Co. Map 14	1609
2. Gortihorky	Charter of Londonderry 391	1613
3. Gort Okorte	Lond. Comp. Valuation 309	1613
4. Gortocork	Phillips MSS (Maps) Plate 28	1622
5. Gortcork	Civ. Surv. iii 174	1654
6. Gortcorke	Civ. Surv. iii 175	1654
7. Gortihorky	Bishop. Der. i 265	1657
8. Gortikorky	Census 135	1659c

9. Gortcork	BSD(c) 61	1661
10. Gortkirk	HMR (Ó Doibhlin 2) 74	1663
11. Gortahurk	Par. Tithe Bk (OSNB) No. 9	1767
12. Gortahork	Sampson's Map	1813
13. Gort-a-'hoirk	OSNB Pron. No. 9	1834c
14. Gorta coirce "the field for oats"	MacCloskey's Stat. Report 61	1821
15. Gort a' choirce "field of the oats"	J O'D (OSNB) No. 9	1834c
16. Gort-a-choirce "The field of the Oats"	Munn's Notes 184	1925
17. ˌgɔrtəˈhɔrk	Local pronunciation	1993
18. ˌgɔrtneˈhərk	Local pronunciation	1993

There seems to be little doubt that this townland derives its name from a field used for the growing of oats. Some of the early spellings, however, appear to suggest a surname as the final element. Most notable among these are the form on the map of 1609 with its capital *I* mimicking Irish *Uí* (from *Ó*), and the form in the 1613 Valuation with its capital *O*. The use of capitals in both these instances seems to indicate that the scribe felt that the final element was a surname, and the *O* reinforces this perception (*O* being occasionally substituted for the grammatically correct genitive *I* < Irish *Uí*). However, no suitable surname is attested in any of the major works on Irish surnames. Moreover, the scribe of the 1609 map elsewhere writes capital *I* in the middle of names where there is no possibility of it forming part of a surname (see **Lecumpher** and **Gortanewry** in the parish of Desertmartin, and possibly **Gortamney** below), and elsewhere scribes occasionally write -*O*- in place-names where they imagine there to be a surname.

Gortamney
H 8595

Gort an tSamhraidh
"the summer field"

1. gortftaury	Esch. Co. Map 14	1609
2. Gortitawry	Charter of Londonderry 391	1613
3. Gourt Tawrey	Lond. Comp. Valuation 309	1613
4. Gort Tawey	Phillips MSS (Maps) Plate 28	1622
5. Gortitaumpher	Civ. Surv. iii 175	1654
6. Gortitanry	Bishop. Der. i 265	1657
7. Gortitamphree	BSD(c) 62	1661
8. Gortanry	HMR (Ó Doibhlin 2) 74	1663
9. Gortamney	Sampson's Map	1813
10. Gort-'tam-ne	OSNB Pron. No. 9	1834c
11. Gortamonadh "the field of division"	MacCloskey's Stat. Report 61	1821
12. Gort-tamhnaigh "garden field"	J O'D (OSNB) No. 9	1834c
13. Gort-tamhnach "The tilled field of the residence"	Munn's Notes 185	1925
14. ˌgɔrˈtaːmni	Local pronunciation	1993

With the aid of the historical spellings assembled here we can see that this name has under-gone some considerable change. There can be little doubt that the original form of the name as represented in our earliest spellings was *Gort an tSamhraidh* "the summer field". Names of the seasons do occasionally occur in Irish place-names. **Annasamry** in the parish of Loughgall, Co. Armagh, is said to derive from *Eanach an tSamhraidh* "summer marsh", and it is hardly coincidental that there is a place within the townland called Summer Island (Ó Mainnín 1989–90, 204). Most noteworthy in the present context is, perhaps, the townland of **Lurgantamry** in the parish of Donaghcloney, Co. Down, which may derive from Irish *Lorgain an tSamhraidh* (see *Joyce* ii 469). In this case, the name may denote a field which dried out only in the summer or which provided a summer crop.

Irish non-palatal *mh* was originally pronounced [v], but at some stage it was vocalized leaving a strong nasal trace on the previous vowel which is still audible in many parts today. This produced some rather unexpected effects in place-names, most of which are reflected in the various forms of this name. Ignoring the *n* of some forms which is clearly a mistran-scription of *u* (6, 8), we can see traces of the nasal quality in the spellings with -*mph*- (cf. *Joyce* i 64–5), and in the *m* of the modern form (cf. **Drumsamney** above).

The change of original *r* to *n* may be due to the effect of the strong nasal element, but reconstruction by analogy with the common place-name element *tamhnach*, gen. sing. *tamh-nai*, is probably more likely. One further development which is worth noting is the shorten-ing of the name from *Gortitawry* to its modern trisyllabic form. This concatenation is here due to haplology, and it seems to have occurred as early as the second decade of the 17th century, although the longer form continued to be used well into the middle of the century. The earliest form, that from the Escheated Counties map of Loughinsholin, has what appears to be *f* where the related sources have *i*, and it is almost certain that this is a mistake for a capital *I* such as is found in other names on the same map (see **Gortahurk** above).

Granny	*Greanaigh*	
H 8195	"gravelly place"	

1. (?)durngrunagh	Esch. Co. Map 14	1609
2. Granny	Civ. Surv. iii 177	1654
3. Cranne	Civ. Surv. iii 187	1654
4. Cranny	Hib. Reg. Loughinsholin	1657c
5. Mirmihellgrany	Census 135	1659c
6. Cranny	BSD(c) 52	1661
7. Grenaghan	Bishop. Der. i 343	1661c
8. Crinney	HMR (Ó Doibhlin 2) 74	1663
9. Cranny	Hib. Del. Derry	1672c
10. Cranny	Lamb Maps Derry	1690c
11. Granny	Sampson's Map	1813
12. 'Gran-ne	OSNB Pron. No. 9	1834c
13. Crannidh "the trees"	MacCloskey's Stat. Report 61	1821
14. Greanach "gravelly"	J O'D (OSNB) No. 9	1834c
15. Greanach "gravelly place"	Joyce ii 374	1875
16. Greanach "The gravelly place"	Munn's Notes 185	1925
17. 'grani	Local pronunciation	1993

The historical spellings show a variation between initial *g* and *c* in this name, and it is tempting to follow McCloskey in positing an origin in the word *Crannach* meaning "abounding in trees" (see *Joyce* i 499). Indeed, if we are correct in identifying *Durngrunagh* (1) as an earlier form of the name, we could add that Granny was once covered in forest as woodland is marked in this townland on the map from the Escheated Counties series.

However, closer examination shows that virtually all the forms beginning with *c* occur in closely related documents, namely, the Civil Survey (3), Petty's maps (4, 9), the Book of Survey and Distribution (6), and Lamb's map of Co. Derry (10). However, the names on Petty's map are derived from those in the Civil Survey and it can be no accident that we find one example of initial *g* there (2). Independent evidence of an initial *c* would seem to be provided by the Hearth Money Rolls, but this is a very unreliable document and *c* for *g* is also found there in the name **Gulladuff** (parish of Maghera). It is distinctly possible that these forms were influenced by the name **Cranny**, a townland in the neighbouring parish of Desertmartin. Initial *g*, on the other hand, is found in a number of independent sources or groups of sources. We may, therefore, propose with some confidence an original Irish *Greanaigh*, an oblique form of *Greanach* which signifies "a gravelly place" in place-names (*Joyce* ii 374-5).

Keenaght
H 8191

Caonach

"mossy place"

1. Cynagh	Esch. Co. Map 14	1609
2. Cynagh	Charter of Londonderry 391	1613
3. Keenah	Lond. Comp. Valuation 309	1613
4. Keenat	Phillips MSS (Maps) Plate 28	1622
5. Keanaught foord	Civ. Surv. iii 174	1654
6. Keanaugh	Civ. Surv. iii 174	1654
7. Cyneigh, the small proportion of	Bishop. Der. i 265	1657
8. Cinagh	Bishop. Der. i 265	1657
9. Cynagh, the small proportion of	Bishop. Der. i 277	1657
10. Keanagh	BSD(c) 61	1661
11. Keenaght	Par. Tithe Bk (OSNB) No. 9	1767
12. Keenagh	Sampson's Map	1813
13. 'Kee-naught	OSNB Pron. No. 9	1834c
14. Canaigh "the pool of water, or caonach, mossy"	MacCloskey's Stat. Report 61	1821
15. Caonach "moss"	J O'D (OSNB) No. 9	1834c
16. Cianachta "The territory of the race of Cian"	Munn's Notes 185	1925
17. 'kʲiːnəx	Local pronunciation	1993

As with **Granny,** our sources present us with a rather confused picture of the history of this name. The current form of the name is clearly suggestive of the Irish tribal name *Cianachta* which is preserved in the name of the neighbouring barony of Keenaght, and at least some of the historical spellings appear to support this derivation (4–5). The spelling on Phillips' map, for example, shows a simple final *t* which we might take to represent the reduction of the consonant group *cht* to *t* which is a feature of some East Ulster dialects, but the fact that

126

these maps are closely related to the earlier Valuation of 1613 (3) suggests that it is merely a mistake for *h*. Moreover, the majority of our early forms show no trace of the final *t*, and where it does occur, it may be erroneous.

The forms in the Civil Survey seem to demonstrate the nature of the error. One spelling shows a final *-ght*, the other just *-gh*. The former is actually a reference to "Keanaught foord", but there can be little doubt that the ford derives its name from the townland. The fact that two different spellings are offered for the same place in a single source should alert us to the possibility of a scribal error and I would suggest that the former spelling has fallen under the influence of the barony name, Keenaght, which would have been well known to those plotting the boundaries of the parishes. Indeed, it seems very likely that the modern form of the townland name has been reformed by analogy with that of the barony. There is some evidence of a parasitic *t* after *ch* in other names such as **Tonaght** in Ballynascreen (Irish *Tonnach* "enclosure/mound"), but the precise nature of this process is unclear and uncertain.

Joyce discusses the word *caonach* "moss" and states that it is applied in its anglicized form, Keenagh, to a number of places in Leinster, Connaught and Ulster (*Joyce* ii 337). He draws our attention to the village of Keenagh, five miles north-west of Ballymahon in Longford, the adjacent demesne of which is called Mosstown, clearly an attempt to translate the Irish (*ibid.*). There seems to be no reason to depart from this interpretation in substance, although we might more reasonably suggest in this context a name derived from the synonym *caonna* (*DIL* sv. *cáenna*) + the adjectival suffix *ach* giving a meaning "mossy place".

Killynumber
H 8494

Cúil an Umair
"recess of the trough or hollow"

1. Coulanamour	Esch. Co. Map 14	1609
2. Cowlanamone	Charter of Londonderry 391	1613
3. Colnumer	Phillips MSS (Maps) Plate 28	1622
4. Cullnumber	Civ. Surv. iii 175,176,178	1654
5. Coulananonie	Bishop. Der. i 265	1657
6. Cooleminiber	Census 135	1659c
7. Cullminiber	BSD(c) 62	1661
8. Cullnamer	HMR (Ó Doibhlin 2) 74	1663
9. Killinumber	Par. Tithe Bk (OSNB) No. 9	1767
10. Killynumer	Sampson's Map	1813
11. Killy-'num-ber	OSNB Pron. No. 9	1834c
12. Coille nuimhir "the great wood"	MacCloskey's Stat. Report 61	1821
13. Cul an Umair "back ... place of the trough"	OSL (Derry) 107	1834
14. Coill an umair "wood of the trough"	J O'D (OSNB) No. 9	1834c
15. Coill-an-umair "the wood of the trough"	Joyce ii 431	1875
16. Coill-an-umair "The wood of the trough"	Munn's Notes 185	1925
17. ˌkʲili'nǫmər	Local pronunciation	1993

The spellings of this name show an extreme degree of variation and confusion, much of it caused by the inability of scribes or editors to correctly distinguish *n*, *u* and *m* in the middle of the name. The representation of the first element, which is probably Irish *cúil* "corner, recess" (see **Coolsaragh** above) varies as we might expect. Its modern form is unusual but not inexplicable, and a similar development is seen in the name **Killyboggin** in the parish of Desertmartin. In unstressed position, the original long *u* of *cúil* would be shortened. We would normally expect the development to stop here, but, perhaps by analogy with other names in the area, such as **Killytoney**, or by a form of dissimilation, a fronting towards the *i*-position has occurred.

O'Donovan takes the last element in the name to be Irish *umar* "a trough" and cites, somewhat sceptically, a claim by a local by the name of Frank Higgins that "there was a trough and the ruins of a Danish mill dug up there" (*OSL (Derry)* 107). However, it is unlikely that the trough referred to in the name is a man-made object and it probably refers to a hollow of some sort (see *Joyce* ii 430–1). There is a noticeable hollow in the townland (OS H 8494). The appearance of a *b* after the original *m* is not unexpected as it occurs in several other place-names such as **Comber** in Co. Down which comes from Irish *Cumar* "ravine" (*Joyce* i 62–3; ii 431).

The Irish word *iomaire* meaning "a ridge" might also be postulated here, but the absence of any definite indication of a final vowel such as -*y* renders it a lesser possibility.

Killytoney	*Coill an Tonnaigh*	
H 8395	"wood of the stockade"	
1. kilitvnny (?)	Esch. Co. Map 14	1609
2. Killitomny	Charter of Londonderry 391	1613
3. Kilteny	Lond. Comp. Valuation 309	1613
4. Killtony	Civ. Surv. iii 174	1654
5. Killytony	Bishop. Der. i 265	1657
6. Killtonney	BSD(c) 62	1661
7. Kilty-Sonthe, Quarter of	HMR (Ó Doibhlin 2) 74	1663
8. Killytoney	Par. Tithe Bk (OSNB) No. 9	1767
9. Killtinny	Sampson's Map	1813
10. Killy-'to-ne	OSNB Pron. No. 9	1834c
11. Coille tonidh "the woody bottom"	MacCloskey's Stat. Report 61	1821
12. Coill Tonnaig "wood of the mound or rampart"	J O'D (OSNB) No. 9	1834c
13. Coille-tonnach "The wood of the mound"	Munn's Notes 185	1925
14. ˌkʲïlə'toni	Local pronunciation	1993

It is tempting to take the final element as *tamhnach* but there is little or no strong evidence in its favour. The form from the Charter of 1613 might suggest such an origin (2), but in closely related sources (1, 5) the spellings are more in accordance with the other early spellings.

There seems to be no reason, therefore, to depart from the suggestion made by O'Donovan. There was formerly a rath in this townland (Speer 1990, 13) and the stockade may have been located at or near this structure. Joyce notes two forms of this word, *tonnach* and *sonnach* (*Joyce* ii 220), the latter being the older, and it is tempting to view the spelling with the *s* in the Hearth Money Roll (7) as an attempt to represent this form, but this source is generally so unreliable that we can put little store by it. Of greater relevance in this regard is the name **Tonaght** in Ballynascreen which shows the use of the form with initial *t* in this area.

The initial element must be either *coill* "a wood" or *cill* "a church" which are indistinguishable in their anglicized guise. However, the former is supported by all previous authorities, including O'Donovan who may have heard the name pronounced in Irish and thus would have been able to make the necessary distinction.

Moneyshanere Of uncertain origin
H 8196

1. mollishanare	Esch. Co. Map 14	1609
2. Mollyshanare	Charter of Londonderry 392	1613
3. Montshenar	Lond. Comp. Valuation 309	1613
4. Moneshenar	Phillips MSS (Maps) Plate 28	1622
5. Manishinor	Civ. Surv. iii 175	1654
6. Molyshanare	Bishop. Der. i 266	1657
7. Monishnare	Census 136	1659c
8. Mannishinore	BSD(c) 62	1661
9. Morishnose	HMR (Ó Doibhlin 2) 74	1663
10. Monishanere	Par. Tithe Bk (OSNB) No. 9	1767
11. Monishanere	Sampson's Map	1813
12. Mun-ny-shan-'air	OSNB Pron. No. 9	1834c
13. Moin a sinner "mountain of yew trees"	MacCloskey's Stat. Report 61	1821
14. Móin na seánoir "bog of the old men"	J O'D (OSNB) No. 9	1834c
15. Muine sean-fhéir "brake of the old grass"	J O'D (OSNB) No. 9	1834c
16. Monga-shean-saighir "The crest, or ridge of the ancient Priest"	Munn's Notes 185	1925
17. ˌmɒniʃïn'air	Local pronunciation	1993

The earliest spellings seem to indicate an initial element *mullach* "summit, hilltop" (1–2, 6), but as they all occur in related sources we may conclude with some certainty that they all stem from a single scribal error (that *mullach* is not intended is further suggested by the use of *o* rather than the usual *u* in the first syllable). Several interpretations of this element have previously been considered (13–16), but the almost consistent use of *o* in the first syllable and the presence here of a considerable portion of bog suggest the word *móin* "bog" or a derivative thereof (*Munn's Notes* 185; *OSM* xxxi 69; *Civ. Surv.* iii 175). Ó Máille cites Moneyshanere as an example of *móin* "bog" + the suffix -*(a)is* (1989–90, 137), but the formation is not clearly attested in any Irish source. The stress on the last syllable, which is probably original, rules out a compound with *sean* "old" as previously suggested (14–16), but the *sh* is otherwise rather difficult to explain.

The final element presents equally serious problems, and a number of suggestions might be made. Local tradition had it that a battle was fought here between the O'Hagans of Calmore and the O'Neills of Tyrone who had come ravaging down the country from

Ballynascreen (*OSM* xxxi 69), and it might be suggested that the final element is *ár* "slaughter". However, although this fits quite neatly with the early spellings, it is rather more difficult to relate it to the later forms. Indeed, the variation between *a*, *o*, and *e* suggests either a short-*a* or *o* followed by a palatal consonant, and among the words which must be considered are *ar* (gen. sing. *air*) "cultivated land" and *oirear* "border, border region". The latter, although disyllabic, is elsewhere reduced by haplology (see *PNI* ii 11), and it might be argued that Moneyshanere takes its name from its location close to the Moyola River which was formerly a significant tribal boundary. However, these are only two of several possible elements, and the original form of the name now seems irretrievable.

| **Mormeal** | *Mír Mhíchíl* | |
| H 8094 | "St Michael's portion" | |

1.	Mirrimeith	Civ. Surv. iii 187	1654
2.	Merinnch	Hib. Reg. Loughinsholin	1657c
3.	Mirmihellgrany	Census 135	1659c
4.	Merrinnieth	BSD(c) 52	1661
5.	Mirmichell	Bishop. Der. i 343	1661c
6.	Mermeth	Hib. Del. Derry	1672c
7.	Meremeale	Bishop. Der. ii 114	1686
8.	Mermeal	Par. Tithe Bk (OSNB) No. 9	1767
9.	Mormeal	Sampson's Map	1813
10.	Mor-'meel	OSNB Pron. No. 9	1834c
11.	"The bog of hares"	MacCloskey's Stat. Report 61	1821
12.	Mór-meall "great knoll or hillock"	J O'D (OSNB) No. 9	1834c
13.	Mor-meall "The great hillock"	Munn's Notes 185	1925
14.	Mór-meall "great hillock"	Joyce iii 512	1925
15.	ˌmɔrˈmeːl	Local pronunciation	1993
16.	ˌmɔrˈmiːl	Local pronunciation	1993

As we shall see, the name Mormeal originates in the phrase *mír Mhíchíl* meaning "portion of food set aside for [the] poor" (*Ó Dónaill* sv. *mír* 1) and, in place-name usage, the term must indicate "land set aside to provide food for the poor". Mormeal was, of course, church land, and it was doubtless the practice of the church here to set aside a portion of land to provide for the poor. *Mír* is not at all common in place-names, and among the few examples in the country are two names of similar origin, namely, Meermihil in the parish of Oughaval, Co. Mayo, and an obsolete townland called *Merimichael* which was formerly held by the Archbishop of Armagh.

The practice of providing for the poor in this manner is traced back as far as the time of St Patrick by native historians. Keating explains it as follows (*Céitinn* iii 39–43; cf. *Trip. Life (Stokes)* ii 557–559). Anghus, wife of Laoghaire, king of Ireland, received the Christian faith from Patrick. One day, while Patrick was visiting, the queen ordered food to be prepared for him and his company. Her son, Lughaidh, began eating the meal with them and a portion stuck in his throat and he died. The distraught queen entrusted her son's body to Patrick who prayed constantly over his body for three days. At the end of the third day, Michael the Archangel appeared in the form of a dove. The dove flew over the boy's mouth and removed the offending morsel from his throat, thereby restoring him to life. Patrick related these events to the jubilant mother who then swore to give a sheep out of every flock she possessed each year and a portion of every meal she would eat during her life to the poor in honour of Michael the Archangel. Furthermore, she enjoined this as a custom on everyone in Ireland who received baptism from Patrick, and this is the origin of the custom of the Michaelmas sheep and the Michael's portion (*mír Mhíchíl*).

The historical spellings suggest that the first element is *mír* "bit, portion". Standing as it is in unstressed position, the originally long-*i* would first have been shortened and then, under the influence of the following final *r*, changed to [ə] (compare [bərθ] birth: Barber 1976, 305). Regarding the second element, as we have seen the historical spellings show that this was originally disyllabic. Several words may be postulated but, as I have suggested, it most probably represents the personal name *Mícheál*. The loss of the *ch* in the name *Mícheál* is found in all varieties of East Ulster Irish, and the reduced form has been recorded in South Derry (*LASID* iv 285; cf. O'Rahilly 1932, 209). It can be clearly seen, therefore, that the historical spellings fully support the suggested derivation from *Mír Mhíchíl*. When we add to this the fact that Mormeal was church land, and that there are comparable names in Cos Armagh and Mayo, there can be little doubt that this is correct.

Moybeg Kirley	*Maigh Bheag* "little plain"	
H 8097	+ *Corrbhaile* "prominent townland"	

1. maybeg	Esch. Co. Map 14	1609
2. Moybegg	Charter of Londonderry 391	1613
3. Moybegkerley	Lond. Comp. Valuation 309	1613
4. Moybegkirlo	Phillips MSS (Maps) Plate 28	1622
5. Moybegg	Civ. Surv. iii 174	1654
6. Moybegg	Bishop. Der. i 266	1657
7. Molock beg Quarter	Census 136	1659c
8. Half Moybegg and Taynaghmore	BSD(c) 62	1661
9. Moybeg	Sampson's Map	1813
10. Moy-beg-'kurley	OSNB Pron. No. 9	1834c
11. Magh beg "little plain"	MacCloskey's Stat. Report 61	1821
12. Mag beag "small plain"	J O'D (OSNB) No. 9	1834c
13. Magh-beg-cian-leath "Little plain of the black coloured half"	Munn's Notes 186	1925
14. ˌmɔiˌbegˈkʲirli	Local pronunciation	1993

This name is a compound of two earlier names, Moybeg and Kirley, the latter of which is still applied to a neighbouring townland in the parish of Maghera. The first name clearly derives from the Irish *Maigh Bheag* "little plain" and probably originally referred to a level piece of ground near the river. On the second name see **Kirley** in Maghera parish.

Moyesset	Of uncertain origin	
H 8395		

1. Mouasaden	Esch. Co. Map 14	1609
2. Moysaden	Charter of Londonderry 391	1613

3. Moyesset	Lond. Comp. Valuation 309	1613
4. Moyessett	Phillips MSS (Maps) Plate 28	1622
5. Moysett	Civ. Surv. iii 175	1654
6. Moyasserden	Bishop. Der. i 265	1657
7. Moyasaden, the small proportion of	Bishop. Der. i 265	1657
8. Mayesset	Par. Tithe Bk (OSNB) No. 9	1767
9. Moyasset	Sampson's Map	1813
10. Moy-'ess-et	OSNB Pron. No. 9	1834c
11. Magh assadh "the plain of the weasel"	MacCloskey's Stat. Report 61	1821
12. Magh-Aisiada "Hasset's plain"	J O'D (OSNB) No. 9	1834c
13. Magh-Assiada "The plain of Hasset"	Munn's Notes 186	1925
14. "Hasset's plain"	Joyce iii 514	1925
15. ˌmɔiˈɛsït	Local pronunciation	1993

The first element is clearly *maigh* "a plain", but it is rather more difficult to suggest an origin for the second element. The early spellings are fairly consistent with one another, but one group of sources (1-2, 6-7) has an additional syllable. Although these documents contain some spelling errors, they frequently supply better forms than many of the other sources cited here and any forms found there must be treated seriously. We might more readily dismiss this group of spellings were the error easily accounted for but the addition of an extra syllable is not in the nature of a normal mistake. On the other hand, it would be peculiar for a final syllable to disappear where it does not end in a vowel, and the development from this form to the more usual spellings is equally hard to explain. However, a name of an obsolete townland in the nearby parish of Desertlyn bears a striking resemblance to the current name (spellings such as *Moyassade* and *Moyesset* are recorded in 17th-century sources) and it might be argued that the form Moyesset arose by analogy with that name (cf. also **Moyasset** in Co. Antrim).

O'Donovan's postulated Irish form, *Magh-Aisiada* "Hasset's plain", is hardly correct. The Co. Clare surname Ó hAiseadha is sometimes anglicized Hassett which seems to have arisen in the 17th century from an earlier anglicization O'Hessedy (MacLysaght 1982, 123). However, by the 17th century we would expect Irish *Ó hAiseadha* to be anglicized O'Hassey, and this is clearly not the case here.

Tamnyaskey
H 8195

Tamhnaigh Oscair
"Oscar's field" (?)

1. Tawneosker	Civ. Surv. iii 187	1654
2. Tawneosker	Hib. Reg. Loughinsholin	1657c
3. Tauniagher	Census 135	1659c
4. Tawneosker	BSD(c) 52	1661
5. Tamlaghoskutt	Bishop. Der. i 343	1661c
6. Tawnaosker	HMR (Ó Doibhlin 2) 74	1663
7. Townasker	Hib. Del. Derry	1672c
8. Tammaskey	Par. Tithe Bk (OSNB) No. 9	1767

9. Tamneyaskey	Sampson's Map	1813
10. Tam-ne-'askee	OSNB Pron. No. 9	1834c
11. Tamnaidh (Temenos) scarrina, a separate field"	MacCloskey's Stat. Report 61	1821
12. Tamhnach eascaigh "field of the quagmire"	J O'D (OSNB) No. 9	1834c
13. Tamhnach-eascaigh "The field of the quagmire"	Munn's Notes 186	1925
14. Tamhnach-eascaigh "field of the quagmire"	Joyce iii 567	1925
15. ˌtamni'aːski	Local pronunciation	1993

The modern form of this name immediately suggests an origin *Tamhnaigh Easca* "field of the wet bog" or the like, but the early forms suggest something quite different. The first element is, indeed, almost certainly *tamhnach* "field" (on which see **Tamnymartin** in Maghera) or, rather, a dative form of this, *tamhnaigh*.

A problem arises, however, with the second element, as it is represented in our sources by a bewildering array of forms. These documents fall into four main groups giving the following pattern: *Tawneosker* (1–2, 4; cf. 7), *Tauniagher* (3), *Tamlaghoskutt* (5), *Tawnaosker* (6). As can be seen, there are two independent witnesses to a form like *Tawneosker*. The forms from the Census of c.1659 are quite erratic, and it could be argued that the spelling *Tauniagher* (3) represents a corruption of this form, with the common mistake of substituting *h* for *k* and the less common error of *g* for tall *s*.

That leaves us with a reference to the townland in the margin of a receipt dated 28 August, 1661 (5). The forms in this document are generally reliable and it supplies us with a particularly faithful spelling of **Mormeal** (see above). The *l* for *n* may be a simple scribal error, or it may reflect a real sound change which occurs sporadically elsewhere in this context. The final *tt* here is probably a mistake for *rr* as a *t* without a bar can be practically indistinguishable from *r* in 17th-century script.

The current pronunciation seems to have arisen in the 17th or 18th century through a process which is not altogether clear. The lowering of *o* to *a* is well-attested in Ulster Irish (O'Rahilly 1932, 192–3), but the loss of final *r* is irregular (cf. Stockman & Wagner 1965, 199). Nevertheless, it may be plausibly explained in terms of the articulation of Irish palatal *r* which Quiggin considered similar to [j] in Donegal speech (1906, 99; also Ó Dochartaigh 1987, 155–9). Although it never became [j] in East Ulster as it has in parts of Donegal, most notably Gweedore, the articulation may have been close enough to this sound to have led, on this occasion at least, to the loss of the *r* in the anglicized form.

It seems, therefore, that all the early spellings are reconcilable, and in general they point towards an original Irish form *Tamhnaigh Oscair*. The meaning of the final element here is uncertain as there are at least two distinct words which take this form, *oscar* "outsider" (see *DIL* sv. 1 *oscar* for possible range of meanings), and *oscar* "leap" (with which compare the use of *léim* "leap" in place-names). However, the most likely origin of the final element is the personal name Oscar, which was used among the Maguires of Fermanagh, and probably further afield, in the 14th century (Ó Corráin & Maguire 1981, 151).

Tobermore
H 8397

Tobar Mór
"large well"

1. tobarnmore	Esch. Co. Map 14	1609
2. Tobarmore	Charter of Londonderry 391	1613
3. ½ Tubbor Moore	Lond. Comp. Valuation 307	1613
4. Tubermor	Phillips MSS (Maps) Plate 24	1622
5. Tobermore	Civ. Surv. iii 175,176	1654
6. Tobarrmore	Bishop. Der. i 265	1657
7. Tobermoore Qr	Census 136	1659c
8. Tobermore	BSD(c) 62	1661
9. Tobermore	HMR (Ó Doibhlin 2) 74	1663
10. Tobermore	Par. Tithe Bk (OSNB) No. 9	1767
11. Tobermore	Sampson's Map	1813
12. Tub-ber-'more	OSNB Pron. No. 9	1834c
13. Tobar mór "great well"	J O'D (OSNB) No. 9	1834c
14. Tobar-mor "The great well"	Munn's Notes 186	1925
15. An Tobar Mór	GÉ 277	1989
16. ˌtọbər'moːr	Local pronunciation	1993

The well which gives name to the village and townland of Tobermore had already dried up by the 19th century (*OSM* xxxi 65; *Munn's Notes* 186).

Tullyroan
H 8294

Tulaigh Uí Ruáin
"O'Rowan's hill"

1. Tillirnan	Civ. Surv. iii 187	1654
2. Tillcran (?)	Hib. Reg. Loughinsholin	1657c
3. Tolleroan	Census 135	1659c
4. Tillernan	BSD(c) 52	1661
5. Tollyrone	Bishop. Der. i 343	1661c
6. Tulleran	HMR (Ó Doibhlin 2) 74	1663
7. Tilleran	Hib. Del. Derry	1672c
8. Tilleroan	Par. Tithe Bk (OSNB) No. 9	1767
9. Tullyrone	Sampson's Map	1813
10. Tullyroan	Custom of County (OSNB) No. 9	1834c
11. Tully-'roan	OSNB Pron. No. 9	1834c
12. Tully rathan "the place of ferns"	MacCloskey's Stat. Report 61	1821
13. Tulaigh Róin "Rowan's hill"	J O'D (OSNB) No. 9	1834c
14. Tullach-Rainain "The hill of Ronan or Rowan"	Munn's Notes 186	1925
15. ˌtọli'rɔːən	Local pronunciation	1993
16. ˌtọli'roːnən (sic)	Local pronunciation	1993

As one of the four townlands belonging to the Bishop of Derry, Tullyroan does not appear in all the usual sources. However, the available forms are fairly consistent and a clear picture of the 17th-century pronunciation is evident. The forms in the Civil Survey, the Book of Survey and Distribution, and Petty's maps (1–2, 4) are, of course, closely related, and contain some common errors, most notably *i* in the first syllable for *u*. The forms in the the the Civil Survey and the Book of Survey and Distribution share a further mistake, *rn* being written for *rr* or, more probably, *ru*. On Petty's maps, the final syllable has been reduced to -*ran*, giving a wholly misleading impression of the pronunciation (the similar spelling in the Hearth Money Rolls is unreliable).

The first element is undoubtedly *tulach* "a hillock", and the feature it denotes is probably the hill now called Belmount Hill. However, even accepting the modern pronunciation as more or less accurate, we are left with a number of possible origins for the second element. There is another **Tullyroan** in the parish of Clonfeacle, Co. Armagh, another townland of the same name in the parish of Kildress, Co. Tyrone, and a Tullyroane in Co. Cavan. O'Donovan suggests *Tulaigh Ruadháin* "Rowan's Hill" for the names in Armagh and Tyrone, but it is highly unlikely that all these names as well as our own can have originated with the same personal name.

Ruán in the sense of "buckwheat" may be appropriate in a number of these names as the relatively well-drained soil on small hills or drumlins would have been ideal for the growing of wheat. We might also consider *ruan*, an early variant of *ruaim*, which appears to have signified "a plant producing red colouring matter", although it is perhaps less likely than the former suggestion. Some commentators have suggested a word *ruán* meaning "red land or soil", which is probably the same word as that translated by Dinneen as "moorland" (see **Roan** in the parish of Clonfeacle, Co. Tyrone). This is perhaps appropriate here as there is a considerable amount of heath in this townland, particularly around Belmount Hill.

However, perhaps the most probable derivation for this element is the surname O'Rowan (Irish *Ó Ruáin*) which the standard surname works have associated with the west of Ireland (Woulfe 1923, 635; MacLysaght 1985, 262). The name is also found in Ulster, and the Hearth Money Rolls record an Own O'Royne in Butcher Street in Derry, and a Knogher O'Rome (for which read O'Roine) in this very parish (*HMR (Ó Doibhlin 2)* 42, 74).

OTHER NAMES

Altagoan River   A hybrid form
H 8093

1. Altnegoa	Civ. Surv. iii 177	1654
2. ˌaltnəˈhoːn	Local pronunciation	1993
3. ˌaltðəˈhoːn	Local pronunciation	1993
4. ˌaltləˈhoːn	Local pronunciation	1993
5. ˌaltəˈgɔːn	Local pronunciation	1993

Both Altagoan Bridge and Altagoan River take their name from a small wooded glen (*allt*) just above the bridge. The forms seem to fluctuate between Irish *Allt an Ghabhann* "glen of the smith" and *Allt na nGabhann* "glen of the smiths", but the precise form remains unclear. The single 17th-century spelling does little to clarify the origin of the name (1), although it seems to rule out the possibility of *Allt na hAbhann* "glen of the river" which might be suggested by some of the local pronunciations. The absence of a final *n* in this form may indicate that it has been mistranscribed, but there is also a variant genitive form *gabha* in Ulster (*Joyce* i 223).

Belmount Hill   A hybrid form
H 8294

135

The name Belmount occurs in several Irish place-names, but it is ultimately of French origin, an old accusative form *Bel Mont* meaning "beautiful mountain". It became popular as a street name in London in Victorian times, mainly for its pseudo-Norman associations (Room 1983, 8), and it is these same pretensions which assured its currency in Ireland.

Crocknamohil	*Cnoc na mBuachailli*	
H 7990	"hill of the herdboys"	
1. "Bo[rsel?] Hill"	OSRNB 40 sh.41	1850c
2. ‚krǫknə'mohəl	Local pronunciation	1993

Crocknamohil, Irish *Cnoc na mBuachailli* "hill of the herdboys" is the name of a substantial hill in the south of the parish. The name may simply refer to the practice of transhumance (boleying) whereby the cattle were driven into the hills and mountains in search of summer pasturage where they were often watched over by boys. On the other hand, the "boys" may have been standing stones, which were sometimes known by the Irish term *buachaill bréige* "false boy" on account of their resemblance from a distance to the figure of a boy (*Joyce* ii 434–5).

Cross Roads	An English form
H 8294	

This village is so called from its location at the junction of several roads (*OSRNB* 40 sh. 41).

Drumbally Hill	A hybrid form	
H 8493		
1. drombally	Esch. Co. Map 14	1609
2. Drombally, ½ of the balliboe of	Charter of Londonderry 391	1613
3. Drom balley	Lond. Comp. Valuation 309	1613
4. Dromballe	Phillips MSS (Maps) Plate 28	1622
5. Drombellifoord East	Civ. Surv. iii 174	1654
6. Drumbally	Civ. Surv. iii 174	1654
7. Drombelly	Civ. Surv. iii 175	1654
8. Drombally	Civ. Surv. iii 176	1654
9. Drumbelly	Civ. Surv. iii 187	1654
10. Drombally	Bishop. Der. i 265,266	1657
11. Drumbally	BSD(c) 61	1661
12. Drumbally	Custom of County (OSNB) No. 8	1834c
13. Drum-'bal-ly	OSNB Pron. No. 8	1834c
14. Druim bhaile "ridge town"	J O'D (OSNB) No. 8	1834c

While not now considered a townland, Drumbally is frequently enumerated as such in documents of the 17th century. There is a rath on top of the hill which MacCloskey describes as the "most remarkable" in the area (*MacCloskey's Stat. Report* 15).

The formation *Droim Baile* "ridge of the townland" is very rare, and occurs as the name of only one other townland in Ireland, that of **Drumbally** in the parish of Creggan, Co.

Armagh. There is a small number of townlands in the North which have a form *droim* + *baile* + a third element (often a surname). In this parish we have **Drumballyhagan** and Drumballyhagan Clark, and there is a **Drumballydonaghy** in the parish of Tamlaght Finlagan in Co. Derry. In addition, there is a Drumballycaslan in Inishowen, Co. Donegal, and a **Drumballyhugh** in Co. Tyrone. The absence of the article meaning "the" from the formation is also noteworthy and suggests that our Drumbally and the one in Armagh are shortened versions of once longer names.

Forge Bridge An English form
H 8097

1. ðə 'foːrdʒˌtəun 'brïdʒ	Local pronunciation	1993

Forge Bridge is named from a smelting furnace which stood on the south side of the bridge in the early part of the 18th century (*OSRNB* 39 sh. 36). The village to the north of the bridge, Forgetown, was also named from it, and the bridge itself has been locally renamed as The Forgetown Bridge. Iron ore from Slieve Gallion, which was found both as bog ore and nearby in its metallic state, was formerly smelted at these ironworks (*MacCloskey's Stat. Report* 5).

Fort William Of Scottish origin
H 8397

1. dounagranan	Esch. Co. Map 14	1609
2. Donnagraven	Charter of Londonderry 391	1613
3. ½ Grenah	Lond. Comp. Valuation 307	1613
4. Grenan	Phillips MSS (Maps) Plate 24	1622
5. Dinigrinan	Civ. Surv. iii 175	1654
6. Dunigrunan	Civ. Surv. iii 175	1654
7. Donnagrannan	Bishop. Der. i 265	1657
8. Dunnigrinane	BSD(c) 62	1661
9. Fort William	Sampson's Map	1813
10. ˌfort'wiljəm	Local pronunciation	1993

Fort William was built in 1795 and named from the nearby fort of the same name (*OSM* xxxi 67). The fort is clearly called after the Scottish Fortwilliam which was named in 1690 in honour of William III (Nicolaisen 1976, 52), and it is this association which undoubtedly encouraged Mr Jackson, the first proprietor, to adopt the name and which contributed to the popularity of the name in Ireland (*OSM ibid.*).

MacCloskey says that the location of the house was called Dunaguny (*sic* for Irish *Dún na Gréine*) which he translates somewhat inaccurately as "the sunny height" (*MacCloskey's Stat. Report* 8-9). This is clearly a mistranscription of the old townland name which appears in our early sources as *Dunnigrinane* etc. The first element is clearly *dún* "fort" which denotes the fort now called Fort William, but the remainder of the name is problematic on account of the strange variation in spelling in the 17th-century sources. It is perhaps *grianán* "eminent place" on which see **Greenan** in the parish of Newry, Co. Down (*PNI* i 28–9).

Nutgrove Wood An English form
H 8293

1. 'nɒtgroːv 'wuːd   Local pronunciation   1993

The wood is named from the nearby settlement of Nut Grove, a late romantic name which refers to a plantation of nut-bearing trees which must have been growing nearby. A plantation of various types of trees, including 125 horse chestnut, was made by Robert Bryan in 1801 (McCracken & McCracken 1984, 42), and the name may have originated then.

Oak Island   An English form
H 8694

Oak Island is a small hill standing in an almost circular hollow through which a small river flows. There may once have been a lake here or the "island" may be metaphoric. The element "island" is frequently used in place-names to denote isolated hillocks, the majority of which are meared by rivers or come within their catchment areas, and some of which are surrounded or partially surrounded by bog (Ó Mainnín 1989–90, 200).

Spring Grove   An English form
H 8194

There is a well here from which the name derives (*OS 1:10,000* sh. 77), but there is now no sign of the grove.

Teiges Hill   An English form
H 8394

1. 'tegz 'hïl   Local pronunciation   1993

So called from a man whose surname was Teague (*OSRNB* 40 sh. 41). The name is incorrectly printed "Telges Hill" on the Ordnance Survey 1:50,000 Series map (cf. *OS 1:10,000* sh. 77).

Tobermore   See TOWNLAND NAMES
H 8397

The oldest house in Tobermore in the mid-19th-century was built in 1727 and belonged to a James Moore (*OSM* xxi 65). Some time after this date, the fair, which had previously been held at the Gort of the parish church, was transferred to Tobermore. At that stage, the village consisted only of Moore's house and a few mud huts, and the growth of the village can be traced to this period.

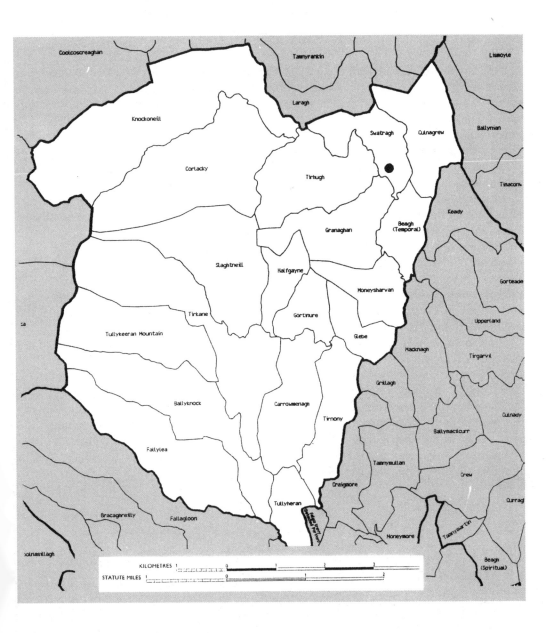

Parish of Killelagh

Townlands
Ballyknock
Beagh (Temporal)
Carrowmenagh
Corlacky
Culnagrew
Fallylea
Glebe

Gortinure
Granaghan
Halfgayne
Knockoneill
Moneysharvan
Slaghtneill
Swatragh
Tirhugh

Tirkane
Tirnony
Tullyheran
Tullykeeran Mountain

Towns
Swatragh

Based upon Ordnance Survey 1:50,000 mapping, with permission of the Director of the Ordnance Survey of Northern Ireland, Crown copyright reserved.

THE PARISH OF KILLELAGH

Little is known about Killelagh before the Plantation. As J.R. Walsh notes in his history of the parish of Maghera, the lack of documentation indicates that Killelagh must have been "a healthy little parish with good priests and faithful people" for medieval ecclesiastical records mostly concern themselves with the rich, the powerful, and the corrupt (1973, 26). Nevertheless, it is mentioned in the Ecclesiastical Taxation of 1302–6 so that it is clearly a parish of some antiquity (*Eccles. Tax. (CDI)* 215). Like other medieval parishes, certain lands were set aside within the parish for the upkeep of the church and its ministers, and these were administered by erenaghs. In Killelagh, the four townlands of Tirnony, Carrowmenagh, Tirkane and Tullyheran constituted the medieval church lands. Nothing is known of the erenaghs, not even their names, and under the terms of the Plantation these four townlands passed into the hands of the Bishop of Derry.

The ruins of a church, probably of medieval date, stand in the townland of Tirnony, about a quarter of a mile south east of Killelagh Lough. It formerly stood in the townland of Carrowmenagh but the boundary with Tirnony was changed at the end of the 18th or beginning of the 19th century (*OSL (Derry)* 63). Hamlin draws attention to the fact that it lies close to the old road across Carntogher Mountain from Maghera to Dungiven (Hamlin 1976, ii 578) and this must have added considerably to its importance.

The patron saint of the church appears to have been a St Muireadhach. In a list of the churches of Derry and their patron saints, the patron of Killelagh is named as St Muireadhach, abbot, whose feast was celebrated on 2 January (*Top. Frag.* 83). Walsh (1973, 22) identifies the good abbot as Muireadhach Ó Cobhthaigh (d. 1173), one time bishop of Maghera, but this is uncertain. Muireadhach was a common name in early Christian Ireland and was borne by many saints, among whom we may note Muireadhach Ó hÉanna, the patron saint of the nearby parish of Banagher (*Colton Vis.* 53n, 107–8; *Top. Frag.* 84). Two 17th-century documents name the church's patron as St Cromurmorius, but it is uncertain how, if at all, this name relates to Muireadhach (*Bishop. Der.* i 405, ii 136; cf. Hamlin 1976, ii 578).

PARISH NAME

Killelagh	*Cill an Locha*	
	"church of the lake"	
1. Cellalacha	Top. Frag. 83	1675c
2. Cill a' Lacha no Locha	Top. Frag. 71	1680c
3. Kellalacha	Eccles. Tax. (CDI) 215	1306c
4. Kyllagh	Colton Vis. 76	1397
5. Kyll-laca	Colton Vis. 82	1397?
6. Killeloghan	CPR Jas I 376b	1609
7. Killelaghan parish	CPR Jas I 377a	1609
8. Killalaghy	Bishop. Der. i 57,62	1610
9. Killalaghy	Bishop. Der. i 80	1611
10. Killalaghy, the termon or erenagh land of	CPR Jas I 279a	1615
11. Killalaghly	CPR Jas I 280a	1615
12. Killalaghy	Bishop. Der. i 102,109	1615

13. Killelaghey, R'c'oria de	Bishop. Der. i 129	1617c
14. Killelaughy	Bishop. Der. i 145	1624c
15. Killalaughy	Bishop. Der. i 145	1624c
16. Killelagh	Civ. Surv. iii 167,191	1654
17. Killealagh	Civ. Surv. iii 179	1654
18. Killealaugh	Civ. Surv. iii 179	1654
19. (?)Killeagh	Civ. Surv. iii 193	1654
20. Killelah, The Parish of	Hib. Reg. Loughinsholin	1657c
21. Killelagh	Census 134	1659c
22. Killeagh	Bishop. Der. i 326	1661
23. Killelagh Parish	BSD(c) 51	1661
24. Killealagh Parish	BSD(c) 64	1661
25. Killelagh	Bishop. Der. i 361,362,364	1663
26. Killelagh, The Parish of	HMR (Ó Doibhlin 2) 66	1663
27. Killilagh	Bishop. Der. i 405	1666
28. Killelagh	Bishop. Der. i 425	1669
29. Killelagh	Bishop. Der. ii 1	1671
30. Killelah	Hib. Del. Derry	1672c
31. Killelagh, Rec' de	Bishop. Der. ii 113	1686
32. Killelah	Lamb Maps Derry	1690c
33. Killelagh	Bishop. Der. ii 136	1692
34. Killelagh, S'ti Cromarmori	Bishop. Der. ii 136	1692
35. Killelagh, the gort of	Bishop. Der. ii 482	1703
36. Killelagh R.	Sampson's Map	1813
37. Kil-le-'lah	OSNB Pron. No. 6	1834c
38. Cill A Lacha "the church of the duck"	OSL (Derry) 64	1834
39. Cill a' lacha "church of the lough"	J O'D (OSNB) No. 6	1834c
40. Cill a' lacha "church of the lake"	Colton Vis. 82n	1850
41. Cill-an-locha "The church of the lake"	Munn's Notes 191	1925
42. ˌkɪliˈlɔx	Local pronunciation	1993

O'Donovan cites a local legend which purports to explain this name. A certain saint, the story goes, repeatedly attempted to erect a church in the parish but an invisible enemy of Christianity used to throw down by night what had been erected during the day. One day, however, a duck removed the mortar and stones to the present site, and so the saint called the church *Cill an Lacha* "the church of the duck" (*OSL (Derry)* 64).

However, *lacha* "duck" becomes *lachan* in the gen. sing. and this rather fanciful suggestion must be dismissed. A much more plausible, if more mundane, interpretation is that the name derives from *Cill an Locha* "church of the lake" (2). The variation between *a* and *o* in *loch* is well-attested from the Early Modern Irish period (*DIL* sv. 1 *loch*), and it appears in a number of place-names (**Drumlough** par. Drumgath, **Drumlough** par. Dromore, **Ballylough** par. Kilmegan and **Ballylough** par. Seapatrick, all in Co. Down). In the modern spelling of Killelagh, we seem to have an archaism based on a long orthographic tradition, for *loch* doubtless came to be pronounced *lough* in the Irish of this area as it did in Tyrone (Stockman & Wagner 1965, 87), and even today the name is pronounced locally as Killylough (42). (Mac Giolla Chomhaill (1968, 4), following Ó Ceallaigh, states that *loch* was pronounced *lach* in the Irish of South Derry. However, Ó Ceallaigh merely observes from the place-name evidence that the 17th-century pronunciation of *loch* was *lach* (*GUH* 29n), and he gives no indication of the modern pronunciation.)

O'Donovan objected to this interpretation on the grounds that the nearest lake, Killelagh Lough, is a quarter of a mile from the church and cannot even be seen from it (*OSL (Derry)* 64). However, the lake is situated beside the old road over Carntogher Mountain and, more significantly, the Ordnance Survey 6-inch map of 1854 shows a small island near the southern end of the lake which might have been a crannog (Ken Neill, pers. comm.). Clearly, the lake was formerly of some importance, and it is not unreasonable to suppose that the nearby church was named from it.

TOWNLAND NAMES

Ballyknock
C 8202

Baile Cnoic
"townland of the hill"

1.	knockitleug	Esch. Co. Map 14	1609
2.	Ballyknock-Icleny	Charter of Londonderry 391	1613
3.	Knock	Lond. Comp. Valuation 307	1613
4.	Knocke	Phillips MSS (Maps) Plate 24	1622
5.	Balliknock	Civ. Surv. iii 179	1654
6.	Belliknuge	Civ. Surv. iii 191	1654
7.	Ballyknock Icleny	Bishop. Der. i 266	1657
8.	Boloknock	Census 134	1659c
9.	Ballyknockeffalely	BSD(c) 64	1661
10.	Billenockley	HMR (Ó Doibhlin 2) 66	1663
11.	Ballynock	Sampson's Map	1813
12.	Bal-ly-'nock	OSNB Pron. No. 6	1834c
13.	Baile an chnuic "town of the hill"	J O'D (OSNB) No. 6	1834c
14.	Baile-an-cnoc "The townland of the hill"	Munn's Notes 191	1925
15.	ˌbaləˈnɔk	Local pronunciation	1993

Ballyknock, from Irish *Baile Cnoic* "townland of the hill", very probably derives its name from the hill in the centre of the townland now known as **Seefin**. Two major variants of the name occur in our 17th-century sources, but both centre on the word *cnoc* "hill" (on the anglicization see *Joyce* i 381–2). The earliest attested form is a longer variant of uncertain origin, but possibly representing *Baile Cnoic an tSléibhe* "the townland of the hill of the mountain". Ballyknock lies at the foot of Carntogher Mountain and the extension, if correct, probably refers to this feature.

It seems likely that the omission of *Bally-* from the Eshceated Counties map is accidental, due in all probability to the frequent abbreviation of this element to *B:* in this source.

The two *Knock(e)* forms, which occur in related documents, have probably arisen in a similar manner (3–4). In the Books of Survey and Distribution (9), the name has been concatenated with that of **Fallylea**, and it has suffered various other corruptions in other sources (6, 10).

Beagh (Temporal)	*An Bheitheach*	
H 8606	"the place of birch trees"	
1. b:nebeghy	Esch. Co. Map 14	1609
2. Balmebeghy	Charter of Londonderry 391	1613
3. Balle ne Behay	Lond. Comp. Valuation 307	1613
4. Ballenebehe	Phillips MSS (Maps) Plate 22	1622
5. Bellagh	Civ. Surv. iii 180	1654
6. Ballinelieghe	Bishop. Der. i 264	1657
7. Bellagh	BSD(c) 65	1661
8. Begh	HMR (Ó Doibhlin 2) 76	1663
9. Beagh	Sampson's Map	1813
10. Beitheach "The place abounding in birch trees"	Munn's Notes 192	1925
11. be:	Local pronunciation	1993
12. bi:ə	Local pronunciation	1993

The townland of Beagh (Temporal), along with Culnagrew, Swatragh, and Knockoneill, lay in the parish of Maghera until it was transferred to Killelagh by Order in Council on Christmas Eve, 1850 (*Der. Clergy* 239). See **Beagh (Spiritual)** in the parish of Maghera.

Carrowmenagh	*Ceathrú Mheánach*	
C 8303	"middle quarterland"	
1. b:neamagh	Esch. Co. Map 14	1609
2. Ballimeanagh	Bishop. Der. i 57	1610
3. Ballymeanagh	CPR Jas I 279a	1615
4. Ballymeanagh	Bishop. Der. i 102	1615
5. Kerrumenagh	Civ. Surv. iii 191	1654
6. Karumenagh	Hib. Reg. Loughinsholin	1657c
7. Kermanagh	Census 135	1659c
8. Kernmenagh	BSD(c) 51	1661
9. Cirinannah	HMR (Ó Doibhlin 2) 66	1663
10. Carnmenagh	Hib. Del. Derry	1672c
11. Kerrowmenagh (x3)	Bishop. Der. ii 113	1686
12. Carrowmenagh	Sampson's Map	1813
13. Car-row-'may-na	OSNB Pron. No. 6	1834c
14. Ceathramha meadonach "middle quarter"	J O'D (OSNB) No. 6	1834c
15. Caethramhadh-meadhonach "The middle quarter land"	Munn's Notes 192	1925

16. Ceathramha-meadhonach "middle quarter"	Joyce iii 187	1925
17. ˌkʲarə'miːnə	Local pronunciation	1993

The term "quarter", Irish *ceathrú*, often denotes a division of a ballybetagh containing three or four townlands (see glossary) but here it almost certainly means "one of four townlands", the four being the erenagh lands of Carrowmenagh, Tirkane, Tirnony, and Tullyheran. This is apparently confirmed by the appearance in our earliest sources of a separate name for the townland which is derived from *Baile Meánach* "middle townland" (1–4). *Meánach* "middle" aptly describes the townland's position in the middle of this group.

Corlacky	*Corr Leacaigh*	
C 8207	"round hill of the flagstony place"	

1. Corra-Leacaidh	OSL (Derry) 68	1740c
2. Corr Leacaigh	DCCU 427	1740c
3. Corlacky	Esch. Co. Map 14	1609
4. Corlacky	Charter of Londonderry 391	1613
5. Corlackey	Lond. Comp. Valuation 307	1613
6. Corlaskey	Phillips MSS (Maps) Plate 24	1622
7. Carleckie	Civ. Surv. iii 179	1654
8. Corleakie	Civ. Surv. iii 179,182	1654
9. Corlackey	Bishop. Der. i 264	1657
10. Carlakie	Census 134	1659c
11. Corleckey	BSD(c) 64	1661
12. Corliskey	HMR (Ó Doibhlin 2) 66	1663
13. Cor-'lack-ky	OSNB Pron. No. 6	1834c
14. Cor leacach "round hill of the flags"	J O'D (OSNB) No. 6	1834c
15. Cor-leacaigh "The round hill of the flagstones"	Munn's Notes 192	1925
16. Cor-leacaigh "hill of flagstones"	Joyce iii 256	1925
17. ˌkɔr'lɛki	Local pronunciation	1993

Corlacky is dismissed in the Ordnance Survey Name Book for this parish as "more productive of grouse and whiskey than of anything else" (*OSNB* No. 6). Munn notes that the whole townland forms a bare, round, stony hill, and there can be little doubt about the origin of this name (*Munn's Notes* 192). *Leacach* (gen. sing. *leacaigh*), is a derivative of *leac* "flat stone or rock" denoting an area of flat rocks or flagstones, and it is commonly used in place-names as such (*Ó Dónaill* sv.; *Joyce* i 417–8).

Culnagrew	*Cúil na gCnumh*	
C 8608	"recess of the worms/maggots"	

1. Coulnagnow	Esch. Co. Map 14	1609

2. Cowlnagnow	Charter of Londonderry 391	1613
3. Coolna Gloo	Lond. Comp. Valuation 307	1613
4. Colnagro	Phillips MSS (Maps) Plate 22	1622
5. Iulnegnuffe	Civ. Surv. iii 181	1654
6. Cullneknuffe	Civ. Surv. iii 181	1654
7. Cowlnagnow	Bishop. Der. i 264	1657
8. Culnegrue	Census 134	1659c
9. Julnegnuffe	BSD(c) 65	1661
10. Cullegrew	HMR (Ó Doibhlin 2) 76	1663
11. Cullnagrew	Par. Reg. (OSNB) No. 11	1794
12. Culnagruadh	Sampson's Map	1813
13. Culnagrew	Custom of County (OSNB) No. 11	1834c
14. Cool-na-'grew	OSNB Pron. No. 11	1834c.
15. Cul na gcraobh "back hill of the bushes or widespreading trees"	J O'D (OSNB) No. 11	1834c
16. Cul-na-g-chraebh "The hill back of the branchy land"	Munn's Notes 192	1925
17. ˌko̲lnəˈgru:	Local pronunciation	1993

Certain difficulties surround the interpretation of this name, most notably the great variety of spellings in our early sources. The interest for us lies in the final element which O'Donovan, followed by Munn, takes to be Irish *craobh* which generally denotes a tree in place-names. While many of the early spellings lend support to this etymology, a significant number of independent forms indicate that we are dealing with a word beginning *cn* or *gn*. In 17th-century Ulster Irish, these consonant clusters developed respectively into *cr* and *gr*, and so the later form of the name is readily explained (O'Rahilly 1932, 22–3). The word *cnó* "nut" might be invoked to account for these spellings, but this would hardly yield a modern form Culnagrew. In addition, we must also attempt to explain the anomalous forms ending in *-uffe* which, although they appear only in a small group of related sources, cannot be easily dismissed as a mere scribal error.

The word *cnóbha*, earlier *cnoghbha*, appears in the names of both Knowth and Crewbane in Co. Meath (Ó Maolfabhail 1990(b)). It is obviously very ancient and, like many other early historical and prehistoric sites, its meaning is uncertain. As is clear from Ó Maolfabhail's article on the growth of the element in the Co. Meath example, a postulated origin in *cnóbha* could easily account for the variety of spellings which we find here (see also Hughes 1989–90). However, this element had probably fallen into disuse by the early Christian period and it is highly unlikely that it would occur in a name such as this, particularly in the plural form which would have been necessary to produce the forms listed above.

Various insects have made their way into local place-names (see *Joyce* ii 291ff.) and it is not unlikely that we have here a form of the word *cruimh* "worm, maggot". The townland of **Culnagrew** in the parish of Killyman, Co. Tyrone, which displays some similar 17th-century spellings, appears to be of identical origin. *Cruimh* took on a variety of forms in its history, including variants beginning *cn-*, and a gen. pl. *cnumh* is attested in the writings of the 17th-century East Ulster writer, Aodh Mac Aingil (*DIL* sv. 1 *cruim*).

Fallylea
C 8201

Fáladh Fhleadha
"enclosure of the chickweed"

1. Fála Fhleadha	OSL (Derry) 67	1740c
2. Falach Fhleadha	DCCU 426	1740c
3. fallatry	Esch. Co. Map 14	1609
4. Fillaley	Charter of Londonderry 391	1613
5. Fallow Leaghe	Lond. Comp. Valuation 307	1613
6. Falloyle	Phillips MSS (Maps) Plate 24	1622
7. ffaleley	Civ. Surv. iii 179	1654
8. Fillaley	Bishop. Der. i 266	1657
9. Fallalee	Census 134	1659c
10. Falleleagh	HMR (Ó Doibhlin 2) 66	1663
11. Fallylea	Sampson's Map	1813
12. Fal-ly-'lea	OSNB Pron. No. 6	1834c
13. Fál liath "grey hedge"	J O'D (OSNB) No. 6	1834c
14. Fala-liath "The grey enclosures made of turf sod banks"	Munn's Notes 192	1925
15. ˌfalə'leː	Local pronunciation	1993

The first element in this name is very rare and is found most commonly in Co. Derry, notably in the two neighbouring townlands of **Fallagloon** and **Falgortrevy** in the parish of Maghera. Joyce takes the first element in two more northerly examples, **Falloward** and **Fallowlea**, to be a byform of *fál* "hedge" (*Joyce* ii 216), and in this he is doubtless correct although the precise form which he proposes is improbable. Both names have changed little since the early 17th century, and their spelling clearly suggests a form *fáladh* with which we may compare *caladh* angl. "callow" and *ceathrú* (earlier *ceathramhadh*) angl. "carrow". The formation is directly analogous to words such as *dúnadh* "encampment" (cf. *dún* "fort") and *bunadh* "origin, basis" (cf. *bun* "bottom"), so that *fáladh* may have the slightly modified meaning of "fenced land" or "enclosure" (cf. *DIL* sv. *fálad* "fencing"). The general body of evidence also seems to rule out a noun ending in *-ach* which is occasionally anglicized [o], as in Sligo (*Sligeach*) and Carlow (*Ceatharlach*) for there is no trace of a *ch* among the historical spellings of any of these names. The 18th-century Irish form cited above (2) is of no relevance here as the editor has simply reinterpreted the obscure earlier form (1).

It seems quite probable, therefore, that *fáladh* is the first element in this name, as well as in the names of the neighbouring townlands of **Fallagloon** and **Falgortrevy**. One early group of sources shows a spelling of the element which is similar to that found in the names **Falloward** and **Fallowlea** (5–6), and Ó Brolcháin's Irish form is a clear attempt to represent the word (1–2). We are also fortunate that Ó Brolcháin's poem unequivocally identifies the second element as *fliodh* "chickweed" (on gen. sing. see *DIL* sv. *flid*).

Glebe   An English form
H 7996

1. (ðə) gliːb	Local pronunciation	1993

Gortinure and Glebe originally formed a single townland but it was divided into two halves which were allotted as glebe lands to the parishes of Termoneeny and Killelagh respectively c. 1624 (*Bishop. Der.* i 145). Leslie states that the glebe of Killelagh in 1693 was the half townland of Ballymacpeake in Tamlaght O'Crilly (Ballymacpeake Lower), but he seems to have been confused by the fact that Killelagh was at this time united with the parish of Maghera which did have a glebe in Ballymacpeake (*Der. Clergy* 239; cf. *Bishop. Der.* i 145). He further states that an informal arrangement existed whereby the glebe in Ballymacpeake Lower which he supposes to have belonged to Killelagh was exchanged with Gortinure which was held by Termoneeny (*ibid.*). However, as we have seen, Killelagh was granted glebe in Gortinure as early as c. 1624, and the exchange noted by Leslie must have been between the parishes of Maghera and Termoneeny.

Gortinure
C 8405

Gort an Úra
"field of the heath"

1. gortinury	Esch. Co. Map 14	1609
2. Gortmarey	Charter of Londonderry 391	1613
3. Gorteneer	Phillips MSS (Maps) Plate 24	1622
4. Gortenure, ½ of	Bishop. Der. i 145	1624c
5. Gortenure one towne land	Civ. Surv. iii 191	1654
6. (?)Gortinnerie	Bishop. Der. i 264	1657
7. Sortnure	Hib. Reg. Loughinsholin	1657c
8. Gortenure (Gleabe Land)	BSD(c) 51	1661
9. Gortenoure	HMR (Ó Doibhlin 2) 66	1663
10. Gortenure	Hib. Del. Derry	1672c
11. Gortinure	Sampson's Map	1813
12. Gor-ti-'nure	OSNB Pron. No. 6	1834c
13. Gort an Iubhair "field of the yew"	J O'D (OSNB) No. 6	1834c
14. Gort-an-iubhair "the field of the yew"	Joyce i 512	1869
15. Gort-an-iubhair "The field of the yew tree"	Munn's Notes 193	1925
16. ˌgɔrtə'njuːr	Local pronunciation	1993

The final element in this name has previously been taken to be *iúr* "yew" (13–15), a common element in Irish place-names, but the earliest forms indicate *úr* (gen. sing. *úra*) "heath" (1–2, 6). This group of sources, although prone to scribal errors, is often the most reliable of all our early documents, and we can probably assume that the final unstressed *a* of the Irish name, which was clearly weak at this stage, was omitted from the other sources (but cf. *-a* for *-e* in **Ballynure** above). The northern portion of the townland consists largely of rocky heath.

The death of Donn Sléibe ua Eochada, king of Ulster, at a place called *Belach Goirt an Ibair* is recorded in the Annals of Ulster under the year 1091 (*AU* (*Mac Airt*) 524). O'Donovan identifies this place with our Gortinure in his edition of the Annals of the Four Masters (*AFM* ii 946n) and is followed in this by Hogan (*Onom. Goed.* 101 sv. *belach goirt in ibair*). However, there are three other townlands in the north of Ireland called Gortinure: one in Leitrim, one in Fermanagh and one in the parish of Clondermot, Co. Derry, and it is clearly impossible that the annals are referring to this Gortinure.

Granaghan   *Greanachán*
C 8406   "little gravelly place"

1. gronsham	Esch. Co. Map 14	1609
2. Gronchan	Charter of Londonderry 391	1613
3. Grenahan	Lond. Comp. Valuation 307	1613
4. Grenahan (x2)	Phillips MSS (Maps) Plate 22	1622
5. Greeneagham	Phillips MSS (Maps) Plate 23	1622
6. Granaghan	Civ. Surv. iii 179	1654
7. Grouchan	Bishop. Der. i 264	1657
8. Granahan	Census 135	1659c
9. Grannaghan	BSD(c) 64	1661
10. Granan	HMR (Ó Doibhlin 2) 66	1663
11. Granaghan	Sampson's Map	1813
12. 'Gra-na-han	OSNB Pron. No. 6	1834c
13. Greanachán "A gravelly place"	J O'D (OSNB) No. 6	1834c
14. Granaghan "The little gravelly place"	Munn's Notes 193	1925
15. 'granəxən	Local pronunciation	1993

Greanach is used in a number of place-names to signify gravelly land (*Joyce* ii 374–5; cf.
Granagh in Cos Down, Antrim, Tyrone, and Limerick, and see **Granny** in parish of
Kilcronaghan above). Here it appears with the diminutive suffix *án* (see *Joyce* ii 33; cf.
Granaghan in Co. Clare, and Granaghan (Dillon) and Granaghan (Martin) in Co.
Roscommon).

Halfgayne   Of uncertain origin
C 8305

1. ½ Nean	Lond. Comp. Valuation 307	1613
2. Nean	Phillips MSS (Maps) Plate 24	1622
3. halfe Gian	Civ. Surv. iii 179	1654
4. Half Lea and Bellegean	HMR (Ó Doibhlin 2) 66	1663
5. Halfgayne	Sampson's Map	1813
6. Half-'gain	OSNB Pron. No. 6	1834c
7. Uibh-cathain "The territory of the...O'Cathains"	Munn's Notes 193	1925
8. haf'ge:n	Local pronunciation	1993

The origin of this name is now obscure. That the first element is English "half" is clear from
the earliest references (1, 3–4). Land units are frequently styled "half" or "quarter" lands in
our early sources and although it is unusual for the fraction to become an integral part of the
name, there are a number of examples where this has happened (**Half Umry** and **Halftown**,
Co. Antrim; **Halftown** Co. Tyrone).

The origin of the second element is less clear. O'Donovan seems to imply that it is the

English word "gain", but this is unlikely and is certainly at variance with the 17th-century forms of the name. The earliest of these, which both occur in related sources, show initial *n*, but this is hard to reconcile with the remainder of the forms. Elsewhere, we see the second element spelt *gian*, and the Hearth Money Rolls seem to record a wholly Irish form, *Bellegean*. The general weight of the evidence, therefore, tends to suggest that the second element has an Irish origin, although what this might be is now impossible to determine.

Knockoneill

C 8008

Cnoc Néill

"Niall's hill"

1.	Cnoc Ui Néill	OSL (Derry) 68	1740c
2.	Cnoc Uí Néill	DCCU 427	1740c
3.	knockneale	Esch. Co. Map 14	1609
4.	Knocknell	Charter of Londonderry 391	1613
5.	Knock Neale	Lond. Comp. Valuation 307	1613
6.	Knockneall	Phillips MSS (Maps) Plate 22	1622
7.	Knocko-Neale	Civ. Surv. iii 180	1654
8.	Knockoneale	Civ. Surv. iii 180,181	1654
9.	Knocknele	Bishop. Der. i 264	1657
10.	Knockeneill	Census 134	1659c
11.	Knock o'Neale	BSD(c) 65	1661
12.	Knoc-Oneill	Sampson's Map	1813
13.	Knockoneil	Custom of County (OSNB) No. 11	1834c
14.	Knock-o-'neel	OSNB Pron. No. 11	1834c
15.	Cnoc Uí Néill "O'Neill's hill"	J O'D (OSNB) No. 11	1834c
16.	Cnoc-ui-Niall "The hill of the O'Neills"	Munn's Notes 193	1925
17.	ˌnɔkə'neːl	Local pronunciation	1993
18.	ˌnɔkə'niːl	Local pronunciation	1993

The absence of the distinctive surname marker *Uí* from the earliest forms (3–6, 9) indicates that the last element is probably not the surname O'Neill but rather the personal name, *Niall* (gen. *Néill*). The O'Neills were the chief sept of the Cineál Eoghain whose control extended over the barony of Loughinsholin, and they were among the principal Irish families in the barony in the 17th century (*Census* 139). The Hearth Money Rolls record no O'Neills in the parish of Killelagh in 1663, but the name is very common in other parts of the barony, particularly in Ballynascreen and Maghera. Given the large number of O'Neills in the barony in the 17th century, it is hardly surprising that the place-name was reinterpreted as *Cnoc Uí Néill* (1–2), producing anglicized forms not unlike the modern form of the name (7–8, 10 etc.).

Knockoneill is a largely mountainous tract of land, but it seems to have taken its name from an eminence in a secluded part of the mountain on which stand the remains of an ancient cashel (*OSM* xviii 10). In the 19th century, the cashel's dry stone wall was up to 5 feet high in parts, and varied in breadth between 3 and 5 feet (*ibid.*). Inside the enclosure there were a number of graves, and other structures could be seen on the outside (*ibid.*). There was a tradition about the place that it was a monument raised over the bodies of Niall

McLaughlin and his followers who were supposedly killed in battle in the townland of **Slaghtneill** (see below). Stories about the names of these two townlands seem to have abounded in the 19th century for O'Donovan heard another version according to which Niall Glúndubh, the progenitor of the O'Neills, was slain at Knockoneill and buried in Slaghtneill, although he was in fact killed in the battle of Islandbridge, Co. Dublin, fighting against the Norse in 919 (*OSL (Derry)* 51; Byrne 1973, 164).

Moneysharvan
C 8505

Muine Searbhán
"thicket of the dandelions"

1. Muine Searbhán	OSL (Derry) 68	1740c
2. Muine Searbhán	DCCU 427	1740c
3. monisarua[n?]	Esch. Co. Map 14	1609
4. Moniservan	Charter of Londonderry 391	1613
5. Mone Sharnan	Lond. Comp. Valuation 307	1613
6. Monesheruan	Phillips MSS (Maps) Plate 22	1622
7. Munisterinall	Civ. Surv. iii 179	1654
8. Monisewan	Bishop. Der. i 264	1657
9. (?)Moryseriant	Census 135	1659c
10. Munisterinall	BSD(c) 64	1661
11. Moneysharven	HMR (Ó Doibhlin 2) 66	1663
12. Moneysharvin	Sampson's Map	1813
13. Mo-ney-'shar-vin	OSNB Pron. No. 6	1834c
14. Móin na Searbhán "Bog of the Dandelion"	J O'D (OSNB) No. 6	1834c
15. Móin-na-searbhán "the bog of the dandelions"	Joyce ii 341	1875
16. Moin-na-shearbhan "The bog of the dandelion"	Munn's Notes 194	1925
17. ˌmǫniˈʃarvən	Local pronunciation	1993

An origin from *Muine Searbhán* is supported by the form used in Ó Brolcháin's 18th-century poem in Irish, but the precise meaning of the second element is unclear. In the medieval period, *searbhán* denoted "oats, wild oats", as well as "dandelion", but elsewhere it is also taken to signify various other plants including "bitter herbs" (*DIL* sv. *serbán*; Ó Dónaill sv.; *Dinneen* sv.). I have followed previous authorities here in translating it "dandelion".

Slaghtneill
C 8205

Sleacht Néill
"Niall's gravemound"

1. slachtneale	Esch. Co. Map 14	1609
2. Slackmele	Charter of Londonderry 391	1613
3. Slot Neale	Lond. Comp. Valuation 307	1613
4. Slatneall	Phillips MSS (Maps) Plate 22	1622
5. Slatenele	Civ. Surv. iii 179	1654
6. Slackmele	Bishop. Der. i 264	1657

7. Slatnerll	Census 134	1659c
8. Slatenole	BSD(c) 64	1661
9. Silotneil	HMR (Ó Doibhlin 2) 66	1663
10. Slaghtneill	Sampson's Map	1813
11. Slaught-'neel	OSNB Pron. No. 6	1834c
12. Sleacht Néill "Niall's monument"	J O'D (OSNB) No. 6	1834c
13. < leacht "sepulchral carn"	Colton Vis. 82n	1850
14. "Niall's monument"	Joyce i 66	1869
15. Leacht-Nial "The sepulchral monument of Niall"	Munn's Notes 194	1925
16. slaxt'ne:l	Local pronunciation	1993

Sleacht, a variant of *leacht* "gravemound", may refer here to the cairn in the north-east of the townland (*Munn's Notes* 194; *NISMR* sh. 32 § 24; see **Slaghtybogy**, Maghera).

Local tradition had it that a Niall McLaughlin and his followers were killed in this townland in a battle with a son of a prince of the O'Neills in revenge for the death of his father at McLaughlin's hands (*OSM* xviii 10, 40). There is a remarkable correspondence between this tradition and a notice in a 17th-century topographical fragment according to which Niall McLaughlin was slain by Brian Catha Dúin (alias Brian O'Neill) at a place called *Slecht Néill* (*Top. Frag.* 69). However, this name appears in a section of the document dealing with O'Cahan's country (*Oireacht Uí Chatháin*), and the context strongly suggests that it was located in the old parish of Banagher rather than at Slaghtneill. There are numerous ancient monuments in the area covered by this section of the fragment, most notably the Aughlish stone circles, and it is possible that *Slecht Néill* refers to one of these. Legends and stories often migrate, sometimes over great distances, attaching significance and prestige to any place they reach, and it is quite likely that the tradition of the death of Niall McLaughlin was falsely attached to Slaghtneill.

Ó Ceallaigh further suggests that Slaghtneill may be the location of the battle of *Caimeirge*, fought in 1241, in which Brian O'Neill defeated the McLaughlins and was installed as lord of Cinéal Eoghain (*AFM* iii 302; Ó Ceallaigh 1950(b), 125). O'Donovan also appears to have considered Slaghtneill as a likely site for the battle (*AFM* iii 302n), although Hogan has some reservations and further postulates a location somewhere on the Donegal/Tyrone border (*Onom. Goed.* 140). However, perhaps the most likely site for the battle is at or near the stronghold of the McLoughlins in Inishowen, Co. Donegal, for O'Neill went to form an alliance with the O'Donnells before his attack on the McLoughlins at *Caimeirge*.

Swatragh
C 8508

An Suaitreach
"the (billeted) soldier"

1. a t-Suaitreach	OSL (Derry) 68	1740c
2. an tSuaithreach	DCCU 427	1740c
3. B:totry	Esch. Co. Map 14	1609
4. Ballitotry	Charter of Londonderry 391	1613
5. Soatrah	Lond. Comp. Valuation 307	1613
6. Swotrah	Phillips MSS (Maps) Plate 22	1622
7. Swatra	Civ. Surv. iii 179–181	1654

8. Ballitotrie	Bishop. Der. i 264	1657
9. Swetragh	Census 134	1659c
10. Swatra	BSD(c) 65	1661
11. Sweetthrugh	HMR (Ó Doibhlin 2) 76	1663
12. Swattragh	Par. Reg. (OSNB) No. 11	1808
13. Swatragh	Custom of County (OSNB) No. 11	1834c
14. 'Swat-ragh	OSNB Pron. No. 11	1834c
15. Suaitreach "a miry place"	J O'D (OSNB) No. 11	1834c
16. Suaithreach "The place of the soldiers"	Munn's Notes 194	1925
17. suaitreach "a hired Scandinavian soldier"	JRSAI lxxx 174	1950
18. An Suaitreach	GÉ 275	1989
19. 'swatrə	Local pronunciation	1993

The meaning "a miry place" has been suggested for this name (15), presumably based on the verb *suaith* "mix, knead", but no such word is attested and, indeed, such a formation is unlikely. A termination *-treach* appears in a number of names, notably in various places called Cullentragh (Irish *Cuileanntrach* "place of holly"), but it is unlikely to have been compounded with a verb. Nevertheless, the name may have been reinterpreted locally along these lines, for the Irish form used by Ó Brolcháin (1–2) indicates a fem. noun of the type commonly found in place-names, but it is clear from our earliest anglicized sources that the modern form is a shortened version of *Baile an tSuaitrigh* "townland of the (billeted) soldier" (3–4, 8). A similar development occurs in the name Saggart, Co. Dublin, which represents a shortened form of *Teach Sagard*, and we may further compare Columbkille in Co. Kilkenny which derives from *Cill Cholm Cille* (*GÉ* 269, *L. Log. C. Chainnigh* 66).

A spurious explanation of the name was recorded here in the 1830s. The name, so the story goes, was given to the place by a traveller who, wearied after a long journey, could find no place to stay until he came to Swatragh. There were only a few houses there at the time but the reception was so warm and hospitable that he named the place Swatragh which, by popular etymology, was understood to come from English "swath" meaning "jovial, merry" (*OSM* xviii 50).

Tirhugh
C 8407

Tír Aodha
"Hugh's land"

1. Tír Aodha	OSL (Derry) 68	1740c
2. Tír Aodha	DCCU 426	1740c
3. direa	Esch. Co. Map 14	1609
4. Dirla	Charter of Londonderry 391	1613
5. Teere	Lond. Comp. Valuation 307	1613
6. Teree	Phillips MSS (Maps) Plate 22	1622
7. Tirhugh	Civ. Surv. iii 179	1654
8. Treugh	Civ. Surv. iii 180	1654
9. Dirla	Bishop. Der. i 264	1657
10. Tirhire	Census 134	1659c

11. Tirhugh	BSD(c) 64	1661
12. Tirkie	HMR (Ó Doibhlin 2) 66	1663
13. Tir-hugh	Sampson's Map	1813
14. Ter-'hu	OSNB Pron. No. 6	1834c
15. Tír Aodha "Hugh's land or district"	J O'D (OSNB) No. 6	1834c
16. Tir-Aeda "The land of Aeda or Hugh"	Munn's Notes 194	1925
17. tər'hju:	Local pronunciation	1993
18. tər'kju	Local pronunciation	1993

Despite the inconsistency of our early spellings, we can be almost certain that Tirhugh derives from Irish *Tír Aodha* "Hugh's land" (see 1–2). The initial *d* in several related sources cited above is unrepresentative of the historical spellings as a whole, and it may be dismissed as a scribal error (3–4, 9). The representation of the final element as *hugh* is obviously by analogy with the personal name Hugh which is commonly used to translate Irish *Aodh*.

Tirkane
C 8203

Tír Chiana
meaning uncertain

1. Tír Chiana	OSL (Derry) 67	1740c
2. Tír Chiana	DCCU 426	1740c
3. tircheamia	Esch. Co. Map 14	1609
4. Treacheana	Bishop. Der. i 57	1610
5. Tirkeana or Tiercheana; except 3a...glebe	CPR Jas I 279a	1615
6. Tiercheana	Bishop. Der. i 102	1615
7. Tiraknogh	Civ. Surv. iii 191	1654
8. Tiraghogh	Hib. Reg. Loughinsholin	1657c
9. Tirkiane	Census 135	1659c
10. Tircrean	HMR (Ó Doibhlin 2) 66	1663
11. Tirkane	Sampson's Map	1813
12. Tir-'kane	OSNB Pron. No. 6	1834c
13. Tír Chathain "Kane's land or district"	J O'D (OSNB) No. 6	1834c
14. Tir-ic-Cathain "The country of the O'Cathains"	Munn's Notes 194	1925
15. Tír Chiana	GÉ 277	1989
16. tər'ke:n	Local pronunciation	1993

In his *Ecclesiastical Antiquities of Down, Connor and Dromore*, William Reeves identifies the place variously spelt as *Tirkehit, Tirkelin*, and *Tirkethin* in King John's grant of 1210 to Alan of Galloway as the barony of Tirkeeran (*EA* 324n), but in his edition of Colton's Visitation of the Diocese of Derry, he suggests, without reference to his previous identification, that it is our Tirkane (*Colton Vis.* 82n). The original identification with the barony is probably correct as the lands granted to Alan are described as "two cantreds beyond the Bann" (*duo cantreda ultra Banum*), namely, the cantreds of *Kunnock* (now the barony of Keenaght) and the aforementioned *Tirkehit* (*EA* 324).

Previous authorities have linked the name with the O'Kanes or O'Cahans (Irish Ó *Catháin*) but this suggestion is not supported by the historical evidence. Although O'Kane is among the most common names in the parish (*OSM* xxvii 99), there is no trace of the original *th* even in the earliest forms. The form suggested here is based on the Irish form used by Ó Brolcháin, but the meaning of the second element is unclear. The old personal name *Cian* might be considered suitable, but this elsewhere has gen. sing. *Céin*. Otherwise, there is a rare byform *ciana* of the word *cian* "distant" but the meaning here seems unsuitable in this context.

Tirnony	*Tir an Omhna*	
C 8403	"land of the tree-trunk"	
1. Tirwuony	Esch. Co. Map 14	1609
2. Tironony	Bishop. Der. i 57	1610
3. Tyronony	CPR Jas I 279a	1615
4. Tyronany	Bishop. Der. i 102	1615
5. Tiranony	Civ. Surv. iii 191	1654
6. Tyranony	Hib. Reg. Loughinsholin	1657c
7. Tyranony	BSD(c) 51	1661
8. Tirmony	HMR (Ó Doibhlin 2) 66	1663
9. Tiranony	Hib. Del. Derry	1672c
10. Tir-nony	Sampson's Map	1813
11. Ter-'no-ny	OSNB Pron. No. 6	1834c
12. Tir an una "land of scarcity or starvation"	J O'D (OSNB) No. 6	1834c
13. Tir-na-inneoin "The land of Inneoin, or...anvil"	Munn's Notes 195	1925
14. ˌtərˈnoːni	Local pronunciation	1993

This name is fairly consistently spelt in our 17th-century sources, and it is clear that, apart from a single syllable which has since been lost, the name has not changed dramatically since then. The first element is undoubtedly *tír* "land" (cf. **Tirkane** above) and the lost syllable probably represents a form of the article *an* "the". The final element is more difficult to establish but it is probably the word *omhna* (masc.) which usually denotes the trunk of a tree (see Ó Dónaill sv.; *DIL* sv. *omna*). This is not a common element in place-names but it does occur in a practically identical name in the Life of St Patrick, namely, *Tír Omna Snitheni* (*Trip. Life (Stokes)* i 82). The phrase *tír omna* appears in a run in the medieval text of Bricriu's Feast where the inability of such trunk-covered land to halt Conall Cernach's horses as his chariot sweeps through it is used to emphasize their power and force (*FB* 58 §47). The Ordnance Survey Memoirs report that timber, mainly fir and oak, was found in the bog in Tirnony (*OSM* xxvii 95) and it is likely that the name refers to a trunk or trunks found in the bog.

A form *Tir an Omhna* "land of the tree-trunk" accords best with the early 17th-century spellings, but we might also consider an origin from *Tír na nOmhnaí* "land of the tree-trunks". This consonant pattern, *r-n-n-n*, is innately unstable, and the loss of the *n* of the article may be explained in a number of ways (assimilation, dissimilation, haplology, metathesis). The later reduction to the modern trisyllabic form has resulted from the further weakening of the already weak vowel between *r* and *n*.

Tullyheran   *Tulaigh Chaorthainn*
C 8301   "hillock of the mountain ash"

1.	tollikerne	Esch. Co. Map 14	1609
2.	Tollikeran	Bishop. Der. i 57	1610
3.	Tollykeran	CPR Jas I 279a	1615
4.	Tollykeran	Bishop. Der. i 102	1615
5.	Tulloghkerran	Civ. Surv. iii 191	1654
6.	Tulloghke	Hib. Reg. Loughinsholin	1657c
7.	Tollokerane	Census 135	1659c
8.	Tullaghkerran	BSD(c) 51	1661
9.	(?)Fallyceivin	HMR (Ó Doibhlin 2) 66	1663
10.	Tullakeran	Hib. Del. Derry	1672c
11.	Tullogh-iren	Sampson's Map	1813
12.	Tul-lo-'e-ren	OSNB Pron. No. 6	1834c

13.	Tulaigh caorthainn "hill of the rowan trees"	J O'D (OSNB) No. 6	1834c
14.	Tulach-therm "The dry hillock"	Munn's Notes 195	1925

15.	ˌtоˌli'hɛrn	Local pronunciation	1993

It is extremely difficult to disentangle the history of the name Tullyheran from that of the nearby townland of **Tullykeeran Mountain**, and suggestions that the two names are ultimately of the same origin seem well-founded if not certain. In a list of the townlands in the parish in the Ordnance Survey Memoirs (1836) there is no mention of Tullykeeran Mountain, and it is noted in the Ordnance Survey Name Books for Killelagh Parish that "there are two townlands of this name or rather perhaps the townland is divided, consisting of a lowland and a mountain portion". In the same entry, Tullyheran is described as "good land renting at an average £1 per acre" while Tullykeeran Mountain is "wholly mountain bog".

References to Tullykeeran Mountain in our historical sources are rare, and the spellings assembled here certainly refer to Tullyheran, although it is not clear if at this time this included Tullykeeran Mountain. Tullyheran was ecclesiastical land, and this is useful in determining the ascription of historical spellings. A church is marked in the townland of *tollikerne* on the Escheated Counties map (1) leaving us in no doubt that this represents modern Tullyheran. It is reckoned as "termon or erenagh land" in a number of documents of ecclesiastical provenance (2–4), and is counted among the lands belonging to the See of Derry in the Civil Survey (5).

Difficulties in determining the correct ascription of 17th-century spellings to Tullykeeran Mountain are discussed below, but it is clear that the English affix "mountain" is at least as old as this period. This affix was almost certainly adopted in order to distinguish the two townlands from one another, and this implies that the two names were either of identical origin or that they were of separate origin but had become indistinguishable by the 17th century, at least in English speech. The fact, however, that Tullykeeran Mountain, with or without the suffix, does not appear independently in any early 17th-century sources, favours a common origin for the two names.

Reeves suggests that Tullykeeran Mountain, and thus by implication Tullyheron, was named after a certain Kieran who, he supposes, was the patron saint of the parish, but he cites no authority for this belief (*Colton Vis.* 82n). Indeed, as we have seen, the patron saint of Killelagh appears to have borne the name Muireadhach. The spellings listed here clearly suggest an origin in *Tulaigh Chaorthainn* "hillock of the mountain ash" (cf. **Moykeeran** above). The vowel *ao*, which came to be pronounced as an unrounded [u:] in Ulster Irish, was earlier pronounced [E:] (O'Rahilly 1932, 31–2). It is most frequently written *e* in place-names in 17th-century documents (cf. **Tirnageeragh** in Maghera), usually becoming *ee* by the 19th century, although a few names preserve the earlier realization (**Scarvagherin**, Co. Tyrone from Irish *Scairbh Chaorthainn* and **Gortaheran**, Co. Antrim from *Gort an Chaorthainn*). Thus, we have here, an example of a single name, *Tulaigh Chaorthainn*, giving two distinct modern forms, Tullyheron and Tullykeeran.

Tullykeeran Mountain C 7904	A hybrid form	
1. Tullaghkarrar, the [M]ountaine of	Hib. Reg. Loughinsholin	1657c
2. (?)Tyrokenny Mt	Hib. Del. Derry	1672c
3. Tully kerin	Sampson's Map	1813
4. Tulach-Chaerthainn "The hill of St. Kieran"	Munn's Notes 195	1925
5. Tulaigh-chaorthainn "hill of quicken-trees"	Joyce iii 590	1925
6. ˌt̥ʊliˈkiːrn məuntn	Local pronunciation	1993
7. ˌt̥ʊliˈhɛrn məuʔn (sic)	Local pronunciation	1993

As noted in the previous entry, Tullykeeran Mountain is an early hybrid of the name *Tullykeran* (later Tullykeeran) and the English word "mountain". It seems to have been considered part of *Tullykeran* during the 17th century and the suffix distinguishes this poor piece of mountainous land from the lower, more profitable, section now called **Tullyheran**.

There is some difficulty in identifying early forms of this name, although it is certain that none of the 17th-century spellings listed under **Tullyheran** belong here. The only spellings which can be assigned to Tullykeeran Mountain with any degree of certainty are those on Petty's maps of c.1657 and c.1672. Unfortunately, there is considerable confusion even here, for the two forms obtained from these maps are substantially different, and we can only conclude that the cartographer has committed a grave error. Petty's map of the barony of Loughinsholin depicts church lands, and the four erenagh lands of Tirnony, Carrowmenagh, Tirkane and Tullyheran, along with the glebe of Gortinure, are shown there. In addition, a place called "the [M]ountaine of Tullaghkarrar" is shown, and this must be our Tullykeeran Mountain. Tirkane is spelt "Tiraghogh" on the barony map (cf. "Tiraknogh" in *Civ. Surv.* iii 191), and it seems unlikely that the "Tyrokenny Mt" of the later county map, despite its apparent similarity, is Tirkane (Tirkane is also missing from the related Book of Survey and Distribution (1661)). On the other hand, "Tyrokenny Mt" bears little or no resemblance to the "Tullaghkarrar" of the barony map which we have identified with Tullykeeran Mountain. In short, "Tyrokenny Mt" must be the result of some spectacular scribal confusion, perhaps involving the name Tullykeeran Mountain, Tirkane and Tirnony. It is included among the spellings here as it nominally signifies the townland of Tullykeeran Mountain but it is, of course, of no use in attempting to ascertain the origin of the name.

Sadly, this leaves us with just a single form from the 17th century on which to base our analysis of this name. The circumstantial evidence strongly suggests that the Irish element of the name is of the same origin as the name **Tullyheran** and, as we have seen, there is nothing among the historical spellings there to contradict an origin in *Tulaigh Chaorthainn* "hillock of the mountain ash".

OTHER NAMES

Altkeeran River C 8004	A hybrid form	
1. Alt a' Chaorthainn "Glen of the rowan trees"	OSRNB 47 sh.32	1850c

Altkeeran River is clearly named after the glen through which it flows which was known in Irish as *Allt an Chaorthainn* "glen of the mountain ash". See **Tullykeeran Mountain**.

Back Parks C 8105	An English form	
1. ðə 'bak ˌparks	Local pronunciation	1993

In English place-names, "park" normally denotes "land enclosed for hunting or as a pleasure ground" (Field 1972, 160), and this is the sense in which it is used in many Irish place-names. Here, however, it probably signifies "field" and is therefore synonymous with the Irish word *páirc* "field" (see *Eng. Dial. Dict.* iv 424). In place-names, "back" is normally applied to land behind a house, field or other feature (Field 1972, 9).

Ballyheige C 8205	*Baile Uí Thaidhg* "Teague's townland"	
1. Baile Thaidhg	OSRNB 46 sh.32	1850c
2. ˌbaliˈhɛːg	Local pronunciation	1993

Ó Taidhg, anglicized Teague etc., was the name of an Ulster family who were anciently chiefs of Fir Lí, the district extending northwards from the Moyola River (Woulfe 1923, 650). The surname appears to have died out here by the 19th century as no one of that name is recorded as living in this townland in Griffith's Valuation (*Griffith's Val.* 46).

Ballynamona C 8104	*Baile na Móna* "townland of the bog"	
1. Ballynaˈmona	OSRNB 47 sh.32	1850c

2. "Bog Town"	OSRNB 47 sh.32	1850c
3. Baile na Móna "town of the Bog"	OSRNB 47 sh.32	1850c
4. ˌbalïnəˈmoːni	Local pronunciation	1993
5. ˌbalənəˈmonə	Local pronunciation	1993
6. ˌbalənəˈmo̞ni	Local pronunciation	1993

Named from a portion of bog (*OSRNB* 47 sh. 32).

Belleview
C 8509

An English form

A fancy name, from French *belle vue* "beautiful view".

Bonny Bush
C 8106

A Scots form

This spreading whitethorn was named from its remarkable aspect (Scots *bonny* "beautiful, pretty, fair"), and its situation in a small indentation in Carntogher mountain contributed towards making it much admired by the lovers of the picturesque in the last century (*OSRNB* 46 sh. 32). It was once believed to have been the haunt of fairies, and many people claimed to have seen it on fire (*OSM* xxvii 99). It no longer exists (Joe Doherty, pers. comm.).

Carn Hill
C 8407

An English form

1. ˈkjarn ˈhïl	Local pronunciation	1993
2. ˈkjɛrn ˈhïl	Local pronunciation	1993

Carn Hill was named from the ruins of a large cairn which formerly stood on its summit (*OSM* xxvii 101). It was already nearly obliterated in 1836 (*ibid.*) and is now completely gone.

Carntogher
C 7906

Carn Tóchair
"cairn of the causeway"

1. (?)co Lae[g] coa thachur	TBC (Rec. I) 1.3460	1100c
2. (?)co Láeg coa thóchur	TBC (LL) 1.4058	1160c
3. go mullach cáirn	OSL (Derry) 68	1740c
4. go mullach an Cháirn	DCCU 427	1740c
5. Carnantagher	Civ. Surv. iii 179	1654
6. Carntagher	Sampson's Map	1813
7. Carn-'togh-her	OSNB Pron. No. 6	1834c
8. Carn Tachair "Tachar's carn or heap"	J O'D (OSNB) No. 6	1834c
9. Carnán Tochair	Éire Thuaidh	1988
10. ˌkjɛrnˈtɔxər	Local pronunciation	1993

Carntogher appears to have been named from a cairn a short distance to the south of its peak near the place called Shane Crossagh's Leap (C 7905; see Chart 1940, 207; *OSL (Derry)* 132). Although there appears to be support for a derivation from *carnán* "little cairn" in the earliest English reference to the name (5), the remaining forms, and particularly the Irish forms (3–4), favour an origin from *carn* "cairn".

O'Donovan's interpretation of the name (13) is based on a local tradition recited to him by an old man called Donogh Roe McKenna according to which a giant called Tachar Mór was buried on **Carntogher**, and that he also gave name to Largantogher (*OSL (Derry)* 132). A comparable legend was recorded by O'Donovan in Glentogher in Inishowen, Co. Donegal, according to which St Patrick destroyed a serpent or demon called Tachar (MacNeill 1962, 146). Both traditions smack of folk etymology. The name Tachar seems to have been abstracted from each of the place-names concerned and there is possibly an intended pun on the word *tachar* "contention, strife". However, there can be little doubt that the final element in both names is *tóchar* "causeway". Wooden causeways have been built in Ireland since the Early Bronze Age and construction seems to have continued well into the Middle Ages and perhaps beyond (Lucas 1985, 44). They were important features in the landscape and they appear in a number of names, chiefly in the Midlands (*IPN* 154-5; Lucas 1985, 55–6). Glentogher lies near the ancient Patrician church of *Domhnach Mór Maí Tóchair* on what was probably the most direct route for travellers between Derry and north Inishowen and it is a natural place for an ancient roadway (MacNeill 1962, 146; *Trip. Life (Stokes)* i 156, 158). Similarly, the old road from Maghera to Dungiven passed over Carntogher close by the cairn (*OSM* xxvii 96).

There may be an early reference to the causeway at Carntogher in the epic tale *Táin Bó Cúailnge* "the cattle-raid of Cooley" (1-2). In one part, the king of Ulster, Conchobar, sends his son throughout his kingdom to rouse the warriors to battle. It is essentially a list of places and people, but the locations generally follow a rough scheme which allows us to locate each of the names within a geographical context (see Muhr 1994, 151 map). Not all the names in the list have been identified, but *Tachur* or *Tóchur* follows several places from the area to the west of Lough Neagh and immediately precedes a reference to the valley of Dungiven (*co Geimen coa glend*), so that it can probably be located somewhere in this area. The element *tóchar* is rare in the North, but there are two instances in this district, Largantogher and Carntogher. Of these two places, the latter is surely the more significant as it occupies a prominent position on an important route and we may tentatively identify the early *Tóchar* as Carntogher.

The early spellings for both Carntogher and **Largantogher** invariably represent the *ó* in *tóchar* as *a*, but although short-*o* is frequently lowered to *a* in Ulster Irish, the lowering of long-*o* is more characteristic of Scottish Gaelic and Manx (O'Rahilly 1932, 193). Variants such as *óg/ág* "young", *fód/fád* "sod" and *bóthar/báthar* "road" are permissible in Classical verse (McManus 1994, 347), but these words invariably retain the older *ó*-sound in Ulster Irish. Nevertheless, *tóchar* is sometimes written *tachar* in Irish MSS (it is never written long). The scribe of the Annals of Connacht, for example, twice writes *a* for *ó* in the name *Tóchar Móna Conneda*, now Templetogher in Co. Galway (*A. Conn.* 16, 138), and a similar variation occurs in the place-name cited from *Táin Bó Cúailnge* above (1–2). It is also interesting that the demon who gave name to Glentogher in Donegal was called Tachar, suggesting that a similar pronunciation was used in that place-name.

Cloghbane	*Cloch Bhán*	
C 7902	"white stone"	

| 1. "White Stone" | OSRNB 47 sh.32 | 1850c |

2. Cloch Bán "white stone"	OSRNB 47 sh.32	1850c

Cloghbane is a large pillar stone about 5 feet 9 inches high, 2½ feet broad and 1½ feet thick. In the last century it was regarded by the peasantry as being placed here by Finn McCool (*OSRNB* 47 sh. 32).

Craignahaltora
C 8305

Creag na hAltóra
"the rock of the altar"

1. "Altar Rock"	OSRNB 46 sh.32	1850c
2. Creag na h-altóra "rock of the altar"	OSRNB 46 sh.32	1850c

Craignahaltora is a steep ledge of rugged rocks (*OSRNB* 46 sh. 32). The final element in the name means "altar" and refers to the mass rock which still exists here (Joe Doherty, pers. comm.; Walsh 1973, 37).

Crockanroe
C 8209

Cnocán Rua
"red hillock"

1. Cnocán Ruadh "Red hillock"	OSRNB 45 sh.26	1850c

The mass of rushes growing on this hill gives it its red colour, and it is from this feature that it was named *Cnocán Rua* "red hillock".

Crockmore
C 8205

Cnoc Mór
"big hill"

1. "Big Hill"	OSRNB 60 sh.35	1850c
2. Cnoc Mor "great hill"	OSRNB 60 sh.35	1850c
3. krɔk'moːr	Local pronunciation	1993

Crockmore is a large hill (Irish *Cnoc Mór*) on the lower slopes of Carntogher Mountain.

Crocknaconspody
C 8009

Cnoc na Conspóide
"hill of the dispute"

Memories of controversies, disputes and squabbles are preserved in a number of Irish place-names, some of which appear to record wrangles over land (*Joyce* ii 459-461).

Doonan
C 8304

Na Dúnáin
"the little forts"

1. "The Forts"	OSRNB 47 sh.32	1850c
2. Dúnán "small fort"	OSRNB 47 sh.32	1850c
3. 'dunǝn	Local pronunciation	1993

This name clearly derives from the Irish word *dúnán* meaning "little fort". The plural form given in the translation (1) predates and is probably more authentic than O'Donovan's Irish form (2) and indicates that we should probably take the original form of the name to be *Na Dúnáin* "the little forts". We may compare the minor name Doonans in Co. Antrim, and Downings in Co. Donegal which, although now known in Irish as *Na Dúnaibh* "the forts" (dat. pl.), probably derives from a form identical to the one suggested here (see *IPN* 78). There are two enclosures or forts within ½ mile of Doonan (*NISMR* sh. 32).

Edendarragh	*Éadan Darach*	
C 8605	"hill-face of the oak"	
1. Edindarne	Civ. Surv. iii 180	1654
2. "The Oak Face"	OSRNB 47 sh.32	1850c
3. Eadan Darach "oak brae"	OSRNB 47 sh.32	1850c

Éadan is the first element in over a hundred townland names, almost all of which are to be found in Ulster (Ó Maolfabhail 1987–8, 80). It is particularly interesting in the current context that a significant proportion of these are of the form *Éadan Doire* "hill-face of the oak-wood" (*ibid.*).

| **Green Water** | An English form |
| C 8008 | |

The adjective "green" is rarely applied to rivers and streams, although we may note the name Green Burn in Co. Antrim (*OS 6-inch* sh. 45).

Lough Bran	*Loch Brain*	
C 8303	"Bran's lake" (?)	
1. lɔx ˈbran	Local pronunciation	1993

There is no longer a lake here, the area it formerly occupied now being swamp. O'Donovan cites a local legend concerning the origin of the name in a letter written in Draperstown in 1834 (*OSL (Derry)* 75). Lough Bran, he says, is called from Finn McCool's celebrated hound, Bran, which tore up the ground where the lake now stands in pursuit of an enchanted doe which, when nearly overtaken by Bran, suddenly sank into the earth by the power of magic. Bran was in such a rage to overtake this enchanted doe that he tore up the earth with his paws. At this time "a leaf of ivy was as large as a griddle, a black-bird's leg as large as that of an ox, and a deer as large as an elephant!" and the lake immediately sprang up where the hound had been digging.

It is quite possible that the name of the lake is purely fanciful in origin as suggested in this story, and we may compare the name of the nearby hill **Seefin** which can only be interpreted as relating to Finn McCool. However, more mundane interpretations may be advanced. Munn cites Scottish Gaelic *bran* meaning "a mountain stream" (*Munn's Notes* 192). We may also think of *bran* "a raven" which commonly occurs in place-names, and *bran* "bream" which is perhaps particularly suitable in the present context. Unfortunately, it is now virtually impossible to choose between these possibilities.

Moneyoran Hill   A hybrid form
C 7907

Joe Doherty of Gorteade informs me that there was once a powerful spring here and this might suggest that the final element in Moneyoran is *fuarán* "spring". In minor names, which are generally anglicized at a later date than townland names, Irish *ua* is sometimes rendered [u:] as in **Roohan** below, and **Lough Ouske** in the parish of Ballynascreen, but it more frequently becomes [o:] as in **Brough**, in Ballyscullion parish, **Boley** and **Crockaghole** in the parish of Ballynascreen, and **Derryhoma** and **Tullyroe Hill** in Maghera. However, we must also consider an origin from *feorainn* (gen. sing. *feorann*) "grassy place" (*Ó Dónaill* sv.) or "a verdant bank or patch on a mountainside" (*Dinneen* sv. *feora*). The identity of the first element cannot be deciphered with certainty, but the nature of the land here may suggest *mónaidh* "bog" (see Toner 1991–3).

Mullans Town   An English form
C 8404

   1. 'molənz 'təun   Local pronunciation   1993

So called from persons named Mullan who resided here for many years (*OSRNB* 47 sh. 32).

Pollan Water   A hybrid form
C 8004

   1. "deep holes"   OSRNB 47 sh.32   1850c

   2. 'polən 'watər   Local pronunciation   1993

The first element in this name derives form Irish *pollán* "a (small) pool", and it occurs in the names of several streams and rivers. A plural form is suggested by the translation recorded by the Ordnance Survey in the last century (1), with which we may compare **Doonan** above and **Pollangorm Hill** below.

Pollangorm Hill   A hybrid form
C 7908

   1. "The Blue Holes"   OSRNB 46 sh.32   1850c
   2. Pollán Gorm   OSRNB 46 sh.32   1850c

This is another instance of the word *pollán* "a (small) pool" (see previous entry). There are two small pools at the foot of Pollangorm Hill (OS C 8008) from which the name appears to derive. A plural form is suggested by the "blue holes" of the name books (1) as well as the existence of two pools, and we may propose an Irish form *Na Polláin Ghorma* "the blue pools". A singular form (2) was later proposed by O'Donovan purely on the basis of the anglicized spelling and does not carry much weight.

Ringsend   An English form
C 8507

   1. rïŋz'en   Local pronunciation   1993

There are a number of places of this name in Ireland, but all seem to have been named from Ringsend in Co. Dublin. This is a hybrid name, from Irish *An Rinn* "the point" (*GÉ* 266) and English "end", so that it denotes "the place at the end of the point". It was formerly a port of some importance and this may have contributed to the adoption of the name in other parts of the country, although its paradoxical nature (a ring has no end) almost certainly would have appealed to those who helped to disseminate it.

Rockfield	An English form	
C 8403		
1. 'rɔkfiːld	Local pronunciation	1993

This name was given to this place by a Mr Clark, a former owner, on account of the great number of stones which then lay about it (*OSRNB* 46 sh. 32). There are a number of places of this name in Antrim, Fermanagh and Down.

Roohan	*Ruachán*	
C 8303	"red land"	
1. Ruadhchan "reddish land"	OSRNB 47 sh.32	1850c
2. 'ruxən	Local pronunciation	1993

It is unlikely that we have here an instance of the word *ruachán* meaning "rocket" (any of numerous plants of the cabbage family). The suggestion here of an original *Ruachán* "red land" is based on O'Donovan's otherwise unattested postulated form (1). A note in the name books states that Roohan contains rough pasture and bog (*OSRNB* 47 sh. 32), and **Roohan** in the parish of Kilrea, which is probably of similar origin, stands on the northern extremity of a small tract of bog (*ibid.* 48 sh. 33). On the termination see **Granaghan** above, and *Joyce* ii 33.

| **Sallyvilla Cottage** | An English form |
| C 8508 | |

Sallyvilla Cottage was built by a Dr Mooney in the 19th century and named from the great number of sally or willow bushes which grew there (Joe Doherty, pers. comm.).

Seefin	*Suí Finn*	
C 8102	"Finn's seat"	
1. Suidhe Fin	OSL (Derry) 75	1834
2. Suidhe Finn "Sessio Finni"	OSL (Derry) 80	1834
3. Suidhe Finn "Sessio Finni"	OSRNB 47 sh.32	1850c
4. sə'f ïn	Local pronunciation	1993

Seefin is an isolated hill on top of which once stood an ancient pillar stone about 4 feet high until it was sent to the foot of the hill by some mischievous boys in 1833 (*OSRNB* 47 sh. 32; *OSM* xxvii 98). A tradition connected with the stone says that Finn McCool threw it from Slieve Gallion to the top of Seefin Hill (*OSM* xxvii 98; *OSL (Derry)* 75).

There was another hill in the parish of Ballynascreen, about a mile or a mile and a half south-west of the old church, called *Suí Ghoill* "Goll's seat" after Finn's arch-rival Goll mac Morna (*OSL (Derry)* 80). Local tradition had it that Finn and Goll occasionally used to sit on the tops of these two hills, a distance of over nine miles, and converse with each other (*ibid.*).

Stranagon	*Srath na gCon*	
C 8408	"river-meadow of the hounds"	
1. Sráth Bhán na gConn	OSL (Derry) 68	1740c
2. Srath Bán na gCon	DCCU 427	1740c
3. Srath na g-con "holm of the dogs"	OSL (Derry) 68	1834
4. "The Hounds Holme"	OSRNB 47 sh.32	1850c
5. Srath na gCon "holme of the hounds"	OSRNB 47 sh.32	1850c
6. ˌstranəˈgɔːn	Local pronunciation	1993

Stranagon takes its name from its low-lying location on the banks of the Knockoneill River. It was believed that it was formerly haunted by wolves which "use to frisk there in the sun" (*OSL (Derry)* 68; cf. *Joyce* i 480).

Wapping	Of English origin
C 8505	

This name may have been transferred from the Wapping in Middlesex which is thought to derive from a word for "marsh" related to Old English *wapol* (Ekwall 1960, 496). There is another Wapping in the townland of Carnanreagh, Co. Derry (*OS 6-inch* sh. 29).

Parish of Maghera

Townlands
Ballymacilcurr
Ballymacpeake Upper
Ballynacross
Ballynahone Beg
Beagh (Spiritual)
Bracaghreilly
Craigadick
Craigmore
Crew
Culnady
Curragh
Curran
Dreenan
Drumard
Drumconready
Drumlamph
Drummuck
Dunglady
Falgortrevy
Fallagloon
Gorteade
Grillagh
Gulladuff
Keady
Kirley
Largantogher
Lisnamuck
Macknagh
Moneymore
Moyagall
Rocktown
Slaghtybogy
Tamnymartin
Tamnymullan
Tirgarvil
Tirnageeragh
Toberhead
Upperland

Towns
Curran
Maghera

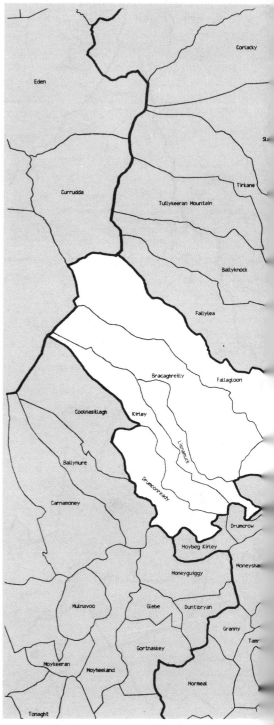

Based upon Ordnance Survey 1:50,000 mapping, with permissio
the Director of the Ordnance Survey of Northern Ireland,
Crown copyright reserved.

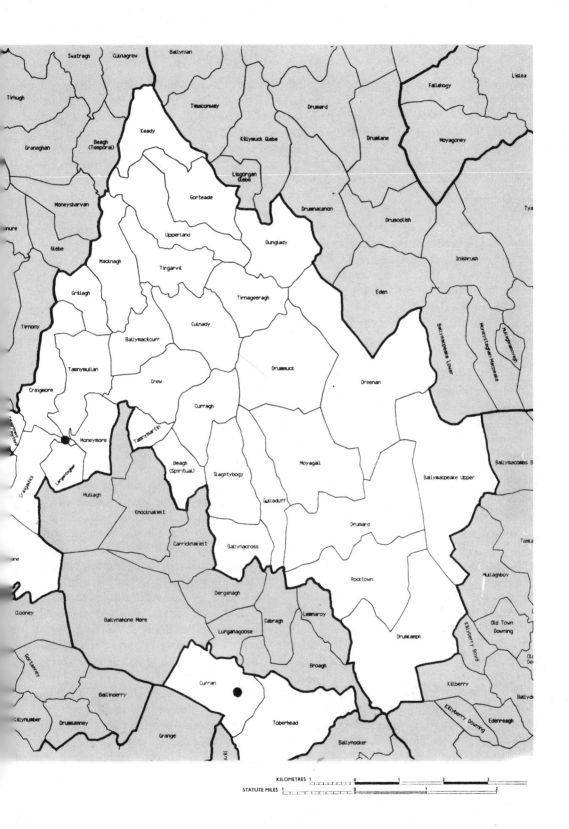

Swatragh Culnagrew Ballynian
Tirhugh
Beagh
(Temporal) Keady Tamaconway Drumard Fallahogy Listea
Granaghan Killymuck Glebe Drumlane Moyagoney
Moneysharvan Lisgorgan
Glebe Gorteade Drumacanon Drumoolish Tya
Upperland Dungiady Eden Inishrush
Glebe
Macknagh Tirgarvil Timageeragh
Grillagh
Tirnony Culnady Ballymacpeake Lower Moneystaghan-Macpeake Mulloghacurragh
Ballymacilcurr Drumuck Dreenan
Tamnymullan Crew
Craigmore Curragh
Moneymore Tamnymartin Ballymacombs B
Lurganboy Beagh
(Spiritual) Moyagall Ballymacpeake Upper
Craigadick Mullagh Slaghtybogy Gulladuff
Knocknakielt Drumard Tamla
Carricknakielt Ballynacross Mullaghboy
Rocktown
Clooney Derganagh Old Town
Downing
Ballynahone More Cabragh Lesnaroy
Lurganagoose Drumlamph Killyberry Boyd Old
Dev
Gortamney Broagh Killberry Ballyd
Curran
Ballinderry Killberry Downing Edenreagh
Killnumber Drumsamney
Grange Toberhead
Ballynocker

KILOMETRES 1   0   1   2   3
STATUTE MILES 1   0   1   2

167

THE PARISH OF MAGHERA

The memory of the 6th-century patron of the parish of Maghera, Lúrach mac Cuanach, is preserved in the earlier name for the parish, *Ráth Lúraigh* "Lúrach's fort". His brother, Bécc, was slain in the battle of Dún Bolg in Leinster in 598, and his nephew, Furudrán, died in 645 (*AU (Mac Airt)* 98, 124). Both were kings of the Uí Macc Uais whose territory extended south to the Moyola River (*ibid.*; *GUH* 21) and so must have included the modern parish of Maghera. Theirs was a family of some political importance in the area, for the medieval genealogies claim that seven descendants of Cuanu, Lúrach's father, were kings of Airgialla (*CGH* LL 333 c 40-46). Their centre of power may well have been located at Maghera, for this same tract states that they ruled all of Airgialla from their fort (*ráth*). The editor of the genealogies is almost certainly correct in taking this to be a common noun meaning "fort" rather than a proper name, but there is considerable circumstantial evidence to suggest that the fort was indeed situated at *Ráth Lúraigh* or Maghera. In one of the manuscripts, Lúrach mac Cuanach is said to have been from *Ráith*, which indicates a shorter, possibly earlier, form of the name (the other MSS have the longer form). Wealthy and influential families frequently endowed the Church with land, but in many instances, such as at Cashel, they even handed over their royal seats to the Church in order to curry favour and stake a moral claim on the territory which would endure for ever (Buckley 1989, 32). Given Lúrach's royal connections, it is not unlikely that he obtained the *ráth* which bears his name in such a manner.

The church was plundered by the Vikings in 832 (*AU (Mac Airt)* 288), and it was among several churches burned in 1135 (*AFM* ii 1050). The ruins of the medieval church still stand in the townland of Largantogher, and the earliest sections belong to the 12th century (Speer 1990, 45; Hamlin 1976, i 139–40; ii 581–4; cf. Walsh 1973, 20).

When a modern diocesan structure was created at the Synod of Rathbrassil in 1111, Maghera was incorporated into the diocese of the Cinéal Eoghain, the seat of which was placed at Ardstraw. About the year 1150, however, the bishop, Muireadhach Ó Cobhthaigh, transferred the seat to his native Maghera (Walsh 1973, 22). The seat remained here until 1254 when, under pressure from the then bishop Germanus Ó Cearbhalláin who complained of its isolation from the mainstream of civilization, it was finally removed to Derry (*ibid.* 23).

Naturally, Maghera decreased in importance after this date but it is still frequently mentioned in ecclesiastical documents of the 15th century. Many of these documents deal with controversies and scandals in the local church at this time, and help us to identify the powerful ecclesiastical families of the later medieval period. Throughout the first half of the 15th century, the ecclesiastical offices in the parish were filled by several priests of the names MacGeoghagan (*Mac Eochagáin*) and O'Keelt (*Ó Caoilte*), the latter of which is also closely associated with the neighbouring parish of Termoneeny (Walsh 1973, 26–7). The obscure surname *Otchegan* was borne by the holders of ecclesiastical office in various churches in south Derry in the 15th century, and is associated with the church of Maghera in the second half of that century (see *GUH* 35–37).

Following the Plantation, the lands in Maghera were divided among three of the London Companies (Mercers, Vintners and Drapers), with a large portion around the modern town of Maghera going to the Established Church, and it is documents relating to these organizations which provide us with the first detailed picture of the townland landscape in this area.

PARISH NAME

Maghera   *Machaire Rátha*
                                   "plain of the fort"

1. Rátha Lúiricch, Fergus	AFM i 426	814
2. Ratha Luraigh, Fergus	AU (Mac Airt) 272	817
3. Rátha Lúirigh, Orgain	AFM i 444	831
4. Ratha Luraigh, Orggain	AU (Mac Airt) 288	832
5. Ráith Lúraigh 7 ilchealla archena	AFM ii 1050	1135
6. ō Rāith Lūrig (vl. Luraig)	CGH LL 333 c 51	1160c
7. Rátha Lúraigh, saccart	AFM iii 192	1218
8. ag Ráith Lúraigh	AFM iii 522	1320
9. Rátha (gen.)	Mart. Gorm. May 19 100n	1630c
10. 'sgo Machaire Arā	Cín Lae Ó M. 10	1645c
11. i bparr[áiste] Machaire a' Rā	Cín Lae Ó M. 15	1645c
12. Machuire Rath Luraidh	Top. Frag. 83	1675c
13. Machaire Ratha	Top. Frag. 72	1680c
14. Rathur'	Eccles. Tax. (CDI) 215	1306c
15. Ratlowry	Colton Vis. 76	1397
16. Rathloury	Colton Vis. 81	1397
17. Rathluraich, the parish church of	Annates Ulst. 211	1411
18. Rathluraygh, par. ecclesie de	Annates Ulst. 189	1426
19. Rathlory	Reg. Swayne 156	1435
20. Raythluraych alias de Raythia	Cal. Papal Letters x 726	1454
21. Rathlubraich	Cal. Papal Letters xii 35	1459
22. Rathlurach	Cal. Papal Letters xii 692	1469
23. Rathlure, bishop of	Cal. Papal Letters xiii 398	1474c
24. Magherira	CPR Jas I 376b,377a	1609
25. Magheria	Bishop. Der. i 57	1610
26. Magheriah	Bishop. Der. i 62	1610
27. Maharry	Speed's Ulster	1610
28. Maharry	Speed's Ireland	1610
29. Magheriaghe	Bishop. Der. i 80	1611
30. Magheryeagh	CPR Jas I 279a	1615
31. Magheriagh	CPR Jas I 280a	1615
32. Magheryeagh, the manor of	CPR Jas I 280a	1615
33. Magheryeagh	Bishop. Der. i 102	1615
34. Magheriagh	Bishop. Der. i 109	1615
35. Magherieagh	Bishop. Der. i 109-112	1615
36. Maghirelagh alias Maghera	Fairs & Markets 54	1615
37. Magherieagh	CPR Jas I 314a	1616
38. Magherieagh, vill' de	Bishop. Der. i 121	1617
39. Magheray, R'c'oria de	Bishop. Der. i 129	1617c
40. Maherah, The Church Lands of	Phillips MSS (Maps) Plate 24	1622
41. Maghera	CPR Jas I 567b	1623
42. Magheragh	Bishop. Der. i 145,146	1624c
43. Magherah	Bishop. Der. i 181	1634?
44. Magheragh	Civ. Surv. iii 167	1654
45. Magherah	Civ. Surv. iii 168,181	1654
46. Magheragh	Civ. Surv. iii 174,180–182	1654
47. Maghera	Civ. Surv. iii 177-180	1654
48. Maghera	Civ. Surv. iii 187,191	1654

49. The parish of Maghera	Hib. Reg. Loughinsholin	1657c
50. Maghara	Census 134	1659c
51. Machara	Bishop. Der. i 326	1661
52. Maghera & Lergantagher	BSD(c) 52	1661
53. Magherieagh or Magheragh	Fairs & Markets 54, 95	1662
54. Maghara	Bishop. Der. i 354	1663
55. Maghera	Bishop. Der. i 357,361	1663
56. Magheregh, The Parish of	HMR (Ó Doibhlin 2) 75	1663
57. Magharah al's Magheragh	Bishop. Der. i 405	1666
58. Maghera	Bishop. Der. i 415	1668
59. Maghera-Matrix	Bishop. Der. i 425	1669
60. Maghera	Bishop. Der. i 425	1669
61. Maghera	Bishop. Der. ii 1	1671
62. Maghera (x2)	Hib. Del. Derry	1672c
63. Maghera	Bishop. Der. ii 34	1677
64. Maghera, church of	Bishop. Der. ii 35	1677
65. Maghera	Bishop. Der. ii 40	1680
66. Rathlawrey, Decanatus de	Bishop. Der. ii 113	1686
67. Magheragh, Rec' de	Bishop. Der. ii 113	1686
68. Maghera	Lamb Maps Derry	1690c
69. Rathlawry, Decanatus de	Bishop. Der. ii 136	1692
70. Maghera, [S'ti] Lurochy	Bishop. Der. ii 136	1692
71. Magherah	Bishop. Der. ii 509	1700c
72. Maghera	Bishop. Der. ii 482	1703
73. Maghera	Par. Reg. (OSNB) No. 11	1785
74. Maghera	Sampson's Map	1813
75. Maghera R.	Sampson's Map	1813
76. Machaire Ratha "plain of the rath"	J O'D (OSNB) No. 11	1834c
77. Lurach's Fort	AFM i 446n	1856
78. Machaire "The plain"	Munn's Notes 220	1925
79. Machaire Rátha	GÉ 250	1989
80. ˌmaxəˈraː	Local pronunciation	1993

Throughout the medieval period, the parish of Maghera was known by the name *Ráth Lúraigh* meaning "Lúrach's fort", but by the 17th century it had acquired its modern name *Machaire Rátha* "plain of the fort" (see above). The reduction of *Machaire Rátha* to its modern form is exactly paralleled by the development of the name **Maghera** in Co. Down which is of identical origin.

TOWNLAND NAMES

Ballymacilcurr
C 8602

Baile Mhic Giolla Choradh
"McGilcorry's townland"

1. bunadh an bhaile...Da sloinntear Mac Ghiolla Chorp	OSL (Derry) 67	1740c

2. bunadh an bhaile...dá sloinntear Mac-Giolla Chuirr	DCCU 426	1740c
3. B:mtgillcorrow	Esch. Co. Map 14	1609
4. Ballinekillycarrow	Charter of Londonderry 391	1613
5. Ba: Mc: Killcarn	Lond. Comp. Valuation 307	1613
6. Ba: McKilcor	Phillips MSS (Maps) Plate 24	1622
7. Bellimcillcuragh	Civ. Surv. iii 180	1654
8. BallimcChury	Civ. Surv. iii 180	1654
9. Ballimcgillecorrow	Bishop. Der. i 264	1657
10. Bolunackilcar	Census 134	1659c
11. Ballymcillcurragh	BSD(c) 65	1661
12. Ballymacgillcur	Par. Reg. (OSNB) No. 11	1788
13. Ballymackilcurr	Par. Reg. (OSNB) No. 11	1790
14. Ballymacelcurr	Sampson's Map	1813
15. Ballymacilcurr	Custom of County (OSNB) No. 11	1834c
16. Bally-mackle-'curr	OSNB Pron. No. 11	1834c
17. Baile mic Giolla Cuirr "MacGilcor's town"	J O'D (OSNB) No. 11	1834c
18. Baile-mic-Giollchuir "Magilcor's Town"	Munn's Notes 220	1925
19. Baile-Mic-Giollchuir "Magilcors' town"	Joyce iii 103	1925
20. ˌbaliˌmakəl'kọr	Local pronunciation	1993
21. ˌbaliˌmakə'kọr	Local pronunciation	1993

Tadhg Ó Brolcháin, in a poem written in exile on his home parish of Maghera, refers to people called Mac Giolla Chuirr (rhyming with *tuinn*):

> Dá gcluineadh bunadh an bhaile úd
> Dá sloinntear Mac-Giolla Chuirr
> Mise bheith gan aon bhraon bainne,
> Leó dob fhaiteach mé dhul ar tuinn. (*DCCU* 426)

(If the folk of that townland who are named MacGilcorry should hear that I am without a drop of milk they would rue my going to sea.)

Ó Ceallaigh takes this to be the surname in the name of this townland and connects it with a certain Giolla Corr whose son or grandson, chief of the Uí Bhranáin of Coleraine, was slain in 1186 (*GUH* 47). It is peculiar, given this reference, that nobody of that name is listed among the inhabitants of Maghera, or any part of the county for that matter, in the Hearth Money Rolls. Moreover, early anglicizations of the name show that it formerly had an extra syllable (3–4, 7–9, 11) and this suggests that the surname used by Ó Brolcháin is not the same as that which gave rise to the name of the townland. The surname *Mac Giolla Choradh*, which is tentatively postulated here, is not attested in any of the surname works, but it seems to be suggested by these early forms. *Giolla* in personal names is most frequently qualified by the name of a saint or a colour (Ó Cuív 1986, 19–20) but very occasionally by a common noun, usually indicating the circumstances of the bearer's birth (e.g. *Mac Giolla Gheimhridh* < *geimhreadh* "winter").

Ballymacpeake Upper H 9399	*Baile Mhic Phéice* "MacPeake's townland"		
1. Go Baile Mic Péice	OSL (Derry) 67	1740c	
2. go Baile Mhic Péice	DCCU 426	1740c	
3. (?)b: vakpeck	Esch. Co. Map 13	1609	
4. Balle Mc: Peakes	Lond. Comp. Valuation 308	1613	
5. Bellimcperke	Civ. Surv. iii 168	1654	
6. the two Bellimcperks	Civ. Surv. iii 180	1654	
7. Ballyvickpeeke	Bishop. Der. i 267	1657	
8. Bally McPeake	Census 134	1659c	
9. Ballymcperke	BSD(c) 65	1661	
10. Ballym'Peake	HMR (Ó Doibhlin 2) 76	1663	
11. Ballymacpeake	Par. Reg. (OSNB) No. 11	1786	
12. Ballymacpeake	Sampson's Map	1813	
13. Ballymacpeake	Custom of County (OSNB) No. 11	1834c	
14. Bally-mac-'peak	OSNB Pron. No. 11	1834c	
15. Baile mic Peice "Mac Peake's town"	J O'D (OSNB) No. 11	1834c	
16. Baile-mac-Fiacha "The town of the MacPeakes"	Munn's Notes 221	1925	
17. ˌbɑləmak'pɛ:k	Local pronunciation	1993	
18. ˌbɑləmək'pe:k 'ʊpər	Local pronunciation	1993	

MacPeake, according to Woulfe, is a rare West Ulster surname meaning "son of *Péic*" (Woulfe 1923, 399), where the name *Péic* is thought to derive from Old English *pēac* "a thick-set man" (MacLysaght 1985, 242; Reaney 1958, 245). The surname MacPeake is clearly of some antiquity in this townland and, while now quite widely dispersed, is still most numerous along the Bann near Lough Beg (see *Griffith's Val.* 103–4).

The division of Ballymacpeake into two parts predates our earliest sources. As one might expect, **Ballymacpeake Lower** in the parish of Tamlaght O'Crilly was usually known as *Baile Mhic Phéice Íochtarach* "lower Ballymacpeake" but the upper portion was known simply as *Baile Mhic Phéice* with no qualifying adjective.

Ballynacross H 8998	*Baile na Croise* "townland of the cross"		
1. b:necrossie	Esch. Co. Map 14	1609	
2. Ballmecrassie	Charter of Londonderry 391	1613	
3. Ballymacrossy, The small proportion called	Charter of Londonderry 391	1613	
4. Ball: ne Crosse	Lond. Comp. Valuation 307	1613	
5. Ballene Cross	Phillips MSS (Maps) Plate 24	1622	
6. Ballnacrosse	Civ. Surv. iii 180	1654	
7. Ballinecrossie	Bishop. Der. i 265	1657	
8. Ballinacrassie	Bishop. Der. i 265,277	1657	

9. Bolynecrosse	Census 134	1659c
10. Ballanacrosse	BSD(c) 65	1661
11. Ballynagrosse	HMR (Ó Doibhlin 2) 76	1663
12. Ballynecrush	Par. Reg. (OSNB) No. 11	1786
13. Ballynacrush	Par. Reg. (OSNB) No. 11	1787
14. Ballinacross	Sampson's Map	1813
15. Ballynacross	Custom of County (OSNB) No. 11	1834c
16. Bally-na-'cross	OSNB Pron. No. 11	1834c
17. Baile na croise "town of the cross"	J O'D (OSNB) No. 11	1834c
18. Baile-na-croise "The town of the Cross"	Munn's Notes 221	1925
19. ˌbalənəˈkrɔs	Local pronunciation	1993

The name Ballynacross clearly originates in Irish *Baile na Croise* "townland of the cross". The final vowel, although now lost, is evident in a number of early forms (1–3, 7–8). Locally, the name "Crush", an anglicization of Irish *An Chrois* "the cross", is given to a hill across which parishioners used to walk to the back door of the church (Ní Mhaolchallann 1993, 20–1). Irish *crois* is frequently anglicized *cross* despite being closer in sound to English "crush", apparently by conscious analogy with the English word *cross* (cf. Adams 1954).

Ballynahone Beg
H 8498

Baile na hAbhann Beag
"little Ballynahone (townland of the river)"

1. b:nehoune	Esch. Co. Map 14	1609
2. Ballmahoun	Charter of Londonderry 391	1613
3. Ballinehone	Bishop. Der. i 145	1624c
4. Ballinahowne	Civ. Surv. iii 175,178	1654
5. Ballinahowne begg	Civ. Surv. iii 176	1654
6. (?)Bellinahowe	Civ. Surv. iii 178	1654
7. Bellinehowne	Civ. Surv. iii 179	1654
8. Bellinehowne	Civ. Surv. iii 187	1654
9. Ballynahouin	Bishop. Der. i 265	1657
10. Ballinchonc	Hib. Reg. Loughinsholin	1657c
11. Bolinhona	Census 134	1659c
12. Boghmyhonc	HMR (Ó Doibhlin 2) 76	1663
13. Ballinehonbeg	Hib. Del. Derry	1672c
14. Ballinehone	Par. Reg. (OSNB) No. 11	1786
15. Ballynahone	Par. Reg. (OSNB) No. 11	1790
16. Ballinahonebeg	Sampson's Map	1813
17. Ballynahone	Custom of County (OSNB) No. 11	1834c
18. Bally-na-'hone-beg	OSNB Pron. No. 11	1834c
19. Baile na habhann "town of the river"	J O'D (OSNB) No. 11	1834c
20. Baile-na-h-abhann "The townland of the river"	Munn's Notes 221	1925

21. ˌbalənəˈhoːn	Local pronunciation	1993

See **Ballynahone More** in the parish of Termoneeny.

Beagh (Spiritual)	*An Bheitheach*	
H 8799	"the place of birch trees"	

1. Air a Bheithigh	OSL (Derry) 66	1740c
2. A Beitheach bhuadhach	OSL (Derry) 68	1740c
3. An Bheitheach bhuadhach	DCCU 427	1740c
4. Behagh piritnall	Civ. Surv. iii 180	1654
5. Beahogh	BSD(c) 52	1661
6. Beagh	HMR (Ó Doibhlin 2) 76	1663
7. Beheagh	Hib. Del. Derry	1672c
8. Beagh	Par. Reg. (OSNB) No. 11	1787
9. Beagh	Sampson's Map	1813
10. Beagh	Custom of County (OSNB) No. 11	1834c
11. 'Bay	OSNB Pron. No. 11	1834c
12. Beitheach "birch land; abounding in birch"	J O'D (OSNB) No. 11	1834c
13. Beitheach "The place abounding in birch trees"	Munn's Notes 221	1925
14. ðə 'beː	Local pronunciation	1993
15. 'bejax	Local pronunciation	1993

The name Beagh is clearly derived from Irish *An Bheitheach* meaning "the place of birch trees" with loss of the original intervocalic *th* as one would expect in the Irish of East Ulster (O'Rahilly 1932, 207–8). It is clearly identical in origin to the name **Beagh (Temporal)**. Although now in the parish of Killelagh, Beagh (Temporal), which then belonged to the company of Mercers, was formerly in the parish of Maghera, so clearly some distinguishing tag was required.

All our earliest references are to Beagh (Temporal). Beagh (Spiritual) is not mentioned until the Civil Survey of 1654 (4), and only occurs as a denomination for the first time in the Books of Survey and Distribution along with **Tamnymartin**.

Bracaghreilly	*An Bhreacach*	
C 8000	"the speckled place"	

1. B:nebracky	Esch. Co. Map 14	1609
2. Ballmabrcky	Charter of Londonderry 391	1613
3. (?)Brackah	Lond. Comp. Valuation 309	1613
4. (?)Prackan	Phillips MSS (Maps) Plate 28	1622
5. Ballynalraky	Bishop. Der. i 266	1657
6. Brackagh	Census 134	1659c
7. Broghah, half	HMR (Ó Doibhlin 2) 75	1663
8. Brogha, half	HMR (Ó Doibhlin 2) 75	1663

9. Brackaghreyly	Sampson's Map	1813
10. Bracaghreilly	Custom of County (OSNB) No. 11	1834c
11. Brac-cagh-'khreel-ly	OSNB Pron. No. 11	1834c

12. Breacach Uí Raighilligh "O'Reilly's speckled land"	J O'D (OSNB) No. 11	1834c
13. Breacach-ui-Ragaillighigh "O'Reilly's speckled townland"	Munn's Notes 221	1925
14. Breacach-Ui-Raghaillighigh "O'Reilly's speckled land"	Joyce iii 148	1925

15. ˌbrakəˈraili	Local pronunciation	1993

It is clear from our 17th-century sources that this townland was known as *Baile na Breacaí* "townland of the speckled place" as well as by a simpler form *An Bhreacach* "the speckled place". More recently it has been given a suffix to distinguish it from other similarly named places (cf. **Brackagh** in Ballynascreen, **Brackagh** in Lissan, **Brackagh Slieve Gallion** in Desertmartin, and **Brackaghlislea** in Kilcronaghan). O'Donovan, Joyce and Munn have all taken this suffix to be the surname O'Reilly (Irish *Ó Raghallaigh*), but Ó Ceallaigh makes the interesting suggestion that it is the place called *Roilgheach*, mentioned by Ó Mealláin, where Cormac O'Neill was attacked by the garrison of Coleraine during the war of 1642 (*GUH* 123n). However, this place is plausibly identified by the editor of Ó Mealláin's text as **Rallagh** in the parish of Banagher (*Cín Lae Ó M.* 55).

Craigadick
H 8499

Creag an Díogha (?)
"rock of the poor land"

1. Cregada	Esch. Co. Map 14	1609
2. Creggada	Bishop. Der. i 57	1610
3. Creggada	CPR Jas I 279a	1615
4. Creggada	Bishop. Der. i 102	1615
5. Cregduff	Civ. Surv. iii 193	1654
6. Cregadig	Hib. Reg. Loughinsholin	1657c
7. Craigadick	Census 134	1659c
8. Cregadig als Cregduffe	BSD(c) 52	1661
9. Cragaduff	HMR (Ó Doibhlin 2) 75	1663
10. Cregadig (a added above line)	Hib. Del. Derry	1672c
11. Cregadick	Par. Reg. (OSNB) No. 11	1787
12. Craigadic	Sampson's Map	1813
13. Craigadick	Custom of County (OSNB) No. 11	1834c
14. Craig-a-'dick	OSNB Pron. No. 11	1834c

15. Creagan dige "rock of the dike"	J O'D (OSNB) No. 11	1834c
16. Craig-a-dearc "The rock of the eye, or cave"	Munn's Notes 221	1925

17. ˌkrɛgəˈdïk	Local pronunciation	1993

The historical spellings gathered here seem to indicate that the townland of Craigadick bore three distinct names at different periods in the 17th century, *Cregada* (1–4), *Cregduff* (5,

8–9), and *Cregadig* or *Craigadick* (6–8, 10–14). However, all these apparently distinct forms are virtually identical in sound, and the only major difference between them is in the realization of the final consonant. If we accept the reading *Cragaduff* (9) over the two forms *Cregduff(e)* which derive from related sources (5, 8), then all the forms are trisyllabic. This raises the very real possibility that the three names are not distinct at all, but mere variants of a single name. However, even allowing for some degree of scribal error, it is difficult to reconcile the remaining differences, and it is perhaps fair to consider the current form of name in isolation.

O'Donovan's suggestion of a final element *díog* "ditch" (15), from Anglo-Norman *digue*, is quite plausible. *Díog* is rare in place-names, but there are a few examples of its use. Bodyke in Co. Clare, for example, is called *Lubán Díge* in Irish, and *Díog Bhuí* "yellow ditch" is the name of a place on Rathlin Island (*GÉ* 192; Mac Giolla Easpaig 1989–90, 42). There are no recorded forts and no linear earthworks in the townland, although this may not be significant as the ditch in question may have been so small as to leave no visible trace.

We may, therefore, tentatively suggest an original form *Creag na Díge* "the rock of the ditch". The loss of the final, unstressed vowel is quite normal in East Ulster place-names, and the devoicing of the resulting final *g* to give *k* may be explained through dissimilation. The shortening of the long-*i* does not present any great problems for it was recorded as half long in Tyrone Irish earlier this century, and there is, in any case, a tendency among English speakers to shorten vowels in place-names, even in stressed position (Stockman & Wagner 1965, 72; Holmer 1940, 12–13). However, the complete absence of the *n* of the article from any of the historical forms is problematic. Although this *n* disappears in many other names after a stop (most commonly *t*) it was usually still audible in the 17th century and can be seen in forms of that date (see **Gortagowan** and **Gortileck**, Co. Tyrone; **Gorticross**, Co. Derry; **Crockacahir** in Ballynascreen above). We encounter similar problems if we take the final element to be *díobhóg* "a stream through boggy land", in addition to which we must note the absence of any indication of the *bh* in the early forms.

It might be possible to take the first element to be plural *creaga* "rocks", but the post-Norman provenance of the noun *díog* would lead us to expect the article in this context (cf. **Drumcrow** in the parish of Kilcronaghan above). O'Donovan's *creagán* "rocky place" may be dismissed on similar grounds and, furthermore, we should surely expect to see some evidence of the -*n* among the 17th-century spellings (15).

In Donegal Irish, medial broad *dh* and *gh* are still pronounced in certain words (Quiggin 1906, 116–7). Although they are now more commonly vocalized, there is some evidence to suggest that they survived even in final position into the 17th century and traces of them can be seen in some place-names. Muff in Co. Donegal, for example, comes from Irish *Magh* "plain", and although the original *dh* in names such as **Drumantine** in Co. Down, and **Feehogue** in Co. Antrim has disappeared, it is apparently preserved in some 17th-century spellings (*PNI* i 99; iv 45). Initially, *gh* regularly gives *g* in anglicized forms of place-names, as occasionally does *dh* (*PNI* i 122), and we could well argue that this has happened non-initially here. Thus, a masc. noun with non-palatal medial or final *gh* or *dh* might explain all the forms listed above.

Díogha (masc.) "the worst (of something)", although now obsolete in speech, is preserved in a number of proverbs in Donegal where it is pronounced [d'i:u] (*Dinneen* sv.; *Ó Dónaill* svv. *díg, díogha*; *DIL* sv. *digu*). In the 17th century, the *gh* would have still been audible, and the name may have been pronounced [ˌkrɛɡəˈdiəɣə] or something approximating to this. This would quite naturally produce forms such as *Cregadig* (6, 8, 10), from which we get *Craigadick* (7, 11–14). The earliest forms (1–4), if they are to be included here, should probably be read as *Creggadue*. The Middle English/Early Modern English diphthong [iu] which became [u:] in words like "due" during the course of the 16th and 17th centuries, closely resembles the pronunciation of *díogha* following vocalization of the *gh*, and this is probably how we should pronounce these forms (see Barber 1976, 299–300; cf. *PNI* i 72–4 for similar variation between *i* and *u*). Forms such as *Cragaduff* (5, 8–9) should probably be interpreted in a similar light, but here a weakened *gh* becomes *f*. The use of this word in place-names has not previously been noted but it surely was applied to a poor piece of land, in this case possibly to that portion of the townland which juts into Ballynahone Bog.

Craigmore
C 8501

Creag Mhór
"large rock"

1. b:cregmora	Esch. Co. Map 14	1609
2. Creggamore	Bishop. Der. i 57	1610
3. Creggamore	CPR Jas I 279a	1615
4. Cregganmore	Bishop. Der. i 102	1615
5. Cregmore	Civ. Surv. iii 193	1654
6. Creganmore	Hib. Reg. Loughinsholin	1657c
7. Craigmoore & Tornymolan	Census 134	1659c
8. Cregmore	BSD(c) 52	1661
9. Cregmore	HMR (Ó Doibhlin 2) 77	1663
10. Creganmore	Hib. Del. Derry	1672c
11. Craigmore	Bishop. Der. ii 113	1686
12. Creigmore	Bishop. Der. ii 113	1686
13. Craigmore	Par. Reg. (OSNB) No. 11	1787
14. Craigmore	Sampson's Map	1813
15. Craigmore	Custom of County (OSNB) No. 11	1834c
16. Craig-'more	OSNB Pron. No. 11	1834c
17. Creag Mhor "great rock"	J O'D (OSNB) No. 11	1834c
18. Craig-mor "The great rock"	Munn's Notes 221	1925
19. krɛg'mo:r	Local pronunciation	1993

Slight but important differences in the early spellings have obscured the precise origin of the first element of this name, but there can be little doubt that it represents some variation on the word *creag* "rock". In the 19th century, a rock known as The Fairies' Castle, in which there was a cliff 1 foot wide and 5½ feet high, was believed to have given name to the townland (*OSM* xviii 60).

An origin from *creagán* "rocky place" is apparently supported by a number of early forms (4, 6, 10), but these may well have resulted from scribal interference. The *n* in form 4 does not appear in related sources (1–3), and the *n* in the forms on Petty's maps (6, 10) is not recorded in related documents such as the Civil Survey (5). The general weight of evidence, therefore, favours an origin from *Creag Mhór* "large rock". We have seen elsewhere that the sources cited under 1-4 above are related, and we might tentatively suggest that they represent an underlying form *Baile (na) Creige Móire* "townland of (the) large rock".

Crew
C 8701

An Chraobh
"the tree/bush"

1. bunadh na Craoibhe gáirdígh	OSL (Derry) 67	1740c

2. bunadh na Craoibhe gáirdighe	DCCU 426	1740c
3. B:nacriuie	Esch. Co. Map 14	1609
4. Ballynacreeny	Bishop. Der. i 57	1610
5. Ballymacreeny	CPR Jas I 279a	1615
6. Ballymacreeny	Bishop. Der. i 102	1615
7. Creeve	Civ. Surv. iii 180,193	1654
8. Creeve	Hib. Reg. Loughinsholin	1657c
9. Criue	Census 134	1659c
10. Creeve	BSD(c) 52	1661
11. (?)Half Scue	HMR (Ó Doibhlin 2) 75	1663
12. (?)half Scue, Half Brogha &	HMR (Ó Doibhlin 2) 75	1663
13. Creeve	Hib. Del. Derry	1672c
14. Crew	Par. Reg. (OSNB) No. 11	1787
15. Crue	Par. Reg. (OSNB) No. 11	1792
16. Crue	Sampson's Map	1813
17. Crew	Custom of County (OSNB) No. 11	1834c
18. 'Crew	OSNB Pron. No. 11	1834c
19. Craobh "a branching tree"	J O'D (OSNB) No. 11	1834c
20. Craebh "The place of the branchy tree"	Munn's Notes 222	1925
21. ðə 'kru	Local pronunciation	1993
22. kru:	Local pronunciation	1993

According to Joyce, *craobh* in place-names was given to trees of religious or inaugural significance, although in many cases it may simply indicate a prominent tree (*Joyce* i 501; *PNI* i 17; iv 101). There is a tradition that Crew Hill in the townland of **Crew**, Co. Antrim, was the inauguration site of the kings of Ulster, and that a great tree had been cut down there (Flanagan 1970, 31). The townland of Creeveroe in Co. Armagh adjoins Navan, the ancient capital of Ulster, and there is a Crew Hill less than two miles south-east of Tullaghoge, Co. Tyrone, which was the inauguration site of the O'Neills (*ibid.*). It is also surely of some significance that great stones are associated with all three of these sites (*ibid.*), although there is no tradition of any such objects here.

Craobh is variously anglicized as both *Crew* and *Creeve*, and both forms are seen among the early spellings of this townland. Final, non-palatal *bh* was originally pronounced [v] and it retained this sound in parts of Ulster into this century but in Donegal and Tyrone it became [w]. The spellings such as *Creeve* may, therefore, point to a dative form *craoibh* (cf. *PNI* i 16–17; Flanagan *loc. cit.*; see also **Creeveroe** Co. Armagh). The earliest English forms show that the townland was also known by a longer form of the name *Baile na Craoibhe* "townland of the tree/bush" (3–6).

Culnady	*Cúil Chnáidí*
C 8802	"recess of the place of burrs"

1. go Cul Cnáimhdídhe	OSL (Derry) 67	1740c
2. go Cúil Cnáimhdidhe	DCCU 426	1740c

3.	Calknady	Esch. Co. Map 14	1609
4.	Culenady	Charter of Londonderry 391	1613
5.	Coolraday	Lond. Comp. Valuation 307	1613
6.	Colerade	Phillips MSS (Maps) Plate 24	1622
7.	Cullknadie	Civ. Surv. iii 181	1654
8.	Culenady	Bishop. Der. i 264	1657
9.	Culknady	Census 134	1659c
10.	Cullknadie	BSD(c) 65	1661
11.	Culknady	HMR (Ó Doibhlin 2) 76	1663
12.	Cullnady	Par. Reg. (OSNB) No. 11	1792
13.	Culnady	Par. Reg. (OSNB) No. 11	1794
14.	Culnaddy	Sampson's Map	1813
15.	Culnady	Custom of County (OSNB) No. 11	1834c
16.	Cool-'nad-y	OSNB Pron. No. 11	1834c

17.	Cuil cnadaidhe "corner or angle of the sluggard	J O'D (OSNB) No. 11	1834c
18.	Cuil-cnadaidhe "The corner of the sluggard"	Munn's Notes 222	1925
19.	Cúil Chnáidí	GÉ 211	1989
20.	Cúil Chnáidí "nook of annoyance"	IPN 198	1994

21.	ˌko̞lˈnadi	Local pronunciation	1993

The second element in this name is extremely rare in Irish place-names but there is little reason to doubt that it is correct. *Cnádán*, which denotes a burr in general or more specifically the head of the burdock or card thistle, has a variant *cnáid*, and it is from this form that we may suppose the second element in this name, *cnáideach* "place of burrs", derives (see Ó *Dónaill* svv.). Ó Brolcháin (1–2) uses a form with a palatal *-mh-* in his poem on various places around Maghera, but this is probably an attempt to account for the nasalization of the vowel which would have accompanied the development of *n* to *r* ([kna:] > [krã:]). Palatal *mh* is still sounded [v'] in Ulster Irish and we should have expected to see some trace of it among the anglicized forms.

Curragh
C 8801

Corrach
"marsh"

1.	Currah	Lond. Comp. Valuation 307	1613
2.	Carragh	Phillips MSS (Maps) Plate 24	1622
3.	Curragh	Civ. Surv. iii 180	1654
4.	Curragh	Census 134	1659c
5.	Curragh	BSD(c) 65	1661
6.	Currugh	HMR (Ó Doibhlin 2) 76	1663
7.	Curragh	Par. Reg. (OSNB) No. 11	1791
8.	Curragh	Sampson's Map	1813
9.	Curragh	Custom of County (OSNB) No. 11	1834c
10.	'Cur-ragh	OSNB Pron. No. 11	1834c

11.	Currach "a moor, or morass"	J O'D (OSNB) No. 11	1834c

12. Currach "The Marsh, or Moor"	Munn's Notes 222	1925

| 13. 'kọrǝx | Local pronunciation | 1993 |
| 14. ðǝ 'kọrǝ | Local pronunciation | 1993 |

Corrach "marsh" is commonly found in place-names throughout Ireland (*Joyce* i 463). The northern boundary of the townland is formed by the Curragh Burn and the marsh was probably located in this vicinity.

Curran	*Curraín*
H 8895	"small tract of wet land"

1. (?)Carrmie	Esch. Co. Map 14	1609
2. Currin	Charter of Londonderry 391	1613
3. Curren	Lond. Comp. Valuation 307	1613
4. Carrin	Phillips MSS (Maps) Plate 24	1622
5. Carren	Civ. Surv. iii 180	1654
6. Currin	Bishop. Der. i 265	1657
7. Carren	BSD(c) 65	1661
8. Curran	HMR (Ó Doibhlin 2) 76	1663
9. Curran	Par. Reg. (OSNB) No. 11	1786
10. Currin	Par. Reg. (OSNB) No. 11	1794
11. Currin	Sampson's Map	1813
12. Curran	Custom of County (OSNB) No. 11	1834c
13. 'Cur-ran	OSNB Pron. No. 11	1834c

14. Carrán "a reaping hook; rocky land"		
	J O'D (OSNB) No. 11	1834c
15. Corran "The reaping hook, or point"	Munn's Notes 222	1925

16. An Corrán	GÉ 211	1989

17. kọrn	Local pronunciation	1993

In an analysis of the element *corrán* "hook, sickle" in place-names, T.S. Ó Máille concludes that names of this type refer to five categories of crescent-shaped objects. He takes our Curran to refer to a crescent-shaped hill or ridge (Ó Máille 1962(a) 83–4) but the hill on the east side of the village of Curran to which he refers can only be so interpreted with some imagination. Strangely, no account is taken in the article of the possibility of a derivation from *corr*, meaning "round hill" or "hollow, pit", and the diminutive suffix *-án*, with which we may compare *corr* + the diminutive suffix *óg* in names such as **Corrog** and **Carrogs** in Co. Down, and **Currogs** in Co. Fermanagh. There is a notable round hill to the south of the village and there is a small round hill at Hill Head in the north-west of the townland, either of which would suggest a connection with *corr* "round hill".

However, final unstressed *áin* or *án* is usually anglicized *an* in place-names (cf. **Drumballyhagan, Kilcronaghan, Dunlogan**), whereas Curran is usually spelt with *i* or *e* in the last syllable suggesting a word ending in the diminutive suffix *ín*. **Correen** is the name of townlands in Antrim, Fermanagh, Leitrim, and Roscommon, and we may also compare Currin in Donegal and Fermanagh (×2), and **Curran** (×2) in the parishes of Tullyniskin and Clonfeacle in Tyrone.

Several places in Donegal are believed to derive their names from a word *currain* which is attested there in the sense of "sodden land, usually supporting only coarse useless grass" (O'Kane 1970, 140). It gives the Irish name for the townland of Currynanerriagh in the parish of Inniskeel (*ibid.* 77), and Currin and Meenacurrin in Donegal are also thought to contain this word (Dónall Mac Giolla Easpaig, pers. comm.). The word *currain* might be taken as a reduced form of *curraichín* "wet land" which occurs in a large number of names in Munster, notably in Cork, Kerry, Limerick, Tipperary and Waterford (see *L. Log. P. Láirge* 70; *L. Log. Luimnigh* 84), but the loss of *ch* would be remarkable in Donegal Irish and it is perhaps more probably a by-form of *cuirrín* with a broad *r*. *Cuirrín* is attested in the name Curreen in the townland of Ballyclare and parish of Cloontuskert, Co. Roscommon. O'Donovan translates it as "moor", and notes that it is often flooded by Lough Ree (*AFM* iii 310n; iv 1182n; *A. Conn.* 80).

As we have seen, there are two round hills in the townland, and an origin from *corr* "round hill" + the diminutive suffix *in* must also be considered. In Irish, the two possibilities would be distinguished by the quality of the *r* but this difference is unlikely to be repeated in the anglicized form. However, the comparative evidence, particularly from Donegal, offers some support for the first of the two options and this is the form recommended here. The townland is bounded by the Moyola River on the north, but the name may refer to a large portion of heath in the west of the townland.

Dreenan · *Draighneán*
C 9201 · "place of blackthorns"

1. go Draoigheanán	OSL (Derry) 67	1740c
2. go Draoighneán	DCCU 426	1740c
3. derrman (?)	Esch. Co. Map 14	1609
4. Derman	Charter of Londonderry 391	1613
5. Drenan	Lond. Comp. Valuation 307	1613
6. Drenan	Phillips MSS (Maps) Plate 24	1622
7. Drynan	Civ. Surv. iii 180	1654
8. Drinan	Civ. Surv. iii 180,186	1654
9. Derman	Bishop. Der. i 265	1657
10. Drenan	Census 134	1659c
11. Drinan	BSD(c) 65	1661
12. Drinan	HMR (Ó Doibhlin 2) 76	1663
13. Dreenan	Sampson's Map	1813
14. Dreenan	Custom of County (OSNB) No. 11	1834c
15. 'Dreen-an	OSNB Pron. No. 11	1834c
16. Draoigheanan "place of black thorns/sloe bushes"	J O'D (OSNB) No. 11	1834c
17. Draighnean "The little blackthorn"	Munn's Notes 222	1925
18. 'dri(:)nən	Local pronunciation	1993

There can be little doubt about the origin of this name despite some corrupt spellings in one group of early sources (3–4, 9). There is a tradition in the townland that the O'Neills and the

O'Cahans were impeded in their progress through Dreenan by the large number of blackthorns growing there (Ní Mhaolchallann 1993, 40; cf. *OSM* xviii 44). The normal word for
blackthorn in Ulster seems to be *draighean* but *draighneán* is recorded in Tyrone (Wagner &
Stockman 1965, 73). Here, we probably have the former word in compound with the suffix
án which in place-names oftens signifies "place of" (*Joyce* i 517–8).

Drumard
H 9198

Droim Ard
"high ridge"

1. dromard	Esch. Co. Map 14	1609
2. Dromard	Charter of Londonderry 391	1613
3. ½ Drum Arde	Lond. Comp. Valuation 307	1613
4. Dromard	Civ. Surv. iii 180	1654
5. Dromard	Bishop. Der. i 265	1657
6. Drumarde	Census 134	1659c
7. Dromard	BSD(c) 65	1661
8. Drummard	HMR (Ó Doibhlin 2) 76	1663
9. Drimard	Sampson's Map	1813
10. Drimard	Custom of County (OSNB) No. 11	1834c
11. Drim-'mard	OSNB Pron. No. 11	1834c
12. Druim árd "high ridge"	J O'D (OSNB) No. 11	1834c
13. Druim-ard "The high ridge"	Munn's Notes 222	1925
14. drọ'maːrd	Local pronunciation	1993

The townland of Drumard may have taken its name from the north-south ridge called
Drumard Hill in the centre of the townland. While not the highest point in the townland, the
land around Drumard Hill falls away on all sides forming a clear and distinct ridge.

Drumconready
H 7998

Droim Con Riada
"Cú Riada's ridge"

1. (?)namroah	Esch. Co. Map 14	1609
2. (?)Namroah	Charter of Londonderry 391	1613
3. 2 Drom Corredy & Agh Clon	Lond. Comp. Valuation 309	1613
4. Dromconrde	Phillips MSS (Maps) Plate 28	1622
5. Drumcowredie	Civ. Surv. iii 177	1654
6. Dromconredie	Civ. Surv. iii 180	1654
7. (?)Namrough	Bishop. Der. i 266	1657
8. Drumconnedy, Quarter of	HMR (Ó Doibhlin 2) 74	1663
9. Drumeconredy	HMR (Ó Doibhlin 2) 75	1663
10. Drumconready	Par. Reg. (OSNB) No. 11	1794
11. Drumconredy	Sampson's Map	1813
12. Drumconready	Custom of County (OSNB) No. 11	1834c
13. Drum-con-'red-dy	OSNB Pron. No. 11	1834c
14. Druim Conriada "Conready's ridge"	J O'D (OSNB) No. 11	1834c
15. Druim-Conriada "Conready's or Reid's ridge"	Munn's Notes 222	1925

16. ˌdrɔmkɔn'rɛdi	Local pronunciation	1993
17. ˌdrɔmkɔn'ri:di	Local pronunciation	1993

The early spellings of this name tend to confirm the origin postulated by O'Donovan, although it is also possible that we have here a reduced form of a name *Droim Mhic Conriada* "MacConready's ridge". According to MacLysaght (1985, 64), MacCready was used as an abbreviated form of MacConready in Co. Derry, but the MacCready (or McReady) which was in use in Maghera in the last century may well be the Co. Donegal name *Mac Riada* which was well represented in the partly contiguous parish of Desertoghill in the 17th century (*OSM* xviii 48; *HMR (Ó Doibhlin 2)* 69–70).

Drumconready is apparently absent from an early group of sources and in these the townland may be represented by a form *namroah*, although this identification is tentative. If this is a separate name, its origin is unclear, but it may be a spectacular corruption of Drumconready with loss of the initial *D*, *n* for *r*, and *a* for *u* in the first syllable, *r* for *c* and *a* for *n* in the second syllable, and the almost total loss of the final two syllables (the significance of the *h* is uncertain).

Drumlamph
Droim Leamhach

H 9296   "ridge of the marsh-mallows"

1. dromlaugha	Esch. Co. Map 14	1609
2. Dromlagha	Charter of Londonderry 391	1613
3. Drum Laugh	Lond. Comp. Valuation 307	1613
4. Dromlaugh	Phillips MSS (Maps) Plate 24	1622
5. Dromlaugh, the foot of	Civ. Surv. iii 168	1654
6. Dromlagh, the foote of the forsd	Civ. Surv. iii 168	1654
7. Drumlaugh, the foote of	Civ. Surv. iii 178	1654
8. Dromlaugh	Civ. Surv. iii 180	1654
9. Dromloagh	Civ. Surv. iii 180	1654
10. Dromlagha	Bishop. Der. i 265	1657
11. Drumlagh	Census 134	1659c
12. Dromloagh	BSD(c) 65	1661
13. Drumlogh	HMR (Ó Doibhlin 2) 76	1663
14. Drumlamph	Sampson's Map	1813
15. Drumlamph	Par. Reg. (OSNB) No. 11	1826
16. Drumlamph	Custom of County (OSNB) No. 11	1834c
17. Drum-'lamph	OSNB Pron. No. 11	1834c
18. Druim leamh "ridge of the elms"	J O'D (OSNB) No. 11	1834c
19. "elm ridge"	Joyce i 508	1869
20. Druim-leamh "The ridge of the elm trees"	Munn's Notes 222	1925
21. drɔm'lamf	Local pronunciation	1993

There is a narrow ridge in the south-west of the townland overlooking the Moyola River to the west and low-lying ground to the east and north-east, and this may be the feature denoted by the first element in this name. Previous writers have identified the second element as *leamh* "elm", but the 17th-century forms seem to suggest *leamhach* "marsh-mallow"

183

(see *Joyce* ii 345). While the final *-gh* of these early spellings might be read as [f] (for bilabial [v]) as in English *laugh*, it would be curious indeed if *f* were never written (cf. **Gulladuff** below), and it seems reasonable to conclude that it represents Irish *ch* as it usually does.

As regards the *mh* of the Irish form, non-palatal *mh*, which was originally pronounced [v], became [w] in Ulster Irish at some time prior to the 17th century, but a strong nasal element was left on the preceding vowel and re-emerged later in many place-names as a nasal consonant (see **Gortamney** and **Drumsamney** in the parish of Kilcronaghan). The conjunction of this nasal and the following *ch*, which is natural neither to Irish or English, came to be pronounced *mph*.

It should be noted that *Leamhach* could be interpreted as an adjectival form of *leamh* "elm" but this is perhaps unlikely, although a small portion of land covered with the stunted remains of a natural wood consisting principally of oak, ash, birch, alder, wild cherry and "a little elm" still existed here in the 1830s (*OSM* xviii 4).

| **Drummuck** | *Droim Muc* | |
| C 8901 | "ridge of pigs" | |

1. drommcke	Esch. Co. Map 14	1609
2. Dromunick	Charter of Londonderry 391	1613
3. Drum Mucke	Lond. Comp. Valuation 307	1613
4. Dromuck	Phillips MSS (Maps) Plate 22	1622
5. Dromucke	Civ. Surv. iii 181	1654
6. Drommucke	Bishop. Der. i 265	1657
7. Drummuck	Census 134	1659c
8. Dromucke	BSD(c) 65	1661
9. Drummuck	HMR (Ó Doibhlin 2) 76	1663
10. Drummuck	Par. Reg. (OSNB) No. 11	1786
11. Drumuck	Sampson's Map	1813
12. Drummuck	Custom of County (OSNB) No. 11	1834c
13. 'Drum-muck	OSNB Pron. No. 11	1834c
14. Druim muc "ridge of the swine"	J O'D (OSNB) No. 11	1834c
15. Druim-muc "The ridge of the pigs"	Munn's Notes 223	1925
16. dro'mok	Local pronunciation	1993

There seems little reason to depart here from the origin proposed by previous commentators. As might be expected, the occurrence side by side of letters such as *m* and *u* has led to some confusion in our early sources, but this is hardly significant.

| **Dunglady** | *Dún gCláidí* | |
| C 9004 | "fort of the Clady River" | |

1. (?)oc Dún Cloitighe	AFM ii 698	972
2. (?)oc Dun Cloitige	AU (Mac Airt) 410	974
3. dounglady	Esch. Co. Map 14	1609
4. Dungladdy	Charter of Londonderry 391	1613
5. Dunglady (ballybetagh)	Lond. Comp. Valuation 307	1613

6. Dongladay	Lond. Comp. Valuation 307	1613
7. Donglade	Phillips MSS (Maps) Plate 22	1622
8. Dongladye	Phillips MSS (Maps) Plate 23	1622
9. Doungladie	Civ. Surv. iii 180	1654
10. Dungleddie	Civ. Surv. iii 181	1654
11. Dunglady	Bishop. Der. i 265	1657
12. Doungladie	Census 134	1659c
13. Downgladie	BSD(c) 65	1661
14. Dunglady	HMR (Ó Doibhlin 2) 76	1663
15. Dunglady	Par. Reg. (OSNB) No. 11	1792
16. Dunglady	Sampson's Map	1813
17. Dun-'glay-dy	OSNB Pron. No. 11	1834c
18. Dún Ghláidídhe	OSL (Derry) 54	1834
19. Dun glaidigh "Glady's fort"	J O'D (OSNB) No. 11	1834c
20. Dun-cloitighe "The fort of Cloitighe"	Colton Vis. 223	1925
21. ˌdɔn'gledi	Local pronunciation	1993

The townland of Dunglady takes its name from a quite remarkable trivallate ringfort overlooking the **Clady River** now known as Dunglady Fort but formerly called *Dún gCláidí* "fort of the Clady River". The nasalization of the second element is doubtless due to the fact that *dún* was neuter in O.Ir., and this indicates that the name is at least 1000 years old.

Dunglady has been identified by O'Donovan as the *Dún Clóitige* (modern *Dún Clóidí*) where Murchadh úa Flaithbheartaigh, king of the Cenél nEogain, died in 974 after being wounded in battle against the Cenél Conaill (*AFM* ii 698n sa. 972). It has been suggested, however, that this place lies further west at the village of Clady on the border between Tyrone and Donegal and, although no such name now exists there, it is perhaps not unreasonable to suppose that the mortally wounded Murchadh was carried across the Finn River to Clady rather than all the way to Dunglady (O'Laverty 1891, 6n). O'Laverty notes that in subsequent centuries the O'Lavertys were closely associated with the area around Clady and attempts to further strengthen the proposed identification by tracing this surname back to Murchadh's grandfather (*ibid.* 4–9). However, he appears to be mistaken in this conclusion, for Murchadh úa Flaithbheartaigh and the Flaithbheartach from whom the O'Lavertys take their name are descended from separate branches of the Uí Néill (*CGH* 140a30 et seq.).

Falgortrevy
H 8399

Fáladh Goirt Riabhaigh
"enclosure of the grey field"

1. follogortrowy (?)	Esch. Co. Map 14	1609
2. Fultagartrewy	Bishop. Der. i 57	1610
3. Tallagartruy	CPR Jas I 279a	1615
4. Fallagartreny	Bishop. Der. i 102	1615
5. ffallgortreagh	Civ. Surv. iii 193	1654
6. Tallgortreagh	Hib. Reg. Loughinsholin	1657c
7. Felgertrewey	Census 134	1659c
8. ffallgorterragh	BSD(c) 52	1661
9. Folgortiony	HMR (Ó Doibhlin 2) 75	1663

10. Talgontea(?)	Hib. Del. Derry	1672c
11. Falgatrevy	Par. Reg. (OSNB) No. 11	1791
12. Falagartrevy	Sampson's Map	1813
13. Falgatrevy	Custom of County (OSNB) No. 11	1834c
14. Fall-gar'trevy	OSNB Pron. No. 11	1834c
15. Falghort riabhach "grey enclosed field"	J O'D (OSNB) No. 11	1834c
16. Fal-guirt-riabhaigh "The hedge or enclosure of the grey field"	Munn's Notes 223	1925
17. Fál-guirt-riabhaigh "hedge of the grey ... field"	Joyce iii 348	1925
18. ˌfalgəˈtrevi	Local pronunciation	1993
19. ˌfaləˌgəˈtrevi	Local pronunciation	1993
20. ˌfaləˌgəˈtriːvi	Local pronunciation	1993

Modern authorities are unanimous in taking the first element in this name to be Irish *fál* "hedge, fence" and this would appear to be supported by a significant number of our early spellings. However, the very earliest forms of the name contain an extra syllable which is, remarkably, retained to the present day in local speech, and this strongly suggests that we have here the same initial element as is found in the names of the neighbouring townlands of **Fallagloon** and **Fallylea**, namely *fáladh* "enclosure".

Conversely, it could be argued that this extra syllable has appeared and reappeared at various times in the name's history by analogy with the names of these adjacent townlands, and that the first element was, indeed, *fál* "hedge, fence". It might further be suggested that *fáladh* as it has been interpreted here in the sense of "enclosure" is largely tautologous beside the second element, which is undoubtedly *gort* "field", but this is not necessarily so. In any case, the form of the name suggests that *fáladh* is here qualifying an older name, *Gort Riabhach* "grey field", so that there is no conflict of meaning (compare names such as Lisdoonvarna in Co. Clare < *Lios Dúin Bhearna* where both *lios* and *dún* have roughly the same significance).

Fallagloon
C 8000

Fáladh Luán
"enclosure of the lambs"

1. Fála Ghlúin	OSL (Derry) 67	1740c
2. Falach Ghlún	DCCU 426	1740c
3. fallaglou[n?]	Esch. Co. Map 14	1609
4. Falaglona	Charter of Londonderry 391	1613
5. Fallow Lowne	Lond. Comp. Valuation 307	1613
6. Fallowloy	Phillips MSS (Maps) Plate 24	1622
7. ffaliglune	Civ. Surv. iii 179	1654
8. ffalliglun	Civ. Surv. iii 180	1654
9. Fallaghoun	Bishop. Der. i 266	1657
10. Falleglone	Census 134	1659c
11. ffalliglune	BSD(c) 65	1661
12. Fallaleene	HMR (Ó Doibhlin 2) 75	1663

13. Fallagloon	Par. Reg. (OSNB) No. 11	1795
14. Fallyglone	Sampson's Map	1813
15. Fallagloon	Custom of County (OSNB) No. 11	1834c
16. Fal-la-'gloon	OSNB Pron. No. 11	1834c
17. Fal a ghlún "hedge or enclosure of the knee"	J O'D (OSNB) No. 11	1834c
18. Fala-ghluin "The hedge or enclosure of the knee"	Munn's Notes 223	1925
19. Fal-a'-ghluin "hedge or enclosure of the knee"	Joyce iii 348	1925
20. Folach Ghlún	GÉ 221	1989
21. ˌfalə'glu:n	Local pronunciation	1993

The most recent interpretation of this name has been from *folach*, presumably in the sense of "hiding place", and there is indeed some evidence of the use of this word in South Derry. A hollow at the foot of Slieve Gallion was known as *Folach Éireann* "hiding or covering of Ireland" and its origin is explained in the story of Cadhan O'Henery's hound. The Carrach O'Neill (probably Brian Carrach O'Neill) offered a grant of all the land that he could see to the man who would deliver the community of Cadhan's ravenous hound. This great deed was finally carried out by Cadhan himself, who then proceeded to O'Neill demanding his reward. O'Neill took him to the aforementioned hollow and ordered him to stand at the very bottom of it. Cadhan looked around him but saw nothing except the sky and the top of Slieve Gallion, and so the hollow and tummocks of Slieve Gallion belonged to the O'Heneries from that day forth (*OSL (Derry)* 77–8).

All previous authorities have taken the second element to be a form of *glúin* "knee", and again there is considerable evidence of the use of this word in place-names where it generally denotes the impression left by the knee of some holy man. In Gorteenagloon in Co. Longford, for example, local people believed that an indentation in a stone there was made by St Patrick's knee, and another stone in Co. Derry with a round depression in the middle was known as *Glúin Phádraig* "St Patrick's knee" (*Joyce* iii 377; *OSRNB* 53 sh. 31).

It is noteworthy, however, that some of our early sources show no trace of the *g* of *glúin*, and this suggests that the *g* originates not with the second element but with the first. Non-palatal *dh* was still occasionally pronounced [γ] in non-initial position in the Irish of Derry and Tyrone in the last century (Mac Giolla Chomhaill 1968, 5), so it is not unlikely that the *g* in this name represents the final *dh* of *fáladh*. Thus, the second element probably begins with *l* rather than *g*. Although we cannot be certain about the origin of this element, it is quite likely that it comes from *luán* "lamb" (see *Joyce* ii 304; *DIL* sv. *lubán*). A plural form is suggested here largely on the strength of the historical spellings which show no trace of the palatal final *n* of the gen. sing., *luáin*. While the anglicized forms of names do not regularly distinguish between palatal and non-palatal consonants, the effect of certain palatal consonants is often manifest in some modification of the preceding vowel (see **Derrynoyd** in the parish of Ballynascreen above).

Several alternative explanations may be explored here. Parts of the body are frequently used in place-names, so we might consider *luan* or *lón* "haunch, rump, buttock" (Ó Maolfabhail 1985; 1987-88; *DIL* sv. 2 *lón*). According to The Cattle Raid of Cooley, the ford at Athlone in Co. Westmeath was named from the rump (*luan*) of the White-Horned Bull which was deposited there after its defeat by the Brown Bull of Cooley. The more usual explanation of this name is from the personal name Luan (*Áth Luain* "Luan's ford"), but both these interpretations require a palatal final *n* which, as we have seen, is not indicated by the historical spellings for Fallagloon. The surname O'Loan (Irish *Ó Luain*), which was fairly common in Cos Monaghan, Armagh, Fermanagh, and Tyrone at least up until the end of the 17th century (MacLysaght 1982, 146–7), is found in this townland in the 19th century (*OSM* xviii 62), but we still have the problem of the final palatal *n*.

Gorteade
C 8805

Of uncertain origin

1. ballinway(?)	Esch. Co. Map 14	1609
2. (?)Ball:Maney	Lond. Comp. Valuation 307	1613
3. (?)Ball:Money	Lond. Comp. Valuation 307	1613
4. Ba Muney	Phillips MSS (Maps) Plate 22	1622
5. Ballivun	Civ. Surv. iii 180	1654
6. Ballyvnne	BSD(c) 65	1661
7. Bollymonny	HMR (Ó Doibhlin 2) 76	1663
8. Gorteade	Par. Reg. (OSNB) No. 11	1790
9. Gortead	Sampson's Map	1813
10. Gorteade	Custom of County (OSNB) No. 11	1834c
11. Gor-'tead	OSNB Pron. No. 11	1834c
12. Gort eada "field of jealousy"	J O'D (OSNB) No. 11	1834c
13. Gort-eada "The field of jealousy, or reproach"	Munn's Notes 223	1925
14. gɔr'tiːd	Local pronunciation	1993

Our earliest sources seem to have had another name for the townland, probably deriving from *Baile Muine* "townland of the thicket" (see Toner 1991–93). The first element in the name Gorteade is clearly *gort* which usually denotes a field of either arable or pasture land (*DIL* sv. 1 *gort*), but the final element presents certain difficulties of interpretation which are severely compounded by the lack of any early references. The original form of the vowel in this element is crucial to its identification, and a selection of 17th-century forms would almost certainly permit us to draw some conclusions about it. If we allow for some speculation, we might consider among the more plausible possibilities words such as *fiod* "aspen tree" and *éid* "cattle" (see *DIL* svv. *fidot*, *éit*). O'Donovan's *éad* "jealousy", although perhaps somewhat fanciful, cannot be entirely dismissed, for several places are named from circumstances which surrounded their acquisition or possession (see *Joyce* ii 459ff.).

Grillagh
C 8503

An Ghriollach
"the muddy place"

1. moyannagrela	Esch. Co. Map 14	1609
2. Mahanegrellah	Charter of Londonderry 391	1613
3. Monishna Grilla	Lond. Comp. Valuation 307	1613
4. Moinshugrilla	Phillips MSS (Maps) Plate 24	1622
5. Mannsnecrulagh	Civ. Surv. iii 180	1654
6. Munishnegrulagh	Civ. Surv. iii 181	1654

7.	Munishnegrulagh	Civ. Surv. iii 181	1654
8.	Manyanagrellagh	Bishop. Der. i 264	1657
9.	(?)Interregrolagh	Census 134	1659c
10.	Monnishnegrallagh	BSD(c) 65	1661
11.	Manisteragrillagh	Sampson's Map	1813
12.	Grillagh	Custom of County (OSNB) No. 11	1834c
13.	'Grill-agh	OSNB Pron. No. 11	1834c
14.	Greallach "a miry place"	J O'D (OSNB) No. 11	1834c
15.	Mainstir "a monastery"	J O'D (OSNB) No. 11	1834c
16.	Greallach "The miry or marshy place"	Munn's Notes 223	1925
17.	(ðə) 'grīləx	Local pronunciation	1993

The "muddy place" from which this townland takes its name probably once lay within the reaches of the Grillagh River which runs through it. *Griollach* is a variant form of *greallach* "muddy place", and is suggested by both the modern form and the historical spellings. We may compare the name Cornagrillagh, a townland in the parish of Inniskeel, Co. Donegal, and **Drumlisnagrilly** in the parish of Seagoe, Co. Armagh, both of which may contain this element. O'Kane (1970, 73) wavers in his interpretation of Cornagrillagh, suggesting among other things the word *greilleach* "a harrow", but this is unlikely here.

A longer form of the name predominated down to the 19th century when it was falsely interpreted as "the monastery (Irish *mainistir*) of the O'Crillys" (*OSM* xviii 38). The final element is obviously *griollcha*, the old gen. sing. of *griollach* (see *DIL* sv. 1 *grellach* and compare the anglicization of *dorcha* in *PNI* iii 50–1), and we might reasonably suggest an origin from Irish *Maigh Inse na Griollcha* "the plain of the island of the muddy place" (compare a parallel structure in the name **Moneysterlin** in the parish of Desertmartin). *Inis* is the normal word used in Irish texts to describe a crannog but no such structure has been located here, nor is there, or is there likely to have been, a lake in the townland. The Ordnance Survey 6-inch map of 1854 shows a small island near the southern end of Killelagh Lough, just over a mile away in Carrowmenagh townland, and it is possible that this was a crannog (Ken Neill, pers. comm.). However, there is no evidence that the townland of Grillagh ever extended so far west. The townland of Tirnony now separates Grillagh and Carrowmenagh, and this situation goes back at least as far as the beginning of the 17th century (*Esch. Co. Map* 14).

A clue to the proper origin of this form of the name is supplied by a separate group of very early sources (1–2, 8) which seem to point to an Irish form *Maigh Eanaigh na Griollcha* "the plain of the marsh of the muddy place". If this is a valid form of the name and not the result of some scribal confusion, then we might plausibly suggest that the second element in the alternative form is a topographical term, *inse* "water meadow" rather than a settlement term. Such an interpretation is supported both by the context of the name and by the presence here of the Grillagh River.

Gulladuff
H 8999

Guala Dhubh
"black shoulder (of a hill)"

1.	galladow	Esch. Co. Map 14	1609
2.	Galladowe	Charter of Londonderry 391	1613

3. Cooladogh	Lond. Comp. Valuation 307	1613
4. Cooladogh	Phillips MSS (Maps) Plate 24	1622
5. Soloduffe	Civ. Surv. iii 180	1654
6. Gallodow	Bishop. Der. i 265	1657
7. Goleduffe	Census 134	1659c
8. Solloduffe	BSD(c) 65	1661
9. Coldiff	HMR (Ó Doibhlin 2) 76	1663
10. Gooladuff	Par. Reg. (OSNB) No. 11	1787
11. Goladuf	Sampson's Map	1813
12. Gulladuff	Custom of County (OSNB) No. 11	1834c
13. Gull-a-'duff	OSNB Pron. No. 11	1834c
14. Guala Dubha "black coals"	OSL (Derry) 90	1834
15. Guala dubha "black shoulders"	J O'D (OSNB) No. 11	1834c
16. Gobhla dubha "black forks"	J O'D (OSNB) No. 11	1834c
17. Guala dubha "The black shoulders"	Munn's Notes 224	1925
18. Guala-dubha "black shoulders (of a hill)"	Joyce iii 390	1925
19. Gaibhle-dubha "black forks"	Joyce iii 390	1925
20. ˌgɒlˈdɒf	Local pronunciation	1993
21. ˌgɒləˈdɒf	Local pronunciation	1993

Parts of the body frequently occur in place-names, usually with some topographical significance (Ó Maolfabhail 1985, 1987–88), and *guala*, together with the later form *gualainn*, is well attested in place-name usage with reference to the brow or shoulder of a hill. *Guala* "shoulder" might be confused with *gabhla*, plural of *gabhal* which usually denotes a fork in a river in place-names, but the topography of the area, with prominent hills in the northern and southern extremities of the townland, indicates that we are probably dealing with the former here. We may compare the names **Gulladuff**, a small outcrop on a hill in Co. Down (J 4480), and **Gulladoo**, a small hill in Tyrone (H 4059), both of which appear to have identical origins to Gulladuff.

Dubh "black" is usually anglicized *duff* in the 17th century, but occassionally it appears as *doo*, even at this early period, and some of the early spellings here seem to indicate such a development (1–2, 6). The spellings with final *gh* (3–4) are ambiguous as the *gh* may have been intended to be read as silent (as in "though") or possibly as *f* (as in "enough").

The variation in spelling between initial *C*, *G*, and *S* in our 17th-century documents is due to scribal error rather than any variation in pronunciation. *S* for *G* in two related sources (5, 8) obviously goes back to a single error, as does *C* for *G* in two earlier related sources (3–4).

Keady
C 8707

An Chéide
"the (flat-topped) hill"

1. b:kediue (?)	Esch. Co. Map 14	1609
2. Ballynekedine	Charter of Londonderry 391	1613
3. (?)Balle ne Kedrey	Lond. Comp. Valuation 307	1613
4. Nekede	Phillips MSS (Maps) Plate 22	1622
5. Kedie	Civ. Surv. iii 180	1654
6. Keadie	Civ. Surv. iii 181	1654

7. Leligin Kedie	Civ. Surv. iii 182	1654
8. Ballynekedine	Bishop. Der. i 264	1657
9. Kedie	Census 134	1659c
10. Kedie	BSD(c) 65	1661
11. Keadie	HMR (Ó Doibhlin 2) 76	1663
12. Keady	Sampson's Map	1813
13. Keady	Custom of County (OSNB) No. 11	1834c
14. 'Kay-dy	OSNB Pron. No. 11	1834c
15. Céide "a small hill level at top"	J O'D (OSNB) No. 11	1834c
16. Ceide "The smooth topped hill"	Munn's Notes 224	1925
17. 'ke:di	Local pronunciation	1993
18. 'ki:di	Local pronunciation	1993

The 17th-century spellings show a considerable amount of variation, but there can be little doubt about the origin of the name. *Céide* usually denotes some form of hill or mound in place-names, and is frequently used of a flat-topped hill. Here, it may refer to any of a number of hillocks in the townland, none of which are distinguished by a level summit. It is usually masculine in Mod. Ir., but feminine forms are attested (*DIL* sv. *céite*) and there is evidence from independent sources that it is feminine here (2–3, 8; we should also probably read 4 as *Ballenekede* and 7 as *Bellynikedie*). Some of the 17th-century forms (1–2, 8) might also suggest an otherwise unattested dental inflection (gen. sing. *céideadh*), but this is not supported by any independent sources.

Kirley   *Corrbhaile*
C 7900   "prominent townland"

1. Correlly	Esch. Co. Map 14	1609
2. Carely	Charter of Londonderry 391	1613
3. Moybegkerley	Lond. Comp. Valuation 309	1613
4. Moybegkirlo	Phillips MSS (Maps) Plate 28	1622
5. Carely	Bishop. Der. i 266	1657
6. Keerly	Census 134	1659c
7. Kirley	Par. Reg. (OSNB) No. 11	1794
8. Kirlea	Sampson's Map	1813
9. Kirley	Custom of County (OSNB) No. 11	1834c
10. 'Kur-ley	OSNB Pron. No. 11	1834c
11. Cor liath "grey round hill"	J O'D (OSNB) No. 11	1834c
12. Cor-liath "The grey round hill"	Munn's Notes 224	1925
13. 'kərli	Local pronunciation	1993
14. 'kʲɛrli	Local pronunciation	1993
15. 'kʲïrli	Local pronunciation	1993

Kirley is a long finger of land stretching from the Moyola River to the top of Coolnasillagh Mountain, but otherwise it contains no remarkable features. Kirley provides the second element in the name of the townland of **Moybeg Kirley** on the opposite bank of the Moyola in the parish of Kilcronaghan, a compound which dates back to the early 17th century (3–4).

191

The emphasis on the first syllable in the local pronunciation is probably original and suggests either a single word or, more probably, a compound of two elements. The word *corr* has a variety of meanings and is used frequently in compounded place-names. Perhaps its best known usage is in the name of the Curlew Mountains, Irish *Corrshliabh* (*GÉ* 77) but it is most frequently found in the form *Corrbhaile* "prominent townland" which is normally anglicized Corbally but occasionally Curley (see *PNI* i 18–19). Indeed, the early spellings here closely resemble those for **Curley** in Co. Down, save that no trace is left here of the *bh*, and it is quite likely that the two names are of identical origin.

Largantogher	*Leargain Tóchair*	
H 8599	"hillslope of the causeway"	
1. Iaragantalis	Esch. Co. Map 14	1609
2. Ioraghgantagha	Bishop. Der. i 57	1610
3. Largagantaghy	CPR Jas I 279a	1615
4. Largagantaghy	Bishop. Der. i 102	1615
5. Lergantagher	Civ. Surv. iii 178,193	1654
6. Largantagher	Civ. Surv. iii 180	1654
7. Largantagher	Census 134	1659c
8. Lergantagher, Maghera &	BSD(c) 52	1661
9. Leamontaer	HMR (Ó Doibhlin 2) 75	1663
10. Largantogher	Sampson's Map	1813
11. Largantogher	Custom of County (OSNB) No. 11	1834c
12. Lar-gan-'togher	OSNB Pron. No. 11	1834c
13. Leargain tachair "Tachar's hill side"	J O'D (OSNB) No. 11	1834c
14. Leargan-tochair "The hill side of the causeway"	Munn's Notes 224	1925
15. "hillside of the causeway (tóchar)"	Joyce iii 462	1925
16. ˌlarn'tɔxər	Local pronunciation	1993
17. ˌlagən'tɔxər	Local pronunciation	1993

The "hillslope" (*leargain*) from which Largantogher is named is probably that which leads up to the present town of Maghera. On the element *tóchar* "causeway" see **Carntogher** in the parish of Killelagh. Wooden causeways were often built close to monasteries (Lucas 1985, 46), and it might be suggested here that a causeway was constructed through the townland of Largantogher to connect the church at Maghera to that at **Mullagh** in the parish of Termoneeny immediately to the south. A small stream separates the two churches, and a small causeway may have crossed wet ground at this point, but it is perhaps more likely that *tóchar* is used here in an extended sense of "path, roadway" (see Lucas 1985, 59). It is perhaps significant that an early alias for **Mullagh** appears to contain the element *droichead* "bridge".

Lisnamuck	*Lios na Muc*	
H 8099	"fort or enclosure of the pigs"	
1. Lisnamue	Sampson's Map	1813

2. Lisnamuc	Custom of County (OSNB) No. 11	1834c
3. Lis-na-'muck	OSNB Pron. No. 11	1834c
4. Lios na muc "fort of the pigs"	J O'D (OSNB) No. 11	1834c
5. Lios-na-muc "The fort of the pigs"	Munn's Notes 224	1925
6. ˌlïsnə'mọk	Local pronunciation	1993

We appear not to have any reference to this name in our 17th-century documentation and it may be a late creation. Nevertheless, there can be little cause for doubting the proposed original *Lios na Muc* "fort or enclosure of the pigs".

Macknagh
C 8604

An Mheacanach
"the place abounding in tubers"

1. air a machnaigh	OSL (Derry) 68	1740c
2. Ar an Mheacnaigh	DCCU 427	1740c
3. B:nemackuy	Esch. Co. Map 14	1609
4. Balememackry	Charter of Londonderry 391	1613
5. Markah	Lond. Comp. Valuation 307	1613
6. Mackah	Phillips MSS (Maps) Plate 22	1622
7. McKnagh	Civ. Surv. iii 180	1654
8. McKnagh	Civ. Surv. iii 181	1654
9. (?)Bellimcrinagh	Civ. Surv. iii 191	1654
10. Ballinemackuy	Bishop. Der. i 264	1657
11. Mackeinagh	Census 134	1659c
12. McKnagh	BSD(c) 65	1661
13. Maghnagh	HMR (Ó Doibhlin 2) 76	1663
14. Macknagh	Par. Reg. (OSNB) No. 11	1796
15. Macknagh	Sampson's Map	1813
16. Macknagh	Custom of County (OSNB) No. 11	1834c
17. 'Mack-nagh	OSNB Pron. No. 11	1834c
18. Meacanach "abounding in carrots"	J O'D (OSNB) No. 11	1834c
19. Meacanach "The place of the parsnips"	Munn's Notes 224	1925
20. 'maknə	Local pronunciation	1993
21. 'mɛknə	Local pronunciation	1993

This name is directly comparable to **Macknagh** in the parish of Aghalurcher, Co. Fermanagh, which also appears to derive from *Meacanach* "place abounding in tubers", and to several other names in various parts of the country (*Joyce* ii 349–50). There is clear evidence here to show that the townland had developed a by-form in the 17th century, namely, *Baile na Meacanaí* "townland of the place abounding in tubers" (3–4, 9–10).

Irish *meacan* can denote any of a number of root vegetables, most commonly *meacan dearg* "carrot" and *meacan bán* "parsnip" (*Ó Dónaill sv.*). Joyce adopts the translation "parsnip" as

193

a matter of convenience (*Joyce* ii 350) but there can be no sure way of knowing which variety of plant is intended. It is perhaps of some relevance that land containing the richest soil was known in early Irish law as "land of the three roots (*meacan*)", that is, thistle, ragwort, and carrot, because these three plants were renowned for their large roots (*DIL* sv. *mecon*). Thus, it is possible that the term *meacanach* denoted, not so much land on which a particular form of tuber grew, but good land with rich soil.

Ó Máille (1967) argues that *meacan* in this and several other names throughout Ireland denotes a hill or short ridge, but the evidence which he produces is overdependent on various transferred uses of the word and no concrete example of this usage is attested in the language. In any case, the form of the name here, with its adjectival suffix -*ach*, is more suggestive of the sense "tuber" than Ó Máille's "hill".

Moneymore		*Muine Mór* (?)	
C 8500		"large thicket"	
1.	b:vommon	Esch. Co. Map 14	1609
2.	Ballywonmore	Bishop. Der. i 57	1610
3.	Ballyvonymore, except 6a. of glebe	CPR Jas I 279a	1615
4.	Ballyvonymore	Bishop. Der. i 102	1615
5.	Minimore	Civ. Surv. iii 193	1654
6.	Munngmore	Hib. Reg. Loughinsholin	1657c
7.	Monymoore	Census 134	1659c
8.	Munnymore	BSD(c) 52	1661
9.	Movwmore	HMR (Ó Doibhlin 2) 76	1663
10.	Munnymore	Hib. Del. Derry	1672c
11.	Moneymore	Par. Reg. (OSNB) No. 11	1788
12.	Moneymore	Sampson's Map	1813
13.	Moneymore	Custom of County (OSNB) No. 11	1834c
14.	Mun-ny-'more	OSNB Pron. No. 11	1834c
15.	Muine mór "great brake or shrubbery"	J O'D (OSNB) No. 11	1834c
16.	Monaidh mór "great bog"	J O'D (OSNB) No. 11	1834c
17.	Moin-mor "The great bog"	Munn's Notes 225	1925
18.	ˌmǫni'mo:r	Local pronunciation	1993

It is virtually impossible to distinguish between the elements *mónaidh* "bog" and *muine* "thicket" in unstressed position in anglicized forms of place-names due to the shortening of the *ó* in the former and the similarity between the resultant vowel and that of *muine* (Toner 1991–3). O'Donovan appears to have been unable to distinguish between the two options and writes both in the Ordnance Survey Name Books (15–16). However, a number of forms are more suggestive of *muine* "thicket" (5–6, 8, 10).

In his letters, O'Donovan translates *muine* as "ridge" and writes from Maghera that the word *muine* "which is not understood in Dungiven, nor in any other parish in which I have been, is well understood here to signify a hill and is almost synonymous with Druim [ridge]" (*OSL (Derry)* 52). However, it is unclear whether the word was in common use in this sense in O'Donovan's time or whether this meaning was merely abstracted from place-names at

O'Donovan's instigation, perhaps on the model of *muin*, gen. sing. *muine*, "back". It is certainly not recorded in this sense in Irish dictionaries. In any case, there is no evidence that this was the meaning of the word over three hundred years or more previously when this name was coined, and so I translate it here with the more usual sense of "thicket".

Moyagall
C 9000

Maigh Ó gColla (?)
"plain of the O'Cullys"

1. moyogalla	Esch. Co. Map 14	1609
2. Moygallo, ⅓ part of the balliboe of	Charter of Londonderry 391	1613
3. Moyagalle	Charter of Londonderry 391	1613
4. Moyegola	Lond. Comp. Valuation 307	1613
5. Moyagola	Phillips MSS (Maps) Plate 24	1622
6. (?)Moyogoll	Civ. Surv. iii 170	1654
7. Moyogola	Civ. Surv. iii 180	1654
8. Moygalloe, one third part of the balliboe of	Bishop. Der. i 265	1657
9. Moyogalls, 2 third parts of the balliboe of	Bishop. Der. i 265	1657
10. Moygoll	Census 134	1659c
11. Moyagola	BSD(c) 65	1661
12. Moyagall	Par. Reg. (OSNB) No. 11	1787
13. Moyagall	Sampson's Map	1813
14. Moyagall	Custom of County (OSNB) No. 11	1834c
15. Moy-a-'gall	OSNB Pron. No. 11	1834c
16. Magh na ngall "plain of the foreigners"	J O'D (OSNB) No. 11	1834c
17. Magh-na-n-gall "The plain of the foreigner"	Munn's Notes 225	1925
18. Magh-na-nGall "plain of the foreigners"	Joyce iii 514	1925
19. Maigh Ghuala	GÉ 255	1989
20. ˌmeə'gɔːl	Local pronunciation	1993

The first element in this name is clearly *maigh* "plain" and it probably originally denoted a portion of the lower ground in the north of the townland. The remainder of the name presents a number of problems, although the early spellings, which seem to indicate an underlying form something like *Moyagola*, give us a reasonably clear picture of the pronunciation in the 17th century. The interchange of *o* and *a* is a feature particularly of Ulster Irish and this seems to have produced the modern form of the name, Moyagall. *Na* is not infrequently intruded into Irish place-names containing a surname (Kelly 1952–53), and this certainly seems to have happened here for Munn claims that the "native Irish" pronounced it Moynagall. This form was subsequently misinterpreted as *Maigh na nGall* "plain of the foreigners" (17).

The most recent attempt to determine the original form of the name, or at least to provide an Irish form, has given us *Maigh Ghuala* (19). It is not certain what we are to take the second element to be, but it is probably intended as the personal name *Guala* which is found in other place-names (see *PNI* ii 166–8; see also *góla* "pit, prison"). However, *guala* might be anglicized *-gole* or *-gool*, but it would not be expected to produce a form *-gall* such as we have here, nor does it account for the second syllable in the name. In addition to the above, we might consider a derivation from *gol* "weeping, wailing" which has an early variant gen. sing. *gola*, but perhaps the most reasonable origin would be from the surname *Ó Colla* (thus *Maigh Ó gColla* "plain of the O'Cullys) which is found in Cos Armagh and Antrim (MacLysaght 1985, 69) and in the parish of Banagher in Co. Derry in the 17th century (*HMR (Ó Doibhlin 2)* 55).

Rocktown
H 9197

Baile na Creige
"townland of the rock"

1. B:nacrighi	Esch. Co. Map 14	1609
2. Ballmaghorihi	Charter of Londonderry 391	1613
3. Balle Cregg	Lond. Comp. Valuation 307	1613
4. Ba Creg	Phillips MSS (Maps) Plate 24	1622
5. Ballinacreg	Civ. Surv. iii 180	1654
6. Ballinagcrihi	Bishop. Der. i 265	1657
7. Bolinekrege	Census 134	1659c
8. Ballynacregg	BSD(c) 65	1661
9. (?)Ballinebriger	HMR (Ó Doibhlin 2) 76	1663
10. Ballinacraig	Sampson's Map	1813
11. Rocktown	Custom of County (OSNB) No. 11	1834c
12. 'Rock-town	OSNB Pron. No. 11	1834c
13. Baile-na-carraige	Munn's Notes 225	1925
14. Tir-a-Carran "The rocky district"	Munn's Notes 225	1925
15. 'rɔktəun	Local pronunciation	1993

This name is of particular interest as it is a direct translation of an earlier Irish name *Baile na Creige* "townland of the rock". Some early spellings (1–2, 6) appear to suggest a form of the name from Irish *Baile na Críche* "townland of the boundary", and indeed Rocktown lies on the boundary with the parish of Termoneeny, but it is quite likely that all these spellings are the result of a single scribal error (see Appendix C).

Slaghtybogy
H 8899

Sleacht an Bhogaigh
"gravemound of the boggy ground"

1. (?)lagtauogolan	Esch. Co. Map 14	1609
2. Laughtanogolan	Charter of Londonderry 391	1613
3. Slata Golan	Lond. Comp. Valuation 307	1613
4. Slatavegolan	Phillips MSS (Maps) Plate 24	1622
5. Slateovoylagh	Civ. Surv. iii 180	1654
6. Laughtonogolan	Bishop. Der. i 265	1657
7. Slaghvoyland	Census 134	1659c
8. Slatoovoglagh	BSD(c) 65	1661
9. Slativoglane	HMR (Ó Doibhlin 2) 76	1663

196

10. Slaghtybogy	Par. Reg. (OSNB) No. 11	1791
11. Slatabogy	Sampson's Map	1813
12. Slatabogy	Custom of County (OSNB) No. 11	1834c
13. Slat-a-'bogy	OSNB Pron. No. 11	1834c
14. Sleacht Uí Bhogaigh "O'Bogy's monument"	J O'D (OSNB) No. 11	1834c
15. Leacht-ui-Bhogaigh "The sepulchral monument of the O'Bogys"	Munn's Notes 225	1925
16. ˌslatə'bogi	Local pronunciation	1993

The first element in this name is clearly *sleacht*, a variant form of *leacht* "gravemound" peculiar to some of the Ulster counties (*Joyce* i 66). The representation of the final element is rather confused in the historical sources and is only vaguely like the modern form.

O'Donovan identifies the final element in the current form of the name as the surname Ó Bogaigh (14), although this is a rare name which has not been connected with Ulster (Woulfe 1923, 439; MacLysaght 1985, 29). Munn considers *bogach* "boggy ground" and notes that all the north of the townland was bog (*Munn's Notes* 225). This might be expected to have produced a name something like *Slaghtybuggy*, but we may compare the name **Portavogie** in Co. Down which comes from Irish *Port an Bhogaigh* "place of the bog" (*PNI* ii 108–9).

Taking all the historical spellings together, a form something like *Slaghtavogolan* emerges. If we assume that this is connected to the modern form of the name, then it seems reasonable to conclude that the final element in the earlier form represents Irish *leathan* "broad" (on the anglicization of this element see **Upperland** below), and we may propose an origin from *Sleacht an Bhogaigh Leathain* "gravemound of the broad bog".

Tamnymartin	*Tamhnaigh Uí Mhártain*	
C 8700	"Martin's field"	

1. Tannymartin	BSD(c) 52	1661
2. Tanemartyn, Half	HMR (Ó Doibhlin 2) 76	1663
3. Tunymarten	Hib. Del. Derry	1672c
4. Tamnymartin	Par. Reg. (OSNB) No. 11	1786
5. Tamneymartin	Sampson's Map	1813
6. Tamnymartin	Custom of County (OSNB) No. 11	1834c
7. Tam-ny-'mar-tin	OSNB Pron. No. 11	1834c
8. Tamhnach Martaín "Martin's field"	J O'D (OSNB) No. 11	1834c
9. "Martin's field"	Joyce i 232	1869
10. Tamnach-Martain "Martin's field"	Munn's Notes 225	1925
11. ˌtani'martən	Local pronunciation	1993
12. ˌtamni'martən	Local pronunciation	1993

The first element in this name is undoubtedly *tamhnach* which probably originally denoted a "clearing" (*DIL* sv.). In Modern Irish, it is associated with mountainous districts and signifies "a grassy upland" or "an arable place in a mountain" (*Ó Dónaill* sv.; cf. *O'Reilly* 708;

Joyce i 231), but in this area John O'Donovan found that *tamhnach* signifies "a cultivated spot in the middle of a wilderness", and equates it with the Scottish croft (*OSL (Derry)* 21). The terrain here is relatively low and flat so that this must be considered the most suitable interpretation in this instance.

In place-names, it seems most commonly to be qualified by a common noun or an adjective, the latter often denoting a colour. However, in a small number of instances, mainly in Co. Derry, it is qualified by a surname, and in these cases the surname undoubtedly denotes ownership or possession. **Tamnagh** in the parish of Learmount, was formerly qualified by the surname McIlmurry, and it is probably a surname which occurs in the names **Tamnymullan**, also in Maghera, **Tamnyagan** in the parish of Banagher, and **Tamniaran** in Ballyscullion.

The qualifier here, therefore, may be the surname Martin which, although frequently of English or Scottish origin in Ulster, can reflect several native Irish names (MacLysaght 1957, 222). Mac Máirtín was the surname assumed by a branch of the O'Neills in Co. Tyrone, and Mac Giolla Mhártain, now usually Gilmartin, was the name of another sept who originally settled in Tyrone from where they spread to Fermanagh, Leitrim and Sligo (*ibid.* 223; Woulfe 1923, 376, 389). However, the names Ó Máirtín, now commonly used as a translation of Martin, and more particularly Ó Mártain, which was borne by the bishop of Clogher who died in 1431 (Woulfe 1923, 613), must be considered the most suitable in the present context.

| **Tamnymullan** | *Tamhnaigh Uí Mhaoláin* | |
| C 8501 | "Mullan's field" | |

1.	Tammencollar	Esch. Co. Map 14	1609
2.	Tawnynymallan	Bishop. Der. i 57	1610
3.	Tawnymullen	CPR Jas I 279a	1615
4.	Tawnymullen	Bishop. Der. i 102	1615
5.	Tawnimullan	Civ. Surv. iii 193	1654
6.	Tornymolan, Craigmoore &	Census 134	1659c
7.	Tannimullan	BSD(c) 52	1661
8.	Tavinmullan	HMR (Ó Doibhlin 2) 77	1663
9.	Toynymullan	Hib. Del. Derry	1672c
10.	Tamnymullen	Par. Reg. (OSNB) No. 11	1787
11.	Tamnaghmullin	Sampson's Map	1813
12.	Tamnymullen	Custom of County (OSNB) No. 11	1834c
13.	Tam-ny-'mullen	OSNB Pron. No. 11	1834c
14.	Tamhnach Uí Mhaoláin "O'Mullan's green field"	J O'D (OSNB) No. 11	1834c
15.	Tamnach-ui-Mhaolain "O'Mullan's field"	Munn's Notes 226	1925
16.	Tamhnach Uí Mhaoláin	GUH 56	1951
17.	ˌtaniˈmɔlən	Local pronunciation	1993
18.	ˌtaniˈmɔln	Local pronunciation	1993
19.	ˌtamniˈmɔlən	Local pronunciation	1993

On the meaning and significance of the first element, see **Tamnymartin** above. The surname *Ó Maoláin* is found in almost every part of Ireland, and they were one of the principal septs under the O'Cahans in Co. Derry (Woulfe 1923, 603; MacLysaght 1957, 233). Although the family's territory lay in the area called the Ballymullans some fifteen miles away in the vicinity of Feeny there is some evidence to suggest that they also held lands as far south as Lough Neagh (*GUH* 56–7 and note).

Tirgarvil	*Tír gCearbhaill* (?)	
C 8704	"Cearbhall's land"	

1. Tirgawly	Esch. Co. Map 14	1609
2. Tirgaraly	Charter of Londonderry 391	1613
3. Terre Garwill	Lond. Comp. Valuation 307	1613
4. Torgorwill	Phillips MSS (Maps) Plate 22	1622
5. Tiregarvell	Civ. Surv. iii 180	1654
6. Tirgaraly	Bishop. Der. i 264	1657
7. Tergarwell	Census 134	1659c
8. Tirgarvill	BSD(c) 65	1661
9. Tirgorvill	HMR (Ó Doibhlin 2) 76	1663
10. Tyrgarville	Par. Reg. (OSNB) No. 11	1803
11. Tirgarvil	Sampson's Map	1813
12. Tirgarvil	Custom of County (OSNB) No. 11	1834c
13. Tir-'gar-vil	OSNB Pron. No. 11	1834c
14. Tír garbhéil "land of gravel"	J O'D (OSNB) No. 11	1834c
15. Tir-gairbheil "The land of gravel"	Munn's Notes 226	1925
16. Tir-gairbhéil "land of gravel"	Joyce iii 575	1925
17. ˌtər'gaːrvəl	Local pronunciation	1993

The first element in this name is clearly *tír* "land, territory", and all previous authorities have agreed in deriving it from Irish *Tír Gairbhéil* "land of gravel" (14–16). *Gairbhéal* is a borrowing from English "gravel", and was in use as early as the 15th century (*DIL* sv. *graibél*). However, it is not widely used in place-names, and several early spellings of the name with internal -*w*-, suggesting a broad *bh*, seem to rule it out as a possibility here (see *Joyce* ii 375).

Tír is commonly used in place-names in association with personal names, less frequently so with surnames (*Onom. Goed.* 635-9). If we allow for the not unlikely possibility that the final *y* in the earliest group of documents (1–2, 6) is spurious, then we might tentatively suggest an origin from *Tír gCearbhaill* "Cearbhall's land". Although *tír* can be masc. or fem. in Mod. Ir., it was originally neuter, and this caused the following consonant to be nasalized. The personal name Cearbhall was popular among the early medieval aristocracy, particularly in Leinster, and was borne by several nobles of the Airgialla (Ó Corráin & Maguire 1981, 50; *CGH* index).

However, several other nouns or compounds must also be considered here, most notably compounds of *garbh* "rough" and *gearr* "short". *Garbh* occurs as the first element in numerous place-names such as **Garvagh** in Co. Derry, from Irish *Garbhachadh* "rough field", and it may be here compounded with *ail* "stone, rock" or possibly *aill* "cliff, precipice" (see *Joyce* ii 475–6). *Gearrbhaile* "short town" is anglicized Garbally in various parts of the country but it would quite naturally give rise to forms such as we see here as well (see Ó Maolfabhail 1990(a) 185).

Tirnageeragh
C 8903

Tír na gCaorach
"land of the sheep"

1.	Tirnagerra	Esch. Co. Map 14	1609
2.	Tirnagerah	Charter of Londonderry 391	1613
3.	Terre ne Gerah	Lond. Comp. Valuation 307	1613
4.	Terenegera	Phillips MSS (Maps) Plate 22	1622
5.	Tirnegiragh	Civ. Surv. iii 180,181	1654
6.	Tirenegiragh	Civ. Surv. iii 181	1654
7.	Ternageragh	Bishop. Der. i 264	1657
8.	(?)Interregrolagh	Census 134	1659c
9.	Tirenegragh	BSD(c) 65	1661
10.	Tirnegoragh	HMR (Ó Doibhlin 2) 76	1663
11.	Ternageeragh	Par. Reg. (OSNB) No. 11	1786
12.	Tirnageeraghan	Sampson's Map	1813
13.	Ternageeragh	Custom of County (OSNB) No. 11	1834c
14.	Tur-na-'geeragh	OSNB Pron. No. 11	1834c
15.	Tír na gcaerach "land or district of the sheep"	J O'D (OSNB) No. 11	1834c
16.	"the land of the sheep"	Joyce ii 381	1875
17.	Tir-na-g-caerach "The land of the sheep"	Munn's Notes 226	1925
18.	ˌtərnəˈgiːrəx	Local pronunciation	1993

There seems to be no doubt concerning the origin of this name (cf. *Joyce* i 473–4).

Toberhead
H 8994

Tobar Thaoide
"St Taoide's well"

1.	tobarhidie	Esch. Co. Map 14	1609
2.	Taberhidy	Charter of Londonderry 391	1613
3.	Tubber Tey	Lond. Comp. Valuation 307	1613
4.	Tubberlyd	Phillips MSS (Maps) Plate 24	1622
5.	Toberteide	Civ. Surv. iii 180	1654
6.	Toherhidy	Bishop. Der. i 265	1657
7.	Towberscide	BSD(c) 65	1661
8.	Tobertide	HMR (Ó Doibhlin 2) 76	1663
9.	Toberhead (x2)	Bishop. Der. ii 113	1686
10.	Tobberide	Par. Reg. (OSNB) No. 11	1786
11.	Toberhead	Sampson's Map	1813
12.	Toberhead	Custom of County (OSNB) No. 11	1834c
13.	To-ber-'head	OSNB Pron. No. 11	1834c
14.	Tiobraid "a well or spring"	J O'D (OSNB) No. 11	1834c
15.	Tiobraid "putens fons"	J O'D (OSNB) No. 11	1834c
16.	Tubrid [The well/spring]	Joyce i 580	1869
17.	Tiobraid "The Well, or Spring"	Munn's Notes 226	1925
18.	ˌtobərˈhɛd	Local pronunciation	1993

The early spellings with internal *t* leave us with little doubt that the second element in this name is the name of the early patron saint of **Church Island** in Ballyscullion parish. There is an ancient well near the main Derry road (*OSM* xviii 45; Ní Mhaolchallann 1993, 63).

Upperland	*Áth an Phoirt Leathain*	
C 8705	"ford of the broad (river) bank"	

1. air Ath A' Phortáin	OSL (Derry) 68		1740c
2. ar Áth an Phortáin	DCCU 427		1740c
3. aghfortlauy	Esch. Co. Map 14		1609
4. Aghfortlany	Charter of Londonderry 391		1613
5. Amford Lame	Lond. Comp. Valuation 307		1613
6. Amfordlan	Phillips MSS (Maps) Plate 22		1622
7. Aportlaughan	Civ. Surv. iii 180		1654
8. Aghfortlany	Bishop. Der. i 264		1657
9. A Port Lawgher	BSD(c) 65		1661
10. Aprotlane	HMR (Ó Doibhlin 2) 76		1663
11. Upperlane	Par. Reg. (OSNB) No. 11		1788
12. Upporlane	Par. Reg. (OSNB) No. 11		1790
13. Apportlane	Par. Reg. (OSNB) No. 11		1793
14. Upperland	Par. Reg. (OSNB) No. 11		1802
15. Ampurtain	Sampson's Map		1813
16. Upperland	Custom of County (OSNB) No. 11	1834c
17. Up-per-'land	OSNB Pron. No. 11		1834c
18. Ath an Phortáin "ford of the bank"	OSL (Derry) 69		1834
19. Ath an Phortáin "ford of the little bank"	J O'D (OSNB) No. 11		1834c
20. Ath-an-purtain "The ford of the little bank"	Munn's Notes 226		1925
21. 'ɒpərˌlənz	Local pronunciation		1993

This name is documented and discussed in one of a series of anonymous articles in *Dinnseanchas* where it is concluded that it derives from Irish *Áth an Phortáin* which we might translate "ford of the little port" (*Dinnsean.* ii (1967), 85–6). Support for this view might be derived from Ó Brolcháin's 18th-century poem and the Ordnance Survey Name Books, both of which give this as the Irish form of the name (1–2, 18–20). While this form seems to have been in use among Irish speakers of the 18th and 19th centuries, and indeed probably gave rise to the name Ampertain House, it cannot be the origin of the current anglicized form of the townland name (OS C 873046; see *OS 1:10,000* sh. 65).

The majority of our sources down to the present day agree in spelling the name with an internal *l*, but this is absent from the Irish form proposed in *Dinnseanchas*. The author of this article admits that it is difficult to explain how the *l* first appeared in the anglicized forms of the name, particularly as it occurs in unrelated sources (*art. cit.* 86), and this must be viewed as a strong objection to the proposed origin. There is no phonological reason why an *l* should be interpolated here, and it cannot be explained as a scribal error. In addition, we may note that the syllable with the strongest stress in the Irish form is unstressed in the English. It is quite likely that the stress did shift onto the first syllable, but the origin proposed in *Dinnseanchas* provides no motivation for such a development.

A much simpler approach is to view the Irish form as a development of an earlier form which more closely resembled the early anglicized versions. The first element is almost certainly *áth* "ford", and the ford in question probably crossed the Knockoneill River which runs the entire length of the townland's southern boundary. The second element is *port* (or possibly a diminutive form of this) which has a variety of meanings. In the present context it probably indicates a river bank, although we might also consider the possibility that it is used in the sense of a "fortified place" and refers to the rath overlooking the Knockoneill River (OS C 869053). The final element is more difficult to determine with certainty due to a considerable variety of spellings in the early 17th-century sources, but some clues have been left to us which may help to determine its form. There is some evidence for the use of the article at this time (5–6), and this suggests that the final element is an adjective rather than a noun. Secondly, the variation in spellings with and without internal *gh* indicates that we are probably dealing with a word with an original intervocalic *th* as this sound was in the process of disappearing from East Ulster Irish during the course of the 17th century (see **Beagh (Spiritual)** above). Both these factors would lead us to believe that the final element is *leathan* "broad". The final *y* in some early related sources (3–4, 8) is almost certainly a scribal error (see **Tirgarvil** above).

It should be clear that this form has a similar, although not identical, stress pattern to the modern name. It is stressed most heavily on the last element, so that in the 17th century it might have been anglicized as *Aportlan* or the like with stress on the final syllable. Following the loss of the *t* from the consonant cluster *rtl*, the name would almost inevitably have been reinterpreted as "Upper Land" among English speakers. The subsequent shift in stress seems to have resulted from the loss of meaning which would have accompanied its adoption as a mere name. In Irish, the original form appears to have been revised or re-analysed to give the attested *Áth an Phortáin*, although one cannot rule out the possibility that all forms of the name go back to an original *Áth an Phortáin Leathain* "ford of the broad little bank".

OTHER NAMES

Annagh-Hilkin   *Eanach Uí Ailleagáin*
C 9300   "Hilligan's marsh island"

1. 'anəh	Local pronunciation	1993
2. ˌanə'hïlkïn	Local pronunciation	1993

Annagh-Hilkin was described in the 19th century as a house and farm on an oval shaped hill nearly surrounded by bog (*OSRNB* 63 sh. 37). The first element is clearly Irish *eanach*, which here means "marsh island" (on which see **Annagh** in parish of Ballyscullion). The final element looks English but it is probably the old Ulster surname, Hilligan (Irish Ó *hAilleagáin*), which is now common in Mayo and Roscommon but is apparently obsolete in Ulster (Woulfe 1923, 549).

Annaghaboggy   *Eanach an Bhogaigh*
H 9395   "marsh-island of the bog"

1. Eanach a' Bhogaigh "soft marsh"	OSRNB 42 sh.42	1850c

A small island of arable land in the middle of a large bog (*OSRNB* 42 sh. 42). Cf. **Slaghtybogy** above.

Annaghfad	*Eanach Fada*	
C 9200	"long marsh-island"	

1. "Long Island"	OSRNB 63 sh.37	1850c
2. Eanach Fada "long moor or marsh"	OSRNB 63 sh.37	1850c
3. ˌanə'faːd	Local pronunciation	1993

A narrow piece of cultivated ground nearly surrounded by bog (*OSRNB* 63 sh. 37).

Back Burn	An English form	
H 8299		

1. 'bɛk bọrn	Local pronunciation	· 1993

See **Back Burn** in the parish of Termoneeny.

Benbradagh	A transferred name	
C 8703		

1. ˌbɛn'bradə	Local pronunciation	1993

The name Benbradagh has been here borrowed from the mountain of that name which lies to the north (OS C 7211). The house was originally owned by the Houstons but was bought over by two brothers by the name of Clark who built a new front in Tudor style. The Clark brothers were keen hunters and had often hunted on Benbradagh, and it was from this association that the house got its name.

Beresfords Bridge	An English form	
C 8703		

1. 'bɛrzfərd brïdʒ	Local pronunciation	1993

A bridge was erected here about 1836 through the influence of Mr Beresford of Learmount, and it was from him that it got its name (*OSRNB* 47 sh. 32).

Big Park	An English form	
H 8097		

See **Back Parks** in the parish of Killelagh above.

Brackagh	*Breacach*	
H 9399	"speckled place"	

1. "Broken or speckled"	OSRNB 63 sh.37	1850c

The hill on which Brackagh is situated was at one time covered with brushwood with forest trees scattered through it, and it was said to have received its name *Breacach* "speckled place" from this circumstance (*OSRNB* 63 sh. 37).

Campbells Bridge   An English form
H 7998

Campbells Bridge was called after a man of that name who formerly resided near it (*OSRNB* 39 sh. 36).

Carnaman   *Carnamán*
H 9299   "cairn place"

1. 'Car-na-man	OSCNB 62 sh.37	1850c
2. Carn na mban "heap of the women"	OSCNB 62 sh.37	1850c
3. Carn na mban	OSRNB 63 sh.37	1850c
4. Carn am an	OSRNB 63 sh.37	1850c
5. 'kjernə,mən	Local pronunciation	1993
6. 'kjarnə,mən	Local pronunciation	1993

The suggestion that the name Carnaman derives from *Carn na mBan* "the cairn of the women" (2–3) is untenable, for it is stressed on the first syllable (5–6). There is a suffix *-amán* which appears in words such as *carracamán* "rocky eminence" (< *carraig* "rock"), *dúramán* "dull-witted person" (< *dúr* "dour, grim"), and *meallamán* "lumpish thing; potato" (< *meall* "lump") and it seems not unlikely that Carnaman is formed from a common noun *carn* "cairn" followed by this suffix. In place-names, the suffix may have a diminutive sense, but it more probably is used in a locative sense as "place of".

Carnbane   *Carn Bán*
C 8705   "white heap or cairn"

1. karn'baːn	Local pronunciation	1993

There is now no sign of a cairn here (see Speer 1990; *OS 1:10,000* sh. 65).

Causin Hill   A hybrid form
C 9201

1. ˌkɔsïn ('kọtïn)	Local pronunciation	1993
2. ˌkɔsïn 'hïl	Local pronunciation	1993

In the relevant Revision Name Book, J. King notes that Causin Hill (or Caution Hill as he calls it) was formerly resorted to by murderers and that, as a result of several killings, travellers became very cautious of themselves (*OSRNB* 63 sh. 37). It is more likely that the first element is *Cosán* "path". Joyce takes this to be the origin of a number of names in various parts of the country, and we may compare *Casán na gCorp* "path of the corpses" in Glenlark, Co. Tyrone, so called from being on the road to the graveyard (*Joyce* i 373; Morton 1959, 55). Joe Doherty of Gorteade informs me that it was originally a very steep hill on the road between Maghera and Portglenone but that, over a century ago, a relief scheme cut a considerable amount off it, thus lowering its height and giving it its alias, Causin Cutting.

Coolderry	*Cúil Darach*	
H 9199	"recess of the oaks"	
1. "Back of the oaks"	OSRNB 63 sh.37	1850c
2. Cul Doir "Back wood, or oakwood"	OSRNB 63 sh.37	1850c
3. ˌkulˈdarə	Local pronunciation	1993

Coolderry sits in a recess (*cúil*) between two hills and must once have been covered with oak trees. The modern spelling of the name suggests that the final element is *doire* "oakwood", but the local pronunciation (3), coupled with the interpretation recorded in the area in the last century (1), favours an origin from *Cúil Darach* "recess of the oaks".

Corby Island	A Scots form	
H 8498		
1. ˌkǫrbi ˈailən	Local pronunciation	1993

The "island" here is a small piece of cultivated ground surrounded by bog (*OSRNB* 39 sh. 36). The first element is the Scots word *corbie* meaning "crow, raven".

Crockcor	*Cnoc Corr*	
C 7902	"conspicuous hill"	
1. Cnoc Corr "odd hill"	OSRNB 46 sh.32	1850c

Crockcor is described as "a small hill conspicuously raised above the ridge of mountain that forms its base" (*OSRNB* 46 sh. 32). *Corr* has a variety of meanings and here it probably means "conspicuous, prominent".

Crockney Hill	See parish of Magherafelt
H 9194	

Crosskeys	An English form	
C 8805		
1. (ðə) krɔsˈkiːz	Local pronunciation	1993

The name Crosskeys appears to originate from a sign over a public house. In 1850, it contained one licensed house, but the name is not recorded (*OSRNB* 47 sh. 32). Cf. **Crosskeys**, Co. Antrim (*PNI* iv 141–2).

Curdian	Of uncertain origin
C 9003	

1. Cur-dy-an	OSRNB 49 sh.33	1850c
2. ˈkọrdʒïn	Local pronunciation	1993
3. ˈkərdʒïn	Local pronunciation	1993

In the absence of any substantial record of this name, it seems futile to speculate on its origin. Although several possibilities present themselves, none can be argued convincingly.

Derryhoma　　　　　　　　*Doire Thuama*
H 9298　　　　　　　　　　　"oakwood of the mound"

| 1. Doire Tuama "Roboretum Tomae" | OSRNB 63 sh.37 | 1850c |
| 2. ˌdɛrəˈhoːmə | Local pronunciation | 1993 |

The origin of the name was not known by any of the inhabitants questioned by members of the Ordnance Survey in the preparation for the revision of the six-inch maps in the middle of the last century, but O'Donovan's suggestion, adopted here, is quite plausible (*OSRNB* 63 sh. 37). The meaning of *tuaim* (gen. sing. *tuama*) is uncertain but in place-names it is thought that it generally denotes a burial mound or tumulus (*Joyce* i 334–6; Mac Giolla Easpaig 1984, 51; *PNI* iv 3; *DIL* sv.). There is now no trace of any such burial.

Derryhurk　　　　　　　　*Doire Thoirc*
H 9297　　　　　　　　　　　"oakwood of the boar"

| 1. ˌdɛriˈhərk | Local pronunciation | 1993 |

Wild boars formerly abounded in Ireland and the word *torc* "boar" occurs in many place-names (*Joyce* i 479). It is now impossible to state definitively whether the form of the last element should be singular or plural (*Doire Thorc* "oakwood of the boars"). The *t* of *torc* is here lenited after the dative. Cf. **Altaturk Glen** in the parish of Ballynascreen.

Dunergan Hill　　　　　　A hybrid form
H 8997

| 1. Donergan | Civ. Surv. iii 180 | 1654 |
| 2. ˌdọnˈɛːrgən | Local pronunciation | 1993 |

There was formerly a rath or fort (*dún*) here, but the site has since completely disappeared due to quarrying (Speer 1990, 7). There is a view to the north over lower ground, and the land to the south and east is very wet (*ibid.*). In the Revision Name Books, the origin of the name is attributed to the shape of the hill – an oblong round-backed ridge – but the second element remains obscure (*OSRNB* 63 sh. 37).

Garrison, The　　　　　　An English form
H 8994

| 1. ðə ˈgjarsən ˌroːd | Local pronunciation | 1993 |

The Garrison reportedly gets its name from a former tenant who fought to retain possession against a considerable force of bailiffs and others who came to evict him (*OSRNB* 42 sh. 42).

Glen	*An Gleann*
C 8200	"the glen"

Glen takes its name from the gentle sloping valley formed by Fallagloon Burn. Irish *gleann* has exactly the same signification as English *glen* (from Scottish Gaelic *gleann*) and with no context it is impossible to establish whether the name is of English or Irish origin (see *Joyce* i 428).

Gortmore	*Gort Mór*
H 8699	"big field"

1. gɔrt'moːr	Local pronunciation	1993

In Maghera, it was believed that the word *gort* signified a piece of ground enclosed by stakes interwoven with brambles and attached to a church which was set aside for the grazing of worshippers' horses (*OSM* xviii 55), but more generally it denotes a small plot of land close to the church, usually a field or two of about five acres, which was set aside for the vicar's use (*Colton Vis.* 118). Gortmore appears to have been a farm attached to the parsonage at Maghera (described as the "Parsonage Farm 68a. 3r. 0p." in *Der. Clergy* 261), and lies approximately 500m south-east of the old glebe called Gort (Irish *Gort* "field"). Gort was thought to have been originally used for the grazing of horses belonging to people attending Mass at the old Roman Catholic house of worship at Maghera before it was enclosed and attached to the parsonage (*OSRNB* 39 sh. 36).

Grove, The	An English form
C 8600	

The Grove, clearly, takes its name from a small plantation of trees.

Heath Mount	An English form
H 8398	

So called on account of its location on a small hill overlooking a large bog.

Hill Head	An English form
H 8895	

1. 'hïl hɛd	Local pronunciation	1993

Hill Head's location on top of a small hill gives rise to its name. Cf. **Hill Head** in the parish of Ballyscullion.

Holly Hill	An English form
H 9398	

1. ðə 'hɔli 'hïl	Local pronunciation	1993

This small village takes its name from its situation on top of a wooded hill, the underwood of which principally consisted of holly (*OSRNB* 62 sh. 37).

Hollyhill Wood   An English form
H 9397

Hollyhill Wood takes its name from the nearby village of **Holly Hill** (see previous entry).

Irish Tirgarvil   A hybrid form
C 8703

  1. ˌairiʃ tərˈgaːrvəl   Local pronunciation   1993

See **Tirgarvil**. Irish Tirgarvil stands in contrast to the neighbouring village of Scotch Tirgarvil, the former having been occupied by Irish Catholics, the latter by Scottish Presbyterians. Such ethnic distinctions are not uncommon in Irish place-names. We have, for example, Irish Cah and Scotch Cah in Co. Derry (OS C 8418, C 8218), Irish Corran and Scotch Corran in Co. Armagh (OS H 9034, H 8935), Irishomerbane and Scotchomerbane in Co. Antrim (OS D 1118, D 1117), and Irishtown and Scotch Town in Co. Tyrone (OS H 5587, H 5487). A Hibernian Hall, bearing the date 1907, still stands in Irish Tirgarvil.

Island   An English form
C 9101

  1. ˈailənd   Local pronunciation   1993

As in so many other places, the element "island" here denotes a piece of cultivated land which is almost surrounded by bog (see *OSRNB* 63 sh. 37).

Killadarkan   *Coillín Dearcán*
H 9297   "little wood of the berries"

  1. "the wood of the berries"   OSRNB 62 sh.37   1850c
  2. Killandarkan, pronounced   OSRNB 62 sh.37   1850c

  3. ˈdarkïn   Local pronunciation   1993

Until some time before the middle of the 19th century, Killadarkan was wooded and we can be reasonably certain that the first element here is a form of *coill* "wood" rather than *cill* "church" (*OSRNB* 62 sh. 37). The pronunciation is recorded in the Revision Name Books where it is noted that an *n* was distinctly heard in the second syllable (2), and this suggests a diminutive form of *coill*.

In the middle of the last century, the name was understood to mean "the wood of the berries" (1) from *dearc* "berry", but it is possible that the final element also represents a form of *dearca* "acorn" (gen. *dearcan*). It is perhaps curious that only the last element appears in the current form of the name, and this might suggest a diminutive form of *dearc* "cave, hollow". However, the name was clearly understood locally in the last century as "the wood of the berries" so that the reduction of the name almost certainly occurred in the English language without reference to the original meaning of the name.

Killard
H 9298

Coill Ard
"high wood"

1.	"Highwood"	OSRNB 62 sh.37	1850c
2.	Coill Ard "high wood"	OSRNB 62 sh.37	1850c
3.	kjïl'a:rd	Local pronunciation	1993

Killard (Irish *Coill Ard* "high wood") takes its name from its location on a hill which was formerly covered with trees (*OSRNB* 62 sh. 37).

Lower Town
H 9099

An English form

This village is called Lower Town in contrast to **Upper Town** which lies a short distance to the south on higher ground (*OSRNB* 62 sh. 37).

Maghera
C 8500

See PARISH NAME.

McKennas Town
H 9399

An English form

So called from people by the name of McKenna who were very numerous here (*OSRNB* 63 sh. 37; *Griffith's Val.* 104).

Milltown
H 8499

An English form

1.	'mil'təun	Local pronunciation	1993

Milltown takes its name from a corn mill which stood here among a cluster of houses in the middle of the last century (*OSRNB* 39 sh. 36).

Milltown Burn
C 8300

An English form

Milltown Burn is named after **Milltown** (see previous entry) which it passes on its way to its confluence with Back Burn.

Ranaghan Bridge
C 7901

A hybrid form

1.	'ranəxən brïdʒ	Local pronunciation	1993

This bridge is named from the northern subdivision of the townland of Fallagloon (*OSRNB* 39 sh. 36). See **Ranaghan More** below.

Ranaghan More
C 8001

Raithneachán Mór
"great Ranaghan"

Ranaghan More is a small village in the townland of Fallylea. Its name is best translated "great Ranaghan" in contradistinction to Ranaghan Beg (Irish *Raithneachán Beag* "little Ranaghan"), a subdivision in the townland of Fallagloon (OS C 7901). *Raithneachán* signifies a place where ferns grow and is found in place-names in all four provinces of Ireland (*Joyce* ii 331).

Rock of Drummuck, The C 8902	A hybrid form	
1. ˈrɔk əv ˌdrọˈmọk	Local pronunciation	1993

Named from the townland of **Drummuck** (see above). It is a high rocky hill, unsuitable for tillage, and formerly the site of a clachan (J. Doherty, pers. comm.; Ní Mhaolchallann 1993, 47).

Rockvale C 8702	An English form	
1. rɔkˈvel	Local pronunciation	1993

I have been unable to ascertain the origin of this name with certainty. The word "vale" is normally used poetically, and Rockvale appears to be a purely fanciful name, being situated on a gently sloping hill. The first element is probably "rock" but Old English *hrōc* "rook" often takes this form in English place-names. Cf. **Rockvale** in Co. Down which is actually a mistake for Rookvale.

Rough Hill C 8900	An English form	
1. (ðə) rọf ˈhïl	Local pronunciation	1993

This hill got its name on account of its rough and uncultivated state (*OSCNB* 62 sh. 37).

Rowans Gift H 9196	An English form	

No traditions are preserved about the name of this place but it undoubtedly derives from the fact that it was given to someone as a gift by a person called Rowan. It was precisely these circumstances which gave rise to the name **Roe's Gift** in the parish of Ballyscullion.

Scotch Tirgarvil C 8803	An English form	

See **Irish Tirgarvil**.

Shanaghan H 9197	An English form	

Shanaghan is named from an old mansion house which formerly stood here (*OSRNB* 62 sh. 37). The house may have been named after the 18th-century architect Michael Shanahan who designed Ballyscullion church, the Earl of Bristol's house at Ballyscullion, and the tower and spire for the church on Church Island in Lough Beg (Curl 1986, 371–2).

Sheskin Bridge   A hybrid form
Sheskin Burn
C 7802, C 7701

The names Sheskin Bridge and Sheskin Burn presuppose the existence of a place called Sheskin from which they were named. The first element in both names is the Irish word *seascann* "marsh", and probably originally referred to some part of this boggy hillside.

Thyme Hill   An English form
H 9397

1. 'taim hïl   Local pronunciation   1993

This place is clearly named from the herb thyme which must have been grown here at one stage.

Tullyroe Hill   A hybrid form
H 9399

1. Tulach Ruadh "red hillock" OSRNB 63 sh.37   1850c

2. ˌtọli'ro: hïl   Local pronunciation   1993
3. ˌtọli'rowi   Local pronunciation   1993

The name Tullyroe (Irish *Tulaigh Rua* "red hillock") was probably originally applied to the hill now somewhat tautologously called Tullyroe Hill. It is likely that the adjective *rua* "red" described the colour of the heather which now partially covers the hill.

Upper Town   An English form
H 9099

1. 'ọpər ˌtəun   Local pronunciation   1993

See **Lower Town** above.

Wood, The   An English form
H 9399

1. ðə 'wud   Local pronunciation   1993

The land here was formerly wooded, from which fact the name is derived (*OSRNB* 63 sh. 37).

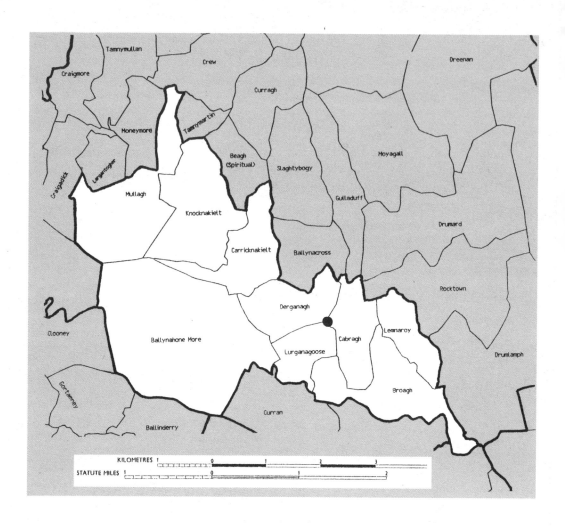

Parish of Termoneeny

Townlands
Ballynahone More
Broagh
Cabragh
Carricknakielt

Derganagh
Knocknakielt
Lemnaroy
Lurganagoose
Mullagh

Towns
Knockloghrim

Based upon Ordnance Survey 1:50,000 mapping, with permission of the Director of the Ordnance Survey of Northern Ireland, Crown copyright reserved.

THE PARISH OF TERMONEENY

The ruins of the old parish church of Termoneeny stand on a prominent hill in the townland of Mullagh overlooking the plain of the Moyola to the south and Maghera to the north (Hamlin 1976, ii 595). Little is known of the church's early history, but it was a medieval parish church, the name of which is documented as early as the Papal Taxation of 1302–6, and again in Colton's visitation of the Diocese of Derry of 1397.

Despite its small size, it was no stranger to controversy in the Middle Ages. In 1411, one John Okahilti (*Ó Caoilte*) was made rector of the parish following the discovery that Peter Omolkallund (*Ó Maolchallann*), the previous incumbent, had concurrently held both the rectory of Termoneeny and that of Tamlaght in the diocese of Armagh (*Cal. Papal Letters* vi 262). However, six years later, he was dismissed from his office when it was discovered that he had bought off Peter's possible opposition by letting him have half the fruits until Peter should obtain another benefice (*ibid.* vii 49). Controversy again arose later in the same century when Patrick Omolachan, then rector of the parish, alleged that his benefice had been conferred on one Philip Othoagan (*Reg. Swayne* 156). In reply, the Archbishop of Armagh enjoined the parishioners of Termoneeny to obey Omolochan as rector under pain of excommunication (*ibid.*). Omolachan later became perpetual vicar of the parish church of Maghera, but subsequently incurred the wrath of the Pope by celebrating Mass and other divine offices despite excommunication for committing simony (*Cal. Papal Letters* xii 692). The complaint had been lodged with the Pope by John Otehegan, then rector of Termoneeny, and very probably a relative of the Philip Othoagan who had some years earlier tried to arrest the rectory from the same Peter Omolachan. Otehegan also complained that the fruits of the church of Termoneeny were insufficient for his maintenance and proposed that the rectory of Termoneeny be united with the vicarage of Maghera (*ibid.*).

The patron of the church is named as St McNessan among Sir James Ware's notes on the Diocese of Derry (*Bishop. Der* i 405), but there is no saint of this name in any of the martyrologies or genealogies. The genealogies of Irish saints make it clear that the patrons came from among the seven sons of Nessán mac Eirc (*Secht meic Nesain*), four of whom dwelt in *Enga* which, as we shall see, is the older name for the parish of Termoneeny, and these became its patrons (*CSH* 284.1; see also *Top. Frag.* 83). The compounding of the sons of Nessán into a single saint is hardly surprising given the prevalence of dedications to single saints.

PARISH NAME

Termoneeny *Tearmann Eanga*
meaning uncertain

1. hi quattuor in Enga sunt	CSH 284.1	1125c
2. Termon Engha	Top. Frag. 83	1675c
3. Euga	Eccles. Tax. (CDI) 215	1306c
4. Eanagea	Colton Vis. 76	1397
5. Ecanage	Colton Vis. 81	1397
6. Henga	Cal. Papal Letters vi 262	1411
7. Enga (x2)	Cal. Papal Letters vii 49	1417
8. Eanga Par.	Reg. Swayne 156	1435
9. Ennya	Reg. Swayne 156	1435

10. Ganga	Reg. Swayne 156, 157	1435
11. Enga	Cal. Papal Letters xii 692	1469
12. Any or Termon-Any	CPR Jas I 376b	1609
13. Termonany	Bishop. Der. i 56	1610
14. Termonany	Bishop. Der. i 80	1611
15. Termonany	CPR Jas I 279a	1615
16. Termonany	CPR Jas I 280a	1615
17. Any parish	CPR Jas I 377a	1615
18. Termonany	Bishop. Der. i 102	1615
19. Termonanny	Bishop. Der. i 109	1615
20. Termonanny, R'c'oria de	Bishop. Der. i 129	1617c
21. Termonany alias Mullahanry	Bishop. Der. i 145	1624c
22. Termonaney	Bishop. Der. i 181	1634?
23. Tarmeny	Civ. Surv. iii 167,178	1654
24. Termonary	Civ. Surv. iii 174	1654
25. Termenenny	Civ. Surv. iii 178	1654
26. Tarmeneny	Civ. Surv. iii 187	1654
27. Termeneny	Civ. Surv. iii 187,193	1654
28. Tarmonery, The parish of	Hib. Reg. Loughinsholin	1657c
29. Turminany	Census 134	1659c
30. Termonenny	Bishop. Der. i 326	1661
31. Tarmoneny Parish	BSD(c) 51	1661
32. Tarmeneny Parish	BSD(c) 64	1661
33. Termonanie, The Parish of	HMR (Ó Doibhlin 2) 74	1663
34. Mullagh Eanadh, S'ti Mcnessan, 9 balliboes	Bishop. Der. i 405	1666
35. Termonany	Bishop. Der. i 415	1668
36. Termonany alias Mulla Henry	Bishop. Der. i 425	1669
37. Termonany	Bishop. Der. ii 1	1671
38. Farrinonerry	Hib. Del. Derry	1672c
39. Termonany al's Mullaghhenry, Rec. De	Bishop. Der. ii 113	1686
40. Termonany (x2)	Bishop. Der. ii 136	1692
41. Termonany	Bishop. Der. ii 509	1700c
42. Tarmoneeny R	Sampson's Map	1813
43. "pronounced Termon-éé-ány"	OSL (Derry) 54	1834
44. Ter-mo-'nee-ny	OSNB Pron. No. 6	1834c
45. Tearmann Uí Éighnigh	OSL (Derry) 54	1834
46. Termon-O-Heney or O'Heney's termon"	OSL (Derry) 54	1834
47. Tearmann Eignigh "Egny's Termon"	J O'D (OSNB) No. 6	1834c
48. "the mensal lands of Heany"	OSM vi 132	1836
49. Tearmann-ui-eighnigh "The sanctuary, or glebe lands, of O'Heaney, or O'Henry"	Munn's Notes 263	1925
50. ˌtərməˈnini	Local pronunciation	1993

214

The name Termoneeny was originally applied only to the parish's termon or erenagh lands, but it later came to signify the parish as a whole (cf. **Ballynascreen** above). The word *tearmann*, which forms the first element of this name, was used in Irish to denote lands belonging to a church or monastic community (*DIL* sv. *termonn*; Flanagan 1981-2(c) 75), and this same element also appears in the parish names **Termonmaguirk** and **Termonamongan** in Co. Tyrone, both of which have as their specific the surname of the associated erenagh family (Flanagan *loc. cit.*).

The early documentation shows that the original name for the parish comes from Irish *Eanga*, but unfortunately its meaning is unclear. It is unlikely that we have here a form of the word *eang* (*ā*-stem, fem.), which in place-names probably denotes a tract of land, as our earliest and most reliable source (1) seems to indicate a dat. sing. *iā*-stem. It is possible, therefore, that the name *Eanga* is of some antiquity and that the word from which it is derived had already become obsolete or obscure at an early date.

In East Ulster Irish, intervocalic *ng* is frequently lost, generally resulting in the lengthening, and sometimes nasalization, of the preceding vowel. This phenomenon is found in several other place-names (de hÓir 1964(a); Flanagan 1981–2(a) 22–3), and we doubtless have another example of it here. In this particular instance, however, the *ng* does not disappear altogether but re-emerges as *n*, much as we find in other place-names where a nasal has been lost. Already by the 17th century, we have evidence of the loss of the *ng*, both in the simple form of the name, *Any* (12, 17), and in the precursor to the modern form, *Termonany*. The modern form has developed from these 17th-century forms by a further modification of the vowel to [ʌ:] and ultimately [i:], a development which is well attested in Tyrone Irish (Stockman & Wagner 1965, 202)

The ruins of the medieval parish church are situated on a hill overlooking the surrounding countryside, and this undoubtedly gave rise to the alias, spelt *Mullahanry* etc., which occurs in a few 17th-century documents (21, 34, 36, 39). *Mullach*, which denotes a hilltop, refers to the eminence on which the old church is perched, and it also gives name to the townland of **Mullagh**. The second element is variously spelt in our documents, but there can be little doubt that it derives once again from the older name of the parish, *Eanga* (see particularly form 34). Some of the later spellings give the impression that it represents the personal name Henry (36, 39), but such an origin is highly unlikely and it is almost certain that these forms are mistranscriptions as both occur in closely related sources containing similar information laid out in the same manner. They seem to be based on the earlier spelling *Mullahanry* which, I would suggest, is a misreading of *Mullahanny*. This variant form then certainly represents an original Irish *Mullach Eanga* "hilltop of *Eanga*".

TOWNLAND NAMES

Ballynahone More
H 8796

Baile na hAbhann Mór
"great Ballynahone (townland of the river)"

1. b:neetollagh (?)	Esch. Co. Map 14	1609
2. Ballinetollagh	Bishop. Der. i 57	1610
3. Ballynetollagh	CPR Jas I 279a	1615
4. Ballinetullagh	Bishop. Der. i 102	1615
5. Bellimihowne	Civ. Surv. iii 187	1654
6. Bellinahownwoghteragh [glebe]	Civ. Surv. iii 187	1654
7. Ballina-hownmore	Civ. Surv. iii 193	1654

8. Ballenehonemore	Hib. Reg. Loughinsholin	1657c
9. Ballynehownmore	BSD(c) 51	1661
10. Belm'here	HMR (Ó Doibhlin 2) 74	1663
11. Ballinehone more	Hib. Del. Derry	1672c
12. Ballinahonemore	Sampson's Map	1813
13. Bal-ly-na-'hone-more	OSNB Pron. No. 6	1834c
14. Baile na h-abhann mór "Town of the river (Big)"	J O'D (OSNB) No. 6	1834c
15. Baile-na-h-ábhann "The townland of the river"	Munn's Notes 263	1925
16. ˌbalnə'hoːn	Local pronunciation	1993

Both *baile* "townland" and *béal átha* "approach to a ford" are sometimes anglicized *bally* and it is, as a result, often difficult to distinguish between them. The Moyola runs directly through Ballynahone More and it is conceiveable that there was once a ford across it from which the townland was named. The forms from the Civil Survey have *e* for *a* in the first syllable, possibly indicating *béal átha* (5–6), but this is common for *baile* in this source and in the Hearth Money Rolls (10; cf. **Drumballyhagan** in the parish of Kilcronaghan).

The use of the elements *mór* "big" and *beag* "little" in the names Ballynahone More and **Ballynahone Beg** suggests that a townland, originally called Ballynahone, was divided into two portions, greater and lesser. However, a close examination of the 17th-century material reveals that the name Ballynahone was probably originally applied solely to the smaller portion, and that the townland now called Ballynahone More was then known by another name, *Baile na Tulcha* "townland of the hillock" (1–4).

Broagh
H 9095

Bruach
"bank/brink"

1. ballinvroyinsikin	Esch. Co. Map 14	1609
2. Broughenishikin	Lond. Comp. Valuation 307	1613
3. Broemshakeen	Phillips MSS (Maps) Plate 24	1622
4. Broghinshekin	Civ. Surv. iii 178	1654
5. Brughinsikeene	Census 134	1659c
6. Broghinshekin	BSD(c) 64	1661
7. Broagh	HMR (Ó Doibhlin 2) 74	1663
8. Broagh	Sampson's Map	1813
9. 'Bro	OSNB Pron. No. 6	1834c
10. Bruach "a brink or margin"	J O'D (OSNB) No. 6	1834c
11. Bruach "The townland of the brink ...of the river"	Munn's Notes 263	1925
12. Bruach "a brink or margin"	Joyce iii 150	1925
13. brux	Local pronunciation	1993
14. brox	Local pronunciation	1993

The name Broagh is derived from Irish *Bruach* "bank/brink". Joyce notes that *bruach* in place-names generally denotes the edge of a glen (*Joyce* ii 210), but here it seems to refer to the bank of the Moyola which forms the southern boundary of the townland.

The earliest references to Broagh show that this is a shortened form of a longer name the origin of which is unclear. The second element might be taken as *inis* "inch, holm, water-meadow", but the very earliest form appears to show the whole name placed in the genitive and qualified by the definite article, which would lead us to expect a form *Baile an Bhruaigh* + adjective. However, we can circumvent this problem by reading *nv* in this form as *w*, giving us *balliwroyinsikin*, which might suggest a dative form *Baile Bhruaigh Inse Caoine* "the townland of the bank of the smooth water-meadow" (see also *caonna* "moss" in *Joyce* ii 63–4).

Cabragh
H 9096

An Chabrach
"poor land"

1. B:necabry	Esch. Co. Map 14	1609
2. Ballmecabry	Charter of Londonderry 391	1613
3. Cabragh	Lond. Comp. Valuation 307	1613
4. Cabragh	Phillips MSS (Maps) Plate 24	1622
5. Cabragh	Civ. Surv. iii 178	1654
6. Ballincrabry	Bishop. Der. i 265	1657
7. Cabragh	Census 134	1659c
8. Cabragh	BSD(c) 64	1661
9. Cabrogh	HMR (Ó Doibhlin 2) 74	1663
10. Cabragh	Sampson's Map	1813
11. 'Car-bra	OSNB Pron. No. 6	1834c
12. Cabrach "bad land; rubbish"	J O'D (OSNB) No. 6	1834c
13. Cabrach "The townland of the bad ...land"	Munn's Notes 263	1925
14. 'kʲabrə(x)	Local pronunciation	1993

The earliest documented form of this name is derived from *Baile na Cabrai* "townland of the poor land" (1–2, 6), but Cabragh was the more usual form, even in the 17th century. On the meaning and distribution of this element see **Cabragh** in the parish of Clonallan, Co. Down (*PNI* i 67).

Carricknakielt
H 8798

Carraig Uí Chaoilte
"O'Keelt's rock"

1. (?)b:Carrige	Esch. Co. Map 14	1609
2. Ballicarigy	Bishop. Der. i 57	1610
3. Ballycareigy	CPR Jas I 279a	1615
4. Ballicareigy	Bishop. Der. i 102	1615
5. Carrogokillty	Civ. Surv. iii 187	1654
6. Caragokilly	Hib. Reg. Loughinsholin	1657c
7. Carrickkeelte	Census 134	1659c
8. Carogokelty	BSD(c) 51	1661
9. Caribe	HMR (Ó Doibhlin 2) 74	1663
10. Caragkelty	Hib. Del. Derry	1672c
11. Caricakielt	Sampson's Map	1813
12. Car-rick-na-'kielt	OSNB Pron. No. 6	1834c

13. Carraic Uí Chaoilte "O'Keilt's rock"	OSL (Derry) 84	1834
14. "rock of concealment"	OSL (Derry) 84	1834
15. Carraig Uí Chaoilte "O'Kealty's Rock"	J O'D (OSNB) No. 6	1834c
16. Carraig-ui-Choillte "The rock of the O'Keilts"	Munn's Notes 263	1925
17. ˌkarĭkəˈki(:)lt	Local pronunciation	1993
18. ˌkarĭgəˈkilt	Local pronunciation	1993

The references assembled here clearly demonstrate that an early form of this name was *Baile na Carraige* "townland of the rock", but by the second half of the 17th century this gives way to a form resembling the modern name more closely. *Carraig* "rock" is a common element in townland names throughout Ireland and, according to Joyce, is generally applied to a large natural rock (*Joyce* i 410–11).

The name Carricknakielt apparently derives from *Carraig Uí Chaoilte* "O'Keelt's rock". The surname Ó Caoilte, although not common, is found in Ulster, Munster and Connacht (Woulfe 1923, 450; Bell 1988, 232–3) and O'Donovan notes that it was very common in Maghera (*OSL (Derry)* 84). Ó Ceallaigh suggests that Ó Caoilte was probably the name of the erenagh family of Termoneeny (*GUH* 37) and, indeed, Bishop Montgomery states that the erenagh here was one Donald O'Keele, for which we should read O'Keelte (*Der. Clergy* 301). They were clearly an important family in the area from as early as the 15th century. In 1411, one John Okahilti was made rector of the parish (*Cal. Papal Letters* vi 262). A certain Geoffrey Okylt is listed among the important members of the parish in a letter of 1435 (*Reg. Swayne* 156), and Patrick Okylt or O Cayelti and Donatus Ocayelti were, about this time, priests of the parish of Maghera (*Reg. Swayne* 156, *Cal. Papal Letters* xii 35). A certain James O'Kiltie of Co. Derry or Tyrone was pardoned in 1622 (*CPR Jas I* 132b), and an Owen O Kiltch of the parish of Kilcronaghan appears in the Hearth Money Rolls (*HMR (Ó Doibhlin 2)* 74).

Some of the 17th-century spellings, albeit all of which come from related sources, might be taken to suggest a form *Carraig Ó gCaoilte* "rock of the O'Keelts" (5–6, 8), but this is less likely than the form proposed here. Scribes seem not uncommonly to write -*o*- in place-names where they recognize or imagine there to be a surname, and the Civil Survey also has an -*o*- in the name **Knocknakielt** for which there is other more conclusive evidence of a singular form of the same surname.

Both this name and the name of the neighbouring townland of **Knocknakielt** have developed an intrusive -*n*- in their modern forms, a phenomenon which has been observed in other place-names which originally contained a surname (Kelly 1952–3(a)). The corrupted form has given rise to a suggestion that the name means "rock of concealment", from Irish *Carraig na Ceilte* (14), despite the fact that none of the local pronunciations collected in the course of fieldwork show any evidence of the -*n*-.

Derganagh
H 8897

An Dearganach
"the red place"

1. b:naderegni	Esch. Co. Map 14	1609
2. Ballmadoregin	Charter of Londonderry 391	1613
3. Dergenah	Lond. Comp. Valuation 307	1613

4. Dergena	Phillips MSS (Maps) Plate 24	1622
5. Dargnagh	Civ. Surv. iii 178	1654
6. Ballinadirgin	Bishop. Der. i 265	1657
7. Red Bog	Hib. Reg. Loughinsholin	1657c
8. Dernagh	Census 134	1659c
9. Dargnagh	BSD(c) 64	1661
10. Dermoygh	HMR (Ó Doibhlin 2) 74	1663
11. Derginagh	Sampson's Map	1813
12. 'Der-ga-na	OSNB Pron. No. 6	1834c
13. Dearg-eanach "red bog or marsh"	J O'D (OSNB) No. 6	1834c
14. Dearg-eanach "The red marsh"	Munn's Notes 264	1925
15. 'dɛːrgïnə	Local pronunciation	1993
16. 'dɛrgən	Local pronunciation	1993

At first glance there would appear to be little doubt that this name derives from Irish *dearg* "red" + *eanach* "marsh". On Petty's map of the barony of Loughinsholin, for example, the name of the townland is omitted but instead we find the words "Red Bog" (7), and the hundred acres of "Redbog" described as "unprofitable and Wast" in the Civil Survey of 1654 probably lay largely within Derganagh (*Civ. Surv.* iii 178).

However, some of the earliest forms (1–2, 6) point to a feminine final element, whereas *eanach* is always masculine. It is likely, therefore, that we have here a compound of the adjective *dearg* "red" and the adjectival suffix *-(e)anach* with which we may compare **Brackenagh** in Co. Down *Breacanach* "speckled/spotted place" (*PNI* iii 30–1). The meaning is obviously not all that different from the alternative suggestion, save that there is no notion of "marsh". The red bog marked on Petty's map and documented elsewhere is doubtless still the referent.

Knocknakielt
H 8799

Cnoc Uí Chaoilte
"O'Keelt's hill"

1. knockichitty	Esch. Co. Map 14	1609
2. Knock Ichilty	Bishop. Der. i 57	1610
3. Knock-Ichilty	CPR Jas I 279a	1615
4. Knockchilty	Bishop. Der. i 102	1615
5. Knockokillty	Civ. Surv. iii 187	1654
6. Knockelty	Hib. Reg. Loughinsholin	1657c
7. Knockakeelty	Census 134	1659c
8. Knockelty	BSD(c) 51	1661
9. Nockoalt	HMR (Ó Doibhlin 2) 74	1663
10. Knockelty	Hib. Del. Derry	1672c
11. Knocnakielt	Sampson's Map	1813
12. Nock-na-'kielt	OSNB Pron. No. 6	1834c
13. Cnoc Ui Chaoilte "O'Keelty's hill"		
	J O'D (OSNB) No. 6	1834c
14. Cnoc-ui-Choillte "The hill of the O'Keilts"		
	Munn's Notes 264	1925

219

15. ˌnɔkənəˈkilt	Local pronunciation	1993
16. ˌnɔknəˈkiːlt	Local pronunciation	1993

There is little reason to doubt the proposed origin of this name. The spelling in the Civil Survey (5) might be taken as an indication of a plural form of the surname, but the -o- seems to have simply been used here, as elsewhere, to indicate a surname. Some of the earlier forms (1–3) have -i- in this position reflecting Irish *Uí*.

As we have seen, the surname Ó Caoilte has long been associated with this district and the family of that name were erenaghs of the church lands of which Knocknakielt formed a part (see **Carricknakielt**). Like Carricknakielt, an -*n*- is intruded into the middle of the name at some late date, although here it is actually reflected in the current pronunciation of the name (see Kelly 1952–3(a)).

Lemnaroy
H 9096

Léim an Eich Rua
"the red horse's leap"

1. lemneghrow	Esch. Co. Map 14	1609
2. Leimmeighry	Charter of Londonderry 391	1613
3. Lemenerogh	Lond. Comp. Valuation 307	1613
4. Laminero	Phillips MSS (Maps) Plate 24	1622
5. Kemineroe	Civ. Surv. iii 178	1654
6. Lemneighry	Bishop. Der. i 265	1657
7. Leamonroye	Census 134	1659c
8. Kemineroe	BSD(c) 64	1661
9. Lamanaroy	HMR (Ó Doibhlin 2) 74	1663
10. Lemenaroy	Sampson's Map	1813
11. Lem-na-ˈroy	OSNB Pron. No. 6	1834c
12. Léim an eich ruaidh "Leap of the reddish horse"	J O'D (OSNB) No. 6	1834c
13. Léim-an-eich-ruaidh "the leap of the red horse"	Joyce ii 317; iii 468	1869
14. Leim-an-eic-ruaidh "The leap of the red horse"	Munn's Notes 264	1925
15. ˌlɛmənəˈrɔi	Local pronunciation	1993
16. ˌlɛmnəˈrɔi	Local pronunciation	1993

Báetán mac Ninnedo, king of Cenél Conaill and of Tara, was slain by the southern Uí Néill in the year 586 at a place called *Léim an Eich* "the horse's leap" (*AU (Mac Airt)* 93; cf. *CGH* 144 f 36). The editors of the Annals place *Léim an Eich* in Leinster, and Hogan identifies it as the townland of Lemnagh in Co. Antrim, but O'Donovan, in his edition of the Annals of the Four Masters, suggests that it is Lemnaroy (*AU* index 204; *Onom. Goed.* 482; *AFM* i 205n). Clearly, it is now impossible to determine the location of *Léim an Eich* with any certainty, but the historical spellings gathered here seem to support a similar origin for Lemnaroy, and in particular there appears to be some evidence for the *ch* of the element *eich* (1–2, 6).

Lurganagoose
H 8996

Leargain na gCuas
"hillslope of the hollows"

1. Carragnagous	Esch. Co. Map 14	1609
2. Caragnagousc	Charter of Londonderry 391	1613
3. Large ne Crosse	Lond. Comp. Valuation 307	1613
4. Larginacos	Phillips MSS (Maps) Plate 24	1622
5. Largan	Civ. Surv. iii 178	1654
6. Caragnagousse	Bishop. Der. i 265	1657
7. Larneguese	Census 134	1659c
8. Largan	BSD(c) 64	1661
9. Cargoose	HMR (Ó Doibhlin 2) 74	1663
10. Lurganagoose	Sampson's Map	1813
11. Lur-gan-a-'goose	OSNB Pron. No. 6	1834c
12. leargain na gcuas "hill side of the caves"	J O'D (OSNB) No. 6	1834c
13. Lurgan-na-g-chuas "The ... ridge of the caves"	Munn's Notes 264	1925
14. Lurgan-na-gcuas "long hill of the caves"	Joyce iii 492	1925
15. ˌlọrgənə'guːs	Local pronunciation	1993

The modern form of the name appears to suggest an original first element *lorgain*, an oblique form of *lorga* "shin" (Ó Maolfabhail 1987–8, 20). However, the early forms are consistent in representing the vowel in the first syllable as *a*, suggesting that the true origin of this element is from *leargain*, an oblique form of *learga* meaning "hillslope". It is interesting that *lorga* does not form the initial element in any townland names in Co. Derry, whereas *learga* occurs in the townland names **Largantea**, **Largy**, and **Largyreagh**, and also in the names **Largybeg**, **Lurganaglare** and **Lurgylea** in Co. Tyrone. In the latter two examples the original *a* of the first element has become *u* in the modern form of the name in precisely the same way as in Lurganagoose. Lurganagoose consists largely of low-lying, flat land in the west, and it doubtless takes its name from the rising ground in the eastern portion.

Mullagh
H 8599

Mullach
"hilltop"

1. lishdroget	Esch. Co. Map 14	1609
2. lisidroghell	Bishop. Der. i 57	1610
3. Lisdroghell	CPR Jas I 279a	1615
4. Sisdroghell	Bishop. Der. i 102	1615
5. Mullagh	Civ. Surv. iii 187	1654
6. Mullagh	Hib. Reg. Loughinsholin	1657c
7. Mullagh	Census 134	1659c
8. Mullagh	BSD(c) 51	1661
9. Mullagh	HMR (Ó Doibhlin 2) 74	1663
10. Mullagh	Hib. Del. Derry	1672c
11. Mullogh	Sampson's Map	1813
12. 'Mul-lock	OSNB Pron. No. 6	1834c
13. Mullach "a summit"	J O'D (OSNB) No. 6	1834c

| 14. Mullach "The hill, or summit" | Munn's Notes 264 | 1925 |
| 15. ðə 'mɒləx | Local pronunciation | 1993 |

The name Mullagh is clearly derived from Irish *Mullach* "hilltop" and denotes the hill on which the ruins of the old church stands (see PARISH NAME above). Mullagh is only documented as a townland in sources of the latter half of the 17th century and later. In earlier documents, those which list the "termon or erenagh" lands of Termoneeny, reference is made to a balliboe called "Lisdroghell", and the Escheated Counties map places a church in it, thereby indicating that this is an old name for Mullagh. Taking the earliest form as generally the most reliable, we can suggest that this name probably originates from *Lios Droichid* "fort of the bridge".

OTHER NAMES

Back Burn
H 8798

An English form

| 1. the Back Burn water | OSM vi 121 | 1836 |

The Back Burn passes behind several villages and houses before falling into the Moyola near Glencarrigan, and it is from this circumstance that it has been named.

Big Hill
H 8597

An English form

The hill referred to by this name rises to approximately 50 metres and is not particularly steep. However, it is slightly larger than many of the hills in the immediate area and this is undoubtedly the reason for its name.

Clover Hill
H 8598

An English form

| 1. Cloverhill | Sampson's Map | 1813 |
| 2. 'klovər ˌhïl | Local pronunciation | 1993 |

Built about 1800 by Anthony Forrester, Clover Hill occupied the site of a house built by Captain Forbes about 1680 (*OSM* vi 122). It was named from the large amount of various types of clover growing in the fields (*ibid.* 130).

Fort, The
H 8896

An English form

| 1. (ðə) forθ | Local pronunciation | 1993 |

Located in the townland of Lurganagoose, the fort denoted by the name is now completely built over (Speer 1990, 4; *NISMR* sh. 36 §1).

222

Glencarrigan	Of uncertain origin	
H 8796		

| 1. ˌglɛnˈkarəxən | Local pronunciation | 1993 |

Glencarrigan and **Glenlarry** were identified by my local informant (an inhabitant of the former) as Upper and Lower Ballynahone. He had not heard them used in 20 years, nor could he identify a glen here. The land around here is generally very flat and boggy, and we might tentatively suggest a first element *cluain* "meadow" (on *cluain* > *glen* see *PNI* iv 238–9). The second element is rather more difficult to establish given the disagreement between the written and the spoken forms, but we might reasonably suggest *carrachán* "rocky patch" or the surname *Ó Corragáin* (angl. Corrigan etc.) which has a variant *Ó Carragáin* (Woulfe 1923, 452).

Glenlarry	*Gleann Láithrigh*
H 8696	"glen of the ruin".

There is a shallow glen to the south, and we might reasonably suggest an origin from *Gleann Láithrigh* "glen of the ruin". See **Glencarrigan** above.

Green Hall	An English form
H 9194	

The word "hall" appears in numerous place-names indicating a big house, and is often qualified by a colour adjective (see **White Hall** below). Although "green" is here probably used to describe the colour of the house, there was a bleach mill here in the 19th century and it is possible that some association with bleaching greens is also intended (*OSM* vi 129; *OSRNB* 42 sh. 42).

Island, The	An English form
H 8596	

The Island is a portion of cultivated land nearly surrounded by bog, and it is from this circumstance that the name is derived (*OSRNB* 39 sh. 36). Cf. **Oak Island** in the parish of Kilcronaghan.

Knockcloghrim	*Cnoc Clochdhroma*
H 8996	"hill of the stony ridge"

1. Knock-loghran	Civ. Surv. iii 178	1654
2. Knockloghrain	Civ. Surv. iii 187	1654
3. (?)Knock	Civ. Surv. iii 187	1654
4. Knockloughrum	Civ. Surv. iii 193	1654
5. Knocleighrim	Sampson's Map	1813
6. Knock-'lock-rim	OSNB Pron. No. 6	1834c
7. Cnoc Liathdhruim "hill of the grey ridge"	J O'D (OSNB) No. 6	1834c
8. Knockcloghgorm "Blue stone hill"	OSRNB 63 sh.37	1850c

9. Cnoc clochraim "stony hill" or cloch-dhruim	OSRNB 63 sh.37	1850c
10. Cnoc Clochdhroma	GÉ 242	1989
11. nə'klɔx,rəm	Local pronunciation	1993

Knockcloghrim, situated on a rough and rocky hill, is aptly named. The first element is Irish *cnoc* "hill", and the second element is clearly related to the word *cloch* "stone", either as a compound of *cloch + droim* (gen. *droma*) "ridge", or from *clochrán* "stony place" (see Ó Dónaill sv. *clochar*; *Joyce* i 415). We possess a number of early spellings of the name, but all come from a single source and do little to settle the matter. There is considerable variation in the representation of the final consonant, but if we read *m* for *in* (2) as we probably should, then the former suggestion seems more likely. The compound *clochdhroim* "stony ridge" is not attested elsewhere, but both words do occur in noun + noun compounds (Mac Giolla Easpaig 1981, 155, 160). The absence of any indication of the final vowel of *droma* "of (the) ridge" is not significant (compare **Killelagh** above).

Knowhead House
H 8798

1. ðə nɔu'hɛːd	Local pronunciation	1993

The first element in this name is a compound of English *knowe* "a small hill, mound, hillock" (*Eng. Dial. Dict.* ii 485) and *head* which here signifies "top (of a hill)". It is the name of several places and is directly comparable to names such as Hillhead.

White Hall
H 8695

1. wait 'hɔl	Local pronunciation	1993

White Hall is the name of a number of places and denotes a white house. The tenant in 1850 was George Stuart (*OSRNB* 40 sh. 41).

White Hill
H 8597

1. wait 'hïl	Local pronunciation	1993
2. 'wait hïl	Local pronunciation	1993

Widow Steeles Bridge
H 8797

This bridge derives its name from a widow Steele who formerly resided nearby (*OSRNB* 39 sh. 36).

APPENDIX A

ASPECTS OF IRISH GRAMMAR RELEVANT TO PLACE-NAMES

The following types of place-names can be identified:

1. Those which consist of a noun only:

> Sabhall "a barn" (Saul, Dn)
> Tuaim "a tumulus" (Toome, Ant.)

There is no indefinite article in Irish, that is, there is no word for *a*, e.g. *Sabhall* means "barn" or "a barn".

English nouns generally have only two forms, singular and plural, and the plural is normally formed by adding s, e.g. *wall, walls; road, roads*. Occasionally a different ending is added – ox, *oxen* – and occasionally the word is changed internally – *man, men;* sometimes there is both addition and internal change – *brother, brethren*. Irish nouns have not only distinctive forms for the plural but also for the genitive singular and sometimes for the dative and vocative as well. These distinctive forms are made by addition, by internal change and sometimes by both. Five principal types of noun change are identified in Irish and nouns are therefore divided into five major groups known as *declensions*. Examples of change will be seen later.

2. Singular article + masculine noun:

> An Clár "the plain" (Clare, Arm.)
> An Gleann "the valley" (Glen, Der.)

The only article in Irish is the definite article, that is, the word corresponding to *the* in English.

The singular article *an* "the" prefixes *t* to masculine nouns beginning with a vowel in certain cases. The nouns *éadan* "front, forehead" and *iúr* "yew tree", for example, appear in the place-names:

> An tÉadan "the face (of a hill)" (Eden, Ant.)
> An tIúr "the yew tree" (Newry, Dn)

3. Singular article + feminine noun:

> An Chloch "the stone" (Clough, Dn)
> An Bhreacach "the speckled place" (Brockagh, Der.)

The article *an* aspirates the first consonant of a following feminine noun.

Aspiration is indicated by putting *h* after the consonant *(cloch* "a stone"; *an chloch* "the stone") and the sound of that consonant is modified, just as in English the sound of *p*, as in the word *praise*, is changed when *h* is added, as in the word *phrase*. Only *b, c, d, f, g, m, p, s,* and *t* are aspirated. The other consonants, and vowels, are not aspirated.

The singular article *an* does not affect feminine nouns beginning with a vowel, e.g.

> An Eaglais "the church" (Eglish, Tyr.)

4. Masculine noun + adjective:

> Domhnach Mór "great church" (Donaghmore, Tyr.)
> Lios Liath "grey ring fort" (Lislea, Arm.)

In Irish the adjective normally follows the noun (but see §8).

225

5. Feminine noun + adjective:

> Bearn Mhín "smooth gap" (Barnmeen, Dn)
> Doire Fhada "long oak-wood" (Derryadd, Arm.)

The first consonant of the adjective is aspirated after a feminine noun.

6. Singular article + masculine noun + adjective:

> An Caisleán Riabhach "the brindled castle" (Castlereagh, Dn)
> An Baile Meánach "the middle town" (Ballymena, Ant.)

7. Singular article + feminine noun + adjective:

> An Charraig Mhór "the large rock" (Carrickmore, Tyr.)
> An Chloch Fhionn "the white stone" (Cloghfin, Tyr.)

Note that the first consonant of the feminine noun is aspirated after the definite article as in §3 above and that the adjective is aspirated after the feminine noun as in §5 above.

8. Adjective + noun:

> Fionnshliabh "white mountain" (Finlieve, Dn)
> Seanchill "old church" (Shankill, Ant.)

Sometimes an adjective precedes a noun. In such cases the two words are generally written as one and the second noun is usually aspirated. In compounds aspiration sometimes does not occur when d, t or s is preceded by d, n, t, l or s.

9. Article + adjective + noun:

> An Seanmhullach "the old summit" (Castledawson, Der.)
> An Ghlasdromainn "the green ridge" (Glasdrumman, Dn)

Dromainn is a feminine noun and the initial consonant of the compound is aspirated in accordance with §3 above.

10. Masculine noun + genitive singular of noun:

> Srath Gabhláin "(the) river valley of (the) fork" (Stragolan, Fer.)
> Port Rois "(the) harbour of (the) headland" (Portrush, Ant.)

These two examples contain the genitive singular forms of the nouns *gabhlán* and *ros*. Many nouns form the genitive singular by inserting *i* before the final consonant.

11. Feminine noun + genitive singular of noun:

> Maigh Bhile "(the) plain of (the) sacred tree" (Movilla, Dn)
> Cill Shléibhe "(the) church of (the) mountain" (Killevy, Arm.)

Note that in these examples the qualifying genitive is aspirated after the feminine noun. However the forms *maigh* and *cill* are also both old datives, and in the older language aspiration followed any dative singular noun.

Two other types of genitive are illustrated here: many nouns which end in a vowel, like *bile*, do not change at all, whereas others, like *sliabh*, form their genitive by adding *e* (and sometimes an internal change is necessary).

12. Noun + *an* + genitive singular:

> Léim an Mhadaidh "(the) leap of the dog" (Limavady, Der.)
> Baile an tSéipéil "(the) town of the chapel" (Chapeltown, Dn)

The noun *an madadh* "the dog" has a genitive *an mhadaidh* "of the dog". Note that, as well as the end of the noun changing as in §10 above, the genitive is aspirated after *an*.

Instead of aspirating *s* the article *an* prefixes *t* to it: *an sac* "the sack", *an tsaic* "of the sack"; *an séipéal* "the chapel", *an tséipéil* "of the chapel".

13. Noun + *na* + genitive singular:

> Muileann na Cloiche "(the) mill of the stone/the stone mill" (Clogh Mills, Ant.)
> Cúil na Baice "(the) corner/angle of the river bend" (Cullybackey, Ant.)

The genitive singular feminine article is *na*. It does not aspirate the following noun: *an chloch* "the stone", *na cloiche* "of the stone".

It prefixes *h*, however, to words beginning with a vowel e.g.

> Baile na hInse "(the) town of the water-meadow" (Ballynahinch, Dn)

The genitive in all these examples is formed by adding *e* to the nominative singular and making a slight internal adjustment.

14. Plural noun:

> Botha "huts" (Boho, Fer.)

The plural form of a substantial group of nouns in Irish is formed by adding *-a*. In the examples in §15 below an internal adjustment has also to be made.

15. *Na* + plural noun:

> Na Creaga "the rocks" (Craigs, Ant.)
> Na Cealla "the churches" (Kells, Ant.)

Na is also the plural article. *Creaga* and *cealla* are the plural forms of the nouns *creig* "rock" and *cill* "church".

16. Noun + genitive plural:

> Droim Bearach "(the) ridge of (the) heifers" (Dromara, Dn)
> Port Muc "(the) harbour of (the) pigs" (Portmuck, Ant.)

As in the case of *bearach* "a heifer" and *muc* "a pig" the genitive plural form is the same as the nominative singular.

17. Noun + *na* + genitive plural:

> Lios na gCearrbhach "(the) fort/enclosure of the gamblers" (Lisburn, Dn)
> Lios na nDaróg "(the) fort/enclosure of the little oaks" (Lisnarick, Fer.)

After *na* the first letter of the following genitive plural is eclipsed. Eclipsis involves adding to the beginning of a word a consonant which obliterates the sound of the original consonant, e.g.

bo "a cow", pronounced like English "bow" (and arrow)

(na) mbó "(of the) cows", pronounced like "mow"

The following are the changes which take place:

Written letter	Is eclipsed by
b	m
c	g
d	n
f	bh
g	ng
p	b
t	d
vowel	n

The other consonants are not eclipsed, e.g.

Áth na Long "(the) ford of the ships" (Annalong, Dn)

18. Noun + genitive of personal name:

Dún Muirígh "*Muiríoch's* fort" (Dunmurry, Ant.)
Boith Mhéabha "Maeve's hut" (Bovevagh, Der.)

In the older language the genitive of a personal name was not aspirated after a masculine noun but it was after a feminine noun. In the above examples *dún* is masculine and *boith* is feminine. In current Irish aspiration of the personal name is also usual after a masculine noun and this is reflected in many place-names in areas where Irish survived until quite recently, e.g.

Ard Mhacha, interpreted as "the height of *Macha*" (Armagh, Arm.)

19. Noun + genitive singular of *Ó* surname:

Baile Uí Dhonnaíle "Donnelly's townland" (Castlecaulfield, Tyr.)
Coill Uí Chiaragáin "Kerrigan's wood" (Killykergan, Der.)

Surnames in *Ó*, e.g. Ó Dochartaigh "(O') Doherty", Ó Flannagáin "Flannagan", etc. form their genitive by changing *Ó* to *Uí* and aspirating the second element – Uí Dhochartaigh, Uí Fhlannagáin .

20. Noun + genitive singular of *Mac* surname:

Lios Mhic Dhuibhleacháin "*Mac Duibhleacháin's* fort/enclosure"
(Lisnagelvin, Der.)
Baile Mhic Gabhann "*Mac Gabhann's* town (angl. McGowan, Smith, etc.)
(Ballygowan, Dn)

Surnames in *Mac,* e.g. Mac Dónaill "McDonnell", Mac Muiris "Morrison, Fitzmaurice", etc. form their genitive by changing *Mac* to *Mhic* and aspirating the second element (except those beginning with *C* or *G).*

21. Noun + genitive plural of *Ó* surname:

Doire Ó gConaíle "the oak-wood of the *Ó Conaíle* family (angl. Connelly)" (Derrygonnelly, Fer.)

In the genitive plural of *Ó* surnames the second element is eclipsed.

22. Neuter noun + genitive or adjective:

Sliabh gCuillinn "mountain of (the) steep slope" (Slieve Gullion, Arm.)
Loch gCaol "(the) narrow lake" (Loughguile, Ant.)

The neuter gender no longer exists in Irish but traces of it are found in place-names. The initials of nouns and adjectives were eclipsed after neuter nouns.

APPENDIX B

LAND UNITS

TERRITORIAL DIVISIONS IN IRELAND

The old administrative system, used in the arrangement of these books, consisted of land units in descending order of size: province, county, barony, parish and townland. Theoretically at least the units fit inside each other, townlands into parishes, parishes into baronies, baronies into counties. This system began piecemeal, with the names of the provinces dating back to prehistoric times, while the institution of counties and baronies dates from the 13th to the 17th century, though the names used are often the names of earlier tribal groups or settlements. Parishes originate not as a secular land-unit, but as part of the territorial organization of the Christian Church. There they form the smallest unit in the system which, in descending order of size, goes from provinces to dioceses to deaneries to parishes. Some Irish parishes derive from churches founded by St Patrick and early saints, and appear as parish units in Anglo-Norman church records: parish units are thus older than counties and baronies. Townlands make their first appearance as small land units listed in Anglo-Norman records. However the evidence suggests that land units of this type (which had various local names) are of pre-Norman native origin.

The 17th-century historian Geoffrey Keating outlined a native land-holding system based on the *tríocha céad* or "thirty hundreds", each divided in Ulster into about 28 *baile biadhtaigh* "lands of a food-provider" or "ballybetaghs", and about 463 *seisrigh* "six-horse plough-teams" or "seisreachs" *(Céitinn* iv 112f.). The term *tríocha céad*, which seems to relate to the size of the army an area could muster, is not prominent in English accounts, though there is a barony called Trough *(Tríocha)* in Co. Monaghan. The ballybetagh (land of a farmer legally obliged to feed his lord and retinue while travelling through the area) is mentioned in Plantation documents for west Ulster, and there is some evidence, from townlands grouped in multiples of three and four, that it existed in Armagh, Antrim and Down (McErlean 1983, 318).

Boundaries of large areas, such as provinces and dioceses, are often denoted in early Irish sources by means of two or four extreme points (Hogan 1910, 279–280; *Céitinn* iii 302). There was also a detailed native tradition of boundary description, listing landmarks such as streams, hills, trees and bogs. This can be demonstrated as early as the 8th century in Tírechán's record of a land grant to St Patrick *(Trip. Life (Stokes)* ii 338–9),[1] and as late as the 17th century, when native experts guided those surveying and mapping Ireland for the English administration. The boundary marks on the ground were carefully maintained, as illustrated in the *Perambulation of Iveagh* in 1618 *(Inq. Ult.* xliii), according to which the guide broke the plough of a man found ploughing up a boundary. However very often Irish texts, for example the "Book of Rights" *(Lebor na Cert)*, the "topographical" poems by Seaán Mór Ó Dubhagáin and Giolla-na-naomh Ó hUidhrín *(Topog. Poems)*, and "The rights of O'Neill" *(Ceart Uí Néill)*, refer to territories by the names of the peoples inhabiting them. This custom has been preserved to the present in some place-names, particularly those of provinces and baronies.

SECULAR ADMINISTRATIVE DIVISIONS

Townlands

Twelfth-century charters provide the earliest documentary evidence for the existence in Ireland of small land units, although we do not know what these units were called. Keating's smallest unit, the *seisreach,* a division of the ballybetagh, is given as 120 acres (the word *acra* is apparently borrowed from English). The size of the *seisreach* seems to have been approximately that of a modern townland, but the word does not occur much outside Keating's *schema.* Many other terms appear in the sources: *ceathrú* "quarter" (often a quarter of a ballybetagh), *baile bó* "land providing one cow as rent" (usually a twelfth of a ballybetagh), *seiseach* "sixth" and *trian* "third" (apparently divisions of a ballyboe). In most of Ulster the ballyboe and its subdivisions are the precursors of the modern townlands, and were referred to in Latin sources as *villa* or *carucata,* and in English as "town" or "ploughland" (the term used for similar units in 11th-century England in the Domesday Book). The Irish term *baile* (see below) seems to have been treated as equivalent to English "town", which had originally meant "settlement (and lands appertaining)"; and the compound term "townland" seems to have been adopted to make the intended meaning clear. It was used in 19th-century Ireland as a blanket term for various local words. In the area of Fermanagh and Monaghan the term for the local unit was "tate". In an English document of 1591 it is stated that the tate was 60 acres in size and that there were sixteen tates in the ballybetagh *(Fiants Eliz.* §5674). Tate appears in place-names in composition with Gaelic elements, but was regarded by Reeves (1861, 484) as a pre-1600 English borrowing into Irish.

There is no evidence for the use of the word *baile* in the formation of place-names before the middle of the 12th century. The earliest examples are found in a charter dating to c. 1150 in the Book of Kells which relates to lands belonging to the monastery of Kells. At this period *baile* seems to mean "a piece of land" and is not restricted to its present-day meaning "hamlet, group of houses", much less "town, village". After the coming of the Normans, *baile* appears more frequently in place-names, until it finally becomes the most prevalent type of townland name. By the 14th century, *baile* had acquired its present-day meaning of "town", probably in reference to small medieval towns, or settlements that had arisen in the vicinity of castles. Price suggests that the proliferation of the use of the word in place-names was a result of the arrival of settlers and their use of the word "town" *(tūn)* in giving names to their lands (Price 1963, 124). When the Irish revival took place in the 14th century many English-language names were translated into Irish and "town" was generally replaced by *baile.* The proportion of *baile* names is greatest in those parts of Ireland which had been overrun by the Anglo-Normans but subsequently gaelicized, and is lowest in the counties of mid-Ulster in which there was little or no English settlement *(ibid.* 125).

Despite attempts at schematization none of the units which predated the modern townlands was of uniform size, and it is clear from the native sources that evaluation was based on an area of good land together with a variable amount of uncultivated land. Thus townlands on bad land are usually larger than those on good land. The average size of a townland in Ireland as a whole is 325 acres, and 357 acres in the six counties of Northern Ireland, though these averages include huge townlands like Slievedoo (4551 acres, Co. Tyrone) and tiny townlands like Acre McCricket (4 acres, Co. Down). There is also considerable local variation: townlands in Co. Down average 457 acres (based on the ballyboe), compared to 184 acres (based on the tate) in Fermanagh (Reeves 1861, 490).

Parishes

Early accounts of the lives of saints such as Patrick and Columcille refer to many church foundations. It seems that land was often given for early churches beside routeways, or on the boundaries of tribal territories. Some of the same church names appear as the names of medieval parishes in the papal taxation of 1302–06 *(Eccles. Tax.).* Some parish names include ecclesiastical elements such as *ceall, domhnach, lann,* all meaning "church", *diseart* "hermitage" and *tearmann* "sanctuary", but others are secular in origin. Parish bounds are not given in the papal taxation, but parishes vary considerably in size, probably depending on the wealth or influence of the local church. The medieval ecclesiastical parishes seem to have come into existence after the reform of the native Irish church in the course of the 12th century; in Anglo-Norman areas such as Skreen in Co. Meath the parochial system had already been adopted by the early 13th century (Otway-Ruthven 1964, 111–22). After the Reformation the medieval parish boundaries were continued by the established Church of Ireland, and used by the government as the bounds of civil parishes, a secular land unit forming the major division of a barony. (The boundaries of modern Roman Catholic parishes have often been drawn afresh, to suit the population of worshippers).

As well as the area inhabited by local worshippers, lands belonging to a medieval church often became part of its parish. These were usually close by, but it is quite common, even in the early 19th century when some rationalization had occurred, for parishes to include detached lands at some distance from the main body (Power 1947, 222–3). Kilclief in the barony of Lecale, Co. Down, for example, has five separate detached townlands, while Ballytrustan in the Upper Ards and Trory in Co. Fermanagh are divided into several parts. While an average parish might contain 30 townlands, parishes vary in the number of townlands they contained; for example, Ballykinler in Co. Down contained only 3 townlands, while Aghalurcher contained 237 townlands (including several islands) in Co. Fermanagh plus 17 townlands in Co. Tyrone. Although most of its townlands are fairly small, Aghalurcher is still much larger than Ballykinler. There were usually several parishes within a barony (on average 5 or 6, but, for example, only 2 in the barony of Dufferin, Co. Down, and 18 in the barony of Loughinsholin, Co. Derry). Occasional parishes constituted an entire barony, as did Kilkeel, for example, which is coterminous with the barony of Mourne. However parish units also frequently extended across rivers, which were often used as obvious natural boundaries for counties and baronies: Newry across the Newry River, Clonfeacle over the Blackwater, Artrea over the Ballinderry River, Blaris over the Lagan. This means that civil parishes may be in more than one barony, and sometimes in more than one county.

Baronies

The process of bringing Irish tribal kingdoms into the feudal system as "baronies" under chieftains owing allegiance to the English crown began during the medieval period, although the system was not extended throughout Ulster until the early 17th century. Many of the baronies established in the later administrative system have population names: Oneilland, Irish *Uí Niulláin* "descendants of Niallán" (Arm.); Keenaght, Irish *Cianachta* "descendants of Cian" (Der.); Clankelly, Irish *Clann Cheallaigh* "Ceallach's children" (Fer.). Others have the names of historically important castles or towns: Dungannon (O'Neills, Tyr.), Dunluce (MacDonnells, Antr.), Castlereagh (Clandeboy O'Neills, Down). The barony of Loughinsholin (Der.) is named after an island fortification or crannog, *Loch Inse Uí Fhloinn* "the lake of O'Flynn's island", although by the 17th century the island was inhabited by the O'Hagans, and the O'Flynn area of influence had moved east of the Bann.

The barony system was revised and co-ordinated at the same time as the counties, so that later baronies always fit inside the county bounds. Both counties and baronies appear on maps from 1590 on. These later baronies may contain more than one older district, and other district or population names used in the 16th and 17th centuries, such as *Clancan* and *Clanbrasil* in Armagh, *Slutkellies* in Down, and *Munterbirn* and *Munterevlin* in Tyrone, gradually fell out of use. Baronies were not of uniform size, though in many cases large baronies have been subdivided to make the size more regular. The barony of Dungannon in Co. Tyrone has three sections (Lower, Middle and Upper) while Iveagh in Co. Down has been divided into four (Lower, Lower Half; Lower, Upper Half; Upper, Lower Half; Upper,

Upper Half). The number of baronies in a county in Ulster varies between five in Co. Monaghan and fifteen in Co. Antrim. Armagh, Fermanagh and Tyrone have eight.

Counties

Over the centuries following the Anglo-Norman invasion the English government created a new administrative system in Ireland, adapting the native divisions of provinces, tribal districts (as baronies), parishes and townlands, and dividing each province of Ireland into counties. The counties were equivalent to the shire in England, where a sheriff exercized jurisdiction on behalf of the King. To begin with the county system applied to only those areas where English rule was strong, but was eventually extended, through the reigns of Elizabeth and James I, to cover the whole of the country. Although a commission to shire Ulster was set up in 1585 *(Fiants Eliz. §4763)*, the situation in 1604 was expressed, rather hopefully, in a document in the state papers:

> "each province, except Ulster and other uncivil parts of the realm, is subdued into counties, and each county into baronies and hundreds, and every barony into parishes, consisting of manors, towns and villages after the manner of England."
> *(CSP Ire. 1603–6, 231).*

Most of the counties created in the north were given the names of important towns: Antrim, Armagh, Coleraine (later Londonderry), Down, Donegal, Monaghan and Cavan. Fermanagh and Tyrone, however, have population names. *Fir Manach* "the men of the *Manaig*" (probably the *Menapii* of Ptolemy's *Geography)* had been important in the area before the Maguires. *Tír Eoghain* "Eoghan's land" derives its name from the *Cenél nEógain* branch of the *Uí Néill*, who had expanded southwards from *Inis Eógain* (Inishowen) during the centuries and whose dominant position continued right up until the Plantation. Counties were generally formed out of an amalgam of smaller territorial units, some of which were preserved as baronies within each county.[2] The bounds of these older units were often of long standing, and usually followed obvious physical features, like the lower Bann, the Blackwater, and the Newry River.

Down and Antrim, as part of the feudal Earldom of Ulster (see below) had been treated as counties since the 13th or 14th century (Falkiner 1903, 189; *Inq. Earldom Ulster* ii 141, iii 60). However other districts within the earldom could also be called counties, and up to the mid-16th-century the whole area was sometimes called the "county of Ulster" *(Cal. Carew MSS 1515–74, 223–4)*. The settling of Down and Antrim with their modern bounds began in 1570–1 *(Fiants Eliz. §1530, §1736)*. Coleraine had also been the centre of an Anglo-Norman county *(Inq. Earldom Ulster* iv 127). Jobson's map of 1590 shows *Antrym, Armagh, Colrane, Downe, Manahan, Farmanaugh, Terconnel,* and *Upper and Nether Terone* as the names of counties. However, Ulster west of the Bann was still referred to as "four seigniories" (Armagh? plus *Terreconnell, Tyren, Formannoche)* in 1603 *(Cal. Carew MSS 1601–3, 446–454)*, although Tyrone had been divided into baronies from 1591 *(Colton Vis. 125–130)*. Armagh was settled into baronies in 1605 *(CSP Ire. 1603–6, 318)*. The "nine counties of Ulster" were first listed in 1608: *Dunegal or Tirconnel, Tirone, Colraine, Antrim, Downe, Ardmagh, Cavan, Monoghan,* and *Fermanagh (CSP Ire. 1606–8, 401)*, and these counties are shown on Hole's adaptation of Mercator's map of Ireland for Camden's atlas *Britannia* (1610). The county of Coleraine was renamed as a result of the plantation grant to the London companies. Under the terms of the formal grant of the area in 1613, the barony of Loughinsholin, which had hitherto been part of Tyrone, was amalgamated with the old county of Coleraine, and Londonderry was made the new county name (Moody 1939, 122–3).

Provinces

Gaelic Ireland, in prehistory and in early historic times, was made up of many small native kingdoms (called *tuatha)*, but a sense of the underlying unity of the island is evident from the name of the earliest division in Ireland, that represented by the four modern provinces of Connaught, Leinster, Munster and Ulster. In Irish each is called *cúige* (older *cóiced)* "a fifth", followed by a district or population name. *Cúige Chonnacht* means "the fifth of the Connaughtmen" *Cúige Laighean* "the fifth of the Leinstermen", *Cúige Mumhan* "the fifth of Munster", *Cúige Uladh* "the fifth of the Ulstermen". The connection between population and place-names is evident at this very early stage. The ancient fifth "fifth" making up the whole was that of Meath, in Irish *Midhe* "middle". The division into these five provinces was taken over when Henry II of England invaded Ireland: Leinster, (North and South) Munster, Connaught, Ulster and Meath *quasi in medio regni positum* (as if placed in the middle of the kingdom), but the number was reduced by the 17th century to the modern four *(CSP Ire.* 1603–6 §402, 231), by incorporating Meath in Leinster.

The Province of Ulster

As mentioned above, the province of Ulster took its name from the tribal name *Ulaid* "Ulstermen" (Flanagan 1978(d)). The earliest record of the tribal name is the form quoted by the 2nd-century Greek geographer Ptolemy, as *Uoluntii* (O'Rahilly 1946, 7). The precise origin of the English form of the name is obscure, though it has been suggested that it derives from something like *Ulaðstir,* an unusual combination of the original Irish name plus the Norse possessive suffix *-s* and the Irish word *tír* "land" (Sommerfelt 1958, 223–227). Ptolemy mentions various other tribes in the north of Ireland, but it appears that the *Ulaid* were the dominant group.

The ancient province of the Ulstermen, according to the native boundary description, stretched south to a line running between the courses of the rivers *Drobaís* (Drowse, on the border between Donegal and Leitrim) and *Bóann* (Boyne, Co. Meath). The "fifth" of the legendary king of the Ulaid, Conchobar, *(Cóiced Conchobair)* thus included modern Co. Louth (Hogan 1910, 279b). It became contracted in historical times, as a result of the expansion of the *Uí Néill* "descendants of Niall", who drove the rulers of the Ulaid from the provincial capital at *Emain Macha* (Navan fort near Armagh) across the Bann into modern Antrim and Down.[3] From the 5th century the area stretching south from Derry and Tyrone to Monaghan and most of Louth belonged to a confederation of tribes called the *Airgialla,* who have been described "as a satellite state of the Uí Néill" (Byrne 1973, 73). Three groups of Uí Néill established themselves in the west, *Cenél Conaill* "Conall's kin" in south Donegal, *Cenél nÉndae* in the area around Raphoe, and *Cenél nEógain* in Inishowen *(Inis Eógain* "Eógan's island"). On the north coast, east of the river Foyle, the *Cianachta* maintained a separate identity, despite continuing pressure from *Cenél nEógain.*

East of the Bann the *Dál Fiatach* (the historic Ulaid) shared the kingship of the reduced Ulster with *Dál nAraide* and *Uí Echach Coba,* both originally *Cruthin* tribes.[4] In the 12th century the Anglo-Norman conquest of Antrim and Down resulted in the creation of a feudal lordship of the area under the English crown called the Earldom of Ulster. During the same period the kings of Cenél nEógain had extended their influence eastward, and after the extinction of the Dál Fiatach kingship in the 13th century they assumed the title of *rí Ulad* "king of the Ulaid" to forward their claim to be kings of the whole of the North. It is this greater Ulster which was the basis for the modern province, although there was some doubt at the beginning of the 17th century as to whether or not this included Co. Louth. By the time of the Plantation in 1609 Ulster had been stabilized as nine counties and Louth had been incorporated into the neighbouring province of Leinster.

ECCLESIASTICAL ADMINISTRATIVE DIVISIONS

Dioceses

Under the Roman Empire Christianity developed an administrative structure of dioceses led by bishops based in the local towns. In early Christian Ireland a bishop was provided for each *tuath,* but since the main centres of population were the monasteries established by the church, the bishop often became part of the monastic community, with less power than the abbot. The invasion of the Anglo-Normans in the 12th century encouraged the re-organization and reform of the native church along continental lines, and by the beginning of the 14th century the territories and boundaries for Irish bishops and dioceses had been settled. Most dioceses are named after important church or monastic foundations: Armagh, Clogher, Connor, Derry, Down, Dromore, Kilmore and Raphoe in the North. The ancient secular province of Ulster was included in the ecclesiastical province of Armagh, which became the chief church in Ireland. The bounds of individual dioceses within the province reflect older tribal areas, for example Derry reflects the development of *Cenél nEógain,* Dromore *Uí Echach Coba.* In the 8th century *Dál Fiatach,* who had settled in east Down, pushed northward into the land of *Dál nAraide,* and the bounds of the diocese of Down reflect their expansion as far north as the river *Ollarba* (the Larne Water). The diocesan bounds differ from those of similarly-named later counties because by the time the county boundaries were settled in the 17th century the leaders of many of the larger native territories had been overthrown. County boundaries were generally not based on large native kingdoms but were put together from an amalgam of smaller districts.

Deaneries

The medieval church divided dioceses into rural deaneries, the names of which often derive from old population names. *Blaethwyc* (modern Newtownards) in the diocese of Down, for example, derives from *Uí Blathmaic* "the descendants of Blathmac", whereas *Turtrye,* in the diocese of Connor, derives from *Uí Thuirtre* "the descendants of (Fiachra) Tort". The deaneries of Tullyhogue (Irish *Tulach Óc*) in the diocese of Armagh and *Maulyne* (Irish *Mag Line*) in Connor are named after royal sites. *Mag Line* was the seat of the *Dal nAraide* and *Tulach Óc* was probably the original seat of the Uí Thuirtre, whose area of influence had by this time moved east across the Bann, as the deanery name reveals. The deanery of Inishowen reflects the earlier homeland of the Cenél nEógain. Deanery names are often a useful source of information on important tribal groups of medieval times. Some of these same population names were used later as the names of baronies, while in other cases the earlier population group had lost its influence and the area had become known by another name.

TRIBAL AND FAMILY NAMES

Many personal or population names of various forms have been used as place-names or parts of place-names in Ireland, from provinces, counties, deaneries and baronies to townlands. As with different types of land divisions, different types of family names have come into being at various times.

The names of early Irish tribal groupings were sometimes simple plurals, for example *Ulaid, Cruthin,* and sometimes the personal name of an ancestor or some other element in composition with various suffixes: *Connachta, Dartraige, Latharna.* Other types prefixed *uí* "grandsons", *cenél* "kin", *clann* "children", *dál* "share of", *moccu* "descendants", *síol* "seed", *liocht* "line" to the name of the ancestor, for example *Dál nAraide* "share of (Fiacha)

Araide", and *Uí Néill* "grandsons of Niall", who are supposedly descended from the 5th-century *Niall Noígiallach* "Niall of the Nine Hostages".

In early Ireland individuals were often identified by patronymics formed by using *mac* "son of" or *ó* (earlier *ua*) "grandson" plus the name of the father or grandfather, rather than by giving the name of the larger group to which the individual belonged. Thus the most straightforward interpretation of *Eoghan mac Néill* is "Eoghan son of Niall", *Eoghan ó Néill* "Eoghan grandson of Niall". Sometimes the same formation can occur with female names. However, in the course of the 10th and 11th centuries patronymics began to be used as surnames. In Modern Irish orthography surnames are distinguished from simple patronymics by using capital *M* or *Ó*: *Eoghan Ó Néill* "Eoghan O'Neill", *Eoghan Mac Néill* "Eoghan MacNeill". However, in early documents, in either Irish or English, it is often difficult to distinguish between surnames and patronymics. This is particularly true of sources such as the *Fiants* where a name such as Donagh M'Donagh may represent the patronymic Donagh, son of Donagh, or the surname Donagh MacDonagh.

As families expanded it was common for different branches to develop their own particular surnames. Some of these have survived to the present, while others, which may have been important enough in their time to be incorporated in place-names, have either died out or been assimilated by similar, more vigorous surnames. In cases such as this the place-name itself may be the only evidence for the former existence of a particular surname in the locality.

Kay Muhr

(1) See also *Geinealach Chorca Laidhe* (O'Donovan 1849, 48–56); *Crichad an Caoilli* (Power 1932, 43–47).
(2) See *Fiants Eliz.* §1736 (1570) for Co. Down; *Colton Vis.* 125–30 (1591) for Cos Derry and Tyrone.
(3) North-east Derry and Louth were also held by the Ulaid, but their influence had been reduced to Down, Antrim and north Louth by the 7th century (Flanagan 1978(d), 41).
(4) The *Cruthin* were a population group widespread in the north of Ireland. The name is of the same origin as "Briton".

APPENDIX C

SOURCES RELATING TO THE PLACE-NAMES OF
THE BARONY OF LOUGHINSHOLIN

This appendix deals with those sources which are important to, or contribute widely to, the study of the place-names in the Barony of Loughinsholin. The aim is to explore the relationships between each of these sources, where such exist, and to assess the reliability of each document as a source for early forms of names. Many of the more useful sources are copied or derived in some way from earlier documents, and clearly spellings of names excerpted from such documents serve only to corroborate forms from related sources and do not provide independent evidence of a name's pronunciation. The 17th-century sources most commonly used in this book fall into a small number of distinct groups or categories, each of which will be dealt with in turn.

The Escheated Counties maps provide us with the earliest comprehensive coverage of townland names in Co. Derry (*Esch. Co. Map*). The survey, which was carried out in 1609 by Josias Bodley, was to be used by the government in making allotments to those involved in the plantation of Ulster (Andrews 1974, 133). It seems that much of the survey was based on verbal information provided by local inhabitants, and this helps to explain many of the errors that occur on the maps (*ibid.*). The method of surveying used is described thus by Bodley:

> For which we thought it our readiest course that ... we should call unto us out of every barony, such persons as by their experience in the country, could give us the name and quality of every ballibo, quarter, tate, or other common measure in any [of] the precincts of the same; with special notice how they butted, or mered interchangeably the one on the other. (cited *ibid.* 145)

Sir John Davies gives us a clearer idea of the kind of person used by the surveyors to obtain their information:

> ... five surveyors were sent forth, into each barony one, who taking with them some of the ancient natives, especially such as had been rent gatherers and sergeants to the Irish lords, did perambulate and view the several baronies, and in their perambulation took notes... These surveyors being returned to the camp, out of their notes drew up cards or maps wherein every ballibo is named and placed in his proper situation. (cited *ibid.* 146)

There exist two charters of 1613 and 1657 which are clearly closely related to the Escheated Counties maps (which, unfortunately, survive only for the barony of Loughinsholin). The Charter of Londonderry formally granting the lands of the new county of Londonderry to the London Companies passed the great seal of England on 29 March 1613, and individually lists each of the townlands that was to be bestowed on the London Companies (*Charter of Londonderry*). The original charter was revoked in 1637 but, following negotiations between the City of London and Oliver Cromwell, a new charter confirming the original rights and possessions was issued on 24th March, 1657 (*Civ. Surv.* iii xvi and note). This charter, which is printed in *Bishop. Der.* i 246–320, is clearly copied from the original charter of 1613 and any difference in the spellings of place-names is purely accidental. In form and spelling the names on the charters differ only in detail from those on the Escheated Counties maps, and any variation may be dismissed as scribal innovation or mistranscription. All three documents belong to a single continuous written tradition and collectively

237

they can give us some idea of the pronunciation of the townland names in Loughinsholin in the early part of the 17th century.

Andrews notes that the place-names on the Escheated Counties maps appear to be "of generally high quality" (Andrews 1974, 153) and Ó Ceallaigh writes that "the spellings and forms of the names are much more reliable than Petty's efforts" (*GUH* 26n). Their comments also apply to the forms in the two charters, although the degree of corruption is greater in these, especially in the charter of 1657. However, all three documents tend to be less reliable in certain areas such as Maghera (see, for example, **Dreenan**, **Largantogher**, **Rocktown**, and **Tirgarvil**). Nevertheless, this group of documents is of particular interest to the study of place-names as it quite frequently contains longer forms of townland names, often with a *Bally-* prefix, which can help in determining or confirming a suspected derivation. While *Bally* is often used in 17th-century documents with no basis in local usage, simply as a townland marker, here it undoubtedly reflects local practice for it is frequently accompanied by a correctly inflected form of the article and noun.

In 1622, Sir Thomas Phillips initiated a survey of the whole county with the intention of showing the miserable and unfinished state of the settlements made by the London Companies (*Phillips' MSS (Maps)* vii). The resulting maps are unsigned but there is considerable evidence to suggest that they were drawn, not by Phillips himself, but by the former surveyor to the Irish Society, Thomas Raven, who almost certainly drew on some of his earlier work for his former employers (Moody 1939, 196). The names on the maps bear a striking resemblance to those in the valuation of the lands of the London Companies extracted from the record of a court of Common Council of the City of London held on 17 December 1613 (*Lond. Comp. Valuation*). The Valuation, which seems to have been compiled without reference to the earlier Escheated Counties Maps or the Charter of 1613, was laid out according to the divisions appropriated to the different companies, and this was the format adopted in Phillips' maps. While the spellings in these two sources exhibit close agreement, they can be shown to differ substantially from other early documents and they clearly offer independent evidence of the pronunciation of the names they contain.

Church lands are omitted from the two charters of Londonderry and from the London Companies' valuation and the Phillips' maps but this gap is filled to a limited extent by two grants to George Montgomery, bishop of Derry, and his successor John Tanner (*Bishop. Der.* i 54–71; *ibid.* 101–116 = *CPR Jas I* 279a–280a). There are very few differences between the names in the two grants, and the grant to Tanner is clearly based on the earlier grant to Montgomery. However, the spellings in both seldom differ significantly from those on the Escheated Counties maps and there can be little doubt that all three sources are somehow related. Thus, the grants do not provide independent evidence for the pronunciation of place-names already shown on the Escheated Counties maps, although they do occasionally serve to confirm dubious spellings on the maps.

The next group of documents to be considered here includes the Civil Survey (*Civ. Surv.*), Sir William Petty's barony and county maps (*Hib. Reg.* and *Hib. Del.*), and the Books of Survey and Distribution (*BSD(c)*). A commission was established on the 22nd June, 1653, directing three surveys to be taken – a Gross Survey described as "a measurement of the surround of whole baronies", a survey by inquisition (the Civil Survey), and a survey by admeasurement (the Down Survey) (*Civ. Surv.* iii viii). The Gross Survey was the first to be made as it was considered of the greatest urgency. It was begun in August 1653 and continued until the following year despite numerous misgivings (*ibid.*). Then, by an Order dated the 14th April, 1654, the other surveys were directed to be begun (*ibid.*).

The Civil Survey of the counties of Donegal, Derry and Tyrone was taken under the authority of Commissions with Instructions, dated 28th of July, 1654, and was apparently completed within eight months (*ibid.* xii). The Survey was to determine and record the possessions of the proprietors of lands and the tenures and titles of their respective estates, and to this end, the local juries were empowered to summon and examine under oath such persons as might be considered competent to assist in the discovery of the facts, and to demand the production of such evidence of title as was considered necessary (*ibid.* iii). Abstracts containing the names of lands and their boundaries taken from the Civil Survey were to be delivered to William Petty for the implementation of the Down Survey (*ibid.* x). Petty produced a series of parish and barony maps of which only the latter are used here (*Hib. Reg.*), followed some years later by an atlas of Ireland based on the earlier maps (*Hib. Del.*; see Price 1951, 94). The place-names in the Down Survey, therefore, are based on those in the Civil Survey, but although the Civil Survey provides comprehensive coverage of the whole county, the Down Survey was concerned only with forfeited lands, and in Loughinsholin only church lands are recorded.

The Books of Survey and Distribution (*BSD(c)*), which were drawn up in 1661, record several particulars abstracted from the Down Survey including place-names. Between all these sources – the Civil Survey, the Books of Survey and Distribution, and Petty's maps, there is little variation in the form of place-names and they are clearly closely related. Occasionally, however, we find that the forms of certain names on Petty's maps have been revised. **Moyard**, for example, is written *Bellnevay* in *Civ. Surv.* but *Moyoghterragh* on Petty's maps and in *BSD(c)*, and **Craigadick** is spelt *Cregduff* in *Civ. Surv.* as against *Cregadig* in Petty (*BSD(c)* gives both forms as aliases). Nevertheless, the spellings used in all these sources seldom vary significantly and we may generally assume that only those names which were found to have radically different forms in subsequent enquiries were revised.

The spellings in the so-called Census of c. 1659, despite being written in a clear, neat hand, are very unreliable (*Census* i). It frequently agrees with other sources of this period, but differences in order, content and spelling indicate that it is independent of all our other sources of the latter half of the 17th century. That this is the case is clear from spellings such as *Ballydermott* beside *Ballidermond* (**Ballydermot**), *Clone* beside *Belliclan* (**Clooney**), and *Mirmihellgrany* beside *Mirrimeith* (**Mormeal**). Thus, in spite of the poor standard of the transcription, it occasionally provides us with useful corroborative evidence of doubtful forms in other sources.

The Hearth Money Rolls of 1663 were destroyed in the fire at the Four Courts, Dublin, in 1922 and Ó Doibhlin's edition, which is used here, is based on a copy of the originals made by Tennison Groves c. 1911 and now preserved in PRONI (*HMR (Ó Doibhlin 2)*). They are of great importance in providing the most complete list of local inhabitants available to us before the 19th century, but the spellings of the place-names are frequently corrupt. As with the Census, it appears to be wholly independent of the other sources used here, but the high degree of corruption inherent in the document considerably reduces its value as a resource for the study of place-names.

An invaluable source for some names in the parishes of Maghera and Killelagh is a poem in Irish written on his deathbed in Bilbao c. 1700 by Fr Tadhg Ó Brolcháin. The poem was first brought to scholarly attention in 1834 when John O'Donovan, while engaged in his work for the Ordnance Survey, came across a copy in Maghera (*OSL (Derry)* 66–7). It was subsequently edited by Seosamh Laoide, presumably from the copy formerly in O'Donovan's possession, and printed in *Dhá Chéad de Cheoltaibh Uladh* (*DCCU* 426–8). Although the copy printed in the Ordnance Survey Letters is clearly corrupt in several regards, it has not suffered the regularization of Laoide's edition which, in many cases, obscures what might be a more genuine form of the place-name, so both copies are cited here.

An important 19th-century source is the series of name books compiled by the Ordnance Survey, the purpose of which was to enable the cartographers to provide a standardized form for each name which was to appear on the OS's 6-inch series. Thomas Larcom, the assistant director of the Survey, believed that this would be best accomplished by basing the anglicized spellings of names on their original Irish forms and so John O'Donovan, then a young but clearly capable Irish scholar, was employed by the Ordnance Survey. He visited Co. Derry in 1834 and travelled throughout the county between July and October of that year questioning local Irish speakers where he could find them about the meanings and origins of place-names, and his conclusions on each name are entered into the Ordnance Survey Name Books (*OSNB*).

O'Donovan spent nearly two months in the barony of Loughinsholin, longer than he spent in the whole of the rest of the county. Most of that time was spent in Maghera and Draperstown, from where he would go out, often accompanied by a local clergyman, to interview the old men of the area. The letters written by O'Donovan during this time show clearly that he met many old men in these two parishes, and while many of them deal with historical events and family names rather than place-names, it is clear that Irish was thriving in these areas. In the parish of Tamlaght O'Crilly, for example, one John O'Crilly of Ballynian was able to tell him "the Irish names of all the townlands" in that parish (*OSL (Derry)* 52). He learnt a great deal about topographical words from a Dr McRory, a native of Ballynascreen, and the Rev. Mr McKenna, parish priest of Maghera and Killelagh, took him to see some old places in his parishes and to converse with some of the most intelligent of the old inhabitants (*OSL (Derry)* 40, 48). He met many Irish speakers on the slopes of Slieve Gallion "where the people are more Irish than in any other part", and these people undoubtedly provided some assistance with the townland names of that area (*ibid.* 104).

While he encountered many Irish speakers in the west of the barony, he seems to have fared less well further east. He remarks that the Irish language had totally disappeared from "the old plain of Moyola", by which he seems to have understood the plain on either side of the Moyola between Curran and Lough Neagh (*ibid.* 117; cf. 100). He hoped that he could make up the loss by speaking with old people in Lissan and Derryloran parishes where, he was told, Irish still survived, but he seems to have been unsuccessful here (*ibid.* 117, 129).

The reliability of O'Donovan's Irish forms is difficult to assess. Forms collected from local Irish speakers are, in general, more deserving of our attention than those postulated by O'Donovan solely on the basis of a few 19th-century spellings and the local pronunciation. Unfortunately, O'Donovan does not anywhere in the name books for the parishes under consideration here attribute his Irish forms to local informants, even in those parishes in which he certainly did find informants. However, where we can judge his Irish forms, either by comparison with 17th-century spellings or other Irish language sources, we see that he does not display any knowledge of the origins of the names other than what might be worked out from the anglicized forms alone. This is particularly noticeable in names which have changed over time, such as **Ballymacpherson**, **Carncose**, **Moneysterlin**, **Coolsaragh**, **Gortamney**, and **Tamnyaskey**, all of which lie in the shadow of Slieve Gallion which was then so strongly Gaelic. Only in a single instance, that of **Upperland** in the parish of Maghera, does he produce a form (*Áth an Phortáin*) that could not have been worked out from the anglicized name alone.

It should be stressed that the fault may not entirely be O'Donovan's. We have no way of knowing to what extent the names had already been corrupted or reinterpreted so that even native speakers may not have been able to divine their original forms. Indeed, in many cases O'Donovan's informants were unaware of the origins of even the most straightforward names. He was given no less than five explanations of the name **Loughinsholin**, including

240

at least two from people who lived nearby, none of which were correct, and it was O'Donovan himself who pointed us in the direction of the correct form of the name (*ibid.* 105). In short, O'Donovan's Irish forms are frequently defective and often misleading, and the fact that they were compiled locally when Irish was still spoken in many parts seems to have had little bearing on the final result.

For the most part, the first Ordnance Survey 6-inch series indicated only townland names, but later issues included a large number of minor names. The procedure for standardizing the spelling of minor names was broadly similar to that used in the first survey for townland names, and it resulted in the production of the Ordnance Survey Revision Name Books (*OSRNB*) and the Contouring Name Books (*OSCNB*), the latter dealing mostly with names of hills and mountains. These have proved particularly valuable in the Loughinsholin area for the study of minor names. Where the names are of English origin, we can be reasonably certain that they were mainly composed within 100 years of the date of the name books and so any derivations offered there are reasonably authoritative. Where the names are Irish, they are sometimes late and frequently more transparent than townland names, and even here the explanations in the name books have proven to be quite reliable. Officers of the Ordnance Survey have entered translations of a great number of names into the name books which they clearly obtained from local people. Although no Irish forms accompany these translations it is usually quite clear what was intended. It should be noted, however, that O'Donovan worked over the name books in Dublin in the 1850s, and his suggestions are generally based on the anglicized spelling alone.

O'Donovan's work for the Ordnance Survey had far-reaching consequences, despite the fact that it was never published, for Joyce drew heavily on it for his *Irish Names of Places*, and Munn makes extensive use of it in his *Notes on the Placenames of Parishes and Townlands of the county of Londonderry*. Although both works have their own deficiencies, they are always cited here (Munn's primary Irish form is cited but his often numerous alternative derivations have generally been omitted to save space). Joyce's work is generally considered to be of immense importance in the study of Irish place-names, but his scope was too wide to consider each name individually and most of his work is presented without any reference to early spellings of the names (Flanagan 1981–2(b) 62). Munn frequently cites early 17th-century documents in his comprehensive survey of Derry place-names, but this is often limited to a single source, usually either the Escheated Counties maps or the related Charter of 1613. As Ó Maolfabhail has noted in the foreword to the reprint of Munn's *Notes*, Munn's Irish forms are often arbitrary and they certainly carry less authority than either O'Donovan's or Joyce's derivations.

One major work which predates O'Donovan, and is therefore totally unrelated to it, is MacCloskey's Statistical Report which contains Irish forms for names in the parishes of Ballynascreen, Desertmartin, and Kilcronaghan in the barony of Loughinsholin (*MacCloskey's Stat. Report*). It is unclear what MacCloskey's source was for these forms but they are almost invariably wrong. Indeed, it is often quite difficult to work out the relationship between his "Irish" form and his translation, and although they are cited among the forms, his suggestions are not discussed.

ABBREVIATIONS

acc.	Accusative	**Mod. Eng.**	Modern English
adj.	Adjective	**Mod. Ir.**	Modern Irish
al.	Alias	**MS(S)**	Manuscript(s)
angl.	Anglicized	**n.**	(Foot)note
Ant.	Co. Antrim	**neut.**	Neuter
Arm.	Co. Armagh	**NLI**	National Library of
art. cit.	In the article cited		Ireland, Dublin
BM	British Museum	**no(s).**	Number(s)
c.	About	**nom.**	Nominative
cf.	Compare	**O. Eng.**	Old English
Co(s).	County (-ies)	**O. Ir.**	Old Irish
col.	Column	**op. cit.**	In the work cited
coll.	Collective	**OSI**	Ordnance Survey, Dublin
d.	Died	**OSNI**	Ordnance Survey, Belfast
dat.	Dative	**p(p).**	Page(s)
Der.	Co. Derry	**par.**	Parish
Dn	Co. Down	**pass.**	Here and there
eag.	Eagarthóir/Curtha in	**pers. comm.**	personal comment
	eagar ag	**pl.**	Plural
ed.	Edited by	**PRO**	Public Record Office,
edn	Edition		London
Eng.	English	**PROI**	Public Record Office, Dublin
et pass.	And elsewhere	**PRONI**	Public Record Office,
et var.	And variations (thereon)		Belfast
f.	Following page	**pt**	Part
fem.	Feminine	**r.**	Correctly
Fer.	Co. Fermanagh	**RIA**	Royal Irish Academy,
ff.	Folios/Following pages		Dublin
fol.	Folio	**s.**	Shilling
gen.	Genitive	**sa.**	Under the year
HMSO	Her Majesty's Stationery	**sect.**	Section
	Office	**ser.**	Series
ibid.	In the same place	**sic**	As in source
IE	Indo-European	**sing.**	Singular
iml.	Imleabhar	**SS**	Saints
IPA	International Phonetic	**St**	Saint
	Alphabet	**sv(v).**	Under the word(s)
l(l).	Line(s)	**TCD**	Trinity College, Dublin
lit.	Literally	**trans.**	Translated by
loc.	Locative	**Tyr.**	Co. Tyrone
loc. cit.	In the place cited	**uimh.**	Uimhir
Lr.	Lower	**Up.**	Upper
masc.	Masculine	**viz.**	Namely
Mid. Eng.	Middle English	**voc.**	Vocative
Mid. Ir.	Middle Irish	**vol(s).**	Volume(s)

PRIMARY BIBLIOGRAPHY

A. Conn.   *Annála Connacht: the annals of Connacht (AD 1224–1544)*, ed. A. Martin Freeman (Dublin 1944).

Acta SS Colgan   *Acta sanctorum veteris et majoris Scotiae seu Hiberniae*, John Colgan (Lovanii 1645).

Adomnán   *Adomnán's Life of Columba* ed. Alan Orr Anderson & Marjorie Ogilvie Anderson (London etc. 1961).

AFM   *Annála Ríoghachta Éireann: annals of the kingdom of Ireland by the Four Masters from the earliest period to the year 1616*, ed. John O'Donovan, 7 vols (Dublin 1848–51; reprint 1990).

AGBP   *Ainmneacha Gaeilge na mbailte poist*, Oifig an tSoláthair (Baile Átha Cliath 1969).

AIF   *The Annals of Innisfallen*, ed. Seán Mac Airt (Dublin 1951).

Ainm   *Ainm: bulletin of the Ulster Place-name Society* (Belfast 1986–)

ALC   *The annals of Loch Cé: a chronicle of Irish affairs from AD 1014 to AD 1590*, ed. William Hennessy, 2 vols (London 1871; reprint Dublin 1939).

Anal. Hib.   *Analecta Hibernica* (Dublin 1930-69; Shannon 1970–).

Annates Ulst.   *De annatis Hiberniae: a calendar of the first-fruits' fees levied on papal appointments to benefices in Ireland, AD 1400–1535*, vol. i (Ulster), ed. Michael A. Costello and Ambrose Coleman (Dundalk 1909; reprint Maynooth 1912).

ASE   "Abstracts of grants of lands and other hereditaments under the acts of settlement and explanation, AD 1666–84", compiled by John Lodge and published in the appendix to the *15th Annual report from the commissioners . . . respecting the Public Records of Ireland* (1825) 45–340.

AU   *Annála Uladh: annals of Ulster; otherwise Annála Senait, annals of Senait: a chronicle of Irish affairs, 431–1131, 1155–1541*, ed. William Hennessy and Bartholomew MacCarthy, 4 vols (Dublin 1887–1901).

AU (Mac Airt)   *The annals of Ulster* (vol. i to 1131 AD), ed. Seán Mac Airt and Gearóid Mac Niocaill (Dublin 1983).

Bar. Coll. (OSNB)   Books of the barony collector, cited in OSNB.

Bartlett Maps (Esch. Co. Maps)   Three maps by Richard Bartlett published together with *Esch. Co. Map*: (i) *A Generalle Description of Ulster*; (ii) South-east Ulster; (iii) North-west Ulster,

(PRO MPF 35–37; copies in PRONI T1652/1–3). These maps have been dated to 1603 by G.A. Hayes-McCoy, *Ulster and Other Irish Maps, c. 1600*, p. 2, n. 13 (Dublin 1964).

BCC — *Betha Colaim Chille/Life of Columcille, compiled by Manus O'Donnell in 1532*, ed. A. O'Kelleher & G. Schoepperle (Illinois 1918).

Béaloid. — *Béaloideas: the journal of the Folklore of Ireland Society* (Dublin 1927–).

Benbradagh — *Benbradagh* (Dungiven 1971–).

Bishop. Der. — *The bishopric of Derry and the Irish Society of London, 1602–1705*, ed. T.W. Moody & J.G. Simms 2 vols (Dublin 1968, 1983).

BSD — *Book of survey & distribution, AD 1661: Armagh, Down & Antrim* (Quit Rent Office copy), PRONI T370/A.

BSD(c) — *Book of survey & distribution, AD 1661: Derry, Donegal & Tyrone* (Quit Rent Office copy), PRONI T370/C.

BUPNS — *Bulletin of the Ulster Place-name Society*, ser. 1, vols i–v (Belfast 1952-7); ser. 2, vols 1–4 (1978–82).

Cal. Carew MSS — *Calendar of the Carew manuscripts preserved in the Archiepiscopal Library at Lambeth*, ed. J.S. Brewer and W. Bullen, 6 vols (London 1867–73).

Cal. Papal Letters — *Calendar of entries in the papal registers relating to Great Britain and Ireland: papal letters AD 1198–1498*, ed. W.H. Bliss, C. Johnson, J.A. Twelmow, Michael J. Haren, Anne P. Fuller, 16 vols (London 1893–1960, Dublin 1978, 1986). In progress.

Ceart Uí Néill — *Ceart Uí Néill*, ed. Myles Dillon, *Stud. Celt.* i (1966) 1–18. Trans. Éamonn Ó Doibhlin, "*Ceart Uí Néill*, a discussion and translation of the document", *S. Ard Mh.* vol. 5, no. 2 (1970) 324–58.

Céitinn — *Foras Feasa ar Éirinn: the history of Ireland by Seathrún Céitinn (Geoffrey Keating)*, ed. Rev. Patrick S. Dinneen, 4 vols, Irish Texts Society (London 1902–14).

Celtica — *Celtica*, Dublin Institute for Advanced Studies (Dublin 1946–).

Census — *A census of Ireland, circa 1659, with supplementary material from the poll money ordinances (1660–1)*, ed. Séamus Pender (Dublin 1939).

Census 1851 — *Census of Ireland, 1851. General alphabetical index to the townlands and towns, parishes and baronies of Ireland . . .* (Dublin 1861).

CGH	*Corpus genealogiarum Hiberniae*, vol. 1, ed. M.A. O'Brien (Dublin 1962).
Charter of Londonderry	The charter of Londonderry of 1613, ed. Rev. George Hill, *An Historical Account of the Plantation in Ulster* (Belfast 1877) 386–392.
Charter of Londonderry (Reed)	"Translation of the Charter of King James the First to the Irish Society, dated the 29th March, 1613", ed. Charles Reed, *An Historical Narrative of the Origin and Constitution of . . . the Honourable the Irish Society* (London 1865) Appendix III 9–138.
Church Lands Arm.	"The Church-lands of Co. Armagh", *S. Ard Mh.* i 67–396.
Cín Lae Ó M.	*Cín lae Ó Mealláin*, ed. Tadhg Ó Donnchadha (alias Torna), *Anal. Hib.* 3 (1931) 1–61.
Civ. Surv.	*The civil survey, AD 1654-6*, ed. Robert C. Simington, 10 vols, Irish Manuscripts Commission (Dublin 1931–61).
CMR	*The Banquet of Dun na nGedh and the Battle of Magh Rath*, ed. John O'Donovan (Dublin 1842).
Colton Vis.	*Acts of Archbishop Colton in his metropolitical visitation of the diocese of Derry, AD 1397*, ed. William Reeves (Dublin 1850).
Comhar	*Comhar* (Baile Átha Cliath 1938–).
Coulter's Ballinascreen	*Ballinascreen and Glendermott*, J.A. Coulter.
CPR Jas. I	*Irish patent rolls of James I: facsimile of the Irish record commissioners' calendar prepared prior to 1830*, with a foreword by M.C. Griffith (Dublin 1966).
CSH	*Corpus genealogiarum sanctorum Hiberniae*, ed. Pádraig Ó Riain (Dublin 1985).
CSP Ire.	*Calendar of the state papers relating to Ireland, 1509–1670*, ed. H.C. Hamilton, E.G. Atkinson, R.P. Mahaffy, C.P. Russell and J.P. Prendergast, 24 vols (London 1860–1912).
Custom of County (OSNB)	Spelling or pronunciation current in the county c. 1834, cited in *OSNB passim*.
DCCU	*Dhá Chéad de Cheoltaibh Uladh*, eag. Énri Ó Muirgheasa (Baile Átha Cliath 1934).
Der. Clergy	*Derry clergy and parishes*, Rev. James B. Leslie (Enniskillen 1937).
Derriana	*Derriana: the journal of the Derry Diocesan Historical Society*.

DIL	*Dictionary of the Irish language: compact edition* (Dublin 1983).
Dinneen	*Foclóir Gaedhilge agus Béarla: an Irish-English dictionary*, Rev. Patrick S. Dinneen (Dublin 1904; reprint with additions 1927 and 1934).
Dinnsean.	*Dinnseanchas*, 6 vols (Baile Átha Cliath 1964–75).
Dongl. Ann.	*Donegal Annual: journal of the County Donegal Historical Society* (1947–).
Duff's Lough Neagh	A map of Lough Neagh made by John Duff (and assisted by James Williamson) for John O'Neill, AD 1785. Copy in Ewart Collection, QUB, Ewart B 1785.
Duty Bk Grange	Estate duty book for Viscount Massereene and Ferrard's property at Grange, Co. Antrim, 1733, PRONI D562/991.
Dwelly	*The illustrated Gaelic-English dictionary*, Edward Dwelly (Glasgow 1901–11; reprint 1920 etc.).
EA	*Ecclesiastical antiquities of Down, Connor and Dromore, consisting of a taxation of those dioceses compiled in the year 1306*, ed. William Reeves (Dublin 1847).
Eccles. Tax.	"Ecclesiastical taxation of the dioceses of Down, Connor, and Dromore", ed. William Reeves, *EA* 2–119.
Eccles. Tax. (CDI)	"Ecclesiastical taxation of Ireland", ed. H.S. Sweetman & G.F. Handcock, *Calendar of documents relating to Ireland . . ., 1302–07* (London 1886), 202–323.
Éigse	*Éigse: a journal of Irish studies* (Dublin 1939–).
Éire Thuaidh	*Éire Thuaidh/Ireland North: a cultural map and gazetteer of Irish place-names*, Ordnance Survey of Northern Ireland (Belfast 1988).
Eng. Dial. Dict.	*The English Dialect Dictionary* ed. Joseph Wright. Published 1898, revised 1970 (Oxford).
EPNS	Publications of the English Place-Name Society.
Esch. Co. Map	*Barony maps of the escheated counties in Ireland, AD 1609*, 28 maps, PRO. Published as *The Irish Historical Atlas*, Sir Henry James, Ordnance Survey (Southampton 1861).
Ét. Celt.	*Études Celtiques* (Paris 1936–).
Fairs & Markets	"Report of the Commissioners appointed to inquire into the State of the Fairs and Markets in Ireland" in *Reports from Commissioners* 1852–3 vol. xli.
FB	*Fled Bricrenn*, ed. George Henderson, Irish Texts Society vol. ii (London 1899).

246

Féil. Torna   *Féilscríbhinn Torna,* eag. Seamus Pender (Cork 1947).

Fiants Eliz.   "Calendar and index to the fiants of the reign of Elizabeth I", appendix to the *11–13th, 15–18th and 21–22nd Reports of the Deputy Keeper of public records in Ireland* (Dublin 1879–81, 1883–86, 1889–90).

Forfeit. Estates   "Abstracts of the conveyances from the trustees of the forfeited estates and interests in Ireland in 1688", appendix to the *15th Annual report from the commissioners . . . respecting the public records of Ireland* (1825) 348–99.

Galvia   *Galvia: irisleabhar Chumann seandalaíochta is Staire na Gaillimhe* (Gaillimh 1954–).

GÉ   *Gasaitéar na hÉireann/Gazetteer of Ireland: ainmneacha ionad daonra agus gnéithe aiceanta,* Brainse Logainmneacha na Suirbhéireachta Ordanáis (Baile Átha Cliath 1989).

GJ   *Gaelic Journal: Irisleabhar na Gaedhilge,* 19 vols (Dublin 1882–1909).

GOI   *A grammar of Old Irish,* Rudolf Thurneysen, trans. D.A. Binchy and Osborn Bergin (Dublin 1946).

Grand Jury Pres. (OSNB)   *Grand jury presentment,* cited in *OSNB passim.*

Griffith's Val.   *General valuation of rateable property in Ireland,* Richard Griffith (Dublin 1849–1864).

GUH   *Gleanings from Ulster History* by Séamus Ó Ceallaigh (Cork 1951), enlarged edition published by Ballinascreen Historical Society (1994).

Harris Hist.   *The antient and present state of the county of Down,* Walter Harris (Dublin 1744).

Hermathena   *Hermathena: a Dublin University review* (Dublin 1873–).

J Louth AS   *Journal of the Louth Archaeological Society* (Dundalk 1904–).

Hib. Del.   *Hiberniae Delineatio*: an atlas of Ireland by Sir William Petty comprising one map of Ireland, 4 maps of provinces and 32 county maps. Engraved c. 1671–72 and published London c. 1685; facsimile reproduction Newcastle-Upon-Tyne, 1968; reprint, with critical introduction by J.H. Andrews, Shannon, 1970.

Hib. Reg.   *Hibernia Regnum*: a set of 214 barony maps of Ireland dating to the period AD 1655–59 (facsimile reproductions by Ordnance Survey, Southampton, 1908).

HMR (Ó Doibhlin 2)   "Hearth Money Rolls (1663): city and county of Derry", *Derriana* ii (1979) 41–91.

Inq. Earldom Ulster	"The earldom of Ulster", Goddard H. Orpen, *JRSAI* xliii (1913) 30–46, 133–43; xliv (1914) 51–66; xlv (1915) 123–42.
Inq. Ult.	*Inquisitionum in officio rotulorum cancellariae Hiberniae asservatarum repertorium*, vol. ii (Ulster), ed. James Hardiman (Dublin 1829).
IPN	*Irish Place Names*, Deirdre Flanagan and Laurence Flanagan (Dublin 1994).
J O'D (OSNB)	Irish and anglicized forms of names attributed to John O'Donovan in the *OSNB*.
Joyce	*The origin and history of Irish names of places*, P.W. Joyce, 3 vols (Dublin 1869–1913).
JRSAI	*Journal of the Royal Society of Antiquaries of Ireland* (Dublin 1849–).
Lamb Maps	*A Geographical Description of ye Kingdom of Ireland Collected from ye actual Survey made by Sir William Petty . . . Containing one General Mapp of ye whole Kingdom, with four Provincial Mapps, & 32 County Mapps . . . Engraven & Published for ye benefit of ye Publique* by Francis Lamb (London [c. 1690]).
LASID	*Linguistic atlas and survey of Irish dialects*, Heinrich Wagner and Colm Ó Baoill, 4 vols (Dublin 1958–69).
Lebor na Cert	*Lebor na Cert: the Book of Rights*, ed. Myles Dillon, Irish Texts Society xlvi (Dublin 1962).
Lewis' Top. Dict.	*A topographical dictionary of Ireland*, ed. Samuel Lewis, 2 vols and atlas (London 1837; 2nd edn 1842).
L. Log. C. Chainnigh	*Liostaí logainmneacha: Contae Chill Chainnigh/County Kilkenny*, arna ullmhú ag Brainse Logainmneacha na Suirbhéireachta Ordanáis (Baile Átha Cliath 1993).
L. Log. Lú	*Liostaí logainmneacha: Contae Lú/County Louth*, arna ullmhú ag Brainse Logainmneacha na Suirbhéireachta Ordanáis (Baile Átha Cliath 1991).
L. Log. Luimnigh	*Liostaí logainmneacha: Contae Luimnigh/County Limerick*, arna ullmhú ag Brainse Logainmneacha na Suirbhéireachta Ordanáis (Baile Átha Cliath 1991).
L. Log. P. Láirge	*Liostaí logainmneacha: Contae Phort Láirge/County Waterford*, arna ullmhú ag Brainse Logainmneacha na Suirbhéireachta Ordanáis (Baile Átha Cliath 1991).
L. Log. Uíbh Fhailí	*Liostaí logainmneacha: Contae Uíbh Fhailí/County Offaly*, arna ullmhú ag Brainse Logainmneacha na Suirbhéireachta Ordanáis (Baile Átha Cliath 1994).

LL

The Book of Leinster, formerly Lebar na Núachongbála, ed. R.I. Best, O. Bergin, M.A. O'Brien & A. O'Sullivan, 6 vols (Dublin 1954–83).

Lochlann

Lochlann: a review of Celtic Studies (Oslo 1958–).

Lond. Comp. Valuation

"Schedules of the lands in Ulster allotted to the London Livery Companies, 1613", ed. T.W. Moody, *Anal. Hib.* viii (1938) 299–311.

MacCloskey's Stat. Report

Statistical reports of six Derry parishes 1821 by John Mac Closkey (1788–1876), ed. David O'Kane (Ballinascreen Historical Society 1983).

Mart. Gorm.

Félire Húi Gormáin: the martyrology of Gorman, ed. Whitley Stokes (London 1895).

Mart. Tal.

The martyrology of Tallaght, ed. R.I. Best and H.J. Lawlor (London 1931).

Mercator's Ire.

Irlandiae Regnum, by Gerard Mercator, first published in his atlas entitled *Atlas sive Cosmographicae Meditationes de Fabrica Mundi et Fabricati Figura*, AD 1595.

Mercator's Ulst.

Ultoniae Orientalis Pars by Gerard Mercator, first published in his *Atlas sive Cosmographicae Meditationes de Fabrica Mundi et Fabricati Figura*, AD 1595.

Met. Dinds.

The metrical Dindshenchas, ed. Edward J. Gwynn, 5 vols (Dublin 1903–35).

Munn's Notes

Notes on the place names of the parishes and townlands of the County of Londonderry (repr. Ballinascreen Historical Society 1985).

NISMR

Northern Ireland sites and monuments record: stage 1 (1979), published privately by the Department of the Environment (NI) and the Archaeological Survey (Belfast 1979).

Nomina

Nomina: a journal of name studies relating to Great Britain and Ireland, Council for Name Studies in Great Britain and Ireland.

Norden's Map

"The plott of Irelande with the confines", formerly included in *A discription of Ireland*, c. 1610, by John Norden. Formerly in the State Paper Office but now in PRO MPF 67. Reproduced in *SP Hen. VIII* vol. ii, pt. 3.

Norsk Tids.

Norsk tidsskrift for sprogvidenskap (Oslo 1928–).

Ó Dónaill

Foclóir Gaeilge-Béarla, eag. Niall Ó Dónaill (Baile Átha Cliath 1977).

O'Reilly

An Irish-English dictionary, Edward O'Reilly. Revised and corrected, with a supplement by John O'Donovan (Dublin 1864).

Onom. Goed.	*Onomasticon Goedelicum locorum et tribuum Hiberniae et Scotiae*, Edmund Hogan (Dublin 1910).
Onoma	*Onoma: bibliographical and information bulletin*, International Centre of Onomastics (Louvain 1950–).
OS 1:10,000	*The Ordnance Survey 1:10,000 series maps*, Ordnance Survey of Northern Ireland (Belfast 1968–).
OS 1:50,000	*The Ordnance Survey 1:50,000 series maps*, also known as *The Discoverer Series*, Ordnance Survey of Northern Ireland (Belfast 1978–88).
OS 6-inch	*The Ordnance Survey six-inch series maps*, first published in the 1830s and 1840s with numerous subsequent editions.
OSCNB	Contouring Name Books in the Ordnance Survey, Phoenix Park, Dublin.
OSL (Derry)	*John O'Donovan's Letters from County Londonderry (1834)* ed. Graham Mawhinney (Ballinascreen Historical Society 1992).
OSM	*Ordnance Survey memoirs of Ireland*, ed. Angélique Day and Patrick McWilliams (Belfast 1990–).
OSM (Loughrey)	*Ordnance Survey Memoir for the Parish of Ballinascreen 1836–1837*, ed. S.V.P. Loughrey (Ballinascreen Historical Society 1981).
OSNB	Name-books compiled during the progress of the Ordnance Survey in 1834–5 and preserved in the Ordnance Survey, Phoenix Park, Dublin.
OSNB Pron.	Local pronunciation as recorded in OSNB.
OSRNB	Ordnance Survey Revision Name Books, compiled c.1850. Reference is to book number and 6-inch sheet number. Originals in Ordnance Survey Headquarters, Phoenix Park, Dublin.
Par. Reg. (OSNB)	Parish register cited in OSNB.
Par. Tithe Bk (OSNB)	Parish tithe book cited in OSNB.
PH	*The passions and the homilies from the Leabhar Breac*, ed. Robert Atkinson, *Todd Lecture Series* ii (Dublin 1887).
Phillips MSS (Maps)	A brief survey of the estate of the Plantation of the County of Londonderry taken by Sir Thomas Phillips and Richard Hadsor Esq., in *Londonderry and the London Companies 1609–1629* (HMSO, Belfast 1928) 147–168 *et passim*.
PNI	*Place-Names of Northern Ireland*, The Northern Ireland Place-Name Project, Queen's University, Belfast, vols 1- (Belfast 1992–).

Poems Giolla Brighde	*The poems of Giolla Brighde Mac Con Midhe*, ed. N.J.A. Williams, Irish Texts Society vol. 51 (Dublin 1980).
Post-Sheanchas	*Post-Sheanchas i n-a bhfuil cúigí, dúithchí, conntaethe, & bailte puist na hÉireann*, Seosamh Laoide (Baile Átha Cliath 1905).
PRIA	*Proceedings of the Royal Irish Academy* (Dublin 1836–). Published in three sections since 1902 (section C: archaeology, linguistics and literature).
Received usage	Received usage cited in OSNB.
Reeves' Ad.	*The Life of St. Columba, founder of Hy, written by Adamnan*, ed. William Reeves (Dublin 1857).
Reg. Deeds	Original bound MSS volumes in the Registry of Deeds, Henrietta St. Dublin (1708–1832). Microfilm copies in PRONI mic.7.
Reg. Dowdall	"A calendar of the register of Primate George Dowdall, commonly called the *Liber Niger* or 'Black Book'", ed. L.P. Murray, *J Louth AS* vi (1925–8) 90–101, 147–58, 211–28; vii (1929–32) 78–95, 258–75.
Reg. Swayne	*The register of John Swayne, Archbishop of Armagh and Primate of Ireland 1418–39*, ed. D.A. Chart (Belfast 1935).
Rent Roll Drapers (OSNB)	Rent Roll of the Drapers' Company, cited in *OSNB*.
S. Ard Mh.	*Seanchas Ard Mhacha: journal of the Armagh Diocesan Historical Society* (Armagh 1954–).
Sampson's Map	George V. Sampson's map of Co. Londonderry, (copy in PRONI D174).
Sampson's Stat. Sur. (OSNB)	Sampson's Statistical Survey, cited in *OSNB*.
Scáthlán	*Scáthlán: iris Chumann Staire agus Seanchais Ghaoth Dobhair* (Béal Átha Seanaigh 1984–).
Sgéalta Mh. L.	*Sgéalta Mhuintir Luinigh*, Éamonn Ó Tuathail (Dublin 1933).
SGS	*Scottish Gaelic Studies* (Oxford 1926–53, Aberdeen 1954–).
Speed's Antrim & Down	A map entitled *Antrym and Downe*, AD 1610, by John Speed. Reproduced in *UJA* ser. 1, vol. i (1853) between pp. 123 and 124.
Speed's Ireland	*The Kingdome of Irland devided into severall Provinces and then againe devided into Counties. Newly described*, AD 1610, by John Speed. Also published in his atlas *The Theatre of the Empire of Great Britain* (Sudbury & Humble 1612).

Speed's Ulster	*The Province Ulster described*, AD 1610, by John Speed. Also published in his atlas *The Theatre of the Empire of Great Britain* (Sudbury & Humble 1612).
SP Hen. VIII	*State Papers published under the authority of His Majesty's Commission: King Henry VIII*, 11 vols (London 1830–52).
TBC (LL)	*Táin Bó Cúalnge from the Book of Leinster*, ed. Cecile O'Rahilly (Dublin 1984).
TBC (Rec. I)	*Táin Bó Cúailnge Recension I*, ed. Cecile O'Rahilly (Dublin 1976).
TCD Gens (H.4.25)	Genealogical tracts from MS TCD 1366 (H.4.25), Trinity College, Dublin.
Title Deeds (OSNB)	Title deeds cited in *OSNB*.
Top. Frag.	"Topographical fragments from the Franciscan Library", ed. Canice Mooney, *Celtica* i (1950) 64–85.
Topog. Poems	*Topographical poems: by Seaán Mór Ó Dubhagáin and Giolla-na-Naomh Ó hUidhrín*, ed. James Carney (Dublin 1943).
Trip. Life (Stokes)	*The tripartite life of Saint Patrick, with other documents relating to that Saint*, ed. Whitley Stokes, 2 vols (London 1887).
UF	*Ulster Folklife* (Belfast etc. 1955–).
UJA	*Ulster Journal of Archaeology*, 1st ser., 9 vols (Belfast 1853–62); 2nd ser., 17 vols (1894–1911); 3rd ser. (1938–).
Ultach	*An tUltach: iris oifigiúil Chomhaltas Uladh* (1923–).
ZCP	*Zeitschrift für Celtische Philologie* (1897–).

252

SECONDARY BIBLIOGRAPHY

Adams, G.B.   1954   "Place-name phonology" in *BUPNS* ser.1 vol.ii pt.2, 30–1.

Andrews, J.H.   1974   "The maps of the escheated counties of Ulster, 1609–10", *PRIA* vol. lxxiv, sect. C, 133–70.

    1975   *A paper landscape; the Ordnance Survey in nineteenth-century Ireland* (Oxford).

    1978   *Irish maps: the Irish heritage series, no. 18* (Dublin).

Arthurs, J.B.   1954(b)   "Sliabh Fuaid" in *BUPNS* ser.1 vol.ii pt.2, 33–8; pt.3, 67.

    1955–6   "The Ulster Place-name Society", *Onoma* vi 80–2.

    1956(b)   "The element Cal- in place-names" in *BUPNS* ser.1 vol. iv pt.2, 28–31.

Barber, Charles   1976   *Early Modern English* (London).

Bell, Robert   1988   *The book of Ulster surnames* (Belfast).

Black, G.F.   1946   *The surnames of Scotland* (New York).

Buckley, Victor M.   1989   "From the Darkness to the Dawn: the later prehistoric and early Christian borderlands", Gillespie and O'Sullivan 1989, 23–39.

Byrne, F.J.   1973   *Irish kings and high-kings* (London).

Camblin, Gilbert   1951   *The town in Ulster* (London).

Chart, D.A.   1940   *A Preliminary Survey of the Ancient Monuments of Northern Ireland* (Belfast).

Curl, J.S.   1986   *The Londonderry Plantation 1609–1914* (Chichester 1986).

Davies, O.   1941(b)   "Ballynascreen Church and Legends" in *UJA* ser. 3. vol. 4 (1941) 57–63.

de hÓir, Éamonn   1964(a)   "An t-athru *onga* > *ú* i roinnt logainmneacha", *Dinnsean.* iml. i, uimh. 1, 8–11.

    1970(a)   "Roinnt nótaí ar *sliabh, binn, cruach* in ainmneacha cnoc" in *Dinnsean.* iml.iv uimh.1, 1–6.

Ekwall, Eilert   1928   *English river-names* (Oxford).

    1960   *The concise Oxford dictionary of English place-names* (Oxford 4th edn).

Falkiner, C.L.   1903   "The counties of Ireland: an historical sketch of their origin, constitution, and gradual delimitation", *PRIA* vol. xxiv, sect. C, 169–94.

Field, John   1972   *English field-names: a dictionary* (Newton Abbot).

Flanagan, Deirdre   1970   "*Craeb Telcha*: Crew, Co. Antrim" in *Dinnsean.* iml.iv uimh.2, 29–32.

	1973	"Three settlement names in County Down: the Turtars of Inishargy; Dunsfort;Tullumgrange", *Dinnsean.* iml. v uimh. iii, 65–71.
	1978(d)	"Transferred population or sept-names: *Ulaidh* (a quo Ulster)", *BUPNS* ser. 2, vol. 1, 40–3.
	1979(f)	Review of *The meaning of Irish place names* by James O'Connell (Belfast 1978), *BUPNS* ser. 2, vol. 2, 58–60.
	1980	"Place-names in early Irish documentation: structure and composition", *Nomina* iv, 41–45.
	1981–2(a)	"Places and their names: Raloo and Ballyarnot", *BUPNS* ser. 2 vol. iv, 22–3.
	1981–2(b)	"Some guidelines to the use of Joyce's *Irish names of places*, vol. i", *BUPNS* ser. 2, vol. 4, 61–9.
	1981–2(c)	"A summary guide to the more commonly attested ecclesiastical elements in place- names", *BUPNS* ser. 2, vol. 4, 69–75.
Fleming, D.I.	1991	*Desertmartin Parish Recalled* (Desertmartin).
Gelling, M., Nioclaisen, W.F.H., Richards, M.	1970	*The Names of Towns and Cities in Britain* (London).
Gillespie, Raymond & O'Sullivan, Harold	1989	*The borderlands: essays on the history of the Ulster-Leinster border* (Belfast).
Goblet,Y.M.	1932	*A topographical index of the parishes and townlands of Ireland in Sir William Petty's Mss. barony maps (c. 1655–9) ... and Hiberniae Delineatio (c. 1672)* (Dublin).
Greene, David	1983	"*Cró, Crú* and similar words", *Celtica* xv, 1–9.
Hamilton, John Noel	1974	*A phonetic study of the Irish of Tory Island, Co. Donegal* (Belfast).
Hamlin, A.	1976	*The Archaeology of Early Christianity* 3 vols. (Ph.D., Queen's University, Belfast).
Hogan, Edmund	1910	*Onom. Goed.*
Holmer, Nils M.	1940	*On some relics of the Irish dialect spoken in the Glens of Antrim* (Uppsala).
Hughes, A.J.	1989–90	"Old Irish *Cnogba* modern townland *Crewbane*: conclusive evidence for a sound change in Meath Irish?", *Ainm* iv 224–6.
Kelly, George	1952-3(a)	"*Na* in place-names" in *BUPNS* ser.1 vol.i, 30.
Kenney, J.F.	1929	*The sources for the early history of Ireland: an introduction and guide*, vol. i: ecclesiastical (New York).
Lewis, Henry & Pedersen, Holger	1937	*A Concise Comparative Celtic Grammar* (Göttingen).
Lucas, A.T.	1985	"Toghers or causeways: some evidence from archaeological, literary, historical and place-name sources", *PRIA* sect. C 37–60.

Mac Airt, Seán   1958   "The churches founded by Saint Patrick" in *Saint Patrick*, ed. John Ryan, 67–80 (Dublin).

M'Aleer, P.   1920   *Townland names of County Tyrone* (c.1920; reprint Portadown & Draperstown 1988).

Mac Aodha, Breandán S.   1986(b)   "Some aspects of the toponomy of the Crannagh district, Glenelly, County Tyrone", *Ainm* i, 83–91.

McCann H.P.   1981-2   "Places and their names: Desertcreat" in *BUPNS* ser.2 vol.iv, 20–2.

McCone, Kim *et al.*   1994   *Stair na Gaeilge* (Maigh Nuad).

McCracken, Eileen   1971   *The Irish woods since Tudor times; distribution and exploitation* (Belfast).

McCracken, Eileen & McCracken, Donal   1984   *A register of trees for County Londonderry, 1768–1911* (PRONI 1984).

MacElhinney, Eugene   1975   "An Buachaill Bréige" in *Benbradagh* v, 3–4.

McErlean, Thomas   1983   "The Irish townland system of landscape organisation" in *Landscape archaeology in Ireland*, ed. Terence Reeves-Smyth and Fred Hamond, 315–39 (Oxford).

Mac Giolla Chomhaill, A.   1968   "Canúintí an Tuaiscirt, XII: Gaeilge Dhoire" in *Ultach* in three parts: vol. 45 (1968) February pp. 5–7; March pp. 4, 6, 15; April pp. 6–7, 18.

Mac Giolla Easpaig, D.   1981   "Noun and noun compounds in Irish place-names", *Ét. Celt.* xviii, 151-63.
    1984   "Logainmneacha na Rosann", *Dongl. Ann.* 36, 48–60.
    1986   "Logainmneacha Ghaoth Dobhair", *Scáthlán* 3, 64–88.
    1989-90   "The place-names of Rathlin Island", *Ainm* iv, 3–89.

McKay, P   1990   *The Names of the Parishes and Townlands of the Baronies of Upper and Lower Toome, Co. Antrim* (Ph.D., University of Ulster at Coleraine).

MacLysaght, Edward   1957   *Irish families: their names, arms and origins* (Dublin).
    1964   *A guide to Irish surnames* (Dublin).
    1982   *More Irish families: a new revised and enlarged edition of "More Irish families" (1960), incorporating "Supplement to Irish families" (1964), with an essay on Irish chieftainries* (Dublin).
    1985   *The surnames of Ireland* (Dublin, 4th edn; 1st edn 1957).

McManus, Damien   1994   "An Nua-Ghaeilge Chlasaiceach" in McCone *et al.* 1994, 335–446.

MacNeill, Máire   1962   *The festival of Lughnasa* (Oxford; reprinted Dublin 1982).

Mallory, J.P. & McNeill, T.E.	1991	*The archaeology of Ulster from colonization to plantation* (Belfast).
Mallory, J.P. & Stockman, Gerard	1994	*Ulidia: proceedings of the first international conference on the Ulster Cycle of tales* (Belfast and Emain Macha).
Mason, William Shaw	1814–9	*A statistical account or parochial survey of Ireland...* in 3 vols (Dublin, Edinburgh).
Mitchell, Brian	1992	*The Surnames of Derry* (Derry).
Mitchell, Frank	1990	*The Shell Guide to Reading the Irish Landscape* (incorporating *The Irish Landscape*) (Dublin 1986; revised 1990).
Moody, T.W.	1939	*The Londonderry plantation, 1609–41: the city of London and the plantation in Ulster* (Belfast).
Morton, Deirdre	1956–7	"Tuath-divisions in the baronies of Belfast and Masserene", *BUPNS* ser. 1, vol. iv 38–44; v 6–12.
	1959	"Some notes on minor place-names in the Glenlark district" in *UF* v 54–60.
Muhr, Kay	1994	"The location of the Ulster Cycle: Part I: Tóchustal Ulad", Mallory & Stockman 1994, 149–58.
Munn, A.M.	1925	*Munn's Notes.*
Nicolaisen, W.F.H.	1976	*Scottish place-names: their study and significance* (London).
Ní Mhaolchallann, M.	1993	*Cúrsaí Staire agus Logainmneacha i bParóiste Leamhaigh i gContae Dhoire* (tráchtas B.Ed., Coláiste Mhuire, Béal Feirste).
Ó Buachalla, B.	1970	"Nótaí ar Ghaeilge Dhoire agus Thír Eoghain" in *Éigse* vol.xiii 249–78.
Ó Ceallaigh, S.	1901	"Irish Christian Names" in *GJ* ii 197–205 (December 1901).
	1927	"Why Gleann Con Chadhain is so called" in *Béaloid.* iml.i uimh.i, 58–60.
	1950(a)	"Old Lights on Place-Names: New Lights on Maps" in *JRSAI* vol. 80 (1950) 172–186.
	1950(b)	"Notes on the Place-names in Derry and Tyrone", *Celtica* i, 118–40.
Ó Ciobháin, Breandán	1978	"Deoise Ard Mhacha sa dara céad déag" in *S. Ard Mh.* vol.9 no.1, 51–69.
Ó Corráin, Donnchadh	1972	*Ireland before the Normans* (Dublin).
Ó Corráin, Donnchadh & Maguire, Fidelma	1981	*Gaelic personal names* (Dublin).

Ó Cuív, Brian   1986   *Aspects of Irish personal names* (Dublin) [reprinted from *Celtica* xviii (1986) 151–84].

Ó Dochartaigh,   1987   *Dialects of Ulster Irish* (Belfast).
Cathair

Ó Doibhlin, É.   1971(b)   "The deanery of Tulach Óg" in *S. Ard Mh.* vol.6 no.1, 141–82.

O'Donovan, John   1849   *Miscellany of the Celtic Society . . .* (Dublin).

Ó Foghludha, Risteard 1935   *Log-ainmneacha .i. dictionary of Irish place-names...* (Dublin).

Ó hÓgáin, Dáithí   1990   *Myth, legend & romance: an encyclopaedia of the Irish folk tradition* (London).

Ó hUrmoltaigh,   1967   "Logainmneacha as Toraí, Tír Chonaill", *Dinnsean.* ii
Nollaig   99–106.

O'Kane, James   1970   "Placenames of Inniskeel and Kilteevoge: A placename study of two parishes in Central Donegal", *ZCP* xxxi 59–145.

O'Laverty, James   1891   *Seancus Cloinne Laithbheartaigh: Some account of the surname anciently written Ua Flaithbheartaigh or Ua Laithbheartaigh but at present written O'Laverty, O'Lafferty, Laverty, or Lafferty, and of its present location as evidenced by the parliamentary registers of voters* (Belfast).

Ó Máille, T.S.   1955(b)   "*Muiceanach* mar áitainm", *JRSAI* lxxxv 88–93.
                       1960   "*Cuilleann* in áitainmneacha", *Béaloid.* xxviii 50–64.
                       1962(a)   "*Corrán, Curraun, Corrane, Craan*", *Béaloid.* xxx 76–88.
                       1962(b)   "Áit-ainmneacha as Condae na Gaillimhe", *Galvia* ix 53–7.
                       1967   "Meacan in áitainmneacha", *Dinnsean.* ii 93–7.
                       1981-2(a)   "*Avish* and *Evish*" in *BUPNS* ser. 2, iv 1–5.
                       1987   "Place-name elements in -*ar*", *Ainm* ii 27–36.
                       1989-90   "Irish place-names in -*as, -es, -is, -os, -us*", *Ainm* iv 125–43.

Ó Mainnín, M.B.   1989-90   "The element *island* in Ulster place-names", *Ainm* iv 200–210.

Ó Maolfabhail, Art   1985   "Baill choirp mar logainmneacha" [béal, bléin & droim] in *Comhar* (Bealtaine, Meitheamh & Iúil).
                       1987-8   "Baill choirp mar logainmneacha", *Ainm* ii 76–82; iii 18–26.
                       1990(a)   *Logainmneacha na hÉireann, iml. I: Contae Luimnigh* (Baile Átha Cliath).
                       1990(b)   "Ilfhás ar ainm clúiteach (Cnogba > Knowth, Craud, Ballinacraud, Crewbane", *Celtica* xxi, 523–32.

Ó Muraíle, Nollaig   1985   *Mayo Places: their names & origins* (Dublin).

Ó Murchadha, Diarmuid   1964   "Ciall bhreise don bhfocal "Cabha"", *Dinnsean.* i 3–5.

O'Rahilly, T.F.   1931   "Etymological Notes – III", *SGS* iii 52–72.
1932   *Irish dialects past and present* (Dublin; reprint 1976).
1933   "Notes on Irish place-names", *Hermathena* xxiii 196–220.
1946   *Early Irish history and mythology* (Dublin; reprint 1976).

Otway-Ruthven, A.J.   1964   "Parochial development in the rural deanery of Skreen", *JRSAI* xciv, 111–22.

Petty, William   1672   *The political anatomy of Ireland,* reprinted in *Tracts and treatises illustrative of Ireland* ii 72-3 (Dublin 1860–1).

Power, Patrick   1932   *Crichad an chaoilli: being the topography of ancient Fermoy* (Cork).
1947   "The bounds and extent of Irish parishes", *Féil. Torna* 218–23.

Price, Liam   1945-67   *The place-names of Co. Wicklow,* 7 fasc., (Dublin).
1951   "The Place-Names of the Books of Survey and Distribution and Other Records of the Cromwellian Settlement", *JRSAI* lxxxi 89–106.
1963   "A note on the use of the word *baile* in place-names", *Celtica* vi 119–26.

Quiggin, E.C.   1906   *A dialect of Donegal, being the speech of Meenawannia in the parish of Glenties* (Cambridge).

Reaney, P.H.   1958   *A dictionary of British surnames* (London).

Reeves, William   1861   "On the townland distribution of Ireland", *PRIA* vii 473–90.

Reid, Professor   1957   "A note on *cinament*", *BUPNS* ser. 1, vol. v 12.

Room, Adrian   1983   *A Concise Dictionary of Modern Place-Names in Great Britain and Ireland* (Oxford).

Sommerfelt, Alf   1929   "South Armagh Irish", *Norsk Tids.* ii 107–91.
1958   "The English forms of the names of the main provinces of Ireland", *Lochlann* i 223–7.

Speer, Deirdre   1990   *Raths & Ruins: a survey of raths, souterrains, crannogs and ecclesiastical sites – extinct and extant – in the south Derry area,* compiled by Deirdre Speer, edited and illustrated by Muriel Bell (Draperstown).

Stockman, Gerard & Wagner, Heinrich   1965   "Contributions to a study of Tyrone Irish", Lochlann iii 43–236.

Taylor, Isaac   1896   *Names and their histories* (1896), reprinted in the Everyman edition of his *Words and places* (1911).

Todd, J.H.	1848	*Leabhar Breathnach annso sis: The Irish Version of the Historia Britonum of Nennius* (Dublin 1848).
Toner, Brian	1990	"Historical notes on Bellaghy from about 1620" (unpublished). Copy in Place-Names Project, QUB.
Toner, Gregory	1991–3	"*Money* in the place-names of east Ulster", *Ainm* v 52–8.
Traynor, Michael	1953	*The English dialect of Donegal: a glossary* (Dublin).
Wagner, Heinrich	1959	*Gaeilge Theilinn* (Baile Átha Cliath).
Walsh, J.R.	1973	*A History of the Parish of Maghera* (John English & Co. Ltd).
Woulfe, Patrick	1923	*Sloinnte Gaedheal is Gall: Irish names and surnames; collected and edited with explanatory and historical notes* (Dublin).

GLOSSARY OF TECHNICAL TERMS

advowson   The right of presenting a clergyman to a vacant benefice.

affricate   A plosive pronounced in conjunction with a fricative; e.g. the sounds spelt with *(t)ch* or *-dge* in English.

alveolar   Pronounced with the tip of the tongue touching the ridge of hard flesh behind the upper teeth; e.g. *t* in the English word *tea*.

analogy   The replacement of a form by another in imitation of words of a similar class; e.g. in imitation of *bake – baked, fake – faked, rake – raked* a child or foreigner might create a form *shaked*.

anglicize   Make English in form; e.g. in place-names the Irish word *baile* "homestead, townland" is anglicized *bally*.

annal   A record of events in chronological order, according to the date of the year.

annates   Later known as First Fruits; a tax paid, initially to the Pope, by a clergyman on appointment to a benefice.

apocope   The loss of the end of a word.

aspiration   (i) The forcing of air through a narrow passage thereby creating a frictional sound; e.g. *gh* in the word *lough* as pronounced in Ireland and Scotland is an aspirated consonant, (ii) the modification of a consonant sound in this way, indicated in Irish writing by putting *h* after the consonant; e.g. *p* aspirated resembles the *ph* sound at the beginning of *phantom;* also called **lenition.**

assimilation   The replacing of a sound in one syllable by another to make it similar to a sound in another syllable; e.g. in some dialects of Irish the *r* in the first syllable of the Latin *sermon-* was changed to *n* in imitation of the *n* in the second syllable, giving a form *seanmóin*.

ballybetagh   Irish *baile biataigh* "land of a food-provider", native land unit, the holder of which had a duty to maintain his lord and retinue when travelling in the area (*Colton Vis.* 130).

ballyboe   Irish *baile bó* "land of a cow", a land unit equivalent to a modern townland, possibly so-named as supplying the yearly rent of one cow (*Colton Vis.* 130).

barony   In Ireland an administrative unit midway in size between a county and a civil parish, originally the landholding of a feudal baron (*EA* 62).

benefice   An ecclesiastical office to which income is attached.

bilabial   Articulated by bringing the two lips together; e.g. the *p* in the English word *pea*.

Brittonic   Relating to the branch of Celtic languages which includes Welsh, Cornish and Breton.

260

calendar   A précis of an historical document or documents with its contents arranged according to date.

carrow   Irish *ceathru* "a quarter". See **quarter.**

cartography   The science of map-making.

cartouche   An ornamental frame round the title etc. of a map.

carucate   Latin *carucata* "ploughland", a territorial unit, the equivalent of a townland.

Celtic   Relating to the (language of the) Irish, Scots, Manx, Welsh, Cornish, Bretons, and Gauls.

centralized   Pronounced with the centre of the tongue raised; e.g. the vowel sound at the beginning of *again* or at the end of *the.*

cess   Tax.

cinament   A territorial unit of lesser size than a **tuogh** (which see). Three derivations have been suggested: (i) from Irish *cine* "a family", (*cineamhain?*) (*EA* 388); (ii) from French *scindement* "cutting up, division" (Morton 1956–7, 39); (iii) from French *(a)ceignement* "enclosure(?)" (Reid 1957, 12).

civil parish   An administrative unit based on the medieval parish.

cluster   See **consonant cluster.**

coarb   Irish *comharba,* originally the heir of an ecclesiastical office, later a high-ranking hereditary tenant of church land under the bishop. The coarb may be in charge of other ecclesiastical tenants called **erenaghs,** which see.

compound   A word consisting of two or more verbal elements; e.g. *aircraft, housework.*

consonant   (i) An element of the alphabet which is not a vowel, e.g. *c, j, x,* etc., (ii) a speech sound in which the passage of air through the mouth or nose is impeded, e.g. at the lips (*b, p, or m*), at the teeth (*s, z*), etc.

consonant cluster   A group of two or more consonants; e.g. *bl* in *blood, ndl* in *handle, lfths* in *twelfths.*

contraction   (i) The shortening of a word or words normally by the omission of one or more sounds, (ii) a contracted word; e.g. *good-bye is* a contraction of *God be with you; can not* is contracted to *can't.*

county   Feudal land division, equivalent to an English shire, created by the English administration in Ireland as the major subdivision of an Irish province.

deanery   Properly called a rural deanery, an ecclesiastical division of people or land administered by a rural dean.

declension A group of nouns whose case-endings vary according to a fixed pattern. (There are five declensions in modern Irish).

delenition Sounding or writing a consonant as if it were not aspirated; see **aspiration.**

dental A sound pronounced with the tip of the tongue touching the upper teeth; e.g. *th* in the English *thumb.*

devoicing Removing the sound caused by the resonance of vocal cords; see **voiced.**

dialect A variety of a language in a given area with distinctive vocabulary, pronunciation or grammatical forms.

digraph A group of two letters expressing a single sound; e.g. *ea* in English *team* or *ph* in English *photograph.*

diocese The area or population over which a bishop has ecclesiastical authority.

diphthong A union of two vowel sounds pronounced in one syllable; e.g. *oi* in English *boil.* (Note that a diphthong cannot be sung on a single sustained note without changing the position of the mouth).

dissimilation The replacing of a sound in one syllable by another to make it different from a sound in another syllable e.g. Loughbrickland comes from an original Irish form, *Loch Bricrenn.*

eclipsis The replacement in Irish of one sound by another in initial position as the result of the influence of the previous word; e.g. the *c* of Irish *cór* "choir" (pronounced like English *core)* is eclipsed by *g* in the phrase *i gcór* "in a choir" due to the influence of the preposition *i,* and *gcór* is pronounced like English *gore*; also called **nasalization.**

elision The omission of a sound in pronunciation; e.g. the *d* is elided in the word *handkerchief.*

emphasis See **stress.**

epenthetic vowel A vowel sound inserted within a word; e.g. in Ireland an extra vowel is generally inserted between the *l* and *m* of the word *film.*

erenagh Irish *airchinnech* "steward", hereditary officer in charge of church lands, later a tenant to the bishop *(Colton Vis.* 4–5).

escheat Revert to the feudal overlord, in Ireland usually forfeit to the English crown.

etymology The facts relating to the formation and meaning of a word.

fiant A warrant for the making out of a grant under the royal seal, or (letters) patent.

fricative A speech sound formed by narrowing the passage of air from the mouth so that audible friction is produced; e.g. *gh* in Irish and Scottish *lough.*

Gaelic   Relating to the branch of Celtic languages which includes Irish, Scottish Gaelic and Manx.

glebe   The house and land (and its revenue) provided for the clergyman of a parish.

glide   A sound produced when the organs of speech are moving from the position for one speech sound to the position for another; e.g. in pronouncing the word *deluge* there is a *y*-like glide between the *l* and the *u*.

gloss   A word or phrase inserted in a manuscript to explain a part of the text.

Goedelic = Gaelic   which see.

grange   Anglo-Norman term for farm land providing food or revenue for a feudal lord, frequently a monastery.

haplology   The omission of a syllable beside another with a similar sound; e.g. *lib(ra)ry*, *deteri(or)ated.*

hearth money   A tax on the number of hearths used by a household.

impropriator   The person to whom rectorial tithes of a monastery etc. were granted after the Dissolution.

inflect   To vary the form of a word to indicate a different grammatical relationship; e.g. *man* singular, *men* plural.

inquisition   A judicial inquiry, here usually into the possessions of an individual at death.

International Phonetic Alphabet   The system of phonetic transcription advocated by the International Phonetic Association.

labial = bilabial which see.

lenition   See **aspiration.**

lexicon   The complete word content of a language.

lowering   Changing a vowel sound by dropping the tongue slightly in the mouth; e.g. pronouncing *doctor* as *dactor.*

manor   Feudal estate (Anglo–Norman and Plantation), smaller than a barony, entitling the landowner to jurisdiction over his tenants at a manor court.

martyrology   Irish *féilire*, also translated "calendar", a list of names of saints giving the days on which their feasts are to be celebrated.

mearing   A boundary.

metathesis   The transposition of sounds in a word; e.g. saying *elascit* instead of *elastic.*

moiety   French *moitié*, "the half of", also a part or portion of any size.

morphology   The study of the grammatical structure of words.

nasalization   See **eclipsis.**

oblique   Having a grammatical form other than nominative singular.

onomasticon   A list of proper names, usually places.

orthography   Normal spelling.

palatal   A sound produced with the tongue raised towards the hard palate.

parish   A subdivision of a diocese served by a single main church or clergyman.

patent   (or letters patent), an official document conferring a right or privilege, frequently here a grant of land.

patronymic   A name derived from that of the father.

phonemic   Relating to the system of phonetic oppositions in the speech sounds of a language, which make, in English for example, *soap* a different word from *soup*, and *pin* a different word from *bin.*

phonetic   Relating to vocal sound.

phonology   The study of the sound features of a language.

plosive   A sound formed by closing the air passage and then releasing the air flow suddenly, causing an explosive sound; e.g. *p* in English *pipe.*

ploughland   Medieval English land unit of about 120 acres, equivalent to a townland.

prebend   An endowment, often in land, for the maintenance of a canon or prebendary, a senior churchman who assisted the bishop or had duties in the cathedral.

precinct   *Ad hoc* land division (usually a number of townlands) used in Plantation grants.

prefix   A verbal element placed at the beginning of a word which modifies the meaning of the word; e.g. *un-* in *unlikely.*

proportion   *Ad hoc* land division (usually a number of townlands) used in Plantation grants.

province   Irish *cúige* "a fifth": the largest administrative division in Ireland, of which there are now four (Ulster, Leinster, Connaught, Munster) but were once five.

quarter   Land unit often a quarter of the ballybetagh, and thus containing three or four townlands, but sometimes referring to a subdivision of a townland. See also **carrow.**

raising   Changing a vowel sound by lifting the tongue higher in the mouth; e.g. pronouncing *bag* as *beg*.

realize   Pronounce; e.g. *-adh* at the end of verbal nouns in Ulster Irish is realized as English *-oo*.

rectory   A parish under the care of a rector supported by its tithes; if the rector cannot reside in the parish he appoints and supports a resident vicar.

reduction   (i) Shortening of a vowel sound; e.g. the vowel sound in *board* is reduced in the word *cupboard*, (ii) = **contraction** which see.

register   A document providing a chronological record of the transactions of an individual or organization.

rounded   Pronounced with pouting lips; e.g. the vowel sounds in *oar* and *ooze*.

Scots   A dialect of Anglo-Saxon which developed independently in lowland Scotland from the 11th to the 16th centuries. By the time of the Union of Crowns in 1603 it was markedly different from southern English.

seize   To put in legal possession of property, especially land.

semantic   Relating to the meaning of words.

semivowel   A sound such as *y* or *w* at the beginning of words like *yet*, *wet*, etc.

sept   Subgroup of people, for instance of a tribe or ruling family.

sessiagh   Irish *seiseach* "a sixth", usually referring to a subdivision of a townland or similar unit. Apparently three sessiaghs were equivalent to a ballyboe (*Colton Vis.* 130).

shift of stress   The transfer of emphasis from one syllable to another; e.g. *Belfast* was originally stressed on the second syllable *fast* but because of shift of stress many people now pronounce it **Bel**fast. See **stress.**

stem   (dental, o-, etc.) Classification of nouns based on the form of their endings before the Old Irish period.

stress   The degree of force with which a syllable is pronounced. For example, the name Antrim is stressed on the first syllable while Tyrone is stressed on the second.

subdenomination   A smaller land division, usually a division of a townland.

substantive   A noun.

suffix   A verbal element placed at the end of a word which modifies the meaning of the word; e.g. *-less* in *senseless*.

syllable A unit of pronunciation containing one vowel sound which may be preceded or followed by a consonant or consonants; e.g. *I*, *my*, *hill*, have one syllable; *outside*, *table*, *ceiling* have two; *sympathy*, *understand*, *telephone* have three, etc.

syncopation The omission of a short unstressed vowel or digraph when a syllable beginning with a vowel is added; e.g. *tiger+ess* becomes *tigress*.

tate A small land unit once used in parts of Ulster, treated as equivalent to a townland, although only half the size.

termon Irish *tearmann*, land belonging to the Church, with privilege of sanctuary (providing safety from arrest for repentant criminals), usually held for the bishop by a coarb as hereditary tenant.

terrier A list of the names of lands held by the Church or other body.

tithes Taxes paid to the Church. Under the native system they were shared between parish clergy and erenagh (as the tenant of the bishop), under the English administration they were payable to the local clergyman of the Established Church.

topography The configuration of a land surface, including its relief and the position of its features.

toponymy Place-names as a subject for study.

townland The common term or English translation for a variety of small local land units; the smallest unit in the 19th-century Irish administrative system.

transcription An indication by written symbols of the precise sound of an utterance.

tuogh Irish *tuath* "tribe, tribal kingdom", a population or territorial unit.

unrounded Articulated with the lips spread or in neutral position; see **rounded**.

velar Articulated with the back of the tongue touching the soft palate; e.g. *c* in *cool*.

vicarage A parish in the charge of a vicar, the deputy either for a rector who received some of the revenue but resided elsewhere, or for a monastery or cathedral or lay impropriator.

visitation An inspection of (church) lands, usually carried out for a bishop (ecclesiastical or episcopal visitation) or for the Crown (regal visitation).

vocalization The changing of a consonant sound into a vowel sound by widening the air passage; akin to the disappearance of *r* in Southern English pronunciation of words like *bird*, *worm*, *car*.

voiced Sounded with resonance of the vocal cords. (A test for voicing can be made by closing the ears with the fingers and uttering a consonant sound. e.g. *ssss*, *zzzz*, *ffff*, *vvvv*. If a buzzing or humming sound is heard the consonant is voiced; if not it is voiceless).

voiceless See **voiced**.

INDEX TO IRISH FORMS OF PLACE-NAMES
(with pronunciation guide)

The following guide to the pronunciation of Irish forms suggested in this book is only approximate. Words are to be sounded as though written in English. The following symbols have the values shown:

ă	as in *above, coma*
ā	as in *father, draught*
ċ	as in *lough, Bach*
ch	as in *chip, church*
ġ	does not occur in English. To approximate this sound try gargling without water, or consider the following: *lock* is to *lough* as *log* is to *loġ.* If you cannot manage this sound just pronounce it like *g* in *go*.
gh	as in *lough, Bach*; not as in *foghorn*
ſ	as in *five, line*
ky	as in *cure, McKeown*
ly	at beginning of words as in *brilliant, million*
ō	as in *boar, sore*
ow	as in *now, plough*

Stress is indicated by writing the vowel in the stressed syllable in bold, e.g., Arm**a**gh, Ballym**e**na, L**u**rgan.

Place-Name	Rough Guide	Page
Abhainn Bhán, An	ăn ōne w**ā**n	57
Abhainn Bheag	ōne v**e**g	40
Abhainn na Scríne	ōne nă skr**ee**nă	52
Abhainn Riabhach, An	ăn ōne r**ee**wagh	35
Achadh Íochtair	aghoo **ee**oċter	97
Áit Tí Néill	ātee n**ai**l	36
Allt an Chaorthainn	alt ă ċ**ee**rhin	157
Allt an Leacaigh	alt ă ly**a**cky	39
Allt an Toirc	alt ă t**u**rk	40
Allt Átha Easca	alt a h**a**skă	41
Allt Bán	alt b**ā**n	40
Allt Dubh	alt d**oo**	40
Allt Mór	alt m**o**re	41
Ard an Ghuail	ard ă ġ**oo**il	47
Áth an Phoirt Leathain	ahă furt ly**a**hin	201
Áth an Phortáin	ahă f**u**rtine	201
Baile an Doire	ballăn d**i**rră	114
Baile an Mhaí	ballăn w**ee**	31
Baile an Mhullaigh Bhuí	ballăn wully w**ee**	69
Baile an tSuaitrigh	ballăn t**oo**tchree	152
Baile Bhruaigh Inse Caoine	ballă wroo inshă k**ee**nă	217

Place-Name	Rough Guide	Page
Baile Cnoic	ballă crick	142
Baile Cnoic an tSléibhe	ballă crick ă tleyvă	142
Baile Eachaidh	ballă aghy	72
Baile Meánach	ballă mānagh	144
Baile Mhic Giolla Chóimdhe Beag	ballă vick gillă ċomă beg	61
Baile Mhic Giolla Chóimdhe Mór	ballă vick gillă ċomă more	62
Baile Mhic Giolla Choradh	ballă vick gillă ċorroo	170
Baile Mhic Phéice	ballă vick feyckă	172
Baile na Breacaí	ballă nă bracky	115
Baile na Cabraí	ballă nă cabry	217
Baile na Cluana	ballă nă cloonă	118
Baile na Coradh	ballă nă corroo	93
Baile na Craoibhe	ballă nă kreevă	178
Baile na Creige	ballă nă kregyă	196
Baile na Creige Móire	ballă nă kregyă mōră	177
Baile na Croise	ballă nă crushă	50
Baile na Croise	ballă nă crushă	172
Baile na hAbhann Beag	ballă nă hōne beg	173
Baile na hAbhann Mór	ballă nă hōne more	215
Baile na hAbhann Riabhaí	ballă nă hōne reewy	35
Baile na Leapa	ballă nă lyapă	26
Baile na Móna	ballă nă mōnă	157
Baile na nGamhna	ballă nă ngawnă	87
Baile na nIúr	ballă năn yoor	9
Baile na Scríne	ballă nă skreenă	7
Baile na Tulaí Brice	ballă nă tully brickă	39
Baile na Tulcha	ballă nă tullăċă	216
Baile Naosa	ballă neesă	63
Baile Thamhlachta Dhuibh	ballă howlaċtă ġiv	71
Baile Uí Dhiarmada	bally yeermadă	61
Baile Uí Scoillín	bally skullyin	59
Baile Uí Scoillín Beag	bally skullyin beg	64
Baile Uí Scoillín Mór	bally skullyin more	64
Baile Uí Thaidhg	bally hayg	157
Béal na Mala	bell nă mală	43
Béal na Sleacht	bell nă shlaċt	43
Bheitheach, An	ă vayhagh	143
Bheitheach, An	ă vayhagh	174
Bhreacach, An	ă vrackagh	114
Bhreacach, An	ă vrackagh	174
Bior	bir	53
Both Bheitheach	boh veyhagh	89
Bóthar an Daill	bōher ă dill	44
Bóthar Buí	bōher bwee	50
Breacach	brackagh	10
Breacach	brackagh	89
Breacach	brackagh	203

Place-Name	Rough Guide	Page
Breacán Ghlas Gaibhleann	brackan ġlas givlen	39
Breacán na Glaise	brackan nă glishă	39
Bruach	brooagh	74
Bruach	brooagh	216
Buaile Cholm Cille	boolyă ċolum killyă	44
Cabhán Riabhach	kawen reewagh	14
Caonach	keenagh	126
Carn Bán	carn bān	204
Carn Chua	carn ċooă	90
Carn Tóchair	carn togher	158
Carnamán	carnăman	204
Carraig na Sionnach	karrick nă shunnagh	45
Carraig Uí Chaoilte	karrick ee ċeeltchă	217
Cathaoir Ruairí	kaher roory	46
Ceathrú Mheánach	kyarhoo vānagh	143
Ceathrú na Móna	kyarhoo nă mōnă	12
Chabrach, An	ă ċabragh	217
Chéide, An	ă ċaydjă	190
Chluanaidh, An	ă ċlooney	117
Chora, An	ă ċorră	93
Chraobh, An	ă ċreeoo	177
Chrois, An	ă ċrush	173
Chuilleann, An	ă ċullion	92
Cill an Locha	kill ă loughă	140
Cill Chruithneacháin	kill ċruhnyaghine	112
Clann Dónaill	clan dōnill	2
Cloch Bhán	clough wān	159
Cloch Fhionn	clough inn	15
Cloch Fhionn	clough inn	118
Cluain	clooin	14
Cnoc an Bhaile	crock ă wallă	47
Cnoc an Cheo	crock ă ċyō	91
Cnoc an Ghuail	crock ă ġooil	47
Cnoc an tSagairt	crock ă taggirtch	47
Cnoc Breac	crock brack	48
Cnoc Clochdhroma	crock cloughrumă	223
Cnoc Corr	crock korr	205
Cnoc Mór	crock more	48
Cnoc Mór	crock more	160
Cnoc na Cathaoireach	crock nă kaheragh	46
Cnoc na Conspóide	crock nă konspodjă	160
Cnoc na Críche	crock nă kreehă	49
Cnoc na Daróige Duibhe	crock nă daroigă divă	43
Cnoc na gCeann	crock nă gyun	99
Cnoc na mBuachaillí	crock nă mooăċilly	136
Cnoc Néill	crock nail	149

Place-Name	Rough Guide	Page
Cnoc Uí Chaoilte	crock ee čeeltchă	219
Cnoc Uí Mhuireáin	crock ee wurine	48
Cnocán Rua	crockan rooă	160
Coill an Tonnaigh	kăl ă tunny	128
Coill Ard	kăl ārd	209
Coill Chreagach	kăl čragagh	50
Coill Íochtarach	kăl eeoghteragh	3
Coillidh Bhearaigh	kălly varry	67
Coillín Dearcán	kăllin jarckan	208
Coll Mór, An	ă cull more	115
Comhrac	cōrăck	16
Corr Leacaigh	corr lyacky	144
Corr na Fearna	corr nă fārnă	45
Corrach	corragh	179
Corrbhaile	corrwallă	131
Corrbhaile	corrwallă	191
Cosán	cussan	204
Crannaigh	cranny	91
Creag an Díogha	crag ă jeeoo	175
Creag Bhán	crag wān	46
Creag Mhór	crag wore	177
Creag na hAltóra	crag nă haltoră	160
Creagach	cragagh	46
Cúil an Bhogáin	cool ă wuggine	98
Cúil an Umair	cool ăn ummer	127
Cúil Bhán	cool wān	74
Cúil Chnáidí	cool črādjee	178
Cúil Darach	cool darragh	205
Cúil na gCnumh	cool nă grew	144
Cúil na Saileach	cool nă sillagh	16
Cúil Sáráin	cool sārrine	118
Curraín	curreen	180
Daróg an Oireachtais	darog ăn irračtish	44
Dearganach, An	ă jarăgănagh	218
Díseart	jeeshărt	18
Díseart Mhártain	jeeshărt wārtin	83
Doire an Fhóid	dirrin odge	17
Doire Cholm Cille	dirră čolum killyă	xix
Doire na Sceallán	dirră nă shkallan	94
Doire Thoirc	dirră hirk	206
Doire Thuama	dirră hooămă	206
Draighneán	dreenyan	181
Droim an Fhia	drim ăn yeeă	66
Droim Ard	drim ārd	19
Droim Ard	drim ārd	182
Droim Baile	drim ballă	136

270

Place-Name	Rough Guide	Page
Droim Bhaile Uí Ágáin	drim wally āgine	120
Droim Con Riada	drim con reeădă	182
Droim Cró	drim crō	121
Droim Dearg	drim jarăg	20
Droim Leamhach	drim lyawagh	183
Droim Mór	drim more	94
Droim Muc	drim muck	184
Droim Muice	drim mwickă	108
Droim Samhna	drim sawnă	122
Dúghlas	dooġlas	44
Dún	doon	19
Dún an Ghiolla Dhuibh	doon ă yillă ġiv	19
Dún gCláidí	doon glāddy	184
Dún Muirígh	doon mwirry	22
Dún Tí Bhriain	doon tee vreeăn	23
Dúnáin, Na	nă doonine	160
Éadan Darach	aydăn darragh	161
Éadan Riabhach, An t	ă chaydan reewagh	66
Eanach	annagh	71
Eanach	annagh	85
Eanach an Bhogaigh	annagh ă wuggy	202
Eanach Fada	annagh fadă	203
Eanach Uí Ailleagáin	annagh ee alyăgine	202
Eanga	angă	215
Fáladh Fhleadha	falloo lyā	145
Fáladh Goirt Riabhaigh	falloo gorch reewy	185
Fáladh Luán	falloo looan	186
Fionnghleann	finġlan	23
Fionnghleann Ó Maolagáin	finġlan o mweelăgine	24
Ghráinseach, An	ă ġrānshagh	96
Ghriollach, An	ă ġrillagh	188
Glaise	glashă	50
Gleann, An	ă glan	207
Gleann Bhigín	glan viggeen	25
Gleann Con Cadhain	glan cun kɼne	2
Gleann Gamhna	glan gownă	24
Gleann Láithrigh	glan lāihry	223
Gort	gort	207
Gort an Aoire	gort ăn eeră	95
Gort an Choirce	gort ă ċirkyă	123
Gort an tSamhraidh	gort ă tawry	124
Gort an Úra	gort ăn ooră	147
Gort Mór	gort more	207
Gort na Sceach	gort nă shkagh	25

Place-Name	Rough Guide	Page
Greanachán	granaghan	148
Greanaigh	granny	125
Guala Dhubh	goolă ġoo	189
Inis Cairn	inish karn	97
Inis Gabhar	inish gōre	40
Inis Taoide	inish teedjă	65
Inis Uí Fhloinn	inish ee linn	102
Leaba, An	ă lyabby	26
Leabaidh na Glaise	lyabby nă glashă	27
Leac Iomchair	lyack umăgher	99
Leamhchoill	lyawċill	100
Leamhnaigh	lyawny	101
Leargain na gCuas	lyarăgin nă gooăs	220
Leargain Tóchair	lyarăgin togher	192
Léim an Eich Rua	lyame ăn eċ rooă	220
Liatroim	lyeeătrim	68
Lios Droichid	lyiss driċid	222
Lios Dubh	lyiss doo	43
Lios Eanaigh	lyiss anny	86
Lios Liath	lyiss lyeeă	114
Lios na Muc	lyiss nă muck	192
Loch Abair	lough abber	109
Loch Beag	lough beg	76
Loch Brain	lough brin	161
Loch Inse Uí Fhloinn	lough inshy linn	1
Loch Phádraig	lough fādrick	51
Loch Uaisce	lough ooăshkă	50
Log Mór	lug more	50
Machaire Bhaile Phearsúin	magheră wallă farsoon	86
Machaire Rátha	magheră rahă	168
Maigh Ard	mwy ārd	30
Maigh Bheag	mwy vegg	131
Maigh Chaoláin	mwy ċeeline	32
Maigh Chaorthainn	mwy ċeerhin	33
Maigh dTamhlachta	mwy dowlaċtă	31
Maigh Eanaigh na Griollcha	mwy anny nă grillăċă	189
Maigh Fhoghlach	mwy ōlagh	78
Maigh Inse na Griollcha	mwy inshy nă grillăċă	189
Maigh Inse Uí Fhloinn	mwy inshy linn	102
Maigh na gCúigeadh	mwy nă gooăgyoo	28
Maigh Ó gColla	mwy o gullă	195
Maigh Uachtarach	mwy ooăċteragh	31
Mheacanach, An	ă vackănagh	193
Mír Mhíchíl	meer veehil	130

Place-Name	Rough Guide	Page
Móin an Chongna	mone ă čō nă	27
Móin na nIonadh	mone nă nyeenoo	29
Muine Mór	mwinnă more	194
Muine Searbhán	mwinnă sharăwan	150
Mullach	mullagh	54
Mullach	mullagh	221
Mullach Buí	mullagh bwee	69
Mullach Eanga	mullagh angă	215
Mullach Leathan	mullagh lyahăn	53
Mullach Mór	mullagh more	53
Mullach Tuirc	mullagh turk	40
Páirc an Mhíodúin	pwark ă veedoon	54
Polláin Ghorma, Na	nă polline ġorumă	162
Raithneachán	rahnyaghan	54
Raithneachán Beag	rahnyaghan beg	210
Raithneachán Mór	rahnyaghan more	209
Ráth Lúraigh	rah loory	168, 170
Ros Gearrán	ross gyārran	103
Ros Iúir	ross yoor	105
Ruachán	rooăghan	163
Scrín Cholm Cille	skreen čolum killyă	6
Sleacht an Bhogaigh	shlačt ă wuggy	196
Sleacht an Bhogaigh Leathain	shlačt ă wuggy lyahin	197
Sleacht Néill	shlačt nail	150
Sliabh gCallann	shleeoo gallon	89
Sliabh Maol	shleeoo mweel	55
Slogán	sluggan	80
Speal Chuach	spal čooăgh	55
Srath	shrah	35
Srath Inis na gCeardaithe	shrah inish nă gyardy	106
Srath Mór	shrah more	36
Srath na gCeardaithe	shrah nă gyardy	105
Srath na gCon	shrah nă gun	164
Sruthán Léana an tSamhaidh	shruhan leynăn tawey	56
Sruthán na gCloch	shruhan nă glough	57
Suaitreach, An	ă sootchragh	151
Suí Finn	see fin	163
Suí Ghoill	see ġill	164
Tamhlacht Dubh	towlačt doo	70
Tamhnaigh Oscair	towny osker	132
Tamhnaigh Uí Eararáin	towny ararine	71
Tamhnaigh Uí Mhaoláin	towny weeline	198
Tamhnaigh Uí Mhártain	towny wārtin	197

Place-Name	Rough Guide	Page
Tearmann Eanga	charmăn **ang**ă	213
Tobar an Mhadaidh Léith	tubber ă waddy **lay**	29
Tobar an Mhadaidh Mhaoil	tubber ă waddy **wee**l	29
Tobar Mór	tubber **more**	133
Tobar Thaoide	tubber **hee**djă	200
Toigh Taisce	tee **ta**shkă	8
Tonnach	**tu**nnagh	37
Torgán	tor**ă**gan	106
Tulaigh Bhric, An	ă tully v**ri**ck	38
Tulaigh Chaorthainn	tully ċ**ee**rhin	155
Tulaigh Rua	tully **roo**ă	211
Tulaigh Uí Ruáin	tully **roo**ine	134
Tír an Omhna	cheer ăn **ō**nă	154
Tír Aodha	cheer **ee**	152
Tír Chiana	cheer ċ**ee**ănă	153
Tír gCearbhaill	cheer gy**ar**ăwill	199
Tír na gCaorach	cheer nă **gee**ragh	200

PLACE-NAME INDEX

Sheet numbers are given below for the OS 1:50,000 map only where the name occurs on that map. Not all the townlands discussed in this volume appear on the published 1:50,000 map and no sheet number is given for those names. The sheet numbers for the 1:10,000 series and the earlier 6-inch series, which is still important for historical research, are also supplied. The 6-inch sheet numbers refer to the Co. Londonderry series except where otherwise stated.

Place-Name	1:50,000	1:10,000	6 inch	Page
Altagoan River	13	77	41	135
Altalacky River	13	77	35	39
Altaturk Glen	13	91	39	40
Altbane Burn	13	91	44	40
Altdoo or Black Glen	8	63	35	40
Altihaskey	13	91	45	41
Altkeeran River	8	64	32	157
Altmore Burn	13	77	35	41
Annagh	14	79	42	71
Annagh and Moneysterlin		77, 78, 93	41	85
Annagh-Hilkin	8	66	37	202
Annaghaboggy	14	78	42	202
Annaghfad	8	65	37	203
Back Burn	13,14	64,78	36	203, 222
Back Parks	8	52	32	157
Ballinderry	14	78	36,41	114
Ballydermot	14	79	37,42	61
Ballyheige	8	64	32	157
Ballyknock	8	64	32,36	142
Ballymacilcurr	8	65	32,36	170
Ballymacombs Beg		66, 79	37	61
Ballymacombs More	14	66, 79	37,38	62
Ballymacpeake Upper		65, 66, 78, 79	73	172
Ballymacpherson	14	93	41	86
Ballynacross	14	78	36,37	172
Ballynacross Bridge	13	77		42
Ballynagown	14	78, 93	41	87
Ballynahone Beg		77, 78	36	173
Ballynahone More	14	78	36,41	215
Ballynamona	8	64	32	157
Ballynascreen Parish				6
Ballynease-Helton	14	66	33,37	63
Ballynease-Macpeake	14	66	33,37,38	63
Ballynease-Strain	8	66	37	63
Ballynure	13	64, 77	35,36	9
Ballyscullion East	14	79	36, 42 (Ant.)	64
Ballyscullion Parish				59
Ballyscullion West	14	79	37,42	64

Place-Name	1:50,000	1:10,000	6 inch	Page
Bancran Glebe	13	76, 77	35, 40	10
Banty Bridge	13	77	36	42
Beagh (Spiritual)	14	65, 78	36	174
Beagh (Temporal)	14	53, 65	32	143
Bealnamala Bridge	13	91	45	42
Bealnaslaght Bridge	13	91	40	43
Bellaghy	14	79	37	72
Belleview	8	53	26	158
Belmount Hill	13	77	41	135
Benbradagh	8	65		203
Beresfords Bridge	8	65	32	203
Big Hill	14	78	36	222
Big Park	13	77	36	203
Bishops Canal	14	79	37	74
Black Fort	13	76	35	43
Black Glen	8	63	35	43
Black Hill, The	13	77	36	43
Black Water	13	92		44
Boheradaile Bridge	13	77	35	44
Boley	13	92	40	44
Bonnety Bush	13	91		45
Bonny Bush	8	52	32	158
Boveagh	13	92	41	89
Bracaghreilly	8	64, 77	31, 35, 36	174
Brackagh	13	92	40, 45	10
Brackagh	14	66	37	203
Brackagh Slieve Gallion	13	92, 93	41, 46	89
Brackaghlislea	13	77, 92	40, 41	114
Broagh	14	78	37, 42	216
Brough	14	94	42	74
Cabragh	14	78	37, 42	217
Cahore	13	77, 92	40	11
Calmore	13	77	36, 41	115
Campbells Bridge	13	77	36	204
Carn Hill	8	53	32	158
Carnaman	14	65	37	204
Carnamoney	13	64, 77	35, 36	12
Carnbane	8	65	32	204
Carncose	13	92, 93	46	90
Carntogher	8	52	32	158
Carricknakielt	14	65, 78	36	217
Carricknashinnagh	13	76	40	45
Carrowmenagh	8	64, 65	32, 36	143
Causin Hill	8	65	33	204
Cavanreagh	13	76, 91	40	14
Church Island	14	79	42	65
Church Island Intake		79	42	65

Place-Name	1:50,000	1:10,000	6 inch	Page
Cloane	13	64,77	35	14
Cloghbane	8	64	32	159
Clooney	13	77,78	36	117
Cloughfin	13	92	40	15
Cloughfin	13	77	41	118
Clover Hill	14	78		222
Cockhill	13	91	40	45
Coney Island	14	79	42	65
Coolcalm House	14	78	41	107
Coolderry	14	65	37	205
Coolnasillagh	13	64, 77	35, 36	16
Coolsaragh	13	77, 78, 92, 93	41	118
Corby Island	13	78	36	205
Corick	13	92	40, 45	16
Corlacky	8	52, 64	26, 32	144
Cornafarna	13	77	40	45
Cow Lough	13	92	45	46
Craigadick		64, 65, 77, 78	36	175
Craigagh Hill	13	76	35	46
Craigbane	13	76	35	46
Craigmore	8	65	32, 36	177
Craignahaltora	8	64	32	160
Cranny	14	93	41, 46	91
Crew	8	65	32, 36	177
Crillys Town	8	66	37	74
Crockacahir	13	92	40	46
Crockaghole	13	91	40	47
Crockanroe	8	52	26	160
Crockataggart	13	76		47
Crockawilla	13	76	35	47
Crockbrack	13	76	35	48
Crockcor	8	64	32	205
Crockmoran	13	91	45	48
Crockmore	13	76		48
Crockmore	8	52	32	160
Crocknaconspody	8	52	26	160
Crocknacreeha	13	91		49
Crocknamohil	13	92	41	136
Crockney Hill	14	78	42	205
Cross Roads	13	77	41	136
Crosskeys	8	65	32	205
Culbane	8	66	37	74
Cullion	13	92	41, 46	92
Culnady	8	65	32, 33, 36, 37	178
Culnagrew	8	53	26, 32	144
Curdian	8	65		205
Curly Hill	14	79	37	75

Place-Name	1:50,000	1:10,000	6 inch	Page
Curr	14	93	41	93
Curragh	8	65	36, 37	179
Curran	14	78	36, 37, 41, 42	180
Cut of the Hill	14	79	37	75
Dan's Brae	13	92	41	108
Derganagh	14	78	36, 37	218
Derryhoma	14		37	206
Derryhurk	14	78	37	206
Derrynoyd	13	76, 77	35, 40	17
Desertmartin	14	93	41	108
Desertmartin Parish				83
Disert	13	77, 92	40	18
Doon	13	76, 77	40	19
Doonan	8	64	32	160
Douglas Bridge	13	77	35	49
Douglas River	13	77	35	49
Downings Borough	14	79	42	75
Doyles Bridge	13	77	35	49
Draperstown	13	77	40	49
Dreenan	8	65	33, 37	181
Dromore		78	41	94
Drumanee Lower		79	27, 42	66
Drumanee Upper		79	37	66
Drumard	13	77, 92	40, 41	19
Drumard	14	65, 78	37	182
Drumbally Hill	13	78	41	136
Drumballyhagan	13	77	36	120
Drumballyhagan Clark		77	36	121
Drumconready		64, 77	36	182
Drumcrow		77	36	121
Drumderg	13	76, 77	35, 40	20
Drumlamph	14	78, 79	37, 42	183
Drummuck	13	92	46	108
Drummuck	8	65	33, 37	184
Drumsamney	14	78	41	122
Dunergan Hill	14	78	37	206
Dunglady	8	65	33	184
Dunlogan	13	76	35	21
Dunmurry	13	64, 77	35	22
Duntibryan	13	77	36, 41	23
Durnascallon	13	92, 93	41	94
Edendarragh	8	65	32	161
Edenreagh		79	42	66
Falgortrevy	13	64, 65, 77	36	185
Fallagloon	8	64, 77	31, 32, 35, 36	186
Fallylea	8	64	15	145
Finglen	13	76	35, 40	23

Place-Name	1:50,000	1:10,000	6 inch	Page
Folly Hill	14	79	37	75
Forge Bridge	13	77		137
Fort William	13	77	36	137
Fort, The	14	78	36	222
Garrison, The	14	78	42	206
Glashagh Burn	13	91	40	50
Glebe	13	77	36, 41	24
Glebe		77	32	146
Glebe East		79	37	67
Glebe West		79	37	67
Glen	8	64		207
Glencarrigan	14	78	36	223
Glengomna	13	76, 91	35, 40	24
Glenlarry	14	78	36	223
Glenview	14	93		109
Glenviggan	13	91	39, 40, 44, 45	25
Gortahurk	13	77, 92	40, 41	123
Gortamney	14	78	36, 41	124
Gortanewry		93	46	95
Gorteade		53, 65	32, 33	188
Gortinure	8	53, 64, 65	32	147
Gortmore	14	65		207
Gortnaskey	13	77	36, 41	25
Granaghan	8	52, 53	32	148
Grange	14	78	41	96
Granny		77	36, 41	125
Green Hall	14	78	42	223
Green Water	8	52	26, 32	161
Grillagh	8	65	32	188
Grove Hill	14	79	42	76
Grove, The	8	65	36	207
Gulladuff	14	65, 78	37	189
Half Quarter	8	66	37	76
Halfgayne		52, 53, 64, 65	32	148
Heath Mount	13	77	36	207
Hill Head	14	79		76
Hill Head	14	79	31, 42	76
Hill Head	14	78	41	207
Holly Hill	14	78	37	207
Holly Mount	14	93	41	109
Hollyhill Wood	14	78		208
Iniscarn	13	92, 93	41, 46	97
Iniscarn Forest	14			76
Intake		79	42	67
Iona House	14	93	41	109
Irish Tirgarvil	8	65		208
Island	8	65	37	208

Place-Name	1:50,000	1:10,000	6 inch	Page
Island, The	14	78	36	223
Keady	8	53	32	190
Keenaght	13	77, 92	41	126
Kilcraigagh	13	63	35	50
Kilcronaghan Parish				112
Killadarkan	14	78	37	208
Killard	14	78	37	209
Killelagh Parish	8			140
Killyberry	14	78, 79	37, 42	67
Killyberry Boyd	14	78, 79	37, 42	67
Killyberry Downing		78, 79	42	67
Killyboggin	14	93	41, 46	98
Killynumber	13	77, 78	41	127
Killytoney	13	77, 78	36, 41	128
Kirley	8	64, 77	35, 36	191
Knockcloghrim	14	78		223
Knocknagin		78, 93	41	99
Knocknakielt	14	65, 78	36	219
Knockoneill	8	52	26, 31, 32	149
Knowhead House	14	78	36	224
Labby	13	76, 77, 91, 92	40	26
Lake View	14	79	42	76
Largantogher		65	36	192
Lecumpher	14	93	41, 46	99
Legmore	13	64	35	50
Leitrim		78, 79, 94	42	68
Lemnaroy		78	37, 42	220
Lisnamuck	13	64, 77	36	192
Long Point	14	79	42	76
Longfield	13	92, 93	41	100
Lough Aber	14	78	41	109
Lough Beg	14	79		76
Lough Bran	8	64	32	161
Lough Ouske	13	76	40	50
Lough Patrick	13	92	40	51
Loughinsholin	13			109
Loughinsholin Barony				1
Lower Town	14	65	37	209
Luney	14	78, 93	41	101
Lurganagoose		78	36, 37, 42	220
Macknagh	8	65	32	193
Maghera	8	65	36	209
Maghera Parish	8	65		168
McConnamys Bridge	13	91	44	51
McKennas Town	14	78	37	209
McNally's Bridge	13	91	44	51
Mile Mountain	13	91	40	52

Place-Name	1:50,000	1:10,000	6 inch	Page
Mill Lough	13	91	45	52
Milltown	13	77	36	52
Milltown	13	65	36	209
Milltown Burn	8	64	36	209
Moneyconey	13	91	39, 40	27
Moneyguiggy	13	77	36	28
Moneymore		65	36	194
Moneyneany	13	63, 64, 76, 77	35	29
Moneyoran Hill	8	52	32	162
Moneyshanere	13	77	36	129
Moneysharvan	8	53, 65	32	150
Moneysterlin, Annagh and		77, 78, 93	41	102
Mormeal	13	77	41	130
Motalee	14	93	41	103
Mountain View	13	76	40	52
Moyagall		65, 78	37	195
Moyard	13	91	39, 40, 44, 45	30
Moybeg Kirley		77	36	131
Moydamlaght	13	63, 64, 76, 77	35	31
Moyesset	13	77, 78	36, 41	131
Moyheeland		77	35, 36, 40, 41	32
Moykeeran	13	77	40	33
Moyola Park	14	78	42	77
Moyola River	13,14	77, 78, 92		52
Moyola Wood	14			78
Mulhollands Town	14	66	37	79
Mullagh	14	65, 78	36	221
Mullaghboy	14	78, 79	37	69
Mullaghlahan	13	77	35	53
Mullaghmore	8	63	35	53
Mullaghshuraren	13	91	40	53
Mullans Town	8	65	32	162
Mulnavoo	13	77	35, 40	34
Newferry	14	79	38	79
Nutgrove Wood	13	77		137
Oak Island	14	78	41	138
Old Church Bridge, The	13	91		54
Oldtown Deerpark	14	78, 79	37, 42	69
Oldtown Downing		79	37, 42	69
Owenreagh	13	91, 92	40	35
Parkaveadan Burn	8	63	35	54
Pollan Water	8	64		162
Pollangorm Hill	8	52	32	162
Ranaghan	13	76	35	54
Ranaghan Bridge	8	64		209
Ranaghan More	8	64		209
Reubens Glen Bridge	14	93	46	109

Place-Name	1:50,000	1:10,000	6 inch	Page
Ringsend	8	53	32	162
Rock Hill	13	76	40	55
Rock of Drummuck, The	8	65	33	210
Rockfield	8	65	32	163
Rocktown	14	78	37	196
Rockvale	8	65	32	210
Roe's Gift	14	79	42	79
Roohan	8	64	32	163
Rose Hill	14	79	42	79
Rosgarran	14	78, 93	41	103
Roshure	14	93	41	105
Rough Hill	8	65	37	210
Rowans Gift	14	78	37	210
Sallyvilla Cottage	8	53	26	163
Sandy Mount	14	79	37	79
Scab Island	14	79	42	70
Scotch Tirgarvil		65		210
Seawright's Hill	14	79	37	80
Seefin	8	64		163
Shanaghan	14	78	37	210
Sheep Hills	8	66	37	80
Sheskin Bridge	8	64		211
Sheskin Burn	8	64	35	211
Six Towns, The	13	91	40	55
Sixtowns Lodge	13	91	40	55
Slaghtneill	8	52, 64	32	150
Slaghtybogy	14	65, 78	36, 37	196
Slievemoyle	13	64	35	55
Slugawn Bridge	14	79	42	80
Spelhoagh	13	76	35	55
Spring Grove	13	77	41	138
Spring Well Bridge	14	79	37	80
Sruhanleanantawey	13	92	45	56
Sruhannaclogh	13	92	40, 45	56
Stone Hill	13	91	40	57
Stranagard		93	41	105
Stranagon	8	53	32	164
Straw	13	77, 92	40	35
Straw Mountain	13	92	40, 41	36
Strawmore	13	77	35, 40	36
Swatragh	8	53	26, 32	151
Tamlaghtduff	14	66, 79	37	70
Tamniaran		78, 79, 93, 94	42	71
Tamnyaskey	13	77	36, 41	132
Tamnymartin		65	36	197
Tamnymullan	8	65	32, 36	198
Teal Lough	13	91	45	57

Place-Name	1:50,000	1:10,000	6 inch	Page
Teiges Hill	13	77	41	138
Termoneeny Parish				213
Thornstown	8	66	37	80
Thyme Hill	14	78	37	211
Tirgan	13	92, 93	46	106
Tirgarvil		65	32, 33	199
Tirhugh		52, 53	32	152
Tirkane	8	52, 64	32, 36	153
Tirnageeragh	8	65	32, 33	200
Tirnony	8	64, 65	32, 36	154
Toberhead	14	78	42	200
Tobermore	13	77, 78	36	133, 138
Tonaght	13	77, 92	40	37
Tory Island	14	66	37	81
Tullybrick	13	91, 92	40, 45	38
Tullyheran	8	64, 65	36	155
Tullykeeran Mountain	8	64	32	156
Tullyroan	13	77	41	134
Tullyroe Hill	14	65	37	211
Upper Town	14	65	37	211
Upperland	8	53, 65	32, 33	201
Wapping	8	53	32	164
Warren Hill	14	79	42	81
Weddell Bridge	13	77	35	57
White Fort	13	77	36	57
White Hall	14	78	41	224
White Hill	14	78	36	224
White Water	13	92	40	57
Widow Steeles Bridge	14	78	36	224
Windy Castle	13	92	46	109
Wood, The	14	79	37	81
Wood, The	14	79	37	211
Woodhill	8	66	37	81